INDEXES
TO
THE COUNTY WILLS
OF
SOUTH CAROLINA

This volume contains a separate index compiled from the W.P.A. copies of each of the County Will Books, except those of Charleston County Will Books, in the South Carolina Collection of the University of South Carolina Library.

Compiled by

MARTHA LOU HOUSTON

CLEARFIELD

Reprinted for
Clearfield Company by
Genealogical Publishing Co.
Baltimore, Maryland
1994, 1996, 2001, 2003, 2007

ISBN-13: 978-0-8063-0185-3
ISBN-10: 0-8063-0185-6

Made in the United States of America

Originally published: Columbia, South Carolina, 1939
Reprinted: Genealogical Publishing Co., Inc.
Baltimore, 1964, 1970, 1975, 1982
Library of Congress Catalogue Card Number 64-19757

The Works Progress Administration, under the general direction of Mrs. Jessie Reed Burnett and Dr. Anne King Gregorie, with the aid and sanction of the South Carolina Civil Works Administration, supervised the typing of verbatim copies of all the available wills of the older counties of South Carolina. Three copies were made and distributed in the following manner; one copy was placed with the original book of wills, one copy was sent to form a depository collection in the South Carolina Room of the University of South Carolina Library, Columbia, South Carolina.

The will books contain the wills of all the counties formed before 1853, with the exception of BEAUFORT COUNTY and of those six counties whose records were destroyed in 1865, namely: CHESTERFIELD, COLLETON, GEORGETOWN, LANCASTER, LEXINGTON, and ORANGEBURG. The BEAUFORT COUNTY records were destroyed by fire soon after the war.

For wills of NINETY SIX DISTRICT, see will books from ABBEVILLE, EDGEFIELD, LAURENS, NEWBERRY, SPARTANBURG, and UNION.

For wills of PENDLETON COUNTY, see will books from ANDER-SON, GREENVILLE, and PICKENS.

The early wills of counties formed since 1853 are to be found among the records of the parent county or counties.

The table of counties on the following page gives the names of all the counties, and the dates of establishment of those which were formed after 1853.

Elizabeth L. Porcher, Librarian
South Carolina Collection
Columbia, S.C.

December 1st, 1939.

EARLY SOUTH CAROLINA WILLS

County	Record of wills.	Date (if formed after 1855)
ABBEVILLE	Copies of wills in S.C. Room	....
AIKEN	Established after 1855	1871
ALLENDALE	Established after 1855	1919
ANDERSON	Copies of wills in S.C. Room	....
BAMBERG	Established after 1855	1897
BARNWELL	Copies of wills in the S.C. Room	....
BEAUFORT	EARLY RECORDS DESTROYED	....
BERKELEY	Established after 1855	1882
CALHOUN	Established after 1855	1909
*CHARLESTON	COPIES OF WILLS IN SOUTH CAROLINA ROOM...........	
CHEROKEE	Established after 1855	1897
CHESTER	Copies of wills in S.C. Room	....
CHESTERFIELD	EARLY RECORDS DESTROYED	....
CLARENDON	Established after 1855	1857
COLLETON	EARLY RECORDS DESTROYED	....
DARLINGTON	Copies of wills in S.C. Room	....
DILLON	Established after 1855	1910
DORCHESTER	Established after 1855	....
EDGEFIELD	Copies of wills in S.C. Room	....
FAIRFIELD	Copies of wills in S.C. Room	....
FLORENCE	Established after 1855	1887
GEORGETOWN	EARLY RECORDS DESTROYED	....
GREENVILLE	Copies of wills in S.C. Room	....
GREENWOOD	Established after 1855	1897
HAMPTON	Established after 1855	1877
HORRY	Copies of wills in S.C. Room	....
JASPER	Established after 1855	1910
KERSHAW	Copies of wills in S.C. Room	....
LANCASTER	EARLY RECORDS DESTROYED	....
LAURENS	Copies of wills in S.C. Room	....
LEE	Established after 1855	1908
LEXINGTON	EARLY RECORDS DESTROYED	....
MARION	Copies of wills in S.C. Room	....
MARLBORO	Copies of wills in S.C. Room	....
McCORMICK	Established after 1855	1914
NEWBERRY	Copies of wills in S.C. Room	....
OCONEE	Established after 1855	1868
ORANGEBURG	EARLY RECORDS DESTROYED	....
PICKENS	Copies of wills in S.C. Room	....
RICHLAND	Copies of wills in S.C. Room	....
SALUDA	Established after 1855	....
SPARTANBURG	Copies of wills in S.C. Room	....
SUMTER	Copies of wills in S.C. Room	....
UNION	Copies of wills in S.C. Room	....
WILLIAMSBURG	Copies of wills in S.C. Room	....
YORK	Copies of wills in S.C. Room	....

*CHARLESTON: In this volume the index for the Charleston
County wills is not included because a cumulative index for the
Charleston county will books has been compiled by the Charleston
Free Library.

INDEX TO CONTENTS

Page

INDEX TO

ABBEVILLE COUNTY WILLS

VOLUME NO. 1
1787-1815

VOLUME NO. 2
1815-1839

VOLUME NO. 3
1839-1855

This index is compiled from W. P. A. copies of
wills filed in the COUNTY PROBATE COURTS.
The volumes indexed are a part of the
South Carolina Collection of the
University of South Carolina
Library.

Columbia, S.C.
1939

7

AME	VOL.	DATE	PAGE
Adams, William (Farmer)	I	1787-1815	123
Adamson, James	1	1787-1815	626
Adamson, Lydia	2	1815-1839	170
Afton, James, see - - - - - - - - - - - - - - - - - -			Aston, James
Ager, John	2	1815-1839	50
Agnew, Samuel	1	1787-1815	70
Akin, Nancy	3	1839-1855	318
Alexander, Aaron	1	1787-1815	151
Alexander, Wm.	1	1787-1815	140
Allen, Edward	3	1839-1855	481
Allen, James	2	1815-1839	323
Allen, Lewis	2	1815-1839	13
Allen, Robert (Sr.)	2	1815-1839	12
Allis, James, see - - - - - - - - - - - - - - - - -			Callis, James
Alston, James	3	1839-1855	386
Anderson, Mary	2	1815-1839	295
Anderson, Samuel	3	1839-1855	277
Anderson, Thomas (Rev.)	2	1815-1839	252
Anderson, Thomas	3	1839-1855	35
Anderson, Wm.	2	1815-1839	184
Armstrong, John H.	3	1839-1855	94
Armstrong, Samuel	1	1787-1815	535
Arnold, Alexander B. (Dr.)	3	1839-1855	446
Arnold, James (Planter)	2	1815-1839	284
Arnold, Jonathan	3	1839-1855	63
Ashley, John	3	1839-1855	31
Ashley, Joshua (Sr.)	3	1839-1855	76
Ashley, Wm. (Sr.)	3	1839-1855	337
Aston, James	1	1787-1815	32
Bailey, Jane, see - - - - - - - - - - - - - - - - - -			Bealy, Jean
Baird, Adam	1	1787-1815	466
Baird, John B.	1	1787-1815	329
Baird, Mary	2	1815-1839	89
Baird, Thomas	1	1787-1815	197
Baker, Caleb	1	1787-1815	324
Baker, John	1	1787-1815	619
Baker, John	2	1815-1839	124
Ball, Elizabeth	2	1815-1839	25
Ball, Lewis	2	1815-1839	7
Ball, Nancy	1	1787-1815	629
Ball, Peter	2	1815-1839	6
Banks, Rivers	1	1787-1815	272
Barksdale, Elizabeth	1	1787-1815	246
Barksdale, Hickerson (Sr.)	1	1787-1815	374
Barksdale, Higgason (Planter)	1	1787-1815	267
Barmore, George	2	1815-1839	16
Barmore, James	2	1815-1839	215
Barmore, William	3	1839-1855	344
Barr, Wm. H. (Minister)	3	1839-1855	316
Bartram, Mary	2	1815-1839	249
Baskin, James S.	3	1839-1855	498
Baskin, John	3	1839-1855	441

Baskins, Hugh (Planter)	1	1787-1815	194
Bates, Fleming	1	1787-1815	364
Bates, Stephen	1	1787-1815	17
Bayle, Mary	1	1787-1815	126
Beack, Hannah	1	1787-1815	613
Beall, Benjamin	2	1815-1839	180
Beall, Sarah	3	1839-1855	13
Bealy, Jean	1	1787-1815	84
Beasley, Wm. (Farmer)	3	1839-1855	511
Beatty, Wm. W.	2	1815-1839	159
Beck, Wm.	1	1787-1815	570
Belcher, Robt. E.	3	1839-1855	380
Bell, John	1	1787-1815	614
Bell, Matthew	1	1787-1815	345
Bell, Sarah	1	1787-1815	527
Bennison, Wm.	2	1815-1839	35
Bentley, Henry	3	1839-1855	396
Bernad, John	1	1787-1815	248
Bickley, Joseph	2	1815-1839	19
Bigbee, Archibald	3	1839-1855	96
Bigby, George	3	1839-1855	393
Bigby, Sarah	2	1815-1839	316
Black, James	3	1839-1855	181
Black, James A.	2	1815-1839	252
Black, James A.	2	1815-1839	296
Black, Mary	2	1815-1839	186
Blain, Wm.	2	1815-1839	202
Blair, Samuel	1	1787-1815	651
Blake, John	3	1839-1855	365
Boggs, Elizabeth	2	1815-1839	86
Boggs, John	3	1839-1855	285
Bole, John	2	1815-1839	228
Boles, John	1	1787-1815	150
Bomar, John	1	1787-1815	43
Bonchillon, John, see - - - - - - - - - - - - - - - - Bouchillon, John			
Bond, Robt.	1	1787-1815	68
Booser, Henry	3	1839-1855	504
Bcuchillon, Jean (Planter)	2	1815-1839	53
Bouchillon, John (Planter)	1	1787-1815	29
Bouchillon, Joseph	1	1787-1815	315
Bowen, Starling	2	1815-1839	103
Bowie, Arthur	3	1839-1855	225
Bowie, George	2	1815-1839	63
Bowie, John (Sr.)	2	1815-1839	182
Bowie, Richard Price	3	1839-1855	520
Bowman, John, see - - - - - - - - - - - - - - - - - Bomar, John			
Bowman, Wm.	1	1787-1815	50
Boyd, James	3	1839-1855	27
Boyd, Mary	2	1815-1839	122
Boyd, Wm.	1	1787-1815	330
Boseman, Susannah	3	1839-1855	262
Brackenridge, David	3	1839-1855	189
Bradly, Isabella	3	1839-1855	57
Bradley, Patrick	2	1815-1839	223
Bradshaw, Wm.	3	1839-1855	314
Branch, Samuel	3	1839-1855	37
Branson, Eli	1	1787-1815	180

Breaseale, Drury	2	1815-1839	93
Breaseale, Willis (Sr.)		1787-1815	124
Bredden, Margery	1	1787-1815	234
Brightman, Thos. (Sr.)	2	1815-1839	120
Brooks, Christopher (Sr.)	1	1787-1815	156
Brooks, Christopher	2	1815-1839	72
Brooks, Sarah R.	2	1815-1839	157
Brough, Thomas (Sr.)	2	1815-1839	259
Brough, Thos. (Farmer)	3	1839-1855	475
Brown, Cornelius	1	1787-1815	92
Brown, Eliz.	1	1787-1815	399
Brown, Joseph	1	1787-1815	401
Brown, Joseph (Sr.)	3	1839-1855	458
Brown, Shadrack	1	1787-1815	657
Brown, Wm. (Sr.)	1	1787-1815	80
Brownlee, George	1	1815-1839	281
Brwonlee, James (Planter)	1	1787-1815	231
Brownlee, John	1	1787-1815	291
Brownlee, Mary	3	1839-1855	19
Brownlee, Wm.	2	1815-1839	266
Buchanan, James	1	1787-1815	385
Buchanan, Martha	3	1839-1855	72
Buchanan, Mary	1	1787-1815	178
Buchanan, Robert	2	1815-1839	317
Buchanan, Robert E.	3	1839-1855	160
Buchanan, Patrick	1	1787-1815	588
Buchanan, William	2	1815-1839	285
Buford, Wm	2	1815-1839	189
Burnett, Littleberry	2	1815-1839	440
Burton, John	2	1815-1839	287
Burton, Joseph	1	1787-1815	564
Burton, Molly	2	1815-1839	209
Burtram, Mary	2	1815-1839	294
Butler, William	3	1839-1855	118
Cain, John	3	1839-1855	11
Cain, Mary	3	1839-1855	214
Caine, Richard	1	1787-1815	106
Caldwell, Edna	3	1839-1855	529
Caldwell, Eliz. (Widow)	1	1787-1815	672
Caldwell, James (Sr.)	1	1787-1815	392
Caldwell, John	1	1787-1815	142
Caldwell, John (Carpenter)	1	1787-1815	220
Caldwell, John	2	1815-1839	11
Calhoun, Downs	3	1839-1855	369
Calhoun, Hugh	1	1787-1815	239
Calhoun, James (Planter)	1	1787-1815	5
Calhoun, James (Sr.)	1	1737-1815	666
Calhoun, James	3	1839-1855	308
Calhoun, Joseph (Planter)	2	1815-1839	23
Calhoun, Martha	2	1815-1839	277
Calhoun, Patrick	1	1787-1815	159
Calhoun, Rebecca	2	1815-1839	199
Calhoun, Wm. (Sr.)	2	1815-1839	175
Calhoun, Wm.	2	1815-1839	252
Calhoun, Wm.	3	1839-1855	52

Callahan, John	3	1839-1855	552
Callis, James	1	1787-1815	622
Calvert, John	3	1839-1855	191
Campbell, Elizabeth	1	1787-1815	459
Campbell, John (Farmer)	1	1787-1815	222
Campbell, John	2	1815-1839	106
Campbell, John	3	1839-1855	421
Campbell, Margery	1	1787-1815	282
Cane, Mary	1	1787-1815	218
Cannon, George Johnson	3	1839-1855	228
Carmichael, Wm. (Planter)	1	1787-1815	274
Carmichael, Wm.	2	1815-1839	73
Carothers, Margaret	2	1815-1839	204
Carson, Wm (Sr.) (Planter)	1	1787-1815	285
Carson, Wm.	2	1815-1839	305
Caruthers, James	2	1815-1839	126
Caruthers, Martha	1	1787-1815	149
Carwile, Josiah	3	1839-1855	55
Chalmers, Martha	2	1815-1839	238
Chambers, Benjamin	2	1815-1839	173
Chambers, John	1	1787-1815	78
Chandler, Jesse	1	1787-1815	369
Chaney, Nathan	2	1815-1839	232
Chatham, Richard	2	1815-1839	288
Chastain, John	2	1815-1839	301
Cheatham, John L.	2	1815-1839	210
Cheatham, Peter	3	1839-1855	50
Cheatham, Robert	1	1787-1815	598
Cheatham, Thomas	2	1815-1839	214
Cheves, Margaret	2	1815-1839	306
Child, Robt.	3	1839-1855	162
Childs, John (Major)	3	1839-1855	186
Childs, Sarah E.	3	1839-1855	190
Chiles, Benjamin	2	1815-1839	99
Chiles, James	1	1787-1815	343
Chiles, John	2	1815-1839	8
Chiles, John (Sr.)	1	1787-1815	327
Chiles, John	1	1787-1815	641
Chiles, Jonathan (Planter)	1	1787-1815	257
Chiles, Nimrod	1	1787-1815	479
Chiles, Reuben	1	1787-1815	510
Chiles, Wm. (Sr.)	1	1787-1815	367
Chiles, Wm.	3	1839-1855	346
Clark, Benjamin	1	1787-1815	163
Clark, John	3	1839-1855	23
Clark, John Huston	1	1787-1815	319
Clark, Samuel	1	1787-1815	336
Clark, Wm.	1	1787-1815	64
Clark, Wm. (Planter)	1	1787-1815	531
Clark, Wm.	3	1839-1855	73
Clarke, Mary	1	1787-1815	304
Clay, John	2	1815-1839	195
Cobb, Edmund (Jr.)	3	1839-1855	343
Cochran, Andres (Planter)	1	1787-1815	152
Cochran, David	2	1815-1839	146
Cochran, James	2	1815-1839	103

Cochran, James	2	1815–1839	195
Cole, Isaac	2	1815–1839	271
Coleman, Peter H.	2	1815–1839	25
Collier, Edward	3	1830–1855	233
Collier, Wm.	1	1787–1815	603
Collins, Charles (Sr.)	2	1815–1839	286
Collins, Charles	2	1815–1839	290
Coney, Samuel, see — — — — — — — — — — — — — — — — Conway, Samuel			
Conn, George (Farmer)	2	1815–1839	54
Conner, Frances	2	1815–1839	191
Conway, Samuel	1	1787–1815	290
Cook, Samuel G.	3	1839–1855	478
Cooper, James	1	1787–1815	463
Cothran, Samuel (Planter)	2	1815–1839	167
Covin, Delila	3	1839–1855	494
Covington, Richard	2	1815–1839	279
Covington, Wm. (Planter)	1	1787–1815	259
Cowan, Andrew	1	1787–1815	19
Cowan, Hannah	2	1815–1839	56
Cowan, Isaac	2	1815–1839	234
Cowan, John	1	1787–1815	85
Cowan, John	1	1787–1815	394
Cowan, Samuel	3	1839–1855	486
Cox, Wm.	1	1787–1815	526
Cosly, Robt.	3	1839–1855	164
Crawford, Agnes	3	1839–1855	307
Crawford, Elizabeth	1	1787–1815	482
Crawford, Enos	2	1815–1839	72
Crawford, Ester	3	1839–1855	280
Crawford, Green B.	3	1839–1855	58
Crayton, Mary	3	1839–1855	62
Creswell, Elihu	2	1815–1839	144
Creswell, George	2	1815–1839	216
Crowther, James (Rev.)	2	1815–1839	208
Crowther, Nancy	3	1839–1855	2
Crosier, James	1	1787–1815	25
Crosier, Michael C.	2	1815–1839	226
Crymes, John	2	1815–1839	87
Cummings, Robt.	2	1815–1839	125
Cunningham, Agnes	1	1787–1815	555
Cunningham, David	1	1787–1815	102
Cunningham, James	1	1787–1815	250
Cunningham, Jane	1	1787–1815	562
Cunningham, Jane	2	1815–1839	32
Cunningham, Robert A.	2	1815–1839	313
Cunningham, Sarah	3	1839–1855	391
Dabbs, Jesse	2	1815–1839	59
Dale, John (Planter)	3	1839–1855	48
Dale, Mary	2	1815–1839	187
Darracott, John	3	1839–1855	329
Davenport, Charles	1	1787–1815	414
Davenport, John (Planter)	1	1787–1815	235
Davis, Chesley	2	1815–1839	294
Davis, Dempsey	2	1815–1839	101
Davis, Garah (Receipt)	2	1815–1839	173

Davis, Israel	2	1815-1839	22
Davis, John	2	1815-1839	229
Davis, Martha	1	1787-1815	347
Davis, Moses	1	1787-1815	372
Davis, William	2	1815-1839	57
Dawkins, John	2	1815-1839	310
Day, Luke	2	1815-1839	309
Deale, James	2	1815-1839	277
Delechaux, Jacob (Blacksmith)	1	1787-1815	56
Delechaux, Sarah	1	1787-1815	91
De La Howe, John (Dr.)	1	1787-1815	167
De La Howe, J. (Bond)	2	1815-1839	
Delph, Henry	2	1815-1839	129
Dendy, Thos. B. (Rev.)	3	1839-1855	414
Devall, Samuel	2	1815-1839	40
Devlin, James	3	1839-1855	335
Devlin, John	3	1839-1855	376
Devlin, Wm. B.	3	1839-1855	231
De Yampert, Lucius	2	1815-1839	200
Dilishaw, James	2	1815-1839	77
Dodson, Enoch	2	1815-1839	10
Donald, Alexander	1	1787-1815	424
Donald, Jane	3	1839-1855	468
Donnald, John	3	1839-1855	535
Donaldson, Jenny	1	1787-1815	542
Donaldson, Matthew	1	1787-1815	307
Donnelly, James (Minister)	3	1839-1855	527
Dorris, Wm.	2	1815-1839	45
Douglass, Agnes	2	1815-1839	285
Douglass, Mary	3	1839-1855	434
Douglass, William	1	1787-1815	458
Downey, John (Planter)	2	1815-1839	181
Dowtin, Thos. P.	3	1839-1855	512
Dosin, James	1	1787-1815	616
Drummond, Benjamin (Planter)	1	1787-1815	332
Drummond, Daniel	2	1815-1839	95
Duncan, James	1	1787-1815	635
Duncan, Thos. M.	3	1839-1855	467
Dunlap, Wm.	1	1787-1815	559
Dunn, James	1	1787-1815	377
Dunn, Jane	3	1839-1855	265
Dunn, John	3	1839-1855	64
Dunn, Robert	3	1839-1855	140
Dunwoody, Samuel (Rev.)	3	1839-1855	500
Eager, John (Sr.)	2	1815-1839	50
Eakins, Joseph	3	1839-1855	216
Edgar, John	2	1815-1839	144
Edmiston, John	1	1787-1815	39
Edwards, Andrew (Planter)	1	1787-1815	76
Edwards, James (Planter)	1	1787-1815	87
Elgin, Ann	1	1787-1815	118
Elgin, Caty	2	1815-1839	204
Ellington, Dewi	1	1787-1815	624
Ellis, Ann, see - Hathorn, Ann			
Ellis, Robt. (Sr.)	2	1815-1839	231
English, Andrew	1	1787-1815	387

Name	Vol	Period	Page
English, Jane	2	1815-1839	163
Evans, Ezekiel (Sr.)	1	1787-1815	451
Evans, Wm. (Sr.)	2	1815-1839	320
Evart, Andrew	1	1787-1815	255
Eymerie, John (Planter)	1	1787-1815	232
Findlay, Jane	3	1839-1855	166
Finley, Thos.	2	1815-1839	235
Finney, Benjamin	2	1815-1839	160
Flinn, David	3	1839-1855	293
Fooshe, Charles	2	1815-1839	110
Fooshe, Robert	3	1839-1855	167
Fooshe, Wm.	2	1815-1839	197
Fooshe, John	3	1839-1855	107
Fooshee, Sarah (Mrs.)	3	1839-1855	93
Foord, Richard (Sr.)	1	1787-1815	556
Foster, John	1	1787-1815	546
Foster, Robert	2	1815-1839	220
Foster, Samuel (Sr.)	2	1815-1839	150
Fox, Elizabeth	3	1839-1855	150
Fox, Mary	2	1815-1839	197
Franklin, James	2	1815-1839	223
Fraser, Donald	1	1787-1815	585
Fraser, John	1	1787-1815	469
Fraser, John.C.	3	1839-1855	41
Fraser, William	1	1787-1815	519
Fraser, James	3	1839-1855	302
Frith, Susannah	1	1787-1815	604
Frithes, Catrena	1	1787-1815	403
Furr, Henry	2	1815-1839	288
Gable, Hernon	1	1787-1815	295
Gaines, Edmund	1	1787-1815	650
Gaines, William	1	1787-1815	338
Gamble, Samuel	1	1787-1815	362
Gant, Wm.	1	1787-1815	525
Gantt, Benjamin (Dr.)	1	1787-1815	325
Gantt, Cador	3	1839-1855	266
Gantt, Frederick	1	1787-1815	645
Garvin, John	3	1839-1855	254
Gibert, Peter	1	1787-1815	668
Gibson, Robert	2	1815-1839	3
Giles, Robert	2	1815-1839	26
Gilespie, Andrew	2	1815-1839	53
Gilespie, Andrew (Sr.)	2	1815-1839	212
Gilkeison, Rebecca	2	1815-1839	203
Gilkeison, Wm.	2	1815-1839	188
Gilkeyson, Wm.	1	1787-1815	498
Gill, Daniel	1	1787-1815	289
Gillam, David	3	1839-1855	75
Gillam, Elizabeth	3	1839-1855	439
Gilmer, Nancy	3	1839-1855	353
Glasgow, James	3	1839-1855	342
Glasgow, John	3	1839-1855	97
Glover, Frederick	1	1787-1815	199
Glover, Jane	2	1815-1839	98

Glover, John	2	1815-1839	60
Glover, Wm. H.	2	1815-1839	222
Golding, Reuben	2	1815-1839	265
Gordon, Robert	1	1787-1815	620
Gordon, Robert C.	3	1839-1855	419
Gordon, Thomas	3	1839-1855	490
Gorley, James (Farmer)	1	1787-1815	54
Gowdey, Robert	1	1787-1815	58
Gowdy, John	3	1839-1855	175
Graham, James (Sr.)	2	1815-1839	4
Graham, James	2	1815-1839	146
Graham, John	3	1839-1855	392
Gray, Arthur	2	1815-1839	165
Gray, Elizabeth	3	1839-1855	34
Gray, Frederick	2	1815-1839	303
Gray, James	1	1787-1815	188
Gray, James	2	1815-1839	82
Gray, James A.	2	1815-1839	231
Gray, John (Sr.)	2	1815-1839	177
Gray, John	3	1839-1855	488
Gray, Wm (Planter)	1	1787-1815	643
Green, Peter	1	1787-1815	182
Green, Sarah	1	1787-1815	520
Greer, David	2	1815-1839	74
Griffen, Owen (Planter)	1	1787-1815	457
Griffen, Robert	1	1787-1815	524
Griffin, Ira	2	1815-1839	210
Griffin, Vincent	3	1839-1855	194
Groves, Joseph	3	1839-1855	381
Guillebeau, Andrew	1	1787-1815	655
Guillebeau, Peter	3	1839-1855	506
Gunnien, Benjamin	1	1787-1815	573
Guttry, Thomas (Sr.)	1	1787-1815	175
Hadden, John	2	1815-1839	289
Hagood, Elisa Ann	3	1839-1855	4
Hagood, Rebecca	2	1815-1839	139
Hairston, James R.	2	1815-1839	267
Hairston, Jane	3	1839-1855	461
Hairston, Wm. (Sr.) (Planter)	1	1787-1815	502
Hall, Sarah	2	1815-1839	285
Hallum, Basil	2	1815-1839	26
Hamilton, Archibald	1	1787-1815	138
Hamilton, John	1	1787-1815	412
Hamilton, John	3	1839-1855	32
Hamilton, Thomas	1	1787-1815	203
Hampton, Washington E.	3	1839-1855	433
Handley, Peter	3	1839-1855	300
Hanks, Luke	1	1787-1815	37
Hannah, Jean	1	1787-1815	284
Harden, Ralph	2	1815-1839	255
Hardy, Miles	3	1839-1855	322
* Harper, Jane	3	1839-1855	447
Harris, John (Minister)	1	1787-1815	66
Harris, John	2	1815-1839	51
* Harper, Lindsey	3	1839-1855	362

15

Harris, John	2	1815-1839	233
Harris, Robert	1	1787-1815	584
Harris, Thomas	2	1815-1839	166
Harris, Wm.	1	1787-1815	201
Harrison, Nathaniel	2	1815-1839	115
Harvick, Wm.	2	1815-1839	131
Haslet, George	2	1815-1839	172
Haslet, Nancy (Widow)	3	1839-1855	120
Hathorn, Ann	1	1787-1815	135
Hathorn, James	1	1787-1815	571
Hatten, Benjamin	2	1815-1839	85
Hawkins, John (Planter)	1	1787-1815	242
Hawthorne, Lary	3	1839-1855	331
Hawthorn, Thos.	3	1839-1855	102
Haynie, Louisa	3	1839-1855	400
Heard, Isaac	1	1787-1815	357
Heard, Richard	2	1815-1839	7
Hearst, John	3	1839-1855	249
Hearst, William	2	1815-1839	106
Hemphill, Andrew	1	1787-1815	277
Hencely, Mary	2	1815-1839	109
Henry, Francis	3	1839-1855	78
Herndon, Stephen	3	1839-1855	272
Herron, Thomas	2	1815-1839	98
Hill, Benjamin	3	1839-1855	3
Hill, Blueford	2	1815-1839	136
Hill, Hamilton	2	1815-1839	234
Hill, Hamilton	3	1839-1855	1
Hill, James	2	1815-1839	211
Hill, John	1	1787-1815	606
Hill, John	2	1815-1839	132
Hill, Joseph	2	1815-1839	147
Hill, Richard	3	1839-1855	79
Hill, Thomas (Carpenter)	2	1815-1839	117
Hill, Uel	2	1815-1839	243
H odges, Elizabeth	2	1815-1839	21
Hodges, James (Sr.)	2	1815-1839	194
Hodges, John (Major)	2	1815-1839	268
Hodges, N. W.	3	1839-1855	69
H olliman, Joseph Whitfield	3	1839-1855	43
Holloway, George (Planter)	3	1839-1855	183
Hopper, Eliz.	3	1839-1855	294
H ose, Elizabeth	2	1815-1839	306
Hose, John	1	1787-1815	435
H ouston, Alexander	3	1839-1855	554
Houston, Benjamin	2	1815-1839	13
Houston, James	1	1787-1815	303
Houston, John	1	1787-1815	313
Houston, John	1	1787-1815	97
Houston, Marthey	3	1839-1855	420
Howard, Benjamin	1	1787-1815	615
Howe, de la, see -			De La Howe
Howell, Lucy	3	1839-1855	286
Howlet, Penix (Carpenter)	2	1815-1839	22
Huey, James (Planter)	3	1839-1855	153
Huey, John	2	1815-1839	255
Huggins, Wm. (Planter)	1	1787-1815	253

Hughes, Eliz.	3	1839-1855	460
Hughs, Catherine	1	1787-1815	179
Hulton, Rebecca	1	1787-1815	633
Hulton, William	1	1787-1815	532
Hunter, Alexander	2	1815-1839	155
Hunter, Elizabeth	3	1839-1855	198
Hunter, John	3	1839-1855	495
Hunter, Wm.	2	1815-1839	240
Huston, James	1	1787-1815	303
Huston, Jonh, see - - - - - - - - - - - - - - - - - - -			Houston, John
Hutchinson, Wm. (Jr.)	1	1787-1815	174
Hutchinson, James (Planter)	2	1815-1839	100
Hutchinson, Wm. (Planter)	1	1787-1815	419
Irwin, Elizabeth	2	1815-1839	272
Irwin, Frances	2	1815-1839	186
Irwin, James	2	1815-1839	315
Irwin, Samuel	3	1839-1855	472
Jackson, Able	1	1787-1815	418
Jarret, Thos.	1	1787-1815	437
Jay, Abigale	3	1839-1855	538
Jeffries, Nathaniel	1	1787-1815	109
Jennings, Caleb	2	1815-1839	17
Jennings, Robt. T.	3	1839-1855	297
Johnson, Henry	2	1815-1839	236
Johnson, Isiah (Planter)	3	1839-1855	136
Johnson, Jonathan	3	1839-1855	220
Johnson, Samuel	2	1815-1839	319
Johnson, Thomas	2	1815-1839	293
J ohnston, Charles	2	1815-1839	62
Johnston, James	1	1787-1815	587
J ones, Ada Crain (Sr.)	2	1815-1839	64
Jones, Harris	1	1787-1815	278
Jones, Isaah	2	1815-1839	228
Jones, James I. (Farmer)	3	1839-1855	259
Jones, John	1	1787-1815	537
Jones, John	2	1815-1839	208
Jopes, Joseph	1	1787-1815	539
Jones, Joseph (Planter)	3	1839-1855	138
Jones, Mary	2	1815-1839	163
Jones, Moses	3	1839-1855	268
Jones, S.T.C.P.	3	1839-1855	483
Jones, Samuel (Sr.)	3	1830-1855	151
Kaise, Maria Eliz.	1	1787-1815	276
Kay, Robt. H.	3	1839-1855	320
Keller, J ohn	3	1839-1855	427
Kelly, Michal	2	1815-1839	269
Kemp, Wiley	3	1839-1855	492
Kennedy, David	1	1787-1815	631
Kennedy, Joseph (Dr.)	1	1787-1815	145
Kerr, David	2	1815-1839	278
Kerr, Mary	1	1787-1815	379
Kerr, Wm. (Sr.)	1	1787-1815	211
Keys, Malcolm	2	1815-1839	93
Kidd, George	2	1815-1839	184
King, Benjamin (Merchant)	1	1787-1815	9

Kolb, Joseph	2	1815-1839	121
Lainey, John	1	1787-1815	427
Lane, Samuel	1	1787-1815	404
Lasey, Zilpah	1	1787-1815	376
Lathers, John L.	3	1839-1855	551
Latimer, Clement T.	3	1839-1855	539
Lawson, Jonas	1	1787-1815	423
Lawson, Wm.	1	1787-1815	492
Lee, Thomas	2	1815-1839	2
Leon, Joseph	3	1839-1855	360
Leroy, Philip (Sr.)	2	1815-1839	200
Lesley, James	1	1787-1815	508
Lesly, Agnes	2	1815-1839	299
Lesly, David	3	1839-1855	469
Lesly, James	2	1815-1839	44
Lesly, Wm.	2	1815-1839	90
Lessley, Joseph	3	1839-1855	374
Lewallen, Richard	1	1787-1815	335
Liddell, George	1	1787-1815	52
Liddell, James	1	1787-1815	192
Liddell, James	2	1815-1839	124
Lilly, David (Minister)	1	1737-1815	486
Lindsay, John	3	1839-1855	54
Lindsay, Thos. (Sr.)	2	1815-1839	91
Link, Thomas	1	1787-1815	521
Lipford, Asa	2	1815-1839	152
Lipford, Royal N.	2	1815-1839	39
Bipscomb, Jemima	3	1839-1855	354
Lipscomb, Nathan	2	1815-1839	78
Lipscomb, Thos.	2	1815-1839	111
Little, Wm. (Weaver)	1	1787-1815	40
Livingston, George	1	1787-1815	225
Livingston, Jane	1	1787-1815	636
Livingston, Thos. (Planter)	1	1787-1815	528
Lockhart, James	3	1839-1855	327
Logan, Andrew	1	1787-1815	18
Logan, Andrew (Chair-maker)	1	1787-1815	563
Logan, Andrew J.	3	1839-1855	368
Logan, Isaac (Sr.)	2	1815-1839	141
Lomax, Aaron	3	1839-1855	269
Lomax, George	3	1839-1855	99
Lomax, James (Sr.)	2	1815-1839	273
Lomax, James (Jr.)	2	1815-1839	276
Lomax, Lucy	3	1839-1855	438
Long, James	1	1787-1815	475
Long, John Reed	2	1815-1839	50
Long, Wm. (Sr.)	3	1839-1855	418
Loosk, James	1	1787-1815	370
Loveless, Noah	2	1815-1839	205
Lyon, Edward	2	1815-1839	111
Lyon, Elijah	3	1839-1855	315
Lyon, Nathaniel N.		1839-1855	437
Lyon, Samuel (Planter)	1	1787-1815	659

McBride, Jean Anderson	3	1839-1855	7
McBride, John	3	1839-1855	451
McBride, Thos.	1	1787-1815	226
McCalla, John	3	1839-1855	17
McAllister, James G.	2	1815-1839	20
McCallister, Alexander	1	1787-1815	545
McCallister, Wm.	3	1839-1855	199
McCaslan, Robt.	3	1839-1855	349
McCarter, Moses (Farmer)	1	1787-1815	11
McCelvey, Hezekiah C.	3	1839-1855	479
McCelvey, James	2	1815-1839	245
McClinton, Mathew	3	1839-1855	456
McClinton, Robt.	2	1815-1839	250
McClinton, Samuel	1	1787-1815	488
McCollough, James	1	1787-1815	384
McCollough, John	2	1815-1839	246
McComb, Robert	2	1815-1839	257
McComb, Wm.	2	1815-1839	301
McCord, Ellen	3	1839-1855	471
McCord, John (Sr.)	1	1787-1815	445
McCord, Mary	2	1815-1839	84
McCormick, Martha	3	1839-1855	98
McCormick, Wm.	1	1787-1815	495
McCoun, Catherine	3	1839-1855	409
McCracken, James	2	1815-1839	46
McCracken, Ann	3	1839-1855	549
McCrone, Wm.	2	1815-1839	283
McCullouh, James	2	1815-1839	33
McCulloch, John (Sr.)	2	1815-1839	246
McCurry, Stephn	3	1839-1855	53
McDill, Thos.	3	1839-1855	324
McDonnell, Wm.	2	1815-1839	149
McElevee, John	1	1787-1815	3
McElroy, Samuel	2	1815-1839	1
McEntire, Daniel	1	1787-1815	439
McFarland, George	2	1815-1839	258
McFarland, John	2	1815-1839	244
McFarlin, Charles	1	1787-1815	297
McGaw, James	2	1815-1839	74
McGaw, John	1	1787-1815	397
McGaw, Sarah	2	1815-1839	80
McGee, Ann	2	1815-1839	316
McGehee, Charles	2	1815-1839	5
McGehee, Joanna	2	1815-1839	261
McGill, Wm.	2	1815-1839	317
McGowan, James	1	1787-1815	309
McGraw, Samuel	1	1787-1815	596
McGreer, Daniel	2	1815-1839	43
McIllivan, John	1	1787-1815	454
McKee, Adam	1	1787-1815	455
McKee, Thomas (Planter)	1	1787-1815	208
McKellar, Donald (Sr.)	3	1839-1855	251
McKinley, Esther	1	1787-1815	74
McKinny, Susanna	2	1815-1839	174
Macklin, James	2	1815-1839	88
McLaren, Agnes	3	1839-1855	385
McLaren, John (Sr.)	3	1839-1855	14
McLennan, John	3	1839-1855	453
McLin, Hugh (Farmer)	2	1815-1839	35

McMaster, Wm.	2	1815–1839	125
McMaster, Wm.	2	1815–1839	128
McMillan, Andrew	2	1815–1839	239
McMullan, James (Planter)	2	1815–1839	131
McMurtrey, John	2	1815–1839	116
McNeil, Jane	2	1815–1839	130
McNeil, John (Sr.)	2	1815–1839	40
McNeill, John	3	1839–1855	433–b
McQuerans, Samuel	2	1815–1839	63
Maddox, Henley	1	1787–1815	431
Maddox, Jennet	1	1787–1815	653
Mann, John	2	1815–1839	214
Mants, Christopher W.	3	1839–1855	411
Marck, John Balthaser	1	1787–1815	41
Margey, Robert O.	2	1815–1839	122
Marion, Nathaniel	3	1839–1855	9
Marshal, John	1	1787–1815	15
Marshall, George	3	1839–1855	415
Marshall, Joseph	3	1839–1855	502
Martin, Alexander	2	1815–1839	234
Martin, Charles	1	1787–1815	514
Martin, Charles	2	1815–1839	57
Martin, Janet	1	1787–1815	575
Martin, John	2	1815–1839	94
Martin, John Alf	2	1815–1839	223
Martin, Nancy	3	1839–1855	81
Martin, Nancy	3	1839–1855	336
Martin, Robert	1	1787–1815	553
Martin, Robt.	3	1839–1855	211
Martin, Thos. P.	2	1815–1839	175
Martin, Wm.	1	1787–1815	216
Martin, Wm.	2	1815–1839	34
Mathew, John	1	1787–1815	101
Mathews, Joseph C.	3	1839–1855	516
Matthews, David	3	1839–1855	378
Matthews, Joseph	2	1815–1839	166
Matthews, Victor (Farmer)	1	1787–1815	144
Mattison, John	2	1815–1839	322
Mattison, Susanna	2	1815–1839	282
Mattison, Wm.	2	1815–1839	311
Maxfield, Susanna	1	1787–1815	112
Maxwell, Hugh	3	1839–1855	388
Maxwell, John	1	1787–1815	449
Maynard, James Madison	3	1839–1855	340
Mayne, Wm.	2	1815–1839	58
Mayson, James	1	1787–1815	261
Mayson, James	1	1787–1815	391
Mayson, John C.	2	1815–1839	31
Means, Wm.	3	1839–1855	425
Meban, John	1	1787–1815	177
Mechlin, David	1	1787–1815	147
Meriwether, Francis	1	1787–1815	98
Meriwether, Francis	2	1815–1839	56
Meriwether, John	1	1787–1815	69
Meriwether, Mary	2	1815–1839	472
Meriwether, Nicholas	2	1815–1839	154
Meriwether, Robt.	2	1815–1839	189
Miller, Elis. Stead	2	1815–1839	129
Miller, John	1	1787–1815	100

Miller, John (Blacksmith)	1	1787-1815	576
Miller, Martha	1	1787-1815	436
Miller, Robt.	2	1815-1839	91
Miller, Samuel	3	1839-1855	147
Milligan, James	1	1787-1815	523
Mills, Gilbert (Planter)	1	1787-1815	53
Milroy, Wm.	1	1787-1815	338
Mitchum, Joshua	3	1839-1855	180
Mitchell, Isaac	1	1787-1815	35
Mitchell, Lewis	2	1815-1839	70
Mitchell, Tanner (Widow)	1	1787-1815	95
Mitchell, Benj.	2	1815-1839	9
Mitchell, Randolph	1	1787-1815	311
Mitchell, Wm.	2	1815-1839	89
Moat, Andrew, see -			Mott, Andrew
Monchet, Samuel	1	1787-1815	270
Montgomery, Thos.	2	1815-1839	272
Moore, James (Dr.)	1	1787-1815	549
Moore, Rosa	3	1839-1855	326
M oore, Thos.	3	1839-1855	410
Moore, Wm.	1	1787-1815	421
Moore, Wm.	1	1787-1815	580
Moore, Wm. Al	3	1839-1855	104
Moragne, Francis	2	1815-1839	38
Moragne, Isaac	3	1839-1855	358
Moragne, Peter (Sr.)	1	1787-1815	489
Moragne, Peter	1	1787-1815	610
More, Robert	3	1839-1855	188
Morgan, John	1	1787-1815	574
Morgan, Malon	2	1815-1839	292
Morrah, Hugh	2	1815-1839	297
Morrah, Jane	3	1839-1855	222
Morris, Margaret	2	1815-1839	174
Morris, Samuel	1	1787-1815	661
Morris, Samuel	3	1839-1855	61
Morris, Wm.	1	1787-1815	340
Morrison, Archibald (Planter)	1	1787-1815	470
Morrison, Wm.	3	1839-1855	429
Morrow, Arthur	1	1787-1815	477
Morrow, Eliz.	2	1815-1839	18
Morrow, George (Planter)	1	1787-1815	48
Morrow, John	1	1787-1815	305
Morrow, Mary	2	1815-1839	97
Morrow, Wm.	2	1815-1839	190
Morton, Thos. W.	3	1839-1855	158
Mosely, Arthur	1	1787-1815	348
Mosely, Charles	1	1787-1815	544
Mosely, Richard	2	1815-1839	230
Mosely, Tarleton	2	1815-1839	161
Mosely, Jordon	3	1839-1855	168
Mott, Andrew	1	1787-1815	6
Mulhern, Charles	1	1787-1815	21
Mullan, Patrick	2	1815-1839	142
Mulland, Mary	2	1815-1839	27
Mullin, John (Planter)	1	1787-1815	516
Murphy, John	2	1815-1839	75
Murphy, Margaret	3	1839-1855	77
Murray, Titus	1	1787-1815	637

Nash, John	1	1787-1815	119
Neely, Wm.	2	1815-1839	92
Nelson, Harvey H.	3	1839-1855	526
Nicholas, Julius	1	1787-1815	354
Noble, James	1	1787-1815	165
Noble, John L. (Dr.)	2	1815-1839	17
Noble, Patrick	3	1839-1855	296
Norris, Andrew (Atty.)	2	1815-1839	133
Norris, Eli	2	1815-1839	318
Norris, Wm.	1	1787-1815	340
Norris, Wm. (Planter)	2	1815-1839	37
Norris, Wilson	1	1737-1815	593
Northout, Benj.	2	1815-1839	264
Northut, Benj.	2	1815-1839	262
Norwood, Eliz.	1	1787-1815	600
Norwood, John	1	1737-1815	205
Norwood, John	3	1839-1855	152
Norwood, Samuel (Planter)	1	1787-1815	62
Norwood, Thoephilus	1	1787-1815	31
Norwood, Wm.	3	1839-1855	255
Ogilsby, Wm. Wesley	3	1839-1855	298
Oliver, Elijah	3	1839-1855	545
Oliver, James	1	1787-1815	322
Oliver, John	3	1839-1855	480
Owen, John	2	1815-1839	157
Owens, John	1	1787-1815	209
Palmer, Dale	2	1815-1839	80
Palmer, George	3	1839-1855	291
Parker, James (Planter)	2	1815-1839	108
Parker, Margaret	3	1839-1855	547
Parker, Thos.	3	1839-1855	110
Parker, Wm. J.	2	1815-1839	56
Partlow, John	3	1839-1855	115
Paschal, Samuel	1	1787-1815	406
Paschall, Milton	2	1815-1839	256
Paterson, Robt.	1	1787-1815	28
Patterson, Alexander	3	1839-1855	5
Patterson, James (Planter)	1	1787-1815	133
Patterson, Josiah	3	1839-1855	207
Patterson, Josiah C.	3	1839-1855	12
Patterson, Napolean	2	1815-1839	309
Patterson, Samuel (Planter)	1	1787-1815	114
Patterson, Samuel (Farmer)	2	1815-1839	132
Patton, Jane	3	1839-1855	124
Paul, Wm. P.	3	1839-1855	312
Paule, Andrew	2	1815-1839	139
Paule, Wm. P.	2	1815-1839	222
Pearson, James	2	1815-1839	27
Perrin, Samuel	2	1815-1839	195
Perryman, Samuel (Dr.)	2	1815-1839	312
Petot, John F.	3	1839-1855	67
Pettigrew, Ebenezer	2	1815-1839	84
Pettigrew, George	3	1839-1855	89
Pettigrew, James	1	1787-1815	23

Pettigrew, John	1	1787-1815	447
Pettigrew, Louisa	2	1815-1839	164
Pettis, James	2	1815-1839	75
Pitman, Mary	2	1815-1839	165
Pollard, James	1	1787-1815	663
Pollard, Richard	1	1787-1815	341
Pollard, Robt.	2	1815-1839	79
Pollard, Robt.	2	1815-1839	114
Poole, Micajah	2	1815-1839	68
Porter, Eliz.	1	1787-1815	429
Porter, Eliz. D.	3	1839-1855	532
Porter, Hugh	1	1787-1815	506
Porter, Hugh	2	1815-1839	143
Porter, John	1	1787-1815	337
Porter, John	2	1815-1839	136
Porter, John	3	1839-1855	200
Porter, Samuel	2	1815-1839	295
Posey, Marse	3	1839-1855	445
Posey, Martha Crenshaw	3	1839-1855	135
Posey, Richard	2	1815-1839	77
Postell, James (Colonel)	2	1815-1839	130
Postell, Rachel	2	1815-1839	41
Power, John (Sr.)	3	1839-1855	525
Pratt, James	2	1815-1839	194
Pratt, John (Jr.)	3	1839-1855	330
Pratt, Joseph	2	1815-1839	158
Presley, John	1	1787-1815	522
Prince, Edward (Sr.)	2	1815-1839	67
Prince, Edward	2	1815-1839	185
Prince, John (Planter)	1	1787-1815	438
Prince, John W.	2	1815-1839	149
Puckett, James	2	1815-1839	207
Pulliam, James	2	1815-1839	244
Pulliam, John (Jr.)	1	1787-1815	228
Pulliam, Lucy L.	2	1815-1839	289
Pulliam, Zachary	2	1815-1839	152
Pulliam, Sarah	1	1787-1815	590
Purdy, Henry (Planter)	2	1815-1839	14
Rabun, David	2	1815-1839	1
Raiford, Wm. P. (Farmer)	3	1839-1855	143
Ragland, Samuel	1	1787-1815	251
Ralston, James	1	1787-1815	121
Ramey, John	3	1839-1855	21
Rampey, John	2	1815-1839	2
Rasor, Christian	3	1839-1855	287
Rasor, James (Farmer)	2	1815-1839	81
Ravlin, John (Planter)	1	1787-1815	88
Ray, Thos.	1	1787-1815	77
Red, George	3	1839-1855	42
Red, Robt.	3	1839-1855	207
Reid, George (Planter)	1	1787-1815	45
Reid, Hugh	2	1815-1839	206
Reighley, Wm.	1	1787-1815	129
Richey, James (Sr.)	1	1787-1815	551
Richey, James	2	1815-1839	251
Richey, Joseph	3	1839-1855	263

Richey, Margaret	3	1839-1855	463
Richey, Robert	2	1815-1839	192
Richey, Robert	3	1839-1855	247
Richey, Wm.	3	1839-1855	202
Riddle, Elis.	2	1815-1839	112
Riddle, Joseph	1	1787-1815	579
Riley, Andrew	3	1839-1855	408
Riley, Thos.	3	1839-1855	470
Robartson, John (Sr.)	1	1787-1815	1
Robenson, Samuel	3	1839-1855	524
Roberts, George	2	1815-1839	191
Roberts, Jane	3	1839-1855	338
Roberts, LeRoy	2	1815-1839	14
Robertson, Andrew Jackson	3	1839-1855	218
Robertson, George	2	1815-1839	30
Robertson, James	1	1787-1815	617
Robertson, Hugh	2	1815-1839	276
Robertson, John	3	1839-1855	399
Robertson, Matilda	2	1815-1839	242
Robertson, Robt. (Farmer)	2	1815-1839	137
Robertson, Samuel	2	1815-1839	224
Robertson, Wm.	1	1787-1815	670
Robinson, Alexander S.	2	1815-1839	179
Robinson, Andrew	3	1839-1855	39
Robinson, Christianna	3	1839-1855	301
Robinson, Nancy	3	1839-1855	402
Robinson, Samuel	3	1839-1855	319
Robinson, Wm.	3	1839-1855	40
Robison, Isaac	3	1839-1855	295
Roden, Leanner	2	1815-1839	298
Roger, Ann Lespine	1	1787-1815	268
Roger, Peter (Planter)	1	1787-1815	280
Rogers, Jeremiah	1	1787-1815	499
Rosemond, James	1	1787-1815	441
Rosemond, Jean	1	1787-1815	90
Ross, Moses Glenn	3	1839-1855	544
Ross, Robt.	1	1787-1815	60
Ross, Stephen	3	1839-1855	88
Ross, Wm. (Planter)	1	1787-1815	186
Ruff, Christian	3	1839-1855	142
Rush, John (Jr.)	3	1839-1855	508
Russell, Abraham	3	1839-1855	282
Russell, David	1	1787-1815	671
Russell, John (Sr.)	1	1787-1815	265
Russell, Timothy (Dr.)	1	1787-1815	240
Rykard, Peter	2	1815-1839	153
Sadler, Wm.	3	1839-1855	80
Sale, Benj. W.	3	1839-1855	509
Sale, John	2	1815-1839	118
Sale, Wm.	2	1815-1839	198
Sales, James	2	1815-1839	161
Sample, Robt.	2	1815-1839	20
Sanders, Adam	1	1787-1815	400
Sanders, Donald	2	1815-1839	101
Sanders, John	2	1815-1839	34
Sanders, Joseph	1	1787-1815	389
Sanders, Joseph	1	1787-1815	611

Saxon, Benjamin T.	2	1815-1839	239
Saxon, D. T.	3	1839-1855	384
Scott, Alexander	1	1787-1815	416
Scott, Archibald	1	1787-1815	504
Scott, Joseph (Sr.)	2	1815-1839	46
Scott, Wm.	2	1815-1839	217
Seawright, James	1	1787-1815	47
Shackelford, Mordicai	3	1839-1855	15
Shanklin, Pheobe	1	1787-1815	473
Shanklin, Thos.	2	1815-1839	201
Shanks, Matthaw	2	1815-1839	116
Shannon, James	2	1815-1839	96
Sharp, Henry	3	1839-1855	111
Sharpe, Edward	1	1787-1815	582
Sharpe, Wm.	1	1839-1855	133
Shaw, Wm.	1	1787-1815	8
Spence, James (Sr.)	2	1815-1839	260
Spence, Samuel	2	1815-1839	126
Spragins, Wm.	2	1815-1839	171
Spruill, John	1	1787-1815	496
Sproul, James	2	1815-1839	145
Stallsworth, Thos.	2	1815-1839	134
Stallsworth, Wm.	2	1815-1839	225
Stallworth, Thos.	3	1839-1855	178
Stalsworth, Joseph	1	1787-1815	157
Stanfield, Wm.	1	1787-1815	433
Stark, Charles	2	1815-1839	321
Starke, Reuben	2	1815-1839	300
Starks, Jeremiah	2	1815-1839	129
Steel, Aaron	1	1787-1815	131
Steele, David	2	1815-1839	179
Steifle, Mary	3	1839-1855	351
Stephenson, James	2	1815-1839	95
Stevens, Martha	2	1815-1839	182
Stewart, B. W.	3	1839-1855	227
Stewart, James (Sr.)	3	1839-1855	92
Stewart, John	2	1815-1839	170
Strain, John	1	1787-1815	238
Strain, Mary	2	1815-1839	245
Strickland, Jacob	1	1787-1815	618
Strickland, Nathan (Planter)	3	1839-1855	454
Stuart, Adam	2	1815-1839	104
Stuart, Alexander,	2	1815-1839	226
Stuart, David	2	1815-1839	307
Stuart, Margaret	2	1815-1839	321
Stuart, Wm.	2	1815-1839	76
Sullivan, D. B.	2	1815-1839	214
Swain, John	2	1815-1839	115
Swain, Nancy	3	1839-1855	534
Swain, Robt.	1	1787-1815	601
Swanzy, Robt.	1	1787-1815	154
Swearingen, Joseph, see - - - - - - - -	Van Swearingen, Joseph		
Swilling, John C.	2	1815-1839	302
Taggart, Moses	2	1815-1839	101
Taggart, Moses	3	1839-1855	65
Tait, Nancy	3	1839-1855	171

Talbert, John	2	1815–1839	113
Talbert, Robt.	3	1839–1855	114
Talbert, Wm.	3	1839–1855	283
Tate, Enos	3	1839–1855	145
Tatom, Orville	2	1815–1839	304
Taton, Wm.	1	1787–1815	349
Taylor, Andrew	2	1815–1839	36
Taylor, Thos.	1	1787–1815	38
Tedards, David	3	1839–1855	465
Tenlon, Charles	1	1787–1815	628
Thacker, Isaac	1	1787–1815	581
Thacker, Joel	1	1787–1815	382
Thomas, Thomas Walter	3	1839–1855	515
Thompson, John	2	1815–1839	29
Thornton, Jonathan	2	1815–1839	127
Thornton, Samuel	1	1787–1815	196
Tilman, Edward	1	1787–1815	647
Tilman, Hiram	2	1815–1839	308
Tiner, Harris	3	1839–1855	131
Tinsley, Thomas	1	1787–1815	244
Todd, Eliz.	3	1839–1855	521
Todd, Eliz.	3	1839–1855	522
Todd, William	2	1815–1839	102
Tolbert, Mary	3	1839–1855	209
Trimble, Esther	2	1815–1839	54
Turnbull, Jane	2	1815–1839	254
Turnbull, John (Planter)	2	1815–1839	80
Turk, John (Planter)	1	1787–1815	128
Van Swearingen, Joseph	1	1787–1815	116
Vernon, James (Sr.)	1	1787–1815	287
Vernon, James (Sr.)	1	1787–1815	13
Vernon, Thomas	2	1815–1839	219
Vick, Fatha	1	1787–1815	561
Vickery, William	1	1787–1815	352
Waite, John	1	1787–1815	409
Walker, David	3	1839–1855	493
Walker, Henry G.	2	1815–1839	167
Walker, Lettice	2	1815–1839	206
Walker, Solomen	3	1839–1855	533
Walkins, Robt.	2	1815–1839	187
Wallace, James (Farmer)	1	1787–1815	122
Wallace, Robt.	3	1839–1855	26
Wallace, Wm. (Sr.)	2	1815–1839	9
Waller, Benj.	1	1787–1815	359
Waller, Eliz.	1	1787–1815	346
Waller, John (Minister)	1	1787–1815	298
Waller, John N.	1	1787–1815	301
Waller, Leonard	2	1815–1839	156
Ward, James (Dr.)	2	1815–1839	167
Ward, Joseph	1	1787–1815	207
Ward, Thomas	2	1815–1839	37
Ward, Wm.	1	1787–1815	411
Ward, Wm.	2	1815–1839	303

Wardlaw, Eliah	1	1787-1815	501
Wardlaw, J. Hugh	1	1787-1815	316
Wardlaw, James	2	1815-1839	63
Wardlaw, James	2	1815-1839	81
Wardlaw, James	3	1839-1855	83
Wardlaw, John (Jr.)	1	1787-1815	72
Wardlaw, Joseph	1	1787-1815	137
Wardlaw, Joseph	3	1839-1855	431
Wardlaw, Polley	1	1787-1839	639
Wardlaw, Wm. B.	2	1815-1839	160
Ware, Edmond (General)	2	1815-1839	246
Ware, Jane	2	1815-1839	240
Waters, Mary	1	1787-1815	237
Watkins, Robt.	2	1815-1839	187
Watkins, Wm.	1	1787-1815	408
Watson, Christopher	1	1787-1815	517
Watson, Edward	3	1839-1855	334
Watson, James	2	1815-1839	119
Watson, James F.	3	1839-1855	404
Watson, Le Roy	3	1839-1855	121
Watson, Stephen	1	1787-1815	461
Watson, Stephen	3	1839-1855	20
Watson, Wm.	2	1815-1839	298
Watson, Wm. Edward	3	1839-1855	436
Watt, Jenneh (Widow)	1	1787-1815	381
Weatherall, John	2	1815-1839	134
Webb, Andrew, (Farmer)	1	1787-1815	512
Webb, B. C.	3	1839-1855	542
Webb, James (Farmer)	1	1787-1815	113
Webb, John	3	1839-1855	443
Wedgworth, Wm. (Farmer)	1	1787-1815	223
Weed, Andrew	3	1839-1855	357
Weed, Martha	1	1787-1815	540
Weed, Nathaniel	1	1787-1815	217
Weed, Nathaniel	2	1815-1839	43
Weed, Reuben (Planter)	1	1787-1815	82
Weems, Emily	2	1815-1839	175
Weems, Margaret	2	1815-1839	123
Wharton, J. C.	2	1815-1839	222
Wharton, Pleasant	2	1815-1839	61
White, Alexander	2	1815-1839	58
White, Agnes	2	1815-1839	68
White, Frances	3	1839-1855	449
White, Francis	1	1787-1815	306
White, James	1	1787-1815	215
White, John	1	1787-1815	107
White, John	2	1815-1839	172
White, John	2	1815-1839	241
White, Margaret	1	1787-1815	592
White, Richard M.	2	1815-1839	127
White, Wm.	2	1815-1839	55
White, Wm.	2	1815-1839	82
Whorton, Pleas G.	2	1815-1839	61
Wideman, Adam (Sr.)	3	1839-1855	299
Wideman, Henry	1	1787-1815	443
Wier, John	3	1839-1855	332
Wier, Thomas	3	1839-1855	394
Williams, James	2	1815-1839	302

Williams, Simeon	1	1787-1815	279
Williams, Thomas W.	3	1839-1855	173
Williamson, Thomas G.	3	1839-1855	56
Willis, Joshua	2	1815-1839	221
Willis, Rachel	2	1815-1839	332
Wills, John	1	1787-1815	484
Wilson, Arabella	2	1815-1839	151
Wilson, Charles	1	1787-1815	566
Wilson, Eliz.	3	1839-1855	396
Wilson, Griezzella	3	1839-1855	224
Wilson, Henry	1	1787-1815	493
Wilson, 'Hugh (Planter)	1	1787-1815	161
Wilson, James	1	1787-1815	594
Wilson, John	1	1787-1815	176
Wilson, John	3	1839-1855	126
Wilson, Mathew	2	1815-1839	263
Wilson, Michael	1	1787-1815	111
Wilson, Nancy	2	1815-1839	141
Wilson, Nathaniel	1	1787-1815	198
Wilson, Samuel	2	1815-1839	274
Wilson, Wm.	1	1787-1815	293
Wilson, Wm. W.	3	1839-1855	499
Wimbush, Alexander	2	1815-1839	28
Winn, Robt.	2	1815-1839	127
Winn, Thomas	1	1787-1815	184
Wire, William (Planter)	3	1839-1855	179
Witts, Stephen	3	1839-1855	46
Woodin, Rebekah	1	1787-1815	26
Woods, Esther	2	1815-1839	6
Woods, Susanna	2	1815-1839	205
Woods, Wm.	1	1787-1815	351
Wooldridge, Gibson	2	1815-1839	18
Wright, Robt.	1	1787-1815	608
Wright, Wm.	1	1787-1815	396
Wums, Margaret	2	1815-1839	123
Yarbrough, Wm.	2	1815-1839	275
Yeldell, Robt. (Sr.)	1	1787-1815	33
Young, Francis	2	1815-1839	96
Young, Isaac	3	1839-1855	60
Young, James	1	1787-1815	213
Young, Jean	1	1787-1815	646
Young, Nancy	3	1839-1855	176
Young, Robt. (Sr.)	1	1787-1815	557
Young, Samuel	2	1815-1839	28
Young, Samuel (Sr.)	2	1815-1839	109
Young, Samuel	3	1839-1855	206
Young, Valentine	2	1815-1839	319
Youngs, Jane	2	1815-1839	315
Youngs, Samuel	2	1815-1839	85
Zimmerman, Henry	2	1815-1839	270
Zimmermah, John	3	1839-1855	462
Zimmerman, Mary	1	1787-1815	275

Copied by:
Mrs. John D. Rogers
/s/   Mrs. John D. Rogers

INDEX TO

ANDERSON COUNTY WILLS.

VOLUME NO. 1
1791-1834

VOLUME NO. 2
1835-1857

This index is compiled from W.P.A.
copies of wills filed in the
COUNTY PROBATE COURTS. The
volumes indexed are a part
of the South Carolina Collection of the University
of South Carolina Library.

Columbia, S. C.
1959

ANDERSON COUNTY

Name	Vol.	Date	Section	Page
Abbot, Margaret	2	1855-1857	B	343
Abbott, Elizabeth	2	1855-1857	B	371
Abbott, Margaret, see	- - - - - - - - - - - - - - - -		Abbot, Margaret	
Adair, John	1	1800-1834	A	195
Adams, John	2	1855-1857	B	274
Alexander, David	1	1791-1798	C	23
Allen, James E.	2	1855-1857	B	391
Anderson, George	1	1800-1834	A	95
Anderson, John	1	1800-1834	A	60
Anderson, Robt. (Gen.)	1	1800-1834	A	145
Armstrong, John	1	1800-1834	A	95
Augusta, Seasor	1	1800-1834	A	54
Auguste, Seasor, see	- - - - - - - - - - - - - - - -		Augusta, Seasor	
Bailey, James	1	1800-1834	A	241
Barr, Samuel	1	1800-1834	A	207
Barry, Richard	1	1800-1834	A	70
Barry, William T.	1	1800-1834	A	258
Barton, Benjamin	1	1800-1834	A	230
Barton, Joseph	1	1800-1834	A	223
Baskins, Jack	1	1800-1834	A	406
Beaty, John (Sr.)	1	1800-1834	A	214
Beaty, Martha	2	1855-1857	B	229
Beaty, Wm.	2	1855-1857	B	225
Beety, John, see	- - - - - - - - - - - - - - - -		Beaty, John	
Bennett, Charles (Sr.)	2	1855-1857	B	213
Bennett, Elisha (Sr.)	1	1800-1834	A	420
Bennett, Wm.	1	1800-1834	A	314
Boone, Mary Sniper	2	1800-1854	Floating wills	312
Bowie, Charles	2	1855-1857	B	78
Bowie, Wesley	2	1855-1857	B	80
Boyd, David L.	1	1791-1798	C	290
Boyse, Alexander	1	1800-1834	A	64
Brimer, Benjamin	1	1800-1834	A	34
Broughton, Willibough	1	1800-1834	A	48
Brown, Charles	2	1855-1857	B	270
Brown, David	1	1791-1798	C	45
Brown, George	2	1855-1857	B	175
Brown, John	2	1800-1854	Floating wills	45
Brown, John	2	1855-1857	B	309
Brown, Joseph (Planter)	1	1800-1834	A	182
Brown, Nancy	2	1855-1857	B	240
Brown, Sarah	1	1800-1834	A	258
Brown, Spencer	1	1800-1834	A	377
Brown, William	1	1791-1798	C	59
Browne, Elijah	2	1855-1857	B	32
Bruce, James (Sr.)	1	1800-1834	A	237
Bruster, John (Sr.)	1	1800-1834	A	205
Bruster, Samuel	1	1800-1834	A	114
Buchanan, Ebenizer	2	1800-1854	Floating wills	131
Burefs, James, see -			Burriss, James	
Burefs, John B., see -			Burriss, John B	

Burefs, Joshua, see -				-Burriss, Joshua
Buris, Joshua, see -				Burriss, Joshua
Burns, Anderson	2	1800-1854	Floating wills	39
Burns, Anderson	2	1835-1857	B	203
Burriss, James	2	1835-1857	B	9
Burriss, John B.	2	1835-1857	B	13
Burriss, Joshua	1	1800-1834	A	38
Burrow, Henry	1	1800-1834	A	367
Burrows, John B., see -				Burriss, John B.
Burt, Francis	2	1835-1857	B	47
Burt, Moody	2	1835-1857	B	159
Burton, Blackman	2	1835-1857	B	233
Caldwell, Nancy M.	2	1791-98	C	315
Calhoun, Alexander	1	1800-1834	A	288
Calhoun, John Ewing	1	1800-1834	A	20
Cannon, Russell	1	1800-1834	A	283
Cantrell, Wm.	1	1800-1834	A	343
Caradine, Thos.	1	1800-1834	A	243
Carpenter, Burwell	1	1800-1834	A	374
Carson, James	1	1800-1834	A	70
Casey, Mary	2	1835-1857	B	349
Chappell, Jesse	1	1800-1834	A	116
Chastain, John	1	1800-1834	A	56
Chestain, John, see -				Chastain, John
Christain, John, see -				Chastain, John
Clark, Joseph	2	1835-1857	B	193
Clarke, Matthew	2	1835-1857	B	108
Clarkson, Wm. (Jr.)	1	1791-1798	C	275
Clement, Isaac, see -				Clements, Isaac
Clements, Isaac	1	1800-1834	A	219
Cleveland, Benj.	1	1800-1834	A	72
Cleveland, William	1	1800-1834	A	259
Clinkscales, Asa	2	1835-1857	B	218
Clinkscales, Francis(Sr.)	2	1835-1857	B	60
Clinkscales, Levi	2	1835-1857	B	145
Cobb, Robt. (Sr.)	1	1800-1834	A	328
Commins, Harmon, see -				Cummins, Harmon
Compton, James	1	1791-1798	C	15
Conwill, James	2	1835-1857	B	284
Cooper, Thos.	1	1800-1834	A	254
Corben, Peter	1	1791-1798	C	17
Corr, John (Sr.)	2	1835-1857	B	75
Cox, Beverly	1	1791-1798	C	30
Cox, Elizabeth	1	1800-1834	A	111
Cox, Elizabeth	2	1835-1857	B	351
Cox, John	1	1800-1834	A	211
Cox, Wm.	1	1800-1834	A	253
Cox, Wm. (Sr.)	2	1835-1857	B	148
Cox, Wm.	2	1835-1857	B	182
Craig, Robt.	1	1791-1798	C	66
Crenshaw, Abraham	1	1800-1834	A	82
Crenshaw, Jesse (Sr.)	1	1800-1834	A	358
Crymes, George	2	1835-1857	B	197
Cummins, Harmon	2	1835-1857	B	280
Cunningham, James	1	1800-1834	A	324
Cunningham, Samuel	2	1835-1857	B	207
Cunningham, Thos.	2	1835-1857	B	377

31

Name	Vol	Years	Type	Page
Dalrunple, Samuel, see				Dalrymple,Samuel
Dalrymple, Samuel	1	1791-1798	C	3
Dalrymple, Sarah	2	1835-1857	B	55
Dane, Gwenney, see				Dean, Gwenney
Dart, Thos. Lynch	1	1800-1834	A	431
Davis, Nathaniel	1	1800-1834	A	246
Davis, Vann (Sr.)	1	1800-1834	A	121
Day, Ballard (Sr.)	1	1800-1834	A	189
Dean, Gwenney	2	1835-1857	B	5
Dean, Samuel	2	1800-1854	Floating wills	28
Dean, Thomas	2	1835-1857	B	334
Dickey, Wm.	1	1800-1834	A	96
Dickson, Elener	2	1835-1857	B	384
Dickson, Margaret	1	1800-1834	A	295
Dickson, Mathew	1	1800-1834	A	378
Dilworth, George(Planter)	1	1800-1834	A	162
Dobbins, James	1	1800-1834	A	224
Dobbs, Lodowick	1	1800-1834	A	172
Doughty, Daniel (Planter)	1	1800-1834	A	52
Doughty, Joseph (Sr.)	1	1800-1834	A	191
Douthit, James	2	1835-1857	B	275
Douthit, John	1	1800-1834	A	161
Dowdle, Robt. (Sr.)	1	1800-1834	A	248
Drennan, David	1	1800-1834	A	110
Duff, James (Sr.)	1	1800-1834	A	42
Duff, James	1	1800-1834	A	176
Duke, Abraham	1	1800-1834	A	218
Durham, David	1	1800-1834	A	376
Earle, Elias	1	1800-1834	A	266
Earle, John B.	2	1835-1857	B	16
Early, Patrick	1	1791-1798	C	72
Earnest, Jacob, see				Ernest, Jacob
Earp, Wesley	2	1835-1857	B	195
Easley, Robt.	1	1800-1834	A	74
Edmiston, Caleb (Farmer)	1	1800-1834	A	12
Edmondson, Thos.	1	1800-1834	A	106
Edmondson, Wm. (Capt.)	2	1800-1854	Floating wills	20
Edmonston, Caleb, see				Edmiston,Caleb
Edwards, Thos.	1	1800-1834	A	76
Edwards,Thos.K. (Planter)	1	1800-1834	A	304
Elliot, Charles	1	1800-1834	A	45
Elliot, Wm. (Jr.)	2	1835-1857	B	91
Elliot, Wm.	2	1835-1857	B	104
Elliott, Ralph E.	2	1835-1857	B	322
Elrod, George	2	1835-1857	B	344
Elrod, Isaac	2	1835-1857	B	162
Elrod, Jeremiah	2	1835-1857	B	141
Elrod, Thomas	2	1835-1857	B	187
Elrod, Wm.	2	1835-1857	B	366
Emerson, Samuel	2	1835-1857	B	176
Ernest, Jacob	1	1800-1834	A	37
Erskine, James (Sr.)	2	1835-1857	B	201
Erskine, Wm.	2	1835-1857	B	390
Evens, Eliz.	1	1800-1834	A	171

Fant, Jessee	2	1825-1857	B	142
Felton, Wm.	1	1800-1834	A	391
Findly, Samuel	1	1791-1798	C	19
Forsythe, Wm.	2	1835-1857	B -	167
Foster, James	1	1830-1834	A	30
Foster, James	1	1800-1834	A	46
Fountain, John	1	1800-1834	A	374
Fretwell, John	2	1835-1857	B	214
Gabee, Robert	2	1800-1854	Floating wills	3
Gambrell, John	1	1800-1834	A	425
Gant, Giles	1	1791-1798	C	7
Gassaway, Benjamin	2	1835-1857	B	300
Gassaway, James	1	1800-1834	A	39
Gentry, Arlhy	2	1835-1857	B	281
Gentry, John	2	1800-1854	Floating wills	37
Gentry, John	2	1835-1857	B	90
George, John	1	1800-1834	A	330
Gibbes, Lewis L.	1	1800-1834	A	365
Gibbs, John	2	1800-1854	Floating wills	35
Gibson, Randle	1	1791-1798	C	14
Gibson, Thos.	1	1800-1834	A	409
Gillison, Archibald	1	1790-1793	Floating wills	5
Gipson, Randle, see — — — — — — — — — — — — — — — — — Gibson, Randle				
Goode, Lewelling	2	1835-1857	B	441
Gordon, Robert	2	1835-1857	B	177
Green, Isham	1	1800-1834	A	92
Green, Mishack	1	1791-1798	C	61
Green, William	1	1800-1834	A	7
Greenlee, Peter	1	1800-1834	A	16
Greer, David (Sr.)	2	1835-1857	B	346
Greer, James	1	1791-1798	C	22
Griffin, James C.	2	1835-1857	B	154
Griffin, Wm. (Planter)	1	1800-1834	A	2
Grissup, Nancy	2	1835-1857	B	254
Guttry, David	2	1835-1857	B	137
Guyton, Aaron	2	1835-1857	B	115
Guyton, Robt.	2	1835-1857	B	106
Hackett, Robert	1	1800-1834	A	407
Halbert, Wm.	1	1800-1834	A	102
Haley, Reuben	2	1835-1857	B	386
Hall, Absalem	1	1800-1834	A	275
Hall, Absalom	2	1835-1857	B	364
Hall, Fenton	1	1800-1834	A	221
Hall, Nancy	1	1835-1857	B	242
Hall, Nathaniel	1	1791-1798	B	41
Hall, Robert	1	1791-1798	C	47
Hallum, John	1	1800-1834	A	193
Hallum, Wm.	1	1800-1834	A	35
Hamilton, Archibald (Planter)	1	1800-1834	A	134
Hamilton, Leonard S. (Farmer)	2	1835-1857	B	318
Hamilton, Luke	1	1800-1834	A	284
Hammond, Lucy	1	1800-1834	A	416
Hammond, Michael	1	1800-1834	A	123

Hammond, Samuel J.	2	1835-1857	B	355
Harbin, Joseph B.	2	1835-1857	B	383
Harkins, Sarah	1	1800-1834	B	383
Harkness, John	2	1835-1857	B	324
Harper, John	2	1835-1857	B	180
Harper, Nancy	2	1835-1857	B	382
Harper, Wm.	2	1835-1857	B	125
Harris, Handy	1	1800-1834	A	58
Harris, James S.	2	1835-1857	B	37
Harris, John	2	1835-1857	B	184
Harris, Nathaniel	2	1835-1857	B	50
Harrison, Hannah	2	1835-1857	B	283
Hasel, Hary	1	1800-1834	A	33
Hayes, John	2	1800-1854	Floating wills	12
Head, George	1	1800-1834	A	226
Headen, Elisha	2	1800-1854	Floating wills	23
Heaton, Nicholas	1	1800-1834	A	303
Heaton, Wm.	1	1791-1798	C	70
Hembree, James (Minister)	2	1835-1857	B	250
Henderson, Robert	1	1800-1834	A	19
Herring, William	1	1800-1834	A	139
Hill, Abel Farmer)	1	1800-1834	A	28
Hillhouse, Joseph	2	1835-1857	B	381
Hipps, Joseph (Sr.)	2	1835-1857	B	257
Hoge, George	1	1800-1834	A	5
Holland, Benjamin	1	1800-1834	A	216
Holland, Moses	1	1800-1834	A	355
Houston, Thomas	1	1800-1834	A	11
Hudgens, Ambrose	1	1800-1834	A	4
Huff, Julius	2	1835-1857	B	268
Humphreys, John	1	1800-1834	A	98
Hunnicutt, Sarah	2	1835-1857	B	393
Hunter, Mary (Sr.)	1	1800-1834	A	276
Hunter, Thos.	1	1800-1834	A	286
Ingram, John	2	1835-1857	B	186
Irwin, Robert	1	1800-1834	A	270
Isaacs, Elijah	1	1791-1798	C	69
James, Elizabeth	1	1800-1834	A	278
James, Griffith	1	1791-1798	C	27
Jennings, John	2	1835-1857	B	74
Johnson, Martha	2	1835-1857	B	304
Johnston, John (Yeoman)	1	1790-1793	Floating wills	3
Jolly, Joseph	1	1800-1834	A	83
Jones, Ambrose	2	1835-1857	B	190
Jones, Lewis	2	1800-1854	Floating wills	10
Junkin, Margaret	2	1835-1857	B	118
Junkin, Robert	2	1835-1857	B	84
Kay, James W.	2	1800-1854	Floating wills	40
Kay, James	2	1835-1857	B	362
Kay, Robert	2	1800-1854	Floating wills	8
Kelly, Elisha	2	1835-1857	B	173

Kemp, Asa (Planter)	1	1800-1834	A	50
Kennemore, George	1	1800-1834	B	337
Keown, Wm.	2	1835-1857	B	150
Kilby, Adam	1	1800-1834	A	265
King, William	2	1835-1857	B	529
Kinnemore, George, see	- - - - - - - - - - - - -		Kennemore, George	
Kirkscy, Christopher	1	1800-1834	A	235
Knox, John	1	1800-1834	A	338
Laboon, Peter	1	1800-1834	A	1
Laboon, Peter (Sr.)	1	1800-1834	A	335
Lawrence, Benjamin (Farmer)		1800-1834	A	300
Lawrence, Joab	1	1800-1834	A	158
Leathers, Michael	1	1800-1834	A	66
Leboon, Peter, see	- - - - - - - - - - - - - -		Laboon, Peter	
Ledbetter, Abner	1	1800-1834	A	359
Ledbetter, Daniel	1	1800-1834	A	316
Ledbetter, Henry	1	1800-1834	A	44
Ledbetter, John	1	1800-1834	A	372
Leonard, Wm.	1	1800-1834	A	129
Lewis, David	1	1800-1834	A	264
Lewis, Eleanor	2	1835-1857	B	82
Lewis, Richard M.	2	1835-1857	B	199
Lewis, Sarah	2	1835-1857	B	112
Liddell, Andrew (Sr.)	1	1800-1834	A	413
Liddle, Moses	1	1800-1834	A	14
Lidell, Thoas.	1	1791-1798	C	51
Linley, John (Yeoman)	1	1790-1793	Floating wills	2
Linn, Robt. M., see	- - - - - - - - - - - - -		Lynn, Robt. M.	
Lorton, Frances	2	1835-1857	P	305
Love, Thomas	1	1800-1834	L	190
Lynch, Wm.	2	1800-1834	Floating wills	25
Lynn, Robt. M.	1	1800-1834	A	404
McAllister, Andrew (Jr.)	1	1800-1834	A	392
McAllister, Daniel (Planter)	1	1800-1834	A	61
McAllister, Nathan	2	1835-1857	B	35
McCallister, Andrew	1	1800-1835	A	417
McCallister, Nathan, see	- - - - - - - - - - - - -		McAllister, Nathan	
McCann, Robert	1	1800-1834	A	389
McCann, Robert	1	1800-1834	A	419
McCarley, James	2	1835-1857	B	205
McCarley, Joseph	2	1835-1857	B	308
McClesky, Joseph	1	1800-1834	A	9
McCollough, John, see	- - - - - - - - - - - - - -		McCullough, John	
McCoy, James (Sr.)	2	1835-1857	B	168
McCoy, Samuel (Sr.)	2	1835-1857	B	2 38
McCulley, Samuel (Farmer)	1	1800-1834	A	68
McCullough, John	1	1800-1834	A	80
McCurday, Wm.	2	1835-1857	B	71
McDaniel, Patsey	1	1800-1834	A	55
McFee, Samuel	2	1835-1857	B	127
McGee, Jesse	2	1835-1857	B	39
McGill, Samuel	2	1835-1857	B	94
McKee, Martha	2	1800-1854	Floating wills	29
McKinstrey, Francis	1	1800-1834	A	269
McLin, James Gamble, see	- - - - - - - - - - - -		Mecklin, James Gamble	

McLinn, Hugh	2	1855-1857	B	164
McMahan, Peter	2	1855-1857	B	189
McMahan, Susannah	2	1855-1857	B	259
McPherson, Elizabeth	2	1855-1857	B	232
McPherson, Wm. (Sr.)	1	1800-1834	A	387
Magill, Samuel, see				McGill, Samuel
Major, Epps	1	1800-1834	A	321
Major, James	2	1855-1857	B	290
Major, John Perry	2	1855-1857	B	306
Major, Joseph M.	2	1855-1857	B	166
Malister, Daniel, see				McAllister, Daniel
Martin, David	2	1855-1857	B	126
Martin, Louis D.	1	1800-1834	A	200
Martin, Roger	2	1800-1854	Floating wills	1
Mason, Ambrose	2	1855-1857	B	49
Masters, Wm.	2	1800-1854	Floating wills	18
Mattison, George B.	2	1855-1857	B	359
Mattison, James	2	1855-1857	B	247
Mattison, James	2	1855-1857	B	254
Mattison, Thos. (Sr.)	2	1800-1854	Floating wills	51
Mauldin, Archibald	2	1855-1857	B	302
Mauldin, John	1	1800-1834	A	396
May, Daniel	2	1855-1857	B	313
May, Wm. (Carpenter)	1	1800-1834	A	85
Mayfield, Abraham	1	1800-1834	A	326
Mecklin, James Gamble	2	1855-1857	B	372
McClin, Hugh, see				McLinn, Hugh
Merritt, James	1	1800-1834	A	422
Middleton, John (Sr.)	1	1791-1798	A	43
Milford, John (Sr.)	2	1855-1857	B	58
Miller, Crosby W.	2	1855-1857	B	87
Miller, Jesse	1	1800-1834	A	239
Miller, John (Printer)	1	1800-1834	A	87
Miller, John (Sr.)	1	1800-1834	A	312
Mills, Elizabeth	2	1855-1857	B	62
Mills, John	1	1800-1834	A	400
Moore, Curtis	1	1791-1798	C	59
Moore, David	2	1855-1857	B	361
Moore, Eliab (Sr.)	1	1800-1834	A	297
Moore, Elijah	2	1855-1857	B	289
Moore, Newman (Merchant)	1	1800-1834	A	209
Moorhead, John	1	1800-1834	A	109
Moorhead, John	2	1855-1857	B	133
Morris, John (Sr.)	1	1800-1834	A	113
Morris, John (Sr.)	2	1855-1857	B	7
Morris, Wm.	2	1800-1854	Floating wills	30
Morrow, John (Farmer)	1	1800-1834	A	144
Mullianax, John, see				Mullinix, John
Mullikin, Benjamin	2	1855-1857	B	286
Mullinix, John	1	1800-1834	A	245
Murry, John, see				Whitten, John
Nash, James	1	1800-1834	A	77
Neel, Samuel	1	1800-1834	A	131
Nelson, Wm. R.	2	1855-1857	B	261
Newell, William	2	1855-1857	B	204
Newman, John	1	1800-1834	A	41

Nicholson, Wm.	1	1800–1854	A	41
Norris, John	1	1791–1798	C	57
North, John Lauren (Planter)	2	1835–1857	B	251
O'Briant, Jesse	2	1835–1857	B	59
Oldham, George (Sr.)	2	1835–1857	B	83
Oliver, Alexander	1	1800–1854	A	370
Orr, Jehu	1	1800–1854	A	320
Paris, Henry (Farmer)	2	1835–1857	B	222
Parker, Mathew	2	1835–1857	B	320
Partain, Hubbard	2	1835–1857	B	245
Patterson, Archibald	2	1800–1854	Floating wills	54
Pepper, John (Sr.)	1	1800–1854	A	205
Perkins, Isaac	1	1791–1798	C	21
Perkins, Wm. (Planter)	1	1800–1854	A	322
Phagins, Phillip	1	1791–1798	C	53
Pickens, Ezekiel	1	1800–1854	A	164
Pickens, Israel	1	1800–1854	A	345
Pickens, John	1	1791–1798	C	28
Pickens, Robert	1	1791–1798	C	9
Pickens, Robt.	1	1800–1854	A	361
Pollock, John	1	1791–1798	C	1
Poole, Robert	2	1835–1857	B	81
Poor, Hugh	2	1835–1857	B	85
Poor, Wm. (Sr.)	1	1800–1854	A	262
Posey, Francis	2	1835–1857	B	64
Prater, Phillip	1	1791–1798	C	58
Pressley, David (Sr.)	1	1800–1854	A	433
Pressley, Rachel M.	2	1835–1857	B	73
Pritchard, Wm.	2	1835–1857	B	111
Pruit, Dudley	2	1800–1854	Floating wills	4
Ragsdale, Frances A.	2	1835–1857	B	139
Rainey, Benjamin	1	1800–1854	A	136
Ralston, Robert	1	1790–1793	Floating wills	1
Ramsay, Alexander (Farmer)	1	1800–1854	A	298
Reece, Wm. G.	2	1835–1857	B	367
Reed, George W.	1	1800–1854	A	367
Reed, Nathaniel	1	1791–1798	C	385
Reese, George	2	1835–1857	B	68
Reese, Thos. (Rev.)	1	1791–1798	C	52
Reese, Thos. Sidney	1	1791–1798	C	55
Reese, Wm. G.	2	1800–1854	Floating wills	48
Reeves, Burges	1	1800–1854	A	150
Reid, Hugh	1	1800–1854	A	347
Richards, Betsy	2	1835–1857	B	269
Richardson, David	2	1835–1857	B	257
Richardson, Mathias	1	1800–1854	A	349
Richardson, Turner	2	1800–1854	Floating wills	56
Richardson, Turner	2	1835–1857	B	77
Riley, Hezekial	2	1835–1857	B	265
Ritchie, John	2	1835–1857	B	53
Rodgers, Jeremiah W.	2	1835–1857	B	227
Roe, John, see — — — — — — — — — — — — — — — — Row, John				

Rogers, Nancy	2	1855-1857	B	357
Rogers, Sarah	2	1800-1854	Floating wills	58
Rogers, Wm. (Sr.)	2	1855-1857	B-	264
Rosamond, Samuel	1	1800-1854	A	141
Row, John	1	1800-1854	A	52
Russell, John	2	1800-1854	Floating wills	13
Russell, Mathew (Sr.)	1	1800-1854	A	156
Rykard, David	1	1800-1854	A	356
Saylor, Leonard (Sr.)	1	1800-1854	A	135
Scott, John	2	1855-1857	B	56
Scuddy, Augustine E.	2	1855-1857	B	66
Sego, Robert	1	1800-1854	A	117
Selmon, Benj., see - - - - - - - - - - - - - - - - Silmon,Benjamin
Sharpe, Elizabeth C., see - - - - - - - - - - - - - Starke,Elizabeth G.
Shelton, Aaron	1	1800-1854	A	159
Shelton, Lewis	1	1791-1798	C	18
Sherrard,Alexander	1	1800-1854	A	100
Sherrill, Lewis	2	1855-1857	B	101
Shirley, John	1	1800-1854	A	91
Shockley, Thomas	2	1800-1854	Floating wills	11
Siddall, Jesse	1	1800-1854	A	340
Siddall, John N.	1	1800-1854	A	292
Silmon, Benjamin	1	1800-1854	A	26
Simms, James	1	1791-1798	C	20
Simpson, John	1	1800-1854	A	402
Simpson, John	1	1800-1854	A	88
Sinkler, Charles	1	1791-1798	C	11
Skelton, Thomas	2	1855-1857	B	296
Sloan, David (Sr.)	1	1800-1854	A	306
Sloan, Nancy	2	1855-1857	B	339
Sloan, Susan	2	1855-1857	B	356
Smith, Davis	2	1855-1857	B	368
Smith, John	1	1790-1793	Floating wills	8
Smith, John	1	1791-1798	C	16
Smith, John	2	1800-1854	Floating wills	6
Smith, John	2	1855-1857	B	235
Smith, Jonathan	1	1800-1854	A	352
Smith, Joseph	2	1800-1854	Floating wills	17
Smith, Nimrod (Sr.)	2	1855-1857	B	211
Smith, Samuel	1	1800-1854	A	62
Smith, Whitaker	2	1800-1854	Floating wills	42
Smith, William	2	1855-1857	B	239
Smithson, Micajah	1	1800-1854	A	268
Spearman, Edmund	1	1800-1854	A	49
Spray, Thomas	2	1855-1857	B	209
Stanton, George	2	1855-1857	B	179
Starke, Elizabeth G.	2	1855-1857	B	326
Steel, Isaac (Sr.)	1	1800-1854	A	29
Steele, Jane	2	1800-1854	Floating wills	27
Steele, William	1	1800-1854	A	255
Stephens, John, see - - - - - - - - - - - - - - - - Stevens, John
Stephenson, Alexander	1	1800-1854	A	403
Stephenson, David	1	1800-1854	A	293
Stephenson, Joseph	2	1855-1857	B	46
Stephenson, Robert	2	1800-1854	Floating wills	16

Stevens, John	1	1800–1834	A	119
Stevenson, Andrew	2	1835–1857	B	392
Stevenson, Joseph, see				Stephenson, Joseph
Stevenson, Wm.	1	1800–1834	A	555
Stigall, Hensley	1	1800–1834	A	505
Storey, Charles	2	1835–1857	B	1
Strawther, Theodisia	2	1835–1857	B	550
Stribling, Thomas	1	1800–1834	A	240
Swords, John (Sr.)	1	1800–1834	A	424
Symmes, F. W.	2	1835–1857	B	375
Taliaferro, Warren	1	1800–1834	A	198
Taliaferro, Zacharias	1	1800–1834	A	579
Tate, James	1	1800–1834	A	107
Tatum, Edward	1	1800–1834	A	128
Taylor, Joseph	2	1835–1857	B	294
Taylor, Samuel (Planter)	1	1791–1798	C	56
Telford, Robert	1	1800–1834	A	550
Terrill, Aaron	1	1800–1834	A	178
Terrill, Henry	1	1791–1798	C	49
Thompson, James	1	1791–1798	C	12
Thompson, Joseph	1	1800–1834	A	118
Thompson, Mary Hale	1	1791–1798	C	65
Thompson, Mathew	1	1791–1798	C	5
Tippen, John	1	1800–1834	A	228
Tippins, Wm.	1	1800–1834	A	544
Todd, Robt.	2	1835–1857	B	170
Towers, Daniel R.	1	1800–1834	A	427
Traynum, Lazarus	2	1835–1857	B	341
Tripp, William	2	1835–1857	B	192
Trotter, Robert (Sr.)	1	1800–1834	A	140
Trussell, Posey	2	1835–1857	B	558
Tucker, Bartley	2	1835–1857	B	105
Turner, James	1	1791–1798	C	25
Turpin, Wm.	2	1835–1857	B	18
Vandiver, Hollingsworth (Sr.)	2	1800–1834	Floating wills	19
Vann, Martha	2	1800–1834	Floating wills	21
Verner, John	1	1791–1798	C	63
Waddle, Wm.	2	1835–1857	B	191
Wade, David	1	1800–1834	A	18
Wakefield, Henry (Planter)	1	1791–1798	C	67
Wakefield, Mary	1	1800–1834	A	79
Wardlaw, Betsy	2	1835–1857	B	287
Wardlaw, James	2	1835–1857	B	352
Warren, Samuel	2	1835–1857	B	122
Warnock, James	2	1835–1857	B	120
Warnock, John	2	1835–1857	B	129
Watkins, David	1	1800–1834	A	115
Watkins, Joseph (Sr.)	2	1800–1834	Floating wills	33
Watson, David	2	1835–1857	B	144
Watson, James	2	1835–1857	B	220
Watson, Thomas	2	1835–1857	B	135
Watson, Jonathan (Sr.)	1	1800–1834	A	232

Watters, Fleming	2	1855-1857	B	216
Webb, Charles	1	1800-1854	A	582
Webb, Wm.	2	1855-1857	B	293
Webster, James R.	2	1855-1857	B	95
Webster, James R.	2	1855-1857	B	98
Weed, Margaret	1	1800-1854	A	81
Welch, David	1	1800-1854	Floating wills	14
West, Jonathan	1	1791-1798	C	15
White, Bartholomew	1	1800-1854	A	104
White, Thomas	2	1855-1857	B	369
Whitefield, Joseph F.	2	1855-1857	B	588
Whitmire, Michael	1	1791-1798	C	35
Whitner, Joseph	1	1800-1854	A	280
Whitten, John	1	1800-1854	A	354
Wilbanks, Isaac	1	1800-1854	A	192
Willbanks, Henry	1	1800-1854	A	254
Williams, Stephen	2	1855-1857	B	52
Williamson, Wm.	2	1855-1857	B	299
Willson, Andrew	1	1800-1854	A	126
Wilson, James	1	1790-1795	Floating wills	7
Wilson, Jane	2	1855-1857	B	263
Wilson, John (Sr.)	1	1800-1854	A	279
Wilson, John	2	1855-1857	B	252
Wilson, Ralph	1	1790-1795	Floating wills	4
Wilson, William	1	1800-1854	A	598
Winter, Dinah	2	1855-1857	B	128
Wood, Jesse (Farmer)	1	1791-1798	C	29
Woodall, John (Sr.)	1	1800-1854	A	67
Woods, Wm. (Planter)	1	1800-1854	A	174
Wright, Larkin	2	1855-1857	B	92
Young, Andrew	1	1800-1854	A	411
Yowell, James	1	1800-1854	A	180

Copied by:

/s/ Mrs. John D. Rogers

INDEX TO

BARNWELL COUNTY WILLS.

VOLUME NO. 1
1787-1826

VOLUME NO. 2
1827-1856

This index is compiled from W.P.A. copies of
wills filed in the COUNTY PROBATE COURTS.
The volumes indexed are a part of the
South Carolina Collection of the
University of South Carolina
Library.

Columbia, S.C.
1939

Name	Vol.	Date	Section	Page
Abney, Nathaniel	1	1787-1826	Bk. I	2
Absten, John	2	1826-1856	C	4
Adams, Francis	2	1826-1856	D	28
Adams, Wm.	1	1787-1826	A	71
Afhley, Nathaniel	1	1787-1826	A	4
Afhley, Nathaniel	1	1787-1826	A	180
Alexander, Raine	1	1787-1826	A	13
Alexander, Wm. H.	1	1787-1826	B	89
Allen, John M.	2	1826-1856	D	257
Allen, Sarah	2	1826-1856	D	275
Anderson, Wm.	1	1787-1826	B	95
Armstrong, William	2	1826-1856	D	242
Ashe, R.C.	2	1826-1856	C	127
Ashley, Nathaniel, see - - - - - - - - - - - - - - - - -				Afley, Nathaniel
Badger, John P.	2	1826-1856	D	101
Bafsett, William (Planter)	1	1787-1826	A	111
Badger, Nathaniel	2	1836-1856	D	20
Bailey, Joseph N.	2	1826-1856	D	90
Banner, Benjamin	2	1826-1856	C	30
Banner, Peter (Planter)	1	1787-1826	B	155
Bassett, William, see - - - - - - - - - - - - - - - - -				Bafsett, William
Bates, Andren	1	1787-1826	A	30
Bates, Howel	1	1787-1826	A	170
Bates, Jesse	2	1826-1856	D	114
Bates, John (Sr.)	1	1787-1826	A	137
Bates, Robert	1	1787-1826	A	168
Bats, Jacob	2	1826-1856	D	181
Baxley, Martha	2	1826-1856	D	133
Baxter, John	1	1787-1826	B	19
Beck, Charles (Sr.)	1	1787-1826	B	102
Beck, Charles	2	1826-1856	D	282
Behannon, Daniel	2	1826-1856	C	78
Bell, Charles	2	1826-1856	D	78
Bellinger, John S. (Doctor)	2	1826-1856	D	22
Bellinger, Joseph	2	1826-1856	C	58
Bellinger, Mary	1	1787-1826	A	129
Bentley, James	2	1826-1856	D	222
Blitchendon, John	1	1787-1826	A	69
Bloom, Darling	2	1826-1856	C	46
Blume, John (Sr.)	1	1787-1826	B	20
Bourdeaux, Isaac	1	1787-1826	B	54
Bowers, John B.	2	1826-1856	D	285
Bowers, Malcolm	2	1826-1856	C	104
Bowie, James	1	1787-1826	A	77
Boyet, Wm.	1	1787-1856	A	104
Boylston, George	2	1826-1856	D	140
Brabham, Martha	2	1826-1856	D	176
Bradley, Robert	1	1787-1826	A	161
Brauda, E.B.	2	1826-1856	D	215
Braxton, Martha	2	1826-1856	D	48
Braxton, Spires (Planter)	2	1826-1856	D	59
Breland, Wm. (Sr.)	1	1787-1826	B	60

Brooker, Leah	1	1787-1826	B	62
Brooker, Wm.	2	1826-1856	C	108
Brown, Bartlett	1	1787-1826	B	100
Brown, Benjamin B.	2	1826-1856	C	64
Brown, Charles J.	1	1787-1826	A	25
Brown, Robert	2	1826-1856	C	81
Brown, Tarlton	2	1826-1856	D	72
Bryan, Fortunatus	1	1787-1826	B	85
Bryan, Lewis	2	1826-1856	D	136
Bryan, Wm.	2	1826-1856	D	267
Bryan, John	1	1787-1826	A	55
Bush, Isaac T.	2	1826-1856	C	86
Bush, John	1	1787-1826	A	35
Bush, John	2	1826-1856	D	198
Burnley, John	1	1787-1826	A	91
Butler, John	1	1787-1826	B	11
Calhoun, Dixon	1	1787-1826	B	130
Calhoun, Henry B.	2	1826-1856	C	57
Calhoun, Micajah	1	1787-1826	B	136
Campbell, James	2	1826-1856	D	103
Canaday, John (Sr.)	1	1787-1826	B	94
Cannon, Reddin	1	1787-1826	A	99
Carrel, Thomas	1	1787-1826	A	10
Cashin, John	2	1826-1856	D	307
Cater, Thos. M.	1	1787-1826	B	16
Cave, David	2	1826-1856	C	79
Cave, John (Sr.)	1	1787-1826	A	126
Cave, William	2	1826-1856	D	291
Chase, Peleg Wood	1	1787-1826	A	115
Chavous, Elisha	2	1826-1856	C	3
Cherry, Jessee	2	1826-1856	D	110
Chette, John	1	1787-1826	A	19
Chitty, John, see - - - - - - - - - - - - - - -				Chette, John
Clayton, John	2	1826-1856	D	80
Cochran, Collins	2	1826-1856	D	280
Cochran, John	2	1826-1856	D	25
Cochran, Mary	2	1826-1856	C	40
Cohen, Barnett A.	2	1826-1856	C	144
Coker, Benjamin	1	1787-1826	B	14
Coker, Elizabeth	2	1826-1856	D	186
Colding, Ann	1	1787-1826	A	83
Coleman, James	1	1787-1826	B	124
Collins, James	1	1787-1826	I	25
Connelly, Joseph	2	1826-1856	D	17
Cooner, Jacob	2	1826-1856	D	226
Cooper, Nichols	1	1787-1826	A	38
Counts, John M. (Merchant)	2	1826-1856	D	195
Coward, Milburn	2	1826-1856	C	73
Crawley, Benj. (Planter)	1	1787-1826	A	132
Creech, Henry	1	1787-1826	B	9
Creech, Wm.	2	1826-1856	C	68
Creel, Wm. (Sr.)	2	1826-1856	C	124
Crofsle, Wm.	1	1787-1826	I	3
Crosbey, Henry	1	1787-1826	B	92
Crossle, Wm., see - - - - - - - - - - - - - - -				Crofsle, Wm.

43

Daniel, Ann	2	1826-1856	C	25
Daniel, James	2	1826-1856	C	1
Daniel, Mary A.	2	1826-1856	D	151
Daniel, Sem (Planter)	2	1826-1856	C	120
Dannelly, David S.	2	1826-1856	D	188
Darlington, Eleanor	2	1826-1856	C	15
Davis, James	1	1787-1826	A	95
Delaveaux, Frances P.	2	1826-1856	D	255
Delk, Kindred	1	1787-1826	B	7
Deveaux, Andrew	1	1787-1826	B	115
Dewees, Sara	1	1787-1826	B	4
Dicks, Josias	2	1826-1856	D	171
Dillard, Barnaba	1	1787-1826	A-	17
Dooling, Elijah, see - - - - - - - - - - - - - - - - - - -				Dowling, Elijah
Dortch, John	2	1826-1856	D	173
Dowling, Elijah	1	1787-1826	B	1
Drummon, John	1	1787-1826	A	127
Duglas, John	1	1787-1826	A	7
Duke, Moses	1	1787-1826	B	83
Dunbar, Andrew (Yeoman)	1	1787-1826	B	71
Dunbar, David M.	2	1787-1826	D	195
Dunbar, John	2	1826-1856	D	251
Dunbar, Samuel F.	2	1826-1856	D	51
Duncan, Joseph	1	1787-1826	B	104
Duncan, Willis J.	2	1826-1856	D	10
Dyches, Issas, see - - - - - - - - - - - - - - - - - - -				Dyckes, Isaac
Dyckes, Isaac	1	1787-1826	A	85
Edwards, David (Sr.)	1	1787-1826	I	27
Ellis, W.D.	2	1826-1856	D	277
Ellis, Wm.	1	1787-1826	B-	87
Enicks, Thomas L.	2	1826-1856	D	64
Enicks, Thomas M.	2	1826-1856	D	294
Enicks, Wm. (Planter)	2	1826-1856	D	15
Enucks, Thomas	1	1787-1826	A	62
Erwin, James (Sr.)	1	1787-1826	A	178
Erwin, James D.	2	1826-1856	D	210
Eubanks, Adam	1	1787-1826	B	73
Everett, Henry	1	1787-1826	B	147
Everitt, Wm.	1	1787-1826	I	10
Evorett, Wm., see - - - - - - - - - - - - - - - - - - -				Everitt, Wm.
Fannon, William	2	1826-1856	C	159
Felder, David	2	1826-1856	D	154
Fennel, Henry	2	1826-1856	C	88
Fiehs, John, see - - - - - - - - - - - - - - - - - - -				Fitts, John
Filput, Thomas	1	1787-1826	I	22
Fitts, John	1	1787-1826	A	26
Fitts, Phillip	2	1826-1856	D	251
Ford, Elijah (Planter)	1	1787-1826	B	141
Foreman, Jacob	1	1787-1826	B	113
Fortune, William	2	1826-1856	D	219
Foster, Benjamin	1	1787-1826	A	18
Free, Jacob	2	1826-1856	C	28

Freeman, Wm.	2	1826-1856	C	140
Furse, James (Sr.)	2	1826-1856	D	169
Futch, Sarah E.B.	2	1826-1856	C	95
Galloway, James P.	2	1826-1856	D	201
Galloway, Peter	2	1826-1856	C	146
Galphin, Thomas	1	1787-1826	A	131
Garvin, James (Planter)	1	1787-1826	B	120
Gavin, Thomas (Planter)	1	1787-1826	A	151
Genkins, Elizabeth	1	1787-1826	A	12
Getsinger, Joseph	1	1787-1826	B	18
Gillett, Elijah	1	1787-1826	B	29
Gomillion, Christian	1	1787-1826	B	125
Googe, Henry G	2	1826-1856	D	296
Gray, James T.	2	1826-1856	D	138
Green, Absolem	2	1826-1856	D	189
Green, Needham	2	1826-1856	C	142
Green, Reuben	2	1826-1856	D	184
Green, William	1	1787-1826	A	152
Guefs, John	1	1787-1826	A	165
Guess, John,	see - - - - - - - - - - - - - - - - - -			Guefs, John
Gust, John,	see - - - - - - - - - - - - - - - - - -			Guefs, John
Guyton, Wm. W.	2	1826-1856	D	191
Hagood, Ann C.	2	1826-1856	D	41
Hagood, Gideon	2	1826-1856	C-	17
Hagood, Johnson	1	1787-1826	A	159
Hagood, Robert	1	1787-1826	B	150
Hair, Daniel	2	1826-1856	D	83
Hair, David	2	1826-1856	D	45
Halford, James H.	2	1826-1856	D	27
Hall, William	2	1826-1856	C	11
Hallford, James H., see - - - - - - - - - - - - - - - -				Halford, J.H.
Hamilton, Samuel N.	1	1787-1826	B	151
Hankerson, Richard	2	1826-1856	C	130
Hankerson, Robt.	1	1787-1826	I	14
Hankinson, Stephen	2	1826-1856	C	20
Harbers, John A.	2	1826-1856	D	233
Harden, Sarah	2	1826-1856	D	98
Hare, Peter	1	1787-1826	A	139
Hargroves, Mary	1	1787-1826	A	94
Harison, Wm.	1	1787-1826-	B	98
Harley, Henry	1	1787-1826	A	171
Harley, Jane A.	2	1826-1856	C	97
Harley, Joseph	1	1787-1826	A	89
Harrison, Henry	1	1787-1826	B	6
Harrison, John (Sr.)	1	1787-1826	D	85
Hart, John	2	1826-1856	C	128
Hartzog, Henry	2	1826-1856	D	92
Hartzog, John	1	1787-1826	B	90
Hartzog, Margaret	2	1826-1856	D	182
Harvey, Wm.	2	1826-1856	C	161
Hasel, Perry	2	1826-1856	D	99

Haskell, Wm.	2	1826-1856	D	168
Hay, Frederick J.	2	1826-1856	D	144
Hay, Lewis S.	2	1826-1856	D	4
Hayes, Joseph	1	1787-1826	A	67
Hays, Edward	2	1826-1856	D	200
Haynes, John	2	1826-1856	C	41
Heath, Benjamin	1	1787-1826	A	50
Henley, John (Sr.)	1	1787-1826	A	107
Hext, Lawrence	2	1826-1856	D	47
Hickman, John	1	1787-1826	A	123
Hicks, Christopher	1	1787-1826	I	24
Hickson, Eliel	2	1826-1856	C	149
Hightower, Thomas	2	1826-1856	C	48
Hogg, John	2	1826-1856	D	95
Holland, James J.	2	1826-1856	D	279
Holland, William	2	1826-1856	D	206
Hollman, Magdalene	2	1826-1856	D	50
Holman, Lewis	2	1826-1856	D	223
Horn, Josiah (Sr.)	2	1826-1856	B	70
Huffman, Solomon	1	1787-1826	A	55
Huggins, John	2	1826-1856	D	121
Hughes, Wm. (Sr.)	2	1826-1856	D	51
Humphreys, James C.	2	1826-1856	D	153
Hussman, Solomon, see - - - - - - - - - - - - - - - - - Huffman, Solomon				
Hutson, Rolin (Planter)	2	1826-1856	C	133
Hutto, Henry	1	1787-1826	A	167
Isnardi, Francis	1	1787-1826	B	88
Jackson, James (Sr.)	1	1787-1826	A	15
Jackson, John	2	1826-1856	C	65
Jelks, Nathanal H.	1	1787-1826	B	10
Jeter, Joseph (Planter)	1	1787-1826	A	122
Johnson, Alexander	2	1826-1856	D	163
Johnson, Ann	2	1826-1856	C	12
Johnson, Jonathan	2	1826-1856	D	269
Johnson, Moore	2	1826-1856	C	91
Johnson, Richard (Sr.)	1	1787-1826	B	143
Johnson, Sarah M.	2	1826-1856	D	57
Johnson, Wm. (Planter)	1	1787-1826	A	95
Jones, Vinson	2	1826-1856	D	308
Jones, William	2	1826-1856	D	108
Jowers, Jonathan	2	1826-1856	D	245
Keadle, Josias	2	1826-1856	C	153
Kearse, William	2	1826-1856	C	157
Kennedy, Henry	2	1826-1856	D	6
Kennedy, Robert	2	1826-1856	C	77
Kennedy, Wm. H.	2	1826-1856	D	232
Kimberhide, Martin	1	1787-1826	I	1
King, John	1	1787-1826	B	145
Kirkland, Benjamin	1	1787-1826	A	23
Kirkland, Edward	1	1787-1826	A	82

Kirkland, Mary	1	1787-1826	A	146
Kirkland, Reuben	1	1787-1826	B	117
Kirkland, Richard C.	1	1787-1826	A	163
Kirkland, Richard	1	1787-1926	A	140
Lain, Osborn	2	1826-1856	D	61
Lard, Adam (Sr.)	2	1826-1856	C	26
Lard, Elizabeth	2	1826-1856	D	46
Lard, Elizabeth	2	1826-1856	D	142
Latham, George	1	1787-1826	A	57
Lee, Levi	2	1826-1856	D	104
Lee, Robert	1	1787-1826	I	12
Lee, Thomas (Yeoman)	1	1787-1826	A	176
Leigh, James	2	1826-1856	D	309
Lewis, Richard	2	1826-1856	D	310
Long, Levi	1	1787-1826	A	39
Long, Thomas (Planter)	1	1787-1826	B	109
McClain, Solomon (Sr.)	1	1787-1826	A	155
McElmurray, Patrick	1	1787-1826	B	21
McElmurray, Andrew	2	1826-1856	D	43
McFail, John	2	1826-1856	D	161
McKenzie, James	2	1826-1856	D	164
McMillan, James	2	1826-1856	D	247
McMillon, Wm.	2	1826-1856	D	116
McNeely, Patrick	1	1787-1826	A	34

Mackelmurray, Patt, see - - - - - - - - - - - - - McElmurray, Patrick

Mallard, George	1	1787-1826	A	154

Matkimberhide, Martin, see - - - - - - - - - - - - Kimberhide, Martin

Martin, David	2	1826-1856	C	60
Martin, Taliaferro	2	1826-1856	C	66
Matthews, Alexander	2	1826-1856	D	312
Maxwell, Jane	1	1787-1826	B	99
Meyers, Johnney	1	1787-1826	B	138
Miley, Robert	1	1787-1826	B	75
Milhous, Charles	2	1826-1856	C	44
Milledge, John	1	1787-1826	B	27
Miller, Jane	1	1787-1826	B	87
Mims, Shadrack	1	1787-1826	A	135
Minor, John	1	1787-1826	B	3
Minors, Elizabeth	2	1826-1856	D	313
Mirick, James	1	1787-1826	A	149
Mixon, Mary	2	1826-1856	C	131
Moody, James	1	1787-1826	A	106
Moore, Margaret	2	1826-1856	B	287
Moore, Samuel	1	1787-1826	B	134
Moore, William	1	1787-1826	A	118
Morgan, Reubon	1	1787-1826	B	135
Morris, Phillip	2	1826-1856	D	205
Moye, Matthew	2	1826-1856	C	33
Murphy, John	2	1826-1856	C	55
Myfser, John	1	1787-1826	I	9

Myrick, James, see - - - - - - - - - - - - - - - - Mirick, James

Myricks, Eli	2	1826–1856	D	8
Mysser, John, see - - - - - - - - - - - - - - - - - -				Myfser, John
Newman, Richard	1	1787–1826	A	21
Newman, Wm. (Planter)	1	1787–1826	A	81
Newsom, Eleanor	2	1826–1856	C	118
Nix, Mary	2	1826–1856	C	165
Nobles, Nicholas	1	1787–1826	A	6
Oakman, Henry W.	1	1787–1826	B	78
O'Bannon, John Thos.	2	1826–1856	D	132
O'Bannon, Lewis	2	1826–1856	D	265
Odom, Abraham	2	1826–1856	D	1
Odom, Daniel (Planter)	2	1826–1856	C	156
Odom, George	2	1826–1856	C	151
Overstreet, Sarah	1	1787–1826	B	59
Odom, Thames	1	1787–1826	A	97
Owens, Griffin	2	1826–1856	D	202
Owens, Jessee	2	1826–1856	D	125
Owens, Solomon	1	1787–1826	B	58
Owens, Stephen	1	1787–1826	B	80
Owens, Stephen (Planter)	1	1787–1826	B	122
Owens, Wm.	2	1826–1856	C	100
Page, Abraham	2	1826–1856	D	119
Page, Jacob	1	1787–1826	A	60
Parker, Alpha	2	1826–1856	D	49
Parker, Burrell	2	1826–1856	C	111
Parker, William	2	1826–1856	C	89
Parker, Wm. L.	2	1826–1856	D	250
Parkinson, John	1	1787–1826	A	64
Parler, Daniel	2	1826–1856	D	137
Parrott, George	2	1826–1856	D	228
Pascalis, Cyril O.	2	1826–1856	C	126
Patrick, Samuel...	2	1826–1856	D	106
Patterson, Angus	2	1826–1856	D	236
Peacock, Mary	1	1787–1826	A	150
Peeples, Darling	2	1826–1856	D	158
Platts, John	1	1787–1826	A	1
Pooser, A.M., see - - - - - - - - - - - - - - - - - -				Pooser, Margaret
Pooser, Margaret	2	1826–1856	D	305
Priester, Wm. (Planter)	2	1826–1856	D	299
Ray, Benjamin	2	1826–1856	D	87
Ray, Jane	2	1826–1856	D	143
Reed, Elizabeth	2	1826–1856	D	217
Reed, Samuel	1	1787–1826	B	111
Rentzs, Simon	1	1787–1826	B	52
Rice, Benjamin	2	1826–1856	D	167
Rice, David (Sr.)	2	1826–1856	D	65
Richards, James Lighton	1	1787–1826	A	66
Riley, G.O.	2	1826–1856	D	11
Riley, Joseph	2	1826–1856	D	127
Roberts, James	1	1787–1826	A	8

Roberts, Stephen	2	1826–1856	C	116
Robertson , Samuel D.	1	1787–1826	A	164
Robison, George, see				Robson, George
Robson, George (Planter)	1	1787–1826	A	45
Roden, William	2	1826–1856	D	314
Rofe, John	1	1787–1826	A	3
Rose, John, see				Rofe, John
Roundtree, Job	2	1826–1856	D	123
Rountree, Levi	2	1826–1856	D	12
Sanders, Nathanial	2	1826–1856	C	106
Sanders, Stephen	2	1826–1856	D	178
Sanders, William	2	1826–1856	D	208
Sandifer, Joseph	2	1826–1856	C	135
Savage, Parker	2	1826–1856	C	98
Scarbrough, Lucy	1	1787–1826	A	174
Scarbrough, Wm.	1	1787–1826	A	114
Scott, John	2	1826–1856	D	89
Sease, Leonard	2	1826–1856	D	18
Shaw, Thomas	1	1787–1826	A	73
Shields, Margaret	1	1787–1826	A	143
Shipes, David	2	1826–1856	C	31
Shipes, Jacob	2	1826–1856	D	225
Shubert, Catharine	2	1826–1856	C	75
Skipir, Nancy	1	1787–1826	A	158
Smith, George P.	2	1826–1856	C	36
Smith, Stephen	1	1787–1826	I	19
Smith, Stephen	2	1826–1856	D	2
Smoke, William	2	1826–1856	D	220
Snelling, Henry	1	1787–1826	B	67
Southwell, Edward (Planter)	1	1787–1826	I	21
Stallings, James	1	1787–1826	A	41
Stallings, Martha	2	1826–1856	D	306
Stallings, Silas	2	1826–1856	D	305
Steed, Charles	1	1787–1826	A	87
Steele, John	2	1826–1856	C	87
Steivender, John E., see				Stivinder, John
Still, Samuel (Sr.)	2	1826–1856	C	43
Stivender, Avreheart	1	1787–1826	A	105
Stivinder, John E.	1	1787–1826	B	149
Stokes, Ezikial	2	1826–1856	C	114
Stokes, John F.	2	1826–1856	D	260
Stokes, Joseph H.	2	1826–1856	L	273
Stone, Marbil	1	1787–1826	A	182
Stringfellow, Richard	2	1826–1856	C	47
Stringfellow, William	1	1787–1826	A	147
Sutton, Sussannah	2	1826–1856	C	76
Syms, James	1	1787–1826	B	82
Tarrant, Benjamin	1	1787–1826	B	66
Taylor, John	1	1787–1826	A	59
Taylor, Mary	1	1787–1826	B	154
Taylor, Rachel	2	1826–1856	C	39
Thomas, Jacob	1	1787–1826	A	72
Thomas, Jane	2	1826–1856	D	37
Thomas, Reubin (Planter)	2	1826–1856	C	122

Thompson, John	1	1787-1826	A	109
Thomson, Jonathan	2	1826-1856	D	35
Tindal, John	1	1787-1826	A	32
Tobin, Cornelius	2	1826-1856	C	50
Touchstone, Frederick Sr.	1	1787-1826	A	79
Tradeway, Richard	1	1787-1826	A	101
Treadaway, Richard, see - - - - - - - - - - - - - - - - Tradeway, Richard				
Trotti, Ann	2	1826-1856	D	39
Trowell, Joseph (Sr.)	2	1826-1856	C	109
Tucker, John	2	1826-1856	C	83
Tucker, Joseph	2	1826-1856	D	33
Turner, Drusilla	1	1787-1826	B	69
Turner, John	1	1787-1826	A	75
Turner, William	1	1787-1826	D	42
Turner, Wm.	2	1826-1856	C	57
Tuten, Wm.	1	1787-1826	A	169
Tyler, Joseph (Sr.)	2	1826-1856	D	233
Ulmer, James	2	1826-1856	D	268
Ussery, Welcom	2	1826-1856	C	81
Varn, Hannah R.	2	1826-1856	D	134
Varn, John (Planter)	2	1826-1856	C	6
Vince, Joseph (Planter)	1	1787-1826	A	119
Walker, George	1	1787-1826	A	28
Walker, Nathan (Planter)	1	1787-1826	B	139
Walker, Nathaniel (Planter)	1	1787-1826	B	43
Walker, Rebecca A.	2	1826-1856	C	62
Ward, George	1	1787-1826	B	48
Ward, Soloman (Merchant)	1	1787-1826	B	50
Way, Amos	1	1787-1826	B	64
Weathersk, Mary	2	1826-1856	C	9
Weathersk, Willis	2	1826-1856	C	16
Weathersbee, Elizabeth	2	1826-1856	C	155
Weathersbee, Sarah	2	1826-1856	D	112
Weathersbee, Thomas (Sr.)	1	1787-1826	A	172
Weissinger, John	2	1826-1856	D	50
Whitney, Malcom	2	1826-1856	C	15
Wilkinson, Reuben	2	1826-1856	C	25
Williams, David	2	1826-1856	D	180
Williams, John	1	1787-1826	A	11
Williams, John	1	1787-1826	B	51
Williams, John	2	1826-1856	D	262
Williams, Zadock	2	1826-1856	C	49
Willis, Elijah	2	1826-1856	D	270
Willis, Robert	2	1826-1856	D	54
Willis, Robert M. (Planter)	2	1826-1856	D	129
Winzer, Anderson	1	1787-1826	A	145
Witney, Malcom, see - - - - - - - - - - - - - - - - Whitney, Malcom				
Wolfe, John	1	1787-1826	B	40
Wood, Jeremeah	1	1787-1826	B	25
Wood, John	1	1787-1826	I	6
Woodroof, Mary	1	1787-1826	B	127

Woolley, Richard	1	1787–1826	B	45
Wroten, Henry H.	2	1826–1856	C	95
Yonge, Susanah	1	1787–1826	B	25
Zorn, Henry (Planter)	1	1787–1826	B	153

Copied by

Mrs. Eileen S. Rogers

/s/   Mrs. Eileen S. Rogers

INDEX
TO
CHESTER COUNTY WILLS.

Volume No. 1
1789-1817

Volume No. 2
1817-1859

Volume No. 5
1833-1853

This index is compiled from W.P.A. copies of
wills filed in the County Probate courts.
The Volumes indexed are a part of the
South Carolina Collection of the
University of South Carolina
Library.

Columbia, S.C.
1939

	Vol.	Date	Section	Page
Adams, James	1	1806-1810	D	33
Adare, James (Sr.)	2	1834-1835	M	6
Aekin, David	1	1799-1802	B	3
Akin, David,   see — — — — — — — — — — — — — — — — Aekin, David
Akin, Thomas	1	1810-1815	E	65
Allen, Jane	3	1833-1843	C	24
Allen, John	3	1838-1845	Wills not recorded	1
Allen, Joseph	2	1829-1851	K	51
Allen, Richard	1	1806-1810	D	9
Anderson, Jane	3	1840-1854	A-1	104
Anderson, John	1	1789-1798	A	134
Andrews, Robert	1	1789-1798	A	108
Archer, Alexander (Farmer)	2	1820-1825	H	62
Archer, William	1	1789-1798	A	96
Armstrong, James (Planter)	2	1829-1851	K	11
Ashcraft, John	1	1815-1817	F-2	127
Atkins, Richard	1	1789-1798	A	121
Atkinson, James (Sr.)	3	1840-1853	A-1	94
Attaberry, William	1	1789-1798	A	82
Baily, Alexander	1	1789-1798	A	77
Baily, John	2	1834-1835	M	10
Bankhead, James	2	1817-1822	G	55
Barber, John M.	2	1834-1835	M	1
Barber, John	3	1840-1853	A-1	287
Barber, Mary	1	1815-1817	F-2	23
Beam, John (Sr.)	2	1826-1828	J	3
Beckham, Benjamin (Jr.)	2	1817-1822	G	1
Beckham, Simon	2	1817-1822	G	16
Beckham, William C., see — — — — — — — — — — — — — — Bukham, William C.
Bell, John	1	1789-1798	A	98
Bell, Valentine	1	1799-1802	B	22
Bigh, James,   see — — — — — — — — — — — — — — — Bigham, James
Bigham, James	3	1838-1845	Wills not recorded	3
Blair, James	1	1810-1815	E	30
Blair, John	3	1838-1845	Wills not recorded	9
Blair, Thomas	1	1789-1798	A	121
Blake, Joshia	3	1840-1853	A-1	72
Bond, Isom	1	1789-1798	A	22
Boyd, Archibald	2	1820-1825	H	21
Boyd, Charles	3	1840-1853	A-1	89
Boyd, David	1	1806-1810	D	46
Boyd, Elizabeth	2	1834-1835	M	12
Boyd, Margaret	3	1838-1845	Wills not recorded	5
Boyd, Robert	1	1799-1802	B	9
Boyd, Sarah	3	1838-1845	Wills not recorded	7
Boyd, William	1	1799-1802	B	32
Boyd, William	1	1815-1817	F-2	32
Boyd, William	2	1817-1822	G	32
Boyd, William (Sr.)	3	1838-1839	P	11
Bradford, Robert	1	1789-1798	A	39
Bradford, William	2	1826-1828	J	8
Bradley, Henry Lewis	2	1817-1822	G	88
Braidy, Alexander, see — — — — — — — — — — — — — — — Baily, Alexander

Breaden, Mary	2	1817-1822	G	30
Brown, Alexander	2	1824-1826	I	1
Brown, Katherine	1	1789-1798	A	26
Brown, James	1	1789-1798	A	94
Brown, John	3	1840-1853	A-1	42
Brown, Joseph	2	1817-1822	G	81
Brown, Stewart	1	1806-1810	D	44
Brown, Thomas	2	1826-1828	J	12
Brown, Walker	3	1838-1845	Wills not recorded	6
Browne, Katherine, see - - - - - - - - - - - - - - - - -			Brown, Katherine	
Buford, Leroy	1	1810-1815	E	9
Bukham, William	2	1820-1825	H	32
Cabean, Thomas	1	1799-1802	B	58
Campbell, John	2	1820-1825	H	8
Campbell, William	2	1820-1825	H	36
Carr, David	1	1803-1805	C	32
Carter, Alexander	2	1824-1826	I	3
Carter, Benjamin	1	1799-1802	B	30
Carter, Churchie (Sr.)	2	1820-1825	H	19
Caskey, Juliane	3	1840-1853	A-1	204
Castles, Barnet	3	1840-1853	A-1	134
Castles, Benjamin	3	1840-1853	A-1	276
Cherry, George	1	1806-1810	D	13
Cherry, John (Hatter)	2	1832-1833	L	1
Cherry, Robert	1	1799-1802	B	16
Chesnut, James	2	1817-1822	G	77
Chestnut, David	3	1838-1845	Wills not recorded	10
Chesholm, Suprey	2	1834-1835	M	3
Chisholm, David	1	1815-1817	F-2	2
Chisolm, Thomas (Planter)	2	1820-1825	H	41
Clark, George	2	1820-1825	H	54
Clifton, William	1	1803-1805	C	1
Cloud, James	1	1806-1810	D	19
Cloud, James	2	1820-1825	H	2
Coats, Notley	1	1806-1810	D	17
Cockrell, John	1	1789-1798	A	151
Coleman, Allen	3	1840-1853	A-1	194
Collins, John (Sr.)	2	1834-1835	M	20
Colvin, Andrew	3	1840-1853	A-1	227
Colvin, John	1	1789-1798	A	81
Colvin, John	2	1817-1822	G	57
Colvin, Martha H.	3	1840-1853	A-1	172
Colvin, Nicholas	3	1838-1839	P	12
Cooper, Hugh (Weaver)	1	1789-1798	A	75
Cooper, John (Planter)	2	1826-1828	J	14
Copeland, John William, see - - - - - - - - - - - - - - -			Copeland, William	
Copeland, William	1	1789-1798	A	142
Corder, William	3	1840-1853	A-1	83
Cowen, John	2	1827-1839	O	15
Cowsert, John	1	1815-1817	F-2	42
Cowsert, Thomas	1	1789-1798	A	130
Crafford, James, see - - - - - - - - - - - - - - - -			Crawford, James	
Crage, George	1	1810-1815	E	21
Craig, George, see - - - - - - - - - - - - - - -			Crage, George	
Crain, Mary	3	1840-1853	A-1	138
Crawford, Edward	3	1840-1853	A-1	121

Crawford, James	1	1810-1815	E	59
Crofly, Thomas, see - - - - - - - - - - - - - - - - - -				Crosly, Thomas
Crook, Elijah	2	1832-1833	L	3
Crook, Elizabeth	3	1840-1853	A	214
Crook, Eliziah	2	1829-1831	K	29
Crosly, John	1	1789-1798	A	143
Crosly, Richard	1	1789-1798	A	34
Crosly, Thomas	1	1789-1798	A	37
Crosset, William	3	1840-1853	A-1	137
Culp, Benjamin	2	1817-1822	G	35
Culp, John	3	1840-1853	A-1	108
Culp, Mary	2	1833-1836	N	10
Culp, Peter	1	1789-1798	A	65
Cupit, John	1	1799-1802	B	73
Curry, Hannah	3	1840-1853	A-1	44
Curry, William	2	1820-1825	H	57
Daniel, David	2	1832-1833	L	5
Darly, Asa	2	1834-1835	M	15
Davidson, William, see - - - - - - - - - - - - - - - -				Davison, William
Davie, F.W.	3	1840-1853	A-1	237
Davie, Hydie A.	3	1840-1853	A-1	203
Davie, William Richardson	2	1817-1822	G	43
Davis, John	3	1838-1845	Wills not recorded	16
Davison, William	1	1815-1815	F-1	4
Debardelaben, John F. (Sr.)	3	1840-1853	A-1	143
Dickey, John	2	1834-1835	M	19
Die, John	3	1838-1845	Wills not recorded	12
Dodds, John	1	1789-1798	A	91
Donald, George	3	1840-1853	A-1	101
Donly, Hugh	1	1789-1798	A	85
Dorder, William, see - - - - - - - - - - - - - - - -				Corder, William
Dorsey, Cornelies (Sr.)	2	1817-1822	G	75
Douglas, Elizabeth	3	1840-1853	A-1	164
Douglas, James	1	1806-1810	D	29
Douglas, James	2	1820-1825	H	24
Dowing, Mary	2	1832-1833	L	26
Downing, Mary (Sr.), see - - - - - - - - - - - - - -				Dowing, Mary
Downing, William	3	1838-1845	Wills not recorded	13
Dunn, Andrew	2	1827-1839	O	11
Dunovant, William	2	1829-1831	K	2
Dye, Elisha	2	1817-1822	G	66
Dye, George (Planter)	3	1840-1853	A-1	147
Eakins, David, see - - - - - - - - - - - - - - - - -				Aekin, David
Eakins, Thomas, see - - - - - - - - - - - - - - - - -				Akin, Thomas
Eakles, Thomas	1	1789-1798	A	109
Eaves, Braxton	1	1815-1815	F-1	1
Eckles, Robert W.	3	1840-1853	A-1	1
Eckley, Robert, see - - - - - - - - - - - - - - - -				Eckles, Robert W.
Edward, Olive	2	1826-1828	J	5
Egger, Andrew	2	1834-1835	M	17
Egger, James	2	1832-1833	L	38
Egger, Nancy	3	1840-1853	A-1	79
Elam, Martin	2	1820-1825	H	78
Elder, Mathew	3	1840-1853	A-1	36

Estes, John	3	1840–1853	A-1	219
Estes, Thomas	2	1820–1825	H	14
Estes, William (Sr.)	1	1806–1810	D	23
Evans, Richard	1	1806–1810	D	10
Evart, Thomas	1	1803–1805	C	31
Fairis, Thomas	2	1820–1825	H	44
Fant, Ephraim	3	1840–1853	A-1	255
Faris, Thomas, see – – – – – – – – – – – – – – –			Fairis, Thomas	
Featherston, John (Jr.)	1	1810–1815	E	17
Featherstone, Lucy	1	1799–1802	B	11
Feemster, Samuel	1	1815–1817	F-2	20
Fergerson, Adam	2	1817–1822	G	85
Fergerson, John (Jr.)	2	1817–1822	G	62
Ferguson, Abraham	2	1832–1835	L	36
Ferguson, Mary	2	1827–1839	O	13
Ferguson, Samuel	1	1815–1817	F-2	43
Ferguson, Sarah	3	1840–1853	A-1	196
Ferguson, William Y.	3	1840–1853	A-1	182
Findley, Isabella	2	1817–1822	G	37
Findley, Thomas	1	1810–1815	E	38
Finlay, Thomas, see – – – – – – – – – – – – – – –			Findley, Thomas	
Flemming, John	1	1789–1798	A	43
Flenniken, Warren (Rev.)	3	1840–1853	A-1	291
Floyd, Reuben	2	1817–1822	G	90
Foote, George (Planter)	1	1806–1810	D	37
Foote, Newton	2	1817–1822	G	87
Forman, Benjamin	1	1810–1815	E	50
Forsyth, Jane	2	1817–1822	G	26
Franklin, Nancy	3	1840–1853	A-1	110
Franklin, Thomas	1	1789–1798	A	12
Galespy, John	1	1810–1815	E	25
Galloway, John	3	1840–1853	A-1	266
Garret, Thomas	1	1789–1798	A	115
Garrot, Hannah	1	1803–1805	C	3
Gaston, John	1	1789–1798	A	58
Gaston, John	1	1806–1810	D	31
Gaston, John (Sr.)	3	1840–1853	A-1	178
Gaston, Joseph	2	1824–1826	I	19
Gaston, William	1	1810–1815	E	57
Gibbs, Wilmot	3	1840–1853	A-1	271
Gibson, Candy	3	1838–1845	Wills not recorded	21
Giles, William	1	1815–1817	F-2	26
Gill, Archabald	1	1803–1805	C	10
Gill, George (Sr.)	3	1840–1853	A-1	76
Gill, Jane	3	1840–1853	A-1	167
Gill, John (Planter)	1	1789–1798	A	48
Gill, John (Farmer)	1	1789–1798	A	145
Gill, Robert (Planter)	1	1803–1805	C	16
Gillmore, Charles	2	1817–1822	G	3
Givens, Edward	1	1789–1798	A	132
Glenn, Gideon	1	1803–1805	C	27
Glenn, James	1	1803–1805	C	24
Glenn, John	2	1820–1825	H	85
Glenn, Robert	3	1840–1853	A-1	103

Goings, Sarah	2	1820-1825	H	6
Gooch, John (Planter)	3	1840-1853	A-1	12
Gore, Clemen	1	1799-1802	B	67
Gore, Elizabeth	1	1789-1798	A	18
Gorrell, Robert	1	1810-1815	E	3
Graham, David (Blacksmith)	1	1799-1802	B	32
Graham, James (Sr.)	2	1820-1825	H	81
Graham, John	1	1806-1810	D	50
Graham, Mary	2	1817-1822	G	85
Gray, Henry (Planter)	2	1834-1835	M	22
Green, Daniel	3	1838-1845	Wills not recorded	17
Gresham, Major	1	1799-1802	B	27
Griffen, Samuel	1	1799-1802	B	12
Griffin, Edward	2	1820-1825	H	37
Grisham, Major, see - - - - - - - - - - - - - - - - - - Gresham, Major				
Grubs, Eurrock (Sr.)	3	1840-1853	A-1	114
Hallsey, Galsiel	2	1824-1826	I	5
Hamilton, James	3	1840-1853	A-1	33
Hamilton, Samuel	1	1799-1802	B	6
Harbin, William (Farmer)	1	1810-1815	E	56
Harbison, Mary	1	1799-1802	B	20
Harden, George (Sr.)	2	1832-1833	L	22
Hardwick, Margeret, see - - - - - - - - - - - - - - Hardwike, Margeret				
Hardwike, Margeret	3	1840-1853	A-1	4
Harper, Daniel	1	1789-1798	A	60
Harper, James	1	1803-1805	C	4
Harper, Robert	1	1799-1802	B	55
Harris, Charles	3	1838-1845	Wills not recorded	22
Hatfield, William	1	1799-1802	B	34
Hays, Charles	2	1820-1825	H	25
Hays, Margaret	3	1838-1845	Wills not recorded	27
Head, Richard	1	1799-1802	B	28
Henderson, Edward (Yeoman)	1	1789-1798	A	46
Heath, Adam	2	1827-1839	O	1
Heath, James	1	1806-1810	D	41
Heath, William (Sr.)	2	1826-1828	J	15
Heeth, James, see - - - - - - - - - - - - - - - Heath, James				
Hemphill, John	2	1832-1833	L	7
Hemphill, William	2	1832-1833	L	52
Henderson, Paterick	2	1824-1826	I	17
Hicklin, William	3	1840-1853	A	127
Hicklin, Zachariah	3	1840-1853	A	231
Hill, Benjamin	2	1827-1839	O	6
Hill, William	1	1803-1805	C	20
Hill, William	3	1840-1853	A-1	128
Hinds, Thomas	2	1832-1833	L	28
Hinkle, Joseph	3	1840-1853	A-1	223
Hitchcock, John (Planter)	1	1789-1798	A	3
Holly, Nathaniel	3	1838-1845	Wills not recorded	76
Holly, Nathaniel	3	1840-1853	A-1	135
Holsey, Gabriel, see - - - - - - - - - - - - - - - Hallsey, Galsiel				
Hope, Allison	3	1840-1853	A-1	54
Hopkins, David	1	1815-1817	F-2	4
Hopkins, Ferdinand	2	1827-1839	O	3
Hopkins, Sarah	3	1840-1853	A-1	239
Howell, Jeremiah	3	1840-1853	A-1	51

Hughes, Andrew	1	1806-1810	D	
Hughes, Thomas	1	1789-1798	A	
Hughes, Thomas	3	1838-1845	Wills not recorded	
Humphries, Bennet	2	1827-1839	O	8
Humphries, John	1	1810-1815	E	60
Hunter, James	1	1810-1815	F-1	6
Hunter, John	2	1820-1825	H	29
Hyatt, David	1	1806-1810	D	4
Hyatt, Hannah	3	1840-1853	A-1	289
Jackson, Benjamin	3	1833-1843	Q	3
Jackson, Gideon G.	3	1840-1853	A-1	262
Jackson, Jacob	3	1840-1853	A-1	22
Jackson, Warren	2	1832-1833	L	29
Jackson, William (Soldier)	1	1815-1817	F-2	24
Jackson, William (Soldier)	3	1838-1845	Wills not recorded	34
Jaggars, Thomas G.	3	1840-1853	A-1	74
Jaggers, John (Sr.)	1	1803-1805	C	13
Jameson, Robert	1	1810-1815	E	44
Jamison, Gardner	2	1826-1828	J	19
Jamison, James	3	1838-1839	P	17
Jamison, James	3	1838-1839	P	17
Johnson, James	1	1815-1817	F-2	14
Johnson, John	1	1815-1817	F-2	18
Johnston, Elizabeth	2	1820-1825	H	70
Johnston, Elizabeth	3	1840-1853	A-1	124
Johnston, Elizabeth	3	1840-1853	A-1	270
Johnston, Thomas	3	1838-1845	Wills not recorded	33
Jones, Jonathan	1	1803-1805	C	18
Jones, Jonathan	3	1833-1843	Q	6
Jorden, Henry	1	1799-1802	B	39
Junkin, William	2	1833-1836	N	8
Kee, Martin	3	1840-1853	A-1	191
Keenam, Mary	3	1840-1853	A-1	205
Keenan, Mary, see			Keenam, Mary	
Kell, James (Yeoman)	1	1810-1815	E	47
Kelsey, Elizabeth	2	1824-1826	I	6
Kelsey, Robert (Planter)	1	1799-1802	B	64
Kennedy, James (Sr.)	2	1820-1825	H	22
Kennedy, James, see			Kinnedy, James	
Kenny, Alexander (Planter)	1	1789-1798	A	148
Kerr, Robert	3	1838-1845	Wills not recorded	78
Kersey, Richard	1	1815-1817	F-2	22
Key, Daniel	2	1826-1828	J	6
Key, David, see			Key, Daniel	
Kidd, Jane	3	1838-1845	Wills not recorded	15
Kidd, John	1	1789-1798	A	89
Kingsburg, Jane	2	1820-1825	H	66
Kingsbury, Jane, see			Kingsburg, Jane	
Kinnedy, James (Planter)	1	1815-1817	F-2	34
Kirk, David	2	1820-1825	H	72
Kirkpatrick, Francis	3	1838-1845	Wills not recorded	36
Knox, Hugh	2	1817-1822	G	58
Knox, John	1	1789-1798	A	69
Knox, John	3	1838-1845	Wills not recorded	38

Knox, John	3	1817-1822	A-1	153
Knox, Samuel	3	1817-1822	A-1	224
Kolb, Harmon	1	1806-1810	D	43
Lacy, Edward (Sr.)	1	1789-1798	A	91
Lamb, William (Ditcher)	2	1832-1833	L	21
Lapsley, George	3	1838-1845	Wills not recorded	44
Lay, James	2	1817-1822	G	56
Lea, John (Planter)	2	1829-1831	K	32
Lea, Mary	3	1838-1845	Wills not recorded	42
Lee, Elliot	2	1832-1833	L	43
Lee, Frederick (Sr.)	1	1815-1817	F-2	36
Lee, Mary, see - - - - - - - - - - - - - - - - - - Lea, Mary				
Leech, David	2	1829-1831	K	1
Lemon, Burnell M., see - - - - - - - - - - - - - - - - McLemone, Burne				
Lemon, Moses	3	1840-1853	A-1	296
Lesly, William	1	1803-1805	C	2
Letsinger, John (Sr.)	1	1806-1810	D	47
Lewis, Titus	3	1840-1853	A-1	98
Lewis, William (Sr.)	2	1817-1822	G	5
Lewis, William (Planter)	2	1829-1831	K	4
Linn, John	2	1820-1825	H	16
Linn, John, see also - - - - - - - - - - - - - - - Lynn, John				
Little, Robert	2	1817-1822	G	42
Lockert, Aaron	1	1799-1802	B	4
Lockert, John	1	1806-1810	D	27
Love, Benjamin	1	1799-1802	B	13
Love, James (Jr.)	1	1799-1802	B	35
Love, Jane	3	1838-1845	Wills not recorded	39
Love, John	1	1799-1802	B	8
Love, John	1	1799-1802	B	69
Love, Mary	3	1840-1853	A-1	215
Love, Richard	3	1840-1853	A-1	65
Love, Thomas H.	3	1840-1853	A-1	211
Loving, Christopher	1	1789-1798	A	36
Lowery, Minerva	3	1838-1845	Wills not recorded	41
Lowry, James	3	1840-1853	A-1	281
Lowry, James	3	1833-1843	3	22
Lowry, James Drayton	2	1832-1833	L	24
Lowry, Joseph	2	1817-1822	G	14
Lowry, Mary	1	1815-1817	F-2	41
Lumpkin, Troy	3	1840-1853	A-1	243
Lyle, William	3	1840-1853	A-1	10
Lynn, John	3	1840-1853	A-1	259
Lynn, John, see also - - - - - - - - - - - - - - - Linn, John				
McAlliley, John	1	1806-1810	D	2
McAlduff, Thomas (Sr.) see - - - - - - - - - - - - - - McKlefuff, Thom				
McCalla, David (Sr.)	2	1820-1825	H	75
McCalla, James	1	1810-1815	E	27
McCalla, Martha	2	1832-1833	L	18
McCannon, John	1	1799-1802	B	50
McCaully, James (Farmer)	2	1832-1833	L	32
McCaw, William	1	1789-1798	A	128

60

McCleur, Mary, see				McClure, Mary
				99
McClintock, James	3	1840-1853	A-1	
McClintock, Matthew, see				McClintoe, Matthew
McClintoe, Matthew	3	1833-1845	Q	8
McClorkin, Elizabeth	2	1832-1853	L	30
McCluney, William	2	1833-1836	N	1
McClure, James	2	1826-1828	J	1
McClure, Mary	1	1799-1802	B	6
McClurkin, Elizabeth, see				McClorkin, Elizabet
McClurkin, James	1	1789-1798	A	110
McClurkin, John	2	1817-1822	G	18
McCollough, John, see				McCullough, John
McCollough, William, see				McCullouch, William
McCown, Alexander	1	1815-1817	F-2	16
McCullouch, William	1	1789-1798	A	137
McCullough, John	2	1827-1838	O	25
McCullough, Mary	2	1826-1828	J	4
McCullough, Samuel	2	1829-1831	K	7
McCully, John	3	1840-1853	A-1	206
McCully, Letty	2	1832-1833	L	11
McDaniel, Charles	1	1799-1802	B	48
McDaniel, Elizabeth	3	1840-1853	A-1	149
McDaniel, John	1	1810-1815	E	22
McDill, John	3	1838-1845	Wills not recorded	51
McDill, John	3	1840-1853	A-1	208
McDill, Thomas (Planter)	1	1789-1798	A	112
McDonald, Charlotte	1	1810-1815	E	34
McDonald, Hugh (Sr.)	1	1810-1815	E	52
McDonald, John, see				McDaniel, John
McDonald, Middleton	2	1817-1822	G	9
McDonald, Timothy (Planter)	1	1789-1798	A	47
McDonald, William (Planter)	1	1799-1802	B	52
McDowell, Elizabeth	3	1840-1853	A-1	177
McElduff, Polly	1	1810-1815	E	28
McElduff, Thomas, see				McKlefuff, Thomas
McElhenny, James	2	1817-1822	G	71
McFadden, Isaac	2	1817-1822	G	50
McFalls, John	2	1820-1825	H	35
McGarah, James	1	1815-1817	F-2	1
McGarity, James	2	1817-1822	G	63
McGarity, William (Sr.)	2	1833-1836	N	5
McGarrah, James, see				McGarah, James
McGerity, William, see				McGarity, William
McGlamcey, John, see				McGlamry, John
McGlamry, Jennet	2	1817-1822	G	40
McGlamry, John	1	1799-1802	B	47
McKee, John	3	1838-1845	Wills not recorded	47
McKeown, John	1	1810-1815	E	5
McKinney, Patrick	1	1789-1798	A	27
McKinney, Samuel	1	1789-1798	A	150
McKinney, William	3	1840-1853	A-1	57
McKinstrey, James	2	1829-1831	K	13
McKlduff, Thomas, see				McKlefuff, Thomas
McKlefuff, Thomas	1	1806-1810	D	35
McKlesuff, Thomas, see				McKlefuff, Thomas
McKow, John, see				McKeown, John
McLemon, Susan	3	1840-1853	A-1	116
McLemone, Burnell	3	1840-1853	A-1	41

McLemore, Susan, see				McLemon, Susan
McLeowery, James, see				Lowry, Jane
McLonen, Forsithe	1	1799-1802	B	37
McLure, Jane	2	1827-1839	O	20
McMillen, Hugh	2	1817-1822	G	20
McMullan, Hugh (Planter)	3	1840-1853	A-1	58
McMullan, Sarah J.	3	1840-1853	A-1	112
McNeel, Samuel	2	1826-1828	J	10
McNinch, Isabella	3	1840-1853	A-1	96
McNinch, John (Sr.)	3	1840-1853	A-1	63
McQuieston, Mary	2	1832-1833	L	13
McQuiston, Andrew, see				McQuiston, Archibald
McQuiston, Ann	2	1829-1831	K	34
McQuiston, Archibald	2	1826-1828	J	22
McQuiston, Archibald	3	1838-1845	Wills not recorded	67
McQuiston, Mary, see				McQuieston, Mary
McWilliams, Mary	3	1840-1853	A-1	189
Maben, Thomas, see				Mayben, Thomas
Mabin, John	2	1817-1822	G	22
Marion, Jannet	3	1840-1853	A-1	268
Marion, William	2	1833-1836	N	3
Marrick, John	1	1789-1798	A	55
Martin, David	2	1817-1822	G	12
Martin, James	3	1840-1853	A-1	69
Martin. Samuel	3	1840-1853	A	257
Martin, William	1	1789-1798	A	20
Martin, William (Rev.)	3	1838-1845	Wills not recorded	45
Mayben, Thomas	2	1820-1825	H	60
Mayes, Robert	2	1824-1826	I	12
Mayfield, Abraham (Sr.)	3	1840-1853	A -1	19
Mayfield, Elisha (Sr.)	2	1829-1831	K	15
Mays, Robert, see				Mayes, Robert
Mays, Eliazbeth	3	1838-1845	Wills not recorded	55
Meek, James (Planter)	1	1803-1805	C	29
Merion, William, see				Marion, William
Merrick, John, see				Marrick, John
Mildoon, Richardson	3	1840-1853	A-1	30
Millen, John, see				Miller, John
Miller, James	3	1838-1845	Wills not recorded	56
Miller, John	3	1840-1853	A-1	80
Miller, Charles (Farmer)	3	1824-1826	I	25
Miller, Josiah	2	1833-1843	Q	17
Miller, Margaret	3	1840-1853	A-1	229
Miller, Robert	3	1832-1833	L	34
Miller, Robert	2	1840-1853	A-1	278
Millier, Josiah, see				Miller, Josiah
Mills, Isabella	3	1840-1853	A-1	20
Mills, John	1	1815-1817	F-2	11
Mills, Mary	3	1840-1853	A-1	21
Mitchell, Alexander	3	1838-1843	Wills not recorded	66
Mitchell, Isaiah	1	1810-1815	E	7
Mobley, Edward	3	1838-1845	Wills not recorded	59
Moffat, Charles	3	1840-1853	A-1	55
Moffat, William	3	1840-1853	A -1	118
Moffat, William	3	1830-1853	A-1	24
Moffet, William	1	1789-1798	A	86

Moffitt, David	2	1829-1831	K	17
Moffitt, Samuel	2	1832-1833	L	9
Montgomery, Elizabeth	2	1820-1825	H	48
Montgomery, Isabella	2	1820-1825	H	52
Montgomery, James (Planter)	2	1820-1825	H	46
Montgomery, John	3	1840-1853	A-1	71
Montgomery, Judith S.	3	1840-1853	A-1	184
Montgomery, Margaret	2	1820-1825	H	50
Montgomery, William	3	1840-1853	A-1	240
Moor, William	3	1840-1853	A-1	141
Moore, James	1	1789-1798	A	1
Moore, Rebecca	3	1840-1853	A-1	264
Moore, Thomas	2	1827-1839	O	16
Moore, William H., see - - - - - - - - - - - - - - - - - - Moor, William				
Morgan, Elizabeth	2	1833-1836	N	7
Morgan, Jarrel	3	1838-1845	Wills not recorded	69
Morgan, William	2	1824-1826	I	21
Morray, William	3	1838-1845	Wills not recorded	53
Morris, Benjamin	2	1820-1825	H	55
Morris, Thomas	1	1789-1798	A	32
Morris, Thomas	3	1840-1853	A-1	23
Morris, Thomas	3	1838-1845	Wills not recorded	49
Morrison, Andrew	1	1810-1815	E	11
Morrison, Thomas	1	1815-1817	F-2	6
Morrow, Joseph (Sr.)	2	1834-1835	M	8
Morrowson, Robert	2	1820-1825	H	12
Morton, John	1	1806-1810	D	6
Murphy, John	2	1824-1826	I	24
Murphy, William	1	1789-1798	A	102
Neal, John	3	1840-1853	A-1	112
Neely, James (Yeoman)	1	1789-1798	A	70.
Neely, Prudence	3	1838-1845	Wills not recorded	71
Neely, Samuel	1	1803-1805	C	8
Neilson, William, see - - - - - - - - - - - - - - - - Nelson, William				
Nelson, William	2	1820-1825	H	65
Nisbet, James	1	1789-1798	A	85
Nix, Ambrose	2	1817-1822	G	33
Oaks, Daniel	1	1789-1798	A	147
Obrient, George	1	1799-1802	B	24
Oliver, James	2	1817-1822	G	89
Orr, John	1	1806-1810	D	1
Owen, John	2	1817-1822	G	27
Owens, Robert	1	1799-1802	B	41
Pardue, Joseph	3	1840-1853	A-1	209
Park, Hugh	2	1820-1825	H	4
Patterson, Margaret	2	1820-1825	H	58
Paul, William	1	1815-1817	F-2	28
Phenny, Patrick (Farmer)	3	1840-1853	A-1	201
Pinchback, John	1	1810-1815	E-	15
Pitman, Wylie	3	1833-1845	Q	19
Porter, James	3	1840-1853	A-1	154
Porter, John	1	1789-1798	A	106

Porter, William	2	1840-1853	A-1	283
Potts, John	3	1840-1853	A-1	1
Powell, Benjamin	1	1815-1817	F-2	230
Powell, George	3	1840-1853	A-1	46
Pratt, John	2	1829-1831	K	19
Pratt, Leonard	3	1840-1853	A-1	159
Price, Cuthbert (Farmer)	2	1834-1835	M	6
Price, John	1	1799-1802	B	1
Price, William	2	1832-1833	L	37
Pride, Jones Halcot	1	1816-1817	F-2	239
Quary, Alexander	2	1829-1831	K	21
Quay, Alexander, see - - - - - - - - - - - - - - - - - -Quay, Andrew				
Quay, Andrew	2	1817-1822	G	60
Quinton, Samuel	1	1789-1798	A	15
Rainey, Mary	3	1840-1853	A-1	52
Rainey, Robert	1	1789-1798	A	67
Rainey, Samuel	1	1810-1815	E	45
Ralph, Samuel	3	1838-1839	P	15
Reed, Hugh	2	1832-1833	L	50
Reedy, John	3	1840-1853	A-1	244
Reives, James	1	1810-1815	E	55
Reives, Mary	2	1817-1822	G	38
Reives, William Cook	2	1817-1822	G	24
Reives, John (Planter)	3	1840-1853	A-1	9
Reives, Nathaniel	1	1789-1798	A	29
Roberson, James	1	1789-1798	A	23
Robins, Thomas	2	1817-1822	G	53
Robinson, Felex	3	1840-1853	A-1	129
Robinson, James, see - - - - - - - - - - - - - - - - Roberson, James				
Robinson, Jane	3	1840-1853	A-1	126
Robinson, Joseph	2	1829-1831	K	24
Robinson, Robert	3	1840-1853	A-1	59
Robinson, David	1	1810-1815	E	32
Robison, Joseph, see - - - - - - - - - - - - - - - - Robinson, Joseph				
Rock, John	2	1817-1822	G	69
Roden, John (Sr.)	2	1817-1822	G	79
Roden, William	1	1789-1798	B	31
Rogers, John R.	1	1789-1798	A	13
Rosborough, Alexander (Sr.)	1	1815-1815	F-1	3
Ross, Abraham	3	1840-1853	A-1	97
Ross, Hugh (Sr.)	3	1840-1853	A-1	253
Ross, Margaret	1	1815-1817	F-2	38
Rowan, Benjamin	2	1832-1833	L	51
Rowel, Benjamin	1	1803-1805	C	6
Rowell, Elizabeth	2	1824-1826	I	22
Rowell, Jerry	3	1840-1853	A-1	169
Rowell, Susanah	3	1840-1853	A-1	175
Sadler, Isaac	1	1789-1798	A	10
Sanders, William (Yeoman)	1	1803-1805	C	15
Sandifer, Mary	3	1840-1853	A-1	85
Sarvis, John, see - - - - - - - - - - - - - - - - - - Servis, John				

Scogin, William	1	1810-1815	E	62
Sealy, Jean	1	1789-1798	A	123
Sealy, John	1	1789-1798	A	62
Sealy, Peters	1	1810-1315	E	19
Servis, John	1	1806-1810	D	21
Simmons, Samuel	2	1824-1826	I	8
Simms, Mathew	1	1799-1802	B	10
Simpson, Charlotte	3	1840-1853	A	125
Simpson, Joseph	3	1833-1853	Q	14
Simpson, Matthew	3	1833-1853	Q	18
Sims, Charles S.	3	1833-1853	Q	12
Slagle, William, see - - - - - - - - - - - - - - - - - - - Sligh, William				
Sleeker, Casper	1	1803-1805	C	34
Sleeker, George	1	1789-1798	A	28
Sleigle, Julay, see - - - - - - - - - - - - - - - - - Sligle, Julia				
Sligh, William	3	1833-1853	A-1	188
Sligle, Julia	3	1840-1853	A-1	251
Sloan, James (Sr.)	2	1817-1822	G	95
Smith, John	1	1789-1798	A	104
Smith, Moses	2	1817-1822	G	64
Standley, Jennet	1	1789-1798	A	141
Steavenson, David	1	1789-1798	A	56
Steedman, Edward	2	1834-1835	M	5
Steel, James	1	1789-1798	A	92
Steel, John	1	1806-1810	D	51
Stenson, William, see - Stinson, William				
Stephenson, James, see - - - - - - - - - - - - - - - - - Stinson, James				
Stewart, John	3	1840-1853	A-1	236
Stewart, Robert	1	1789-1798	A	7
Stinson, Elizabeth	3	1840-1853	A-1	119
Stinson, James	1	1789-1798	A	16
Stinson, William	1	1806-1810	D	48
Stockdale, John	3	1840-1853	A-1	25
Stokes, Sarah	3	1840-1853	A-1	225
Stokes, Thomas, see - - - - - - - - - - - - - - - - - - Strokes, Thomas				
Storment, John	1	1789-1798	A	120
Stormont, David	1	1810-1815	E	14
Strange, Edmon (Sr.)	1	1806-1810	D	8
Stringfellow, William	1	1840-1853	A-1	220
Strokes, Thomas (Farmer)	2	1820-1825	H	13
Strong, James	1	1789-1798	A	73
Strong, James (Sr.)	2	1820-1825	H	33
Strong, John	1	1803-1805	C	5
Strong, Letty	3	1833-1843	Q	11
Strong, Robert	2	1820-1825	H	73
Stroud, Sarah	3	1833-1843	Q	10
Tanner, Samuel	3	1840-1853	A-1	35
Taylor, Sarah	1	1789-1798	A-1	114
Taylor, William	1	1789-1798	A	51
Terry, Priscilla	3	1840-1853	A-1	217
Terry, Thomas	3	1840-1853	A-1	234
Thompson, Christopher (Sr.)	2	1832-1833	L	39
Thorn, Thomas	1	1815-1817	F-2	8

Timms, James G.	2	1824-1826	I	10
Tims, Amos	2	1820-1825	H	1
Tims, Amos (Yeoman)	2	1829-1831	K	26
Tims, Joseph	1	1799-1802	B	45
Tims, Joseph	3	1840-1853	A-1	92
Triplett, John	1	1799-1802	B	66
Trussell, William	1	1810-1815	E	36
Walker, Adam	1	1799-1798	A	125
Walker, Agnes	3	1838-1845	Wills not recorded	74
Walker, Alexander	1	1789-1798	A	152
Walker, Alexander	1	1789-1798	A	18
Walker, Charles (Planter)	2	1817-1822	G	92
Walker, Charles	3	1838-1839	P	20
Walker, Isabella	2	1827-1839	O	17
Walker, James	2	1817-1822	G	8
Walker, Jane	2	1820-1825	H	39
Walker, Jeremiah	3	1838-1839	P	18
Walker, John (Jr.)	1	1789-1798	A	8
Walker, John (Yeoman)	1	1799-1802	B	71
Walker, Joseph	1	1789-1798	A	53
Walker, Robert	1	1789-1798	A	79
Walker, Robert (Sr.)	1	1810-1815	E	1
Walker, Robert (Sr.)	2	1817-1822	G	73
Walker, Rody	3	1833-1843	Q	21
Wall, Charles	3	1840-1853	A-1	86
Wall, John	1	1806-1810	D	25
Wallace, Thomas	2	1824-1826	I	14
Walls, Drury	1	1789-1798	A	88
Wear, John, see - Weir, John
Weer, William (Planter)	1	1789-1798	A	5
Weir, David	1	1789-1798	A	135
Weir, John	1	1803-1805	C	21
Weir, William (Planter)	1	1789-1798	A	41
Wells, Mary	3	1840-1853	A-1	82
Wells, Thomas	2	1832-1833	L	16
Westbrook, Arthur	3	1838-1843	Wills not recorded	79
Westbrook, Jacob	3	1838-1845	Wills not recorded	75
Westbrooks, Nancy	3	1840-1853	A-1	67
Wham, Benjamin	2	1820-1825	H	7
White, Abraham	3	1840-1853	A	151
White, Robert	3	1840-1853	A-1	156
White, Thomas	2	1829-1831	K	10
White, Thomas (Sr.)	3	1840-1853	A-1	213
White, William	3	1833-1843	Q	1
White, William R.	3	1840-1853	A-1	176
Whitehead, John	2	1832-1833	L	27
Whiteside, Hugh	1	1799-1802	B	75
Wiley, Elizabeth	1	1799-1802	B	21
Wilye, Frances, see - - - - - - - - - - - - - - - - - - - Wylie, Frances
Wilks, Richard	3	1840-1853	A	7
Willans, Benjamen, see - - - - - - - - - - - - - - - Williams, Benjamin
Williams, Martha	3	1838-1845	Wills not recorded	73
Williams, Benjamin	1	1789-1798	A	118
Williams, Moses	2	1817-1822	G	70
Wilson, James (Sr.)	2	1820-1825	H	10
Wilson, John (Planter)	1	1810-1815	E	42

Wilson, John	3	1840–1853	A–1	106
Wilson, Robert	2	1829–1831	K	28
Wood, Agnes	3	1840–1853	A–1	186
Wood, Rolly	3	1840–1853	A–1	199
Woodward, Williams (Rev.)	2	1820–1825	H	27
Worthy, William	3	1840–1853	A–1	48
Wright, Clabourn	2	1820–1825	H	71
Wright, James	3	1840–1853	A–1	50
Wright, John (Planter)	1	1806–1810	D	39
Wright, John (Sr.)	3	1830–1853	A–1	230
Wright, Mabrey	3	1840–1853	A–1	261
Wylie, Adam	3	1840–1853	A–1	152
Wylie, Duncan	3	1840–1853	A–1	6
Wylie, Frances	3	1840–1853	A–1	62
Wylie, James	1	1806–1810	D	14
Wylie, James	2	1817–1822	G	94
Wylie, William	1	1806–1810	D	15
Young, James	1	1815–1817	F–2	12
Young, William (Sr.)	3	1840–1853	A–1	130

Copied by:

Mrs. John D. Rogers

/s/ Mrs. John D. Rogers

INDEX
TO
DARLINGTON COUNTY WILLS.

Volume No. 1
1785-1840

Volume No. 2
1838-1853

This index is compiled from W.P.A. copies of
wills filed in the COUNTY PROBATE COURTS.
The volumes indexed are a part of the
South Carolina collection of the
University of South Carolina
Library.

Columbia, S.C.
1939

Name	VOL.	Date	Section	Page
Adams, Birgess	1	1812-1817	4	3
Adams, Kinchin	2	1838-1853	10	102
Anderson, William	2	1838-1853	10	151
Atkinson, Samuel	1	1812-1817	4	45
Bacot, Anna W.	2	1838-1853	10	186
Beasley, John	1	1798-1812	2	42
Beck, James	1	1819-1819	5	3
Belk, Jeremiah	2	1838-1853	10	139
Berry, William	1	1798-1812	2	56
Blackwell, Hannah	1	1817-1825	7	10
Blackwell, Samuel	1	1819-1820	6	26
Brockington, Mary H.	2	1838-1853	10	209
Brockington, Richard	2	1838-1853	10	34
Brown, James	2	1838-1853	10	192
Brown, Jesse	1	1811-1813	3	3
Brown, Thomas	1	1812-1817	4	49
Bryant, Jesse	2	1838-1853	10	169
Burnet, John	1	1830-1837	8	34
Burris, William	2	1838-1853	10	12
Cannon, George	1	1798-1812	2	7
Cannon, Henry E.	2	1838-1853	10	69
Cannon, William H. (Sr.)	2	1838-1853	10	37
Casack, Adam (Sr.)	2	1838-1853	10	91
Catlett, Sarah T.	2	1838-1853	10	25
Chandler, John	1	1830-1837	8	5
Chapman, Henry	1	1819-1820	6	24
Chapman, Wiley	2	1838-1853	10	185
Coggeshall, Peter C.	1	1827-1840	9	16
Coker, Caleb	1	1830-1837	8	35
Coker, Thomas	2	1838-1853	10	101
Cole, James	1	1798-1812	2	18
Cole, Mary	2	1838-1853	10	207
Coleman, James	1	1812-1817	4	11
Connell, William	1	1798-1812	2	52
Cook, Jacob	2	1838-1853	10	180
Cooper, Frances, see - - - - - - - - - - - - - - - - - - Cooper, Francis				
Cooper, Francis	2	1838-1853	10	149
Cooper, Nancy	1	1827-1840	9	1
Cooper, Nancy	2	1838-1853	10	155
Crow, John (Jr.)	1	1817-1825	7	31
Currie, Mary Anne	1	1819-1819	5	7
Cuttino, Elisa	1	1798-1812	2	51
Dalrimple, John	1	1827-1840	9	9
Dalrymple, John, see - - - - - - - - - - - - - - - - - DALRIMPLE, John				
Dargan, Ann	1	1819-1819	5	21
Dargan, Timothy	1	1827-1840	9	11
DeWitt, Charles	1	1798-1812	2	23
DeWitt, William	1	1819-1819	5	13

DeWitt, William	1	1827-1840	9	14
Divine, John B.	1	1827-1840	9	7
Dowling, John	1	1817-1825	7	20
Doyal, John	1	1812-1817	4	25
Doyl, John, see - Doyal, John				
Dubose, Andrew (Sr.)	1	1798-1812	2	2
DuBose, Daniel	1	1830-1837	8	19
DuBose, Elias	1	1830-1837	8	25
Edwards, Margaret M.	1	1830-1837	8	9
Edwards, Peter	1	1817-1825	7	1
Edwards, Thomas H.	1	1830-1837	8	8
Ervin, Elizabeth	2	1838-1853	10	4
Evan, Samuel	1	1812-1817	4	17
Fort, Margaret	2	1838-1853	10	167
Fountain, Alexander	2	1838-1853	10	26
Fountain, William (Planter)	1	1798-1812	2	39
Gainey, Isaac	1	1798-1812	2	58
Galloway, Absalom (Planter)	1	1785-1793	1	6
Ganey, Isaac, see - Gainey, Isaac				
Garland, William	1	1817-1825	7	23
Garner, Absalem	1	1812-1817	4	34
Garner, John	1	1817-1825	7	24
Garner, William (Sr.)	2	1838-1853	10	15
Gee, Edmund	1	1830-1837	8	7
Gee, John	1	1819-1820	6	17
Gee, Judith	1	1830-1837	8	33
Gee, Nevel	2	1838-1853	10	29
Gee, Thomas	2	1838-1853	10	201
Gee, William	1	1798-1812	2	82
Good, Susanah	2	1838-1853	10	119
Graham, Peter S.	2	1838-1853	10	131
Griggs, William (Sr.)	2	1838-1853	10	173
Hafs, John	1	1798-1812	2	54
Hafe, John, see - Hayes, John				
Hale, William	2	1838-1853	10	11
Hales, Silas	2	1838-1853	10	122
Halloway, James	2	1838-1853	10	196
Ham, Briley	2	1838-1853	10	75
Ham, Henry	1	1798-1812	2	43
Harrell, John	1	1798-1812	2	4
Harrell, Lewis	1	1812-1817	4	54
Harrell, Spencer	2	1838-1853	10	113
Harts, James	1	1798-1812	2	22
Hase, John, see - Hafe, John				
Hatchell, Morris	1	1798-1812	2	53
Hawkins, John	2	1838-1853	10	138
Hayes, John	1	1798-1812	2	55
Hayes, John	1	1819-1820	6	13
Hayes, John, see - Hafe, John				

71

Heath, Keziah	1	1817-1825	7	21
Hendrix, Hasten	2	1838-1853	10	172
Herron, James (Sr.)	1	1819-1819	5	5
Hewitt, Francis M.	2	1838-1853	10	200
Hicks, John	2	1838-1853	10	23
Hill, Amos (Farmer)	2	1838-1853	10	217
Hill, Benjamin	1	1812-1817	4	56
Hill, John (Planter)	2	1838-1853	10	146
Hill, John, see also -Hafe, Joh				
Hinds, Dawson	1	1830-1837	8	43
Hinds, Orison	1	1812-1817	4	44
Hixon, Thomas	1	1793-1812	2	60
Holloman, Kindred	1	1830-1837	8	1
Hooton, Littleton	2	1838-1853	10	73
Huggins, John	1	1817-1825	7	12
Hughes, John	1	1812-1817	4	5
Hunter,A.N.	2	1838-1853	10	80
Hunter, Andrew (Sr.)	1	1812-1817	4	26
Hunter, Andrew	1	1830-1837	8	18
Hunter, James	2	1838-1853	10	158
Hunter, Thomas	1	1830-1837	8	16
Huse, John, see - Hughes, John				
Jackson, John	1	1830-1837	8	52
James, Enox	1	1812-1817	4	1
James, George	2	1838-1853	10	109
James, William	1	1785-1893	1	1
Johnson, Samuel	1	1817-1825	7	17
Jordan, Alexander	2	1838-1853	10	126
Jordan, Peter	2	1838-1853	10	20
Kea, Thomas	1	1830-1837	8	51
Kennedy, Thomas (Sr.)	1	1819-1820	6	1
Kerly, George (Sr.)	2	1838-1853	10	28
Kilgore, James (Sr.)	1	1819-1819	5	34
Kimbrough, Hannah, see - - - - - - - - - - - - - - - - Kinborough,Hannah				
Kinborough, Hannah	1	1798-1812	2	70
King, John (Sr.)	1	1798-1812	5	9
King, Samuel	2	1819-1819	10	36
King, Stephen R.	2	1838-1853	10	83
Kirven, John	1	1819-1820	6	10
Kirven, Caid	1	1817-1825	7	28
Lane, Rachel	1	1830-1837	8	21
Langston, Ridick	2	1838-1853	10	153
Lawhorn, John	2	1838-1853	10	71
Lewis, James	1	1830-1837	8	54
Lides, Hugh	2	1838-1853	10	31
McArtha, Alexander	1	1817-1825	7	4
McBride, Archibald	1	1798-1812	2	25
McBride, Sally	1	1798-1812	2	28
McCall, Duncan	2	1838-1853	10	13
McCall, George	1	1830-1837	8	57

McCall, John	1	1798-1812	2	68
McCall, Solomen	2	1838-1853	10	129
McCall, Solomon, see also - - - - - - - - - - - - - McCall, Duncan				
McCallum, Elizabeth	2	1838-1853	10	215
McCown, John	1	1812-1817	4	36
McGuire, Hugh (Merchant)	1	1812-1817	4	52
McIntosh, John, see - - - - - - - - - - - - - - - Mackintosh, John				
McIntosh, Sarah E.	2	1838-1853	10	174
McIver, Evander (Sr.)	1	1817-1825	7	2
McIver, John K.	2	1838-1853	10	115
McIver, Mary A.W.	1	1830-1837	8	49
Mackintosh, John	1	1798-1812	2	16
McLachlin, John	1	1812-1817	4	14
McLenaghan, Matilda Ann	2	1838-1853	10	202
McPherson, Sarah	1	1817-1819	7	18
Marshall, Mary	1	1819-1819	5	1
Marshall, William	1	1819-1819	5	25
Mercer, Jesse	1	1798-1812	2	61
Mercer, Thomas (Sr.)	1	1830-1837	8	14
Miers, Daniel	1	1812-1817	4	31
Mikell, Anne	1	1798-1812	2	50
Mims, Jacob	2	1838-1853	10	182
Miscon, Jehu	1	1830-1837	8	11
Mixon, Micah (Planter)	1	1798-1812	2	32
Mixon, Simpson	1	1830-1837	8	50
Morris, Stephen	1	1812-1817	4	22
Mozingo, William	2	1838-1853	10	188
Muldrew, Hugh	1	1812-1817	4	47
Muldrew, John	1	1819-1819	5	16
Muldrew, William (Planter)	1	1798-1812	2	84
Muldrew, William (Planter)	1	1812-1817	4	7
Muse, Elias P.	2	1838-1853	10	133
Muse, Martha	2	1838-1853	10	166
Myers, David, see - - - - - - - - - - - - - - - - - - - Miers, David				
Nettles, James	1	1819-1820	6	28
Nettles, Zachariah	1	1798-1812	2	11
Newbery, James	2	1838-1853	10	204
Newberry, Jesse	1	1798-1812	2	31
Nipper, Jacob	2	1838-1853	10	85
Norwood, John (Sr.)	1	1817-1825	7	37
Odom, Jacob	1	1819-1819	5	19
Oliver, Elizabeth	1	1819-1820	6	21
Onails, John	1	1830-1837	8	61
Orr, John	1	1798-1812	2	20
Parnal, James	1	1811-1813	3	1
Parrott, Benjamin	2	1838-1853	10	96
Parrott, Jacob (Sr.)	1	1819-1820	6	6
Pawley, James	1	1798-1812	2	76
Pearce, Jesse	2	1838-1853	10	184

Perritt, Martha	2	1838-1853	10	190
Phillips, Joel (Farmer)	2	1838-1853	10	219
Phillips, Stephen	2	1838-1853	10	177
Pierce, Copeland	2	1838-1853	10	22
Pigot, Margaret	2	1838-1853	10	111
Pippins, Micajah	2	1838-1853	10	18
Pollard, Joshua	1	1819-1819	5	11
Powell, John	1	1830-1837	8	41
Pugh, Evan	1	1798-1812	2	5
Revell, Mathew	1	1798-1812	2	9
Reynolds, Winneford	2	1838-1853	10	9
Rhodes, Joseph E.	2	1838-1853	10	78
Rollings, Richard	1	1830-1837	8	65
Ruffin, Rachel	1	1812-1817	4	51
Rufsell, James (Jr.)	1	1798-1812	2	77
Rufsell, Michael	1	1798-1812	2	63
Russell, James, see - - - - - - - - - - - - - - - - - Rufsell, James				
Russell, Michael, see - - - - - - - - - - - - - - - - Rufsell, Michael				
Sammons, Hansel	1	1830-1837	8	63
Sanders, Hannah	2	1838-1853	10	104
Sanders, Moses	2	1838-1853	10	1
Sanders, Nathaniel	1	1798-1812	2	36
Sansbury, Daniel	1	1812-1817	4	20
Sansbury, John	2	1838-1853	10	
Scaff, John, see - Scoff, John				
Scoff, John	2	1838-1853	10	117
Scott, Moses	1	1787-1793	1	3
Segars, Burrell	2	1838-1853	10	144
Skinner, Benjamin	1	1817-1825	7	26
Skinner, Mary	1	1830-1837	8	62
Smith, John	1	1798-1812	2	73
Smith, Martha	1	1819-1820	6	3
Snipes, Sorah	1	1819-1820	6	14
Standard, John	1	1812-1817	4	9
Standley, Thomas	1	1798-1812	2	46
Stanly, Elizabeth	1	1812-1817	4	39
Stephenson, Jepthah	2	1838-1853	10	2
Stewart, John	1	1830-1837	8	40
Talevast, Adolph (Farmer)	2	1838-1853	10	178
Taylor, Robert	1	1817-1825	7	16
Teele, Christopher	1	1798-1812	2	15
Thomas, Hesekiah	2	1838-1853	10	128
Thomas, John Parker	1	1812-1817	4	19
Thomas, Micheal	1	1817-1825	7	6
Thomas, Solomon	1	1798-1812	2	45
Thompson, Elizabeth	1	1812-1817	4	33
Thornhill, John	1	1798-1812	2	30
Trader, Dennis	2	1838-1853	10	93
Trawick, George	1	1830-1837	8	46
Trivitt, Elijah	1	1798-1812	2	79

Vancannon, John	2	1838–1853	10	89
Walters, Moses	1	1819–1820	6	22
Ward, Theopholus	1	1812–1828	4	15
Webb, Jolly (Planter)	1	1785–1893	1	4
Welch, Henry	2	1838–1853	10	198
White, William	2	1838–1853	10	124
Wilds, Martha	1	1819–1820	6	11
Wilds, Mary (Mrs.)	1	1798–1812	2	80
Wilkins, A. (Sr.)	2	1838–1853	10	86
Williams, David R.	1	1830–1837	8	2
Williams, Elisabeth	2	1838–1853	10	7
Williams, Stephen	1	1817–1825	7	7
Williams, William	1	1817–1825	7	33
Williamson, Lydia	1	1817–1825	7	36
Williamson, Samuel A.	2	1838–1853	10	156
Wilson, Augustin	2	1838–1853	10	136
Wingate, Edward	1	1798–1812	2	1
Wingate, William	2	1838–1853	10	87
Witherspoon, Garvin, see – – – – – – – – – – –			Withuspoon, Gavin	
Withuspoon, Gavin	1	1830–1837	8	47
Wood, Frame	1	1812–1817	4	22
Wood, Joseph (Farmer)	1	1798–1812	2	37
Woodham, Ariss	1	1812–1817	4	41
Woods, Andrew B.	1	1817–1825	7	9
Wright, Benjamin	1	1798–1812	2	49
Wright, Gillis	1	1819–1820	6	19
Wright, Jonathan	1	1817–1825	7	14
Wright, Josiah	1	1830–1837	8	37
Wright, Sarah	1	1812–1817	4	57
Zimmerman, William	1	1812–1817	13	

Copied by:
Mrs. John D. Rogers

/s/ Mrs. John D. Rogers

INDEX

TO

EDGEFIELD COUNTY WILLS.

Book A - Volume No. 1
1785-1818

Book A - Volume No. 2
1785-1818

Book C - Volume No. 1
1817-1835

Book C - Volume No. 2
1817-1835

Book D - Volume No. 1
1836-1853

Book D - Volume No. 2
1836-1853

This index is compiled from W.P.A. copies of
wills filed in the COUNTY PROBATE COURTS.
The volumes indexed are a part of the
South Carolina Collection of the
University of South Carolina
Library.

Columbia, S.C.
1939

Edgefield County Wills

	Vol.	Date	Section	Page
Abney, Azariah	2	1836-1853	D	344
Abney, Joel	2	1785-1818	A	651
Abney, John (Merchant)	2	1785-1818	A	581
Abney, Lark	1	1817-1835	C	184
Abney, M. M.	2	1836-1853	D	379
Abney, Nathaniel	1	1785-1818	A	399
Abney, Paul	1	1817-1835	C	91
Abney, Walter	2	1817-1835	C	399
Abney, William (Planter)	2	1836-1853	D	535
Adam, William (Sr.)	1	1836-1853	D	227
Adams, Charles (Planter)	2	1817-1835	C	371
Adams, Drury	1	1785-1818	A	632
Adams, James	2	1836-1853	D	579
Adams, John (Sr.)	1	1817-1835	C	173
Adams, Mary G.	2	1836-1853	D	581
Adams, Thomas	2	1785-1818	A	478
Addison, Allen B.	2	1836-1853	D	520
Addison, John (Sr.)	2	1817-1835	C	422
Addison, Joseph R.	2	1817-1835	C	617
Aiton, Robert	2	1836-1853	D	525
Allen, Aaron	1	1817-1835	C	205
Allison, Richard	1	1785-1818	A	19
Anderson, Allen	2	1836-1853	D	519
Anderson, Allen (Sr.)	1	1836-1853	D	245
Anderson, Robert	1	1817-1835	C	1
Anderson, Samuel	1	1785-1818	A	223
Anderson, Thomas	1	1785-1818	A	193
Anderson, William (Planter)	2	1785-1818	A	745
			Inv. & Wills	
Ardagh, Patrick (Merchant)	2	1785-1818	A	506
Ardis, Abram	2	1785-1818	A	188
Ardis, Christian	1	1785-1818	A	171
Ardis, David	2	1785-1818	A	764
Ardis, John	1	1818-1835	C	292
Arledge, John	1	1817-1835	C	123
Ashburry, James (Planter)	1	1817-1835	C	134
Atkinson, Joanna	1	1817-1835	C	156
Bacon, Nathaniel (Planter)	2	1785-1818	A	428
Bailey, Allen	1	1785-1818	A	380
Bailey, John	1	1836-1853	D	271
Baker, James	1	1785-1818	A	326
Banks, Amos	1	1836-1853	D	239
Banks, Thomas (Planter)	2	1785-1818	A	791
			Inv. & Wills	
Barker, Jesse	2	1817-1835	C	624
Barksdale, Susannah	2	1785-1818	A	563
Barnes, John (Farmer)	2	1785-1818	A	671
Barnes, Reason	1	1817-1835	C	269
Barronton, Elisha	2	1836-1853	D	559
Barronton, Wilson	2	1817-1835	C	489
Barronton, James	2	1817-1835	C	565
Barrott, Elizabeth	2	1817-1835	C	363
Bartlett, Richason	1	1817-1835	C	87
Barton, Thomas	1	1817-1835	C	270

Bates, Catherine	1	1817-1835	C	276
Bean, James (Sr.)	2	1836-1853	D	315
Beasley, Jonathan	1	1785-1818	A	271
Beckham, Thomas	1	1785-1818	A	156
Belcher, Robert	1	1785-1818	A	17
Bell, Catherine	2	1836-1853	D	423
Bender, George	1	1785-1818	A	395
Berry, Jacob	2	1785-1818	A	620
Berry, Thomas (Sr.)	1	1817-1835	C	34
Bettis, Jesse	1	1836-1853	D	75
Bird, Hezekiah	2	1785-1818	A	457
Bird, Soloman	2	1785-1818	A	521
Bishop, Joseph	1	1785-1818	A	294
Black, John H.	1	1836-1853	D	169
Blackbury, Elias	2	1817-1835	C	408
Blackston, Commodore D.	2	1836-1853	D	317
Blalock, John	1	1817-1835	C	203
Blalock, Reubin	2	1785-1818	A	647
Bland, Pressley	2	1817-1835	C	459
Bland, Randal W.	1	1836-1853	D	125
Blocker, David L.	2	1817-1835	C	437
Blocker, James	2	1736-1853	D	538
Blocker, John (Sr.)	2	1817-1835	C	547
Blocker, Michiel (Sr.)	2	1785-1818	A	618
Bodie, Nathan	1	1785-1818	A	318
Bolger, Elizabeth	1	1836-1853	D	196
Bolware, James	1	1836-1853	D	11
Bones, James	1	1785-1818	A	80
Bortner. Lewis	2	1785-1818	A	785
			Inv. & Wills	
Borrum, Higdom	2	1785-1818	A	412
Borrum, William	2	1785-1818	A	713
Bostick, Talaver	2	1785-1818	A	576
Boswell, David	2	1785-1818	A	443
Bouknight, Daniel	2	1836-1853	D	527
Boulware, James	1	1785-1818	A	80
Boulware, Spencer	2	1836-1853	D	469
Bowers, David (Planter)	1	1785-1818	A	85
Bowers, David	2	1817-1835	C	589
Boyd, Edmund	2	1785-1818	A	771
			Inv. & Wills	
Boyd, Edmund	2	1836-1853	D	586
Boyd, Henry K.	1	1817-1835	C	279
Boyd, John	1	1817-1853	C	150
Boyd, John (Jr.)	1	1817-1853	C	315
Boyd, Susannah	2	1836-1853	D	393
Bracknel, John	1	1817-1835	C	108
Bridges, Sarah	2	1817-1835	C	370
Briethaupt, Christian	2	1817-1835	C	632
Brooks, Whitfield	2	1836-1853	D	565
Brooks, Zachariah Smith	2	1835-1853	D	433
Brunson, Daniel (Sr.)	1	1836-1853	D	250
Brunson, William	2	1836-1853	D	361
Buckhalter, Christian	1	1785-1818	A	235
Buckhalter, Michiel	1	1785-1818	A	393
Bullock, James	2	1817-1835	C	344
Bullock, John	2	1785-1818	A	751
			Inv. & Wills	
Bostick, Washington	2	1785-1818	A	717

Bunting, Benjamin (Planter)	2	1817-1835	C	395
Bunting, Ruth	2	1836-1853	D	335
Burgess, Ann	2	1836-1853	D	490
Burgess, James (Carpenter)	1	1785-1818	A	233
Burgess, John	1	1836-1853	D	69
Burkhalter, Christian, see - - - - - - - - - - Buckhalter, Christian				
Burkhalter, William	2	1836-1853	D	447
Burnell, Cradock	1	1817-1835	C	58
Burnes, John	2	1785-1818	A	677
Burnett, Elizabeth	1	1817-1835	C	66
Burnett, Hezekiah	1	1817-1835	C	265
Burney, Mary	2	1836-1853	D	426
Burns, Crecy	1	1817-1835	C	237
Burns, John, see - - - - - - - - - - - - - - - - - Burnes, John				
Burress, John	2	1817-1835	C	359
Burress, John, see also - - - - - - - - - - - - - Burgess, John				
Burress, Martin	2	1836-1853	D	456
Burt, Armstead	1	1836-1853	D	129
Burt, Harwood	2	1785-1818	A	664
Burt, Philip	2	1817-1835	C	455
Burt, Robert, see - - - - - - - - - - - - - - - - Burts, Roberts				
Burton, Allen (Sr.)	2	1785-1818	A	422
Burton, Allen Y.	1	1836-1853	D	137
Burton, William	2	1785-1818	A	681
Burts, Mathew (Sr.)	1	1785-1818	A	118
Burts, Roberts	1	1785-1818	A	221
Bush, Bibby	2	1785-1818	A	569
Bush, Elizabeth	2	1817-1835	C	532
Bush, Isaac	1	1836-1853	D	6
Bush, John B.	1	1836-1853	D	300
Bush, William	1	1836-1853	D	52
Bussey, Charles	2	1785-1818	A	768
			Inv.& Wills	
Bussey, George	2	1836-1853	D	337
Bussey, George (Sr.)	1	1785-1818	A	207
Bussey, Martha	2	1836-1853	D	417
Bussey, Wade	1	1817-1835	C	32
Bussey, Zadoc	1	1817-1835	C	280
Bulter, Daniel	1	1817-1835	C	189
Bulter, Frank	2	1817-1835	C	377
Bulter, James (Farmer)	2	1785-1818	A	533
Bulter, John	2	1817-1835	C	534
Bulter, Robert	1	1785-1818	A	314
Bulter, Thomas (Major)	2	1785-1818	A	675
Bulter, William M.	1	1836-1853	D	121
Bulter, Winnefrey	2	1817-1835	C	518
Busbie, Benjamin	2	1785-1818	A	641
Callaham, Morris	1	1817-1835	C	191
Cain, William	1	1785-1818	A	161
Canfield, John	1	1785-1818	A	51
Cantelow, Peter	2	1817-1835	C	444
Cappel, Henry, see - - - - - - - - - - - - - - - Chappell, Henry				
Carpenter, Adam	2	1836-1853	D	560
Carroll, Mary	2	1836-1853	D	550
Carson, James (Sr.)	1	1817-1835	C	247
Carson, John	2	1785-1818	A	451

Name		Date		No.
Carson, William	1	1836-1853	D	213
Carter, Eliza	2	1836-1853	D	408
Carter, Nancy	2	1785-1818	A	697
Carter, Patience	1	1817-1835	C	202
Carter, Patience	2	1817-1835	C	481
Carter, Thomas	2	1785-1818	A	792

Inv. & Wills

Name		Date		No.
Cartledge, Isaiah	1	1817-1835	C	253
Cary, William H.	1	1836-1853	D	17
Chappell, Henry	1	1817-1835	C	102
Cheatham, John	1	1836-1853	D	221
Childs, Henry	1	1785-1818	A	59
Christian, Gideon	1	1817-1835	C	118
Christian, Jesse	1	1836-1853	D	118
Christian, Sarah	1	1817-1835	C	308
Christie, Susanah	1	1836-1853	D	264
Clackler, John (Sr.)	1	1785-1818	A	50
Clackèr, John (Sr.)	1	1817-1835	C	175
Clark, David	2	1785-1818	A	584
Clark, Elizabeth	2	1817-1835	C	384
Clark, Henry	1	1836-1853	D	144
Clark, John	1	1785-1818	A	103
Clark, John (Sr.)	1	1817-1835	C	179
Clark, Lewis	1	1785-1818	A	127
Clark, Lewis	1	1785-1818	A	252
Clarke, John (Sr.)	2	1817-1835	C	328
Clement, Obediah	1	1785-1818	A	266
Cloud, Martin	1	1785-1818	A	359
Cloud, Noah	1	1836-1853	D	78
Coats, James	2	1785-1818	A	715
Cobb, Thomas	1	1836-1853	D	163
Cockram, Benjamin	1	1785-1818	A	27
Cochran, Robert	1	1836-1853	D	110
Cogburn, Hannah	1	1836-1853	D	37
Cogburn, Jessie	1	1817-1835	C	124
Cogburn, John	2	1785-1818	A	524
Coleman, Daniel	1	1785-1818	A	267
Coleman, Edward	2	1817-1835	C	382
Coleman, Mary	2	1817-1835	C	462
Coleman, Mathew	1	1836-1853	D	146
Coleman, Richard (Planter)	2	1836-1853	D	498
Coleman, Thomas (Planter)	1	1817-1835	C	46
Coleman, William	1	1817-1836	C	309
Collier, Hillary	1	1836-1853	D	180
Collier, Joseph	1	1836-1853	C	38
Collier, William John	1	1785-1818	A	110
Collins, Horatio	2	1817-1835	C	566
Collum, Uriah	2	1785-1818	A	447
Conner, Ann	2	1817-1835	C	351
Cook, Samuel	2	1785-1818	A	596
Cooker, Timothy	2	1785-1818	A	544
Cooper, Charles	1	1817-1835	C	62
Cooper, Elizabeth	2	1817-1835	C	561
Cooper, Reuben	1	1817-1835	C	243
Cooper, Timothy, see - - - - - - - - - - - - - - -			Cooker, Timothy	
Corley, Bultett	2	1785-1818	A	459
Corley, Catlett	2	1817-1835	C	537

Corley, Elizabeth,	1	1817-1835	C	208
Corley, Sarah	2	1836-1853	D	503
Corley, Sherwood	1	1785-1818	A	335
Cox, Christopher (Sr.)	1	1817-1835	C	41
Cox, Clement	2	1836-1853	D	530
Cox, Edmund	1	1785-1818	A	113
Cox, James	1	1785-1818	A	225
Cox, Toliver M.	2	1817-1835	C	410
Cox, William (Jr.)	1	1785-1818	A	188
Crafton, Archibald T.	2	1836-1853	D	501
Crofton, Samuel	2	1785-1818	A	472
Crookshanks, John	1	1785-1818	A	387
Cross, Feather Stone	1	1785-1818	A	132
Crouch, John	1	1785-1818	A	61
Cruther, Isaac	1	1785-1818	A	111
Culbreath, John	2	1836-1853	D	327
Culbreath, Joseph	1	1817-1835	C	169
Culpepper, Joicy	1	1836-1853	D	166
Cunningham, Agnes	1	1817-1835	C	64
Cunningham, Joseph (Planter)	1	1785-1818	A	305
Cunningham, Joseph (Planter)	2	1817-1835	C	411
Cunningham, Sarah	1	1836-1853	D	254
Dagnel, Charles H.	1	1836-1853	D	296
Dagnel, Samuel	1	1817-1835	C	114
Dalton, Mary	1	1836-1853	D	164
Daly, Mary	2	1817-1835	C	556
Daniel, James	2	1785-1818	A	649
Daniel, Josiah L.	2	1785-1818	A	602
Daniel, William	1	1785-1818	A	384
Darby, Benjamin	2	1785-1818	A	612
Darby, Benjamin	2	1785-1818	A	627
Davis, Chesley	2	1817-1835	C	367
Davis, Francis	1	1817-1835	C	122
Davis, Samuel	1	1817-1835	C	282
Dawson, James C.	1	1836-1853	D	140
Day, Peter	1	1785-1818	A	55
Dean, William	2	1817-1835	C	486
Deen, Thomas	1	1836-1853	D	135
Deen, William (Jr.)	2	1817-1835	C	599
Dees, Shadarack	1	1785-1818	A	200
DeLaughter, Charity	2	1836-1853	D	324
DeLaughter, George (Sr.)	2	1817-1835	C	497
DeLoach, Thomas (Preacher)	1	1817-1835	C	51
Denore, John	2	1785-1818	A	455
Denore, Mathew (Sr.)	2	1785-1818	A	426
Doolittle, Samuel	2	1785-1818	A	754
			Inv.& Wills	
Doolittle, Samuel (Sr.)	2	1785-1818	A	695
Dorn, John (Sr.)	2	1836-1853	D	374
Dorn, Peter	1	1817-1835	C	303
Douglas, Lewis	1	1785-1818	A	68
Douglass, John	1	1785-1818	A	242
Downer, Alexander	1	1817-1835	C	97
Downer, Margaret	1	1817-1835	C	86
Dozier, William	1	1817-1835	C	93
Dugles, Lewis, see - - - - - - - - - - - - - - - -			Douglas, Lewis	
Dunton, Mary L.	1	1836-1853	D	172

Eddins, James	2	1785-1818	A	621
Edmonds, Alexander	1	1817-1835	C	192
Edwards, Benjamin	2	1785-1818	A	770
			Inv. & Wills	
Edwards, Jarrott	2	1817-1835	C	559
Elam, George G. (Sr.)(Planter)	2	1836-1853	D	390
Elam, John	1	1817-1835	C	249
Elam, William	2	1785-1818	A	480
Elligood, Thomas	1	1817-1835	C	187
Ernest, Jacob	2	1817-1835	C	346
Etheridge, William	2	1836-1853	D	472
Ethridge, Aaron	1	1817-1835	C	120
Evans, Nathaniel	2	1817-1835	C	577
Evans, Stephen	2	1817-1835	C	386
Everett, Martin	2	1817-1835	C	601
Fauqua, Mary	1	1785-1818	A	115
Ferguson, William	1	1836-1853	D	33
Fester, Lawrence	1	1785-1818	A	74
Fleek, John	1	1785-1818	A	245
Flin, William (Sr.)	1	1836-1853	D	48
Forman, Mary	1	1785-1818	A	130
Fortner, William (Sr.)	1	1836-1853	D	273
Fox, John	1	1836-1853	D	39
Fox, Martha	1	1785-1818	A	283
Franklin, Edmond	1	1785-1818	A	320
Frazier, Benjamin	2	1836-1853	D	304
Frazier, Jessie	2	1785-1818	A	731
Frazier, John	1	1817-1835	C	261
Frazier, John	2	1785-1818	A	772
			Inv. & Wills	
Freeman, Henry F.	2	1836-1853	D	561
Freeman, Thomas	1	1817-1835	C	283
Fudge, Jacob (Sr.)	1	1785-1818	A	46
Fuller, Elizabeth B.	2	1836-1853	D	378
Gale, Lugretia	2	1785-1818	A	476
Gallman, Daniel	2	1817-1835	C	438
Gardner, James	2	1785-1818	A	493
Gardner, Robert	1	1785-1818	A	372
Gardner, Samuel	2	1785-1818	A	767
			Inv. & Wills	
Gardon, Ambrose (Merchant)	2	1785-1818	A	587
Garrett, Edward	1	1836-1853	D	20
Garrett, Elizabeth	1	1836-1853	D	287
Garrett, John C.	2	1817-1835	C	575
Garrett, John W.	2	1836-1853	D	465
Garrett, Stephen	1	1817-1835	C	213
Garrett, William	2	1836-1853	D	569
Gentry, Hezekiah (Planter)	1	1817-1835	C	228
Gentry, Reynol	1	1817-1835	C	299
Gentry, Thomas, see - - - - - - - - - - - - - - - -			Genty, Thomas	
Genty, Thomas (Planter)	1	1817-1835	C	60
Gibbs, James W.	2	1836-1853	D	467
Gibson, John (Sr.)	1	1817-1835	A	258
Gillon, Milley	2	1817-1835	C	564-A
Gitty, Henry	2	1817-1835	C	368
Glanton, Jonathan	1	1817-1835	C	296

Glenn, William	1	1817-1835	C	104
Glover, Wiley (Planter)	1	1785-1818	A	366
Glover, William (Planter)	2	1785-1818	A	778
			Inv. & Wills	
Glover, William J.	1	1836-1853	D	231
Goggins, James	1	1836-1853	D	277
Goleman, James	2	1785-1818	A	488
Gomillion, Andrew	2	1785-1818	A	720
Goode, Garland	1	1785-1818	A	173
Goode, Lewelling	2	1785-1818	A	566
Goode, Mackerness	1	1785-1818	A	138
Goode, Phillip	1	1785-1818	A	91
Goode, Samuel (Planter)	2	1785-1818	A	760
			Inv.& Wills	
Gordon, Ambrose, see - - - - - - - - - - - - - -			Gardon, Ambrose	
Gorman, John (Sr.)	1	1785-1818	A	278
Gray, John (Sr.)	1	1817-1835	C	235
Gray, John	2	1817-1835	C	587
Gray, John J.	1	1836-1853	D	283
Gray, William W.	2	1836-1853	D	359
Green, Bryant	1	1785-1818	A	136
Griffin, Jesse	1	1785-1818	A	401
Griffin, Rivhard	2	1836-1853	D	582
Griffin, Sumpter M.	2	1836-1853	D	532
Griffin, William	2	1785-1818	A	548
Griffis, John	1	1836-1853	D	94
Griffis, Mary	2	1836-1853	D	558
Griffith, David	1	1785-1818	A	352
Griffith, Joseph	2	1785-1818	A	528
Grigsby, Enoch	1	1785-1818	A	167
Grigsby, Rhydon, see - - - - - - - - - - - - - -			Grisby, Rhydon	
Grisby, Rhydon	2	1817-1835	C	321
Grisham, James P.	2	1836-1853	D	578
Grubbs, Joel H.	2	1785-1818	A	485
Guyton, Jacob	1	1817-1835	C	17
Gwyn, William	2	1785-1818	A	550
Hagan, Thomas	1	1785-1818	A	160
Hagens, William	1	1836-1853	D	13
Hagood, Benjamin (Sr.)	2	1785-1818	A	700
Hagood, George	2	1817-1835	C	508
Hall, Alexander	1	1785-1818	A	397
Hall, Esekile M.	2	1785-1818	A	679
Hall, James	1	1785-1818	A	140
Hall, Tebitha	2	1836-1853	D	322
Hall, Thomas	2	1817-1835	C	416
Hamilton, David	2	1836-1853	D	412
Hamilton, Richard	2	1836-1853	D	410
Hamilton, William	1	1836-1853	D	25
Hammond, Charles	1	1785-1818	A	122
Hammond, Charles (Sr.)	1	1836-1853	D	29
Hammond, John	2	1785-1818	A	773
			Inv. & Wills	
Hammond, LeRoy	1	1785-1818	A	43
Hampton, John	1	1836-1853	D	289
Hampton, Richard	1	1 836-1853	D	148
Hancock, Martha	2	1817-1835	C	388
Hannah, Alexander (Planter)	2	1785-1818	A	449

Hardy, John	1	1785–1818	A	248
Hargrove, Charles	1	1785–1818	A	227
Hargrove, Temple	2	1836–1853	D	485
Harrin, William	1	1817–1835	C	116
Harris, Moses	2	1836–1853	D	310
Harrison, Benjamin	2	1817–1835	C	474
Harrison, Edward H.	2	1817–1835	C	464
Harrison, James	1	1785–1818	A	344
Harrison, James	1	1836–1853	D	279
Harrison, James	2	1785–1818	A	743

Inv. & Wills

Harrison, Robert (Jr.)	1	1817–1835	C	129
Harrison, Robert	2	1817–1835	C	605
Harry, Benjamin (Sr.)	2	1785–1818	A	531
Hart, James	2	1817–1835	C	513
Harter, Adam	2	1785–1818	A	661
Harvey, William	1	1785–1818	A	12
Harvins, John	1	1785–1818	A	355
Hatcher, Benjamin	1	1836–1853	D	72
Hatcher, John	1	1817–1835	C	289
Hatcher, Lucy	1	1836–1853	D	111
Haviard, John	1	1817–1835	C	273
Haws, Isaac	2	1836–1853	D	425
Haws, Spencer	1	1785–1818	A	364
Heard, George	1	1817–1835	C	80
Hearn, Druey	1	1836–1853	D	156
Henderson, Nathaniel	1	1785–1818	A	287
Herbert, William	2	1836–1853	D	573
Hester, John	1	1817–1835	C	28
Hibbler, Jacob	2	1817–1835	C	619
Hicks, Charles	2	1785–1818	A	466
Hicks, James M. (Planter)	1	1817–1835	C	154
Hightower, Benjamin	1	1817–1835	C	224
Hightower, Joseph	2	1785–1818	A	538
Hiles, Sophia	1	1785–1818	A	14
Hill, Aaron	2	1836–1853	D	536
Hill, Abil	1	1817–1835	C	16
Hill, Dannett (Planter)	1	1785–1818	A	408
Hill, Darcas	1	1785–1818	A	309
Hill, Jesse	11	1817–1835	A	78
Hill, Joel D.	2	1836–1853	D	431
Hill, John (Sr.)	2	1785–1818	A	424
Hill, John	2	1785–1818	A	561
Hill, Lodowick	1	1817–1835	C	168
Hill, Mary	1	1817–1835	C	166
Hill, Theophilus	2	1836–1853	D	606
Hinton, Allen	1	1785–1818	A	169
Hogans, William	1	1785–1818	A	357
Holladay, James, see – – – – – – – – – – – – – –			Holloday, James	
Hollingsworth, Alexander	1	1785–1818	A	321
Hollingsworth, James	1	1785–1818	A	342
Hollingsworth, James (Sr.)	1	1817–1835	C	131
Hollingsworth, John	1	1836–1853	D	202
Holloday, James	2	1817–1835	C	349
Holloway, Asa	2	1817–1835	C	340
Holloway, Caleb	1	1836–1853	D	151
Holloway, Jesse	1	1817–1835	C	27
Holloway, John H.	2	1785–1818	A	520

loway, William	1	1836-1853	D	76
mes, Edward	1	1817-1836	C	162
lmes, William (Planter	1	1785-1818	A	39
Howard, John	2	1817-1835	C	511
Howard, Samuel (Planter)	1	1785-1818	A	24
Howerton, James	1	1785-1818	A	349
Howle, Esther	1	1836-1853	D	243
Howle, William (Sr.)	1	1836-1853	D	297
Hubbard, James (Sr.)	2	1836-1853	D	364
Hudson, James	1	1817-1835	C	293
Hudson, William	2	1785-1818	A	559
Huff, John	2	1785-1818	A	635
Hull, Gideon, H.	1	1836-1853	D	170
Jackson, John	1	1785-1818	A	120
Jay, Jesse	1	1836-1853	D	47
Jennings, Robert	2	1785-1818	A	637
Jennings, Thomas	2	1817-1835	C	614
Jennings, William	1	1836-1853	D	236
Jernegan, Angelie	1	1785-1818	A	187
Jeter, William	1	1785-1818	A	178
Jeter, William (Planter)	1	1817-1835	C	69
Johns, Obadiah	1	1817-1835	C	3
Johnson, Haly	1	1785-1818	A	370
Johnson, James	2	1817-1835	A	732
Johnson, John	2	1817-1835	C	432
Johnson, Rachel	1	1785-1818	A	230
Johnson, Samuel	2	1817-1835	C	546
Johnson, Thomas (Shoemaker)	1	1785-1818	A	191
Johnson, William S.	1	1836-1853	D	198
Jones, Francis	2	1785-1818	A	765
			Inv. & Wills	
Jones, Hicks	2	1817-1835	C	348
Jones, James L.	2	1817-1835	C	365
Jones, John	1	1785-1818	A	163
Jones, Leana	1	1817-1835	C	170
Jones, Mathias	2	1817-1835	C	439
J ones, Richard	1	1836-1853	D	81
Joor, Sarah C.	2	1836-1853	D	413
Joor, William W.	2	1836-1853	D	318
Jordan, John	2	1836-1853	D	539
Kay, John	2	1785-1818	A	699
Keating, Edward	1	1785-1818	A	36
Kerblay, Madame	1	1817-1835	C	160
Key, Henry	1	1785-1818	A	36
Key, Henry (Sr.)	2	1785-1818	A	800
			Inv. & Wills	
Key, John	1	1836-1853	D	210
Key, Thomas	1	1817-1835	C	125
Kilcrease, Arthur (Planter)	1	1785-1818	A	78
Kilcrease, James E. (Planter)	2	1836-1853	D	420
Kilcrease, John (Planter)	2	1817-1835	C	446
Kilcrease, Lewis	2	1817-1835	C	543
Kilcrease, Mary	2	1836-1853	D	463
Kilcrease, Sampson	2	1836-1853	D	505
King, Henry	1	1817-1835	C	56
King, James	2	1817-1835	C	571
King, William (Sr.)	2	1817-1835	C	626

Kirkland, Thomas	1	1785-1818	A	26
Kyser, George (Sr.)	2	1785-1818	A	418
Labarde, Peter	1	1817-1835	C	89
Lake, Joseph	1	1817-1835	C	199
Lakey, Thomas	1	1817-1835	C	30
Lamar, James	2	1785-1818	A	646
Lamar, Jamina	1	1817-1835	C	188
Lamar, Jeremiah	1	1785-1818	A	377
Lamar, Lydia	2	1817-1835	C	612
Lamar, Robert (Sr.)	2	1785-1818	A	435
Lamar, Thomas (Minister)	2	1785-1818	A	786
			Inv. & Wills	
Lamar, Thomas G.	2	1817-1835	C	568
Lamkin, Helen	2	1817-1835	C	519
Lamkin, Peter	1	1817-1835	C	319
Landrom, Reuben	1	1836-1853	D	269
Landrum, John (Sr.)	2	1836-1853	D	386
Lane, Margaret	2	1817-1835	C	545
Lang, James	1	1785-1818	A	289
Langley, David	1	1817-1835	C	177
Langley, Josiah (Sr.)	2	1817-1835	C	419
Lanham, Rezin	2	1836-1853	D	377
Lanier, Richard	1	1785-1818	A	165
Laremon, Edward	1	1785-1818	A	8
Largent, Thomas	1	1785-1818	A	261
Lark, John	1	1817-1835	C	255
Lasseter, Isaac	2	1817-1835	C	597
Lasuer, James	2	1785-1818	A	518
Leavenworth, Ann	1	1836-1853	D	61
Leavenworth, Melines C.	1	1817-1835	C	194
Lee, Andrew	1	1785-1818	A	152
Lee, Thomas	1	1785-1818	A	351
Lee, Wilson	2	1785-1818	A	574
Leftone, Edward, see - - - - - - - - - - - - - - -			Lofton, Edward	
Lesley, Maria	2	1836-1853	D	395
Lesuer, James, see - - - - - - - - - - - - - - -			Lasuer, James	
Lewis, Richard	1	1836-1853	D	80
Lightfoot, Francis	1	1785-1818	A	316
Lightfoot, Patsy	2	1836-1853	D	350
Limbecker, Christian	1	1817-1835	C	8
Lindsey, Benjamin	1	1836-1853	D	191
Lindsey, William	2	1817-1835	C	403
Little, William	1	1836-1853	D	49
Livington, James	2	1785-1818	A	598
Lofton, Edward	2	1817-1835	C	470
Long, Catherine (Sr.)	2	1817-1835	C	567
Long, George	2	1785-1818	A	643
Long, Jacob (Sr.)	2	1836-1853	D	437
Long, Michael	1	1817-1835	C	152
Longmire, John	2	1785-1818	A	722
Lott, Ensley	2	1817-1835	C	467
Lott, Jesse	2	1785-1818	A	552
Lott, Sarah	2	1817-1835	C	530
Low, James	1	1785-1818	A	224
Low, Polly	2	1817-1835	C	504
Lowe, Henry W.	2	1817-1835	C	524
Lowe, Nicholas	1	1836-1853	D	258
Lowe, Trechy	2	1836-1853	D	533

Lowery, James	2	1785-1818	A	672
Lowry, Lucy	1	1785-1818	A	211
Lowry, Richard	1	1785-1818	A	41
Lucas, John (Sr.)	2	1785-1818	A	741
			Inv. & Wills	
Lyon, Benj. F.	1	1817-1835	C	251
Lyon, John	1	1836-1853	D	178
McCary, Benjamin	1	1785-1818	A	293
McCary, Dolly	2	1785-1818	A	495
McCreless, John (Sr.)	2	1785-1818	A	482
McDaniel, Angus	1	1785-1818	A	134
McDaniel, John	2	1785-1818	A	725
McFailands, Mary	1	1785-1818	A	331
McGilton, James	1	1785-1818	A	4
McGinnis, Joseph	2	1785-1818	A	653
McGregor, Alexandra (Ferryman)	1	1785-1818	A	37
McGinnie, Roger	1	1836-1853	D	261
McLewarth, Francis	1	1785-1818	A	254
McManus, Goddy	2	1836-1853	D	487
McMillan, Matthew, see - - - - - - - - - - - - - -			McMillar, Matthew	
McMillar, Matthew	1	1785-1818	A	182
McMurphey, George Y.	2	1785-1818	A	591
McWhorter, Moses	1	1785-1818	A	195
Mann, Elizabeth (Sr.)	1	1785-1818	A	229
Mantz, C. Stephen	1	1817-1835	C	175
Marchant, John	2	1817-1835	C	514
Marcus, Ellis	1	1785-1818	A	16
Marlow, William	1	1836-1853	D	93
Marsh, Samuel	1	1785-1818	A	23
Marshall, Howell R.	2	1817-1835	C	476
Martin, Betty	1	1785-1818	A	196
Martin, George	2	1785-1818	A	723
Martin, John	1	1817-1835	C	82
Martin, John F.	2	1836-1853	D	381
Martin, Joshua	2	1817-1835	C	380
Martin, Mathew	2	1836-1853	D	429
Martin, Sarah	1	1836-1853	D	299
Martin, Thomas (Sr.)	2	1817-1835	C	451
Martin, William	1	1785-1818	A	5
Martin, William	2	1817-1835	C	405
Martin, William	2	1785-1818	A	788
			Inv. & Wills	
Mason, Elizabeth	2	1817-1835	C	422
Mathews, Drury (Planter)	2	1817-1835	C	495
Mathews, James	2	1836-1853	D	495
Mathews, Lewis	2	1817-1835	C	544
Mathews, Mourning	2	1835-1853	D	387
Mathews, Susannah	1	1785-1818	A	67
Mathews, Susannah	1	1836-1853	D	122
Matthews, Hardy	2	1817-1835	C	541
Maynard, James (Planter)	2	1836-1853	D	356
Maynard, John	2	1817-1835	C	478
Mays, Abney	1	1785-1818	A	312
Mays, John J.	2	1836-1853	D	483
Mays, Mathew	2	1817-1835	C	544
Mays, Samuel	2	1785-1818	A	666
Mays, Samuel	2	1785-1818	A	738

Mays, Stephen	2	1785-1818	A	710
Mays, William	2	1785-1818	A	780
			Inv. & Wills	
Mays, William B. (Planter)	2	1836-1853	D	354
Mealing, John H.	2	1817-1835	C	417
Melton, Nathan (Planter)	1	1785-1818	A	382
Meriwether, Francis L.	2	1836-1853	D	547
Meriwether, Thomas	2	1817-1835	C	521
Messersmith, John Jacob	1	1785-1818	A	88
Meyer, Catherine	2	1785-1818	A	749
			Inv. & Wills	
Meyer, Jonathan	2	1785-1818	A	798
Meyers, Elizabeth (Jr.)	1	1785-1818	A	53
Middleton, John (Planter)	2	1836-1853	D	368
Miller, George	1	1785-1818	A	363
Miller, Jacob	1	1785-1818	A	69
Miles, Aquilla	2	1785-1818	A	794
			Inv. & Wills	
Miles, Margaret	2	1817-1835	C	602
Mins, Beheathland	1	1836-1853	D	23
Mins, Dabid	2	1817-1835	C	485
Mins, Elizabeth	2	1836-1853	D	402
Mins, M.	2	1836-1853	D	453
Minter, William	1	1785-1818	A	28
M itchel, Green B.	1	1836-1853	D	193
Mitchell, Littleberry	2	1785-1818	A	705
Mitchell, Mary	2	1836-1853	D	446
Mitchell, Reziah	2	1836-1853	D	430
Mobley, Rachel	2	1817-1835	C	350
Mobley, Sarah	2	1817-1835	C	350
Mobley, Whitfield	2	1836-1853	D	383
Mock, George (Sr.)	1	1785-1818	A	54
Moore, Creswell	1	1836-1853	D	133
Moore, John C.	2	1836-1853	D	325
Moore, Joseph	2	1836-1853	D	563
Moore, Martha	2	1817-1835	C	324
M oore, Patty	2	1785-1818	A	607
Moore, Richard	1	1785-1818	A	391
Morgan, Elias	1	1785-1818	A	303
Morgan, Evan	1	1785-1818	A	241
Morgan, Evan	1	1836-1853	D	8
Morgan, Ozias	2	1817-1835	C	500
Morris, James	2	1836-1853	D	440
Morris, Joseph	2	1836-1853	D	510
Morris, Joseph (Sr.)	1	1836-1853	D	150
Mosely, Benjamin	1	1785-1818	A	131
Mosley, James	2	1817-1835	C	453
Mosley, John	2	1836-1853	D	444
Mosley, Robert	1	1785-1818	A	158
Moss, Rachel	1	1836-1853	D	298
Murphy, Lewis	2	1817-1835	C	407
Murphy, William	2	1785-1818	A	756
Myers, Mary	1	1785-1818	A	231
Nail, Barbara	1	1785-1818	A	157
Nail, Casper (Sr.)	1	1785-1818	A	183
Nail, Casper	1	1836-1853	D	224
Neal, Daniel	2	1785-1818	A	487

Newport, Robert	1	1785-1818	A	281
Newton, Robert	1	1836-1853	D	238
Nicholls, Sarah	2	1836-1853	D	319
Nicholson, John O.	2	1836-1853	D	542
Nicholson, Shemual	2	1836-1853	D	400
Nicholson, Urbane	2	1785-1818	A	734
Nicholson, Wright	2	1785-1818	A	416
Nobles, Hesekiah	2	1817-1835	C	562
Norrell, Isaac	1	1785-1818	A	177
Norris, Nathan	2	1836-1853	D	540
Norris, Stephen	2	1785-1818	A	579
Nunn, Ingram	1	1836-1853	D	105
Oden, Hesekiah, see - - - - - - - - - - - - - - -			Odom, Hesekiah	
Odom, Hesekiah (Sr.)	1	1785-1818	A	203
Odom, Martha	2	1785-1818	A	728
Ogilbia, Thomas, see - - - - - - - - - - - - - -			Ogilvie, Thomas	
Ogilvie, James	1	1785-1818	A	338
Ogilvie, Thomas	1	1817-1835	C	312
Ogle, William	1	1785-1818	A	285
Oliphant, John	2	1785-1818	A	657
Oliphant, William	2	1817-1835	C	392
Oliver, Dionecious	2	1785-1818	A	662
Oliver, Dionysios	2	1785-1818	A	500
Ousts, Martin (Sr.)	2	1836-1853	D	314
Ousts, Peter (Sr.)	2	1817-1835	C	433
Owens, Jonathan	2	1785-1818	A	439
Padgett, Dryden	2	1836-1853	D	416
Palmer, Ellis	2	1785-1818	A	762
			Inv. & Wills	
Palmer, Thomas	1	1785-1818	A	346
Pardue, Joel	1	1785-1818	A	189
Parker, Daniel	2	1785-1818	A	433
Parker, Isaac (Planter)	2	1785-1818	A	701
Parkins, Milton (Planter)	2	1836-1853	D	506
Parkman, Elisabeth	2	1817-1835	C	461
Partin, Charles, see - - - - - - - - - - - - - -			Pastin, Charles	
Pastin, Charles (Planter)	2	1785-1818	A	557
Perkins, Charles (Merchant)	2	1785-1818	A	420
Perrin, George	1	1785-1818	A	198
Perrin, Robert	2	1817-1835	C	361
Perrin, Sarah	2	1817-1835	C	424
Perrin, William	1	1785-1818	A	1
Perry, Esekiel	2	1817-1835	C	573
Perryman, Munsford	1	1817-1835	C	73
Peterson, Thomas	2	1817-1835	C	357
Phillips, John	2	1817-1835	C	323
Phillips, Joseph	1	1836-1853	D	127
Phillips, Michajak	2	1785-1818	A	555
Pickens, Andrew	1	1836-1853	D	84
Pipers, Willis (Planter)	2	1836-1853	D	512
Pitts, David	2	1785-1818	A	410
Pope, George	1	1836-1853	D	302
Pope, Jacob	2	1836-1853	D	504
Pope, Samson	1	1785-1818	A	311
Pope, Soloman	1	1785-1818	A	128
Posey, Francis	1	1785-1818	A	10
Posy, William C.	2	1817-1835	C	608

Pow, James	2	1817-1835	C	404
Pow, Robert	1	1785-1818	A	291
Powel, Charles	1	1817-1835	C	18
Prince, Daniel	1	1836-1853	D	272
Pryor, John	1	1785-1818	A	142
Pursell, Edward	2	1785-1818	A	784
			Inv. & Wills	
Pursell, John	1	1785-1818	A	125
Purvis, John	1	1785-1818	A	81
Quarles, James	2	1785-1818	A	609
Quarles, Nancy	2	1836-1853	D	442
Quarles, Richard (Sr.)	1	1785-1818	A	213
Quarles, Richard	1	1817-1835	C	25
Quarles, William	1	1817-1835	C	145
Raiford, Philip	1	1817-1835	C	230
Rainsford, John	1	1817-1835	C	4
Rainsford, Thomas	1	1836-1853	D	65
Rakestraw, John	1	1817-1835	C	172
Ramage, James	1	1836-1853	D	35
Rambo, Mary	2	1836-1853	D	450
Rampy, Peter	1	1836-1853	D	266
Ramsey, Barbara R.	1	1817-1835	C	300
Ramsey, John	1	1817-1835	C	295
Ramsey, Mathew	1	1785-1818	A	209
Ramsey, Thomas	2	1817-1835	C	457
Randall, George	1	1817-1835	C	206
Ravencraft, William (Sr.)	2	1785-1818	A	499
Rawl, Philip	1	1817-1835	C	112
Ray, Elizabeth M.	2	1785-1818	A	712
Raybourn, Joseph	1	1785-1818	A	83
Reavencraft, William, see - - - - - - - - - - -			Ravencraft, William	
Reed, John Byan	2	1817-1835	C	563
Rees, John (Farmer)	1	1785-1818	A	301
Reiser, George	2	1785-1818	A	686
Reynolds, Thomas (Sr.)	1	1836-1853	D	190
Rhoden, John	2	1836-1853	D	406
Rhodes, William	2	1817-1835	C	611
Richardson, Amos	1	1817-1835	C	238
Richardson, Daniel	2	1817-1835	C	466
Richardson, David	1	1836-1853	D	293
Richardson, Jefferson	1	1836-1853	D	1
Richardson, William	2	1785-1818	A	655
Riley, James	2	1785-1818	A	659
Riley, William (Sr.)	2	1785-1818	A	684
Rinehart, John	2	1817-1835	C	445
Risor, George	1	1817-1835	C	105
Rivers, John	1	1785-1818	A	38
Rivers, Mary	1	1785-1818	A	264
Roberson, James	1	1785-1818	A	323
Roberson, John	2	1785-1818	A	685
Robertson, John, see - - - - - - - - - - - - -			Roberson, John	
Roberson, William	2	1817-1835	C	335
Roberts, Shelton G.	2	1836-1853	D	508
Robertson, Elisha, see - - - - - - - - - - - -			Robinson, Elisha	
Roberts, Thomas	1	1785-1818	A	7
Roberts, Thomas	1	1785-1818	A	21

Robertson, James, see	- - - - - - - - - - - - - - - -		Roberson, James	
Robertson, Moses	2	1785-1818	A	758
			Inv. & Wills	
Robertson, William	1	1836-1853	D	175
Robertson, William (Sr.)	1	1836-1853	D	233
Robertson, William	2	1785-1818	A	571
Robinson, Elisha	1	1785-1818	A	175
Robinson, Martha	2	1817-1835	C	578
Robinson, William, see	- - - - - - - - - - - - -		Roberson, William	
Roe, Cornelous (Planter)	2	1817-1835	C	358
Rogers, Daniel	1	1836-1853	D	274
Rogers, Daniel (Sr.)	2	178501818	A	469
Rogers, William B.	2	1836-1853	D	411
Roper, Benjamin	1	1836-1853	D	200
Roper, Joel	2	1836-1853	D	341
Roper, William	1	1785-1818	A	300
Roper, William	2	1785-1818	A	536
Ross, James	1	1817-1835	C	182
Ross, Thomas	2	1785-1818	A	782
			Inv. & Wills	
Rotton, William	2	1836-1853	D	351
Rountree, Christian	1	1785-1818	A	246
Rountree, Jesse	2	1785-1818	A	628
Roundtree, Jesse, see	- - - - - - - - - - - - -		Rountree, Jesse	
Roundtree, John	1	1817-1835	C	36
Rowe, Mary	2	1836-1853	D	394
Rowell, Edward	2	1817-1835	C	440
Rosier, Isham	2	1836-1853	D	419
Rushton, Gaines F.	1	1836-1853	D	220
Rutherford, Henry W.	2	1836-1853	D	488
Rutherford, James	1	1785-1818	A	212
Rutherford, Joseph (Planter)	2	1817-1835	C	629
Ryan, Benjamin, see	- - - - - - - - - - - - -		Ryon, Benjamin	
Ryan, John	2	1817-1835	C	372
Ryon, Benjamin	2	1785-1818	A	604
Samuel, Robert (Sr.)	2	1785-1818	A	503
Sanders, William	2	1785-1818	A	673
Satcher, Samuel	2	1785-1818	A	614
Savage, Samuel (Planter)	1	1785-1818	A	328
Scott, Elizabeth	2	1817-1835	C	552
Scott, James	1	1785-1818	A	406
Scott, Samuel	2	1785-1818	A	463
Scurry, Thomas (Sr.)	1	1836-1853	D	54
Scurry, Thomas (Jr.)	1	1836-1853	D	229
Scurry, William	1	1817-1835	C	135
Searles, John	1	1817-1835	C	53
Seef, Daniel	1	1836-1853	D	14
Sentell, Jonathan (Planter)	1	1785-1818	A	236
Sharpton, Jeptha	1	1836-1853	D	100
Shelcy, Mathias	2	1836-1853	D	339
Shelnut, Henry	2	1836-1853	D	461
Shelton, Lewis S.	2	1836-1853	D	580
Shibly, Jacob B.	2	1836-1853	D	312
Ships, Phillip	1	1817-1835	C	318
Sigler, George	1	1836-1853	D	241
Simkins, Arthur (Sr.)	1	1817-1835	C	332
Simkins, Eldred (Sr.)	2	1817-1835	C	549
Simkins, Eliza H.	1	1836-1853	D	56

Simkins, John	2	1817-1835	C	580
Sisson, Frederick	1	1785-1818	A	76
Slappy, John G.	2	1817-1835	C	506
Slapy, Frederick	2	1817-1835	C	330
Smith, George	1	1817-1835	C	241
Smith, Jacob	1	1785-1818	A	361
Smith, James (Sr.)	1	1817-1835	C	209
Smith, James M.	1	1836-1853	D	68
Smith, Luke	2	1785-1818	A	467
Smyley, James	1	1836-1853	D	96
Snalgrove, Edward, see - - - - - - - - - - - - -			Snulgrove, Edward	
Snead, John	1	1785-1818	A	146
Snulgrove, Edward	1	1785-1818	A	274
Spann, Elizabeth	1	1836-1853	D	256
Spann, Henry	2	1785-1818	A	736
Spann, John	2	1785-1818	A	589
Spraggins, Thomas	1	1785-1818	A	389
Stallsworth, William, see - - - - - - - - - - -			Stollworth, William	
Starr, John (Sr.)	1	1817-1835	C	107
Stephens, Sarah	1	1785-1818	A	101
Stevens, Abraham	1	1817-1835	C	259
Stevens, Benjamin	2	1836-1853	D	553
Stevens, Elisha	2	1817-1835	C	621
Stevens, Sarah, see - - - - - - - - - - - - - - -			Stephens, Sarah	
Steward, William, see - - - - - - - - - - - - - -			Stewart, William	
Stewart, Alexander (Planter)	1	1817-1835	C	245
Stewart, Sally	1	1817-1835	C	130
Stewart, William	2	1785-1818	A	514
Stewart, William (Planter)	2	1817-1835	C	320
Still, John	1	1785-1818	A	201
Stoker, Mathew, see - - - - - - - - - - - - - - -			Stokes, Mathew	
Stokes, Greenberry	1	1817-1835	C	252
Stokes, Mathew (Planter)	1	1785-1818	A	98
Stollworth, William	2	1785-1818	A	461
Stone, John (Sr.)	2	1817-1835	C	415
Street, John	1	1785-1818	A	256
Strom, Mary	2	1836-1853	D	526
Stringer, John	1	1785-1818	A	260
Strother, William (Planter)	1	1785-1818	A	116
Stuart, Rebecca S.	2	1836-1853	D	507
Sturgennegger, John	2	1836-1853	D	602
Stursenegger, Elizabeth	2	1785-1818	A	437
Sullivan, John	1	1836-1853	D	123
Sullivan, Pressley G.	1	1836-1853	D	10
Summers, James	2	1817-1835	C	326
Swearingen, Vann	1	1785-1818	A	166
Swearingen, Vann	1	1836-1853	D	5
Swearingen, Vann	2	1785-1818	A	445
Swillevant, Mary	1	1817-1835	C	95
Talbert, see - - - - - - - - - - - - - - - - - - -			Tolbert	
Tarrance, John	1	1817-1835	C	266
Tate, Henry	1	1836-1853	D	27
Taylor, Abraham (Planter)	1	1785-1818	A	333
Taylor, John	1	1836-1853	D	219
Taylor, Josiah	1	1817-1835	C	143
Taylor, William Forbes	2	1785-1818	A	541
Teague, Addison M.	2	1836-1853	D	404

Teer, Anna	2	1817-1835	C	458
Teer, Stephen	2	1785-1818	A	680
Terry, Anna Maria	1	1836-1853	D	285
Thomas, James	1	1785-1818	A	325
Thomas, Roberts	2	1785-1818	A	32
Thomas, William (Sr.)	2	1785-1818	A	553
Thompson, Marshall	2	1836-1853	D	556
Thompson, Wiley	2	1836-1853	D	384
Thornton, Abraham	1	1785-1818	A	185
Thorton, Thomas	1	1817-1835	C	138
Thurman, Elizabeth, see - - - - - - - - - - - - -			Thurmond, Elizabeth	
Thurmond, Elizabeth	1	1785-1818	A	339
Thurmond, John	1	1785-1818	A	109
Thurmond, Pleasant	2	1817-1835	C	502
Tillman, Benjamin, see - - - - - - - - - - - - -			Tilliman, B. R.	
Tilliman, B. R.	2	1836-1853	D	516
Tillman, Ann Sebell	2	1817-1835	C	472
Tillman, Jonathan	1	1836-1853	D	158
Timmerman, Jacob	2	1817-1835	C	342
Timmerman, Jonathan	2	1836-1853	D	460
Timmerman, Peter (Sr.)	2	1836-1853	D	492
Tobler, John Joacorn (Planter)	2	1785-1818	A	526
Tobler, Ulrie	1	1817-1835	C	215
Tobler, William (Planter)	1	1785-1818	A	368
Tolbart, Joseph	1	1785-1818	A	106
Tolbert, Ansel (Sr.)	2	1836-1853	D	329
Tolbert, William	1	1785-1818	A	22
Tomkins, Augustus M.	1	1836-1853	D	257
Tomkins, Samuel	2	1817-1835	C	483
Trotter, Jeremiah	1	1817-1835	C	133
Trotter, Nathan	1	1817-1835	C	305
Trowbridge, E. S.	1	1817-1835	C	242
Tucker, Martha	1	1836-1853	D	153
Tullice, Moses	2	1785-1818	A	719
Turk, Thomas	1	1817-1835	C	211
Turner, George	1	1817-1835	C	298
Turner, John E.	1	1836-1853	D	276
Turner, Robert	1	1836-1853	D	248
Tutt, Richard	2	1785-1818	A	414
Twiggs, George L.	2	1836-1853	D	590
Uts, Peter (Planter)	2	1785-1818	A	789
Vann, Isaac	1	1836-1853	D	217
Vaughn, James (Blacksmith)	2	1785-1818	A	674
Vessels, Mickell	2	1785-1818	A	624
Wade, Henderson	2	1817-1835	C	515
Waldo, Elizabeth	2	1836-1853	D	493
Walker, John	1	1785-1818	A	350
Walker, John	2	1785-1818	A	516
Walker, Samuel	2	1785-1818	A	593
Wall, John	1	1817-1835	C	68
Wallace, Beaufort A.	1	1836-1853	D	186
Wallace, James (Planter)	2	1836-1853	D	588
Walling, William W.	2	1836-1853	D	576
Ward, Frederick	1	1785-1818	A	297
Ware, Henry	2	1785-1818	A	600
Ware, Margarett	2	1817-1835	C	468

Ware, Nickolas (Sr.)	2	1785-1818	A	776
			Inv. & Wills	
Ware, Robert (Sr.)	1	1817-1835	C	10
Warren, Charles	1	1836-1853	D	142
Warren, Joshua	2	1836-1853	D	338
Warren, Thomas	1	1817-1835	C	84
Wash, John (Planter)	2	1836-1853	D	514
Watkins, Anderson	2	1817-1835	C	426
Watkins, Elijah (Sr.)	1	1836-1853	D	183
Watkins, Richard	1	1836-1853	D	74
Watson, Arthur	1	1785-1818	A	404
Watson, John	1	1785-1818	A	63
Watson, Michael	2	1836-1853	D	398
Watson, Stanmore	2	1836-1853	D	476
Watts, Robert	1	1836-1853	D	115
Weaver, Elizabeth	2	1817-1835	C	539
Weaver, Jonathan	1	1836-1853	D	173
Webb, Hendley	2	1817-1835	C	397
Weeks, Aron	1	1817-1835	C	226
West, Joseph	1	1817-1835	C	109
West, William	1	1785-1818	A	94
Whatley, Fersey	1	1836-1853	D	268
Whatley, Philis	2	1817-1835	C	482
Whatley, Sheerwood	1	1785-1818	A	276
Wheeler, Daniel (Sr.)	1	1836-1853	D	291
White,Blumer (Sr.)	1	1817-1835	C	263
White, Blumer	1	1836-1853	D	131
White, Burges	2	1817-1835	C	516
White, Nathan (Sr.)	1	1785-1818	A	639
White, William	1	1785-1818	A	238
White, William (Planter)	1	1785-1818	A	375
Whitehead, James	1	1817-1835	C	55
Whitley, Elizabeth	1	1817-1835	C	136
Whitley, John	2	1785-1818	A	537
Whitlock, Winfrey	1	1836-1853	D	114
Wiggins, James	2	1817-1835	C	430
Wilborn, William	2	1817-1835	C	402
Williams, Anna Maria	1	1785-1818	A	257
Williams, Daniel	1	1817-1835	C	157
Williams, Daves	2	1817-1835	C	463
Williams, Frederick	2	1785-1818	A	441
Williams, John	1	1785-1818	A8	147
Williams, Lud	1	1785-1818	A	219
Williams, Roger M.	1	1836-1853	D	22
Williamson, Humphry	2	1785-1818	A	585
Wills, Jones	2	1785-1818	A	726
Wills, Mathew	2	1817-1835	C	353
Wills, Nancy	2	1836-1853	D	320
Wilson, Hamital	2	1785-1818	A	490
Wilson, Rebecca	1	1785-1818	A	353
Wilson, Thomas	1	1785-1818	A	216
Wimberly, William	1	1785-1818	A	269
Winfrey, Thomas Lamar	2	1785-1818	A	496
Wise, Jacob	2	1836-1853	D	348
Wise, Rachel	1	1836-1853	D	215
Wise, Sarah	1	1836-1853	D	67
Woodroof, Wilson (Planter)	2	1785-1818	A	546

Wootan, Joat (Planter)	2	1785-1818	A	452
Worthington, Elisha	1	1817-1835	C	159
Wright, James	2	1836-1853	D	352
Wright, John	2	1785-1818	A	796
			Inv. & Wills	
Wright, Jonathan	1	1785-1818	A	57
Wright, Meshack (Planter)	2	1785-1818	A	616
Wynn, William	2	1817-1835	C	355
Yancy, Benjamin	2	1785-1818	A	707
Yarbrough, Gilson	1	1836-1853	D	107
Yeldell, Mary L.	2	1817-1835	C	627
Yon, Martin	1	1836-1853	D	161
Young, Jacob	1	1785-1818	A	72
Youngblood, James (Planter)	1	1785-1818	A	66
Youngblood, Lewis	1	1817-1835	C	139
Youngblood, Mary	1	1836-1853	D	228
Youngblood, Thomas	1	1817-1835	C	141
Zimmerman, Henry	1	1785-1818	A	250
Zimmerman, Philip	1	1785-1818	A	205
Zinn, Elizabeth	1	1785-1818	A	97
Zubly, David (Planter)	1	1785-1818	A	29

Copied by:

/s/ Mrs. John D. Rogers

Mrs. John D. Rogers

INDEX

TO

FAIRFIELD COUNTY WILLS.

Volume No. 1
1787-1819

Volume No. 2
1820-1859

Volume No. 5
1840-1857

This index is compiled from W.P.A. copies
of wills filed in the COUNTY PROBATE
COURTS. The Volumes indexed are
a part of the South Carolina
collection of the University
of South Carolina Library.

Columbia, S. C.
1939

WILLS.

Name	Vol.	Date	Sec.	Page
Adger, William	2	1820–1839	II	1
Aiken, Charles	1	1787–1819	2	1
Aiken, Esther	3	1840–1857	19	1
Allen, James (Saddler)	1	1787–1819	5	3
Akin, Elisabeth	1	1787–1819	5	1
Akin, Walter	1	1787–1819	5	5
Allen, Thomas	1	1787–1819	5	7
Alston, James	3	1840–1857	19	3
Amick, John	1	1787–1819	5	9
Andrews, Edward (Sr.)	2	1840–1839	10	1
Andrews, James	1	1787–1819	2	3
Andrews, John	1	1787–1819	2	5
A rick, Mary	2	1820–1839	14	1
Arick, Sarah	3	1840–1857	19	8
Arledge, Clemment	2	1820–1839	8	1
Arledge, Isaac (Sr.)	1	1787–1819	1	1
Arledge, Isaac (Jr.)	3	1840–1857	19	10
Arledge, Joseph	1	1787–1819	5	13a
Arledge, Moses	1	1787–1819	1	3
Armstrong, John	3	1840–1857	19	15
Arnet, Samuel	1	1787–1819	5	15
Arnett, John Q.	3	1840–1857	19	17
Arskin, Petter	1	1787–1819	4	1
Ashford, Bennett	3	1840–1857	19	19
Ashford, James	2	1820–1839	14	4
Ashford, George (Planter)	1	1787–1819	6	1
Ashford, William (Planter),	see — — — — — — — — — — — Ashley, William
Ashley, William (Planter)	2	1820–1839	14	7
Aston, Samuel	1	1787–1819	5	16
Austen, James	1	1787–1819	4	4
Austin, Elizabeth	1	1787–1819	4	2
Auston, Elisabeth	1	1787–1819	2	6
Banks, Samuel	3	1840–1857	19	24
Barber, James	2	1820–1839	9	1
Barkley, Hugh (Sr.)	1	1787–1819	7	1
Barkley, Hugh	2	1820–1839	11	7
Barkley, Mary	2	1820–1839	10	4
Bean, Sarah (Widow)	2	1820–1839	8	3
Bean, Sarah	2	1820–1839	18	1
Beard, James	3	1840–1857	19	26
Beasley, George	2	1820–1839	13	1
Beasley, Jacob	1	1787–1819	1	4
Beaty, James	2	1820–1839	14	10
Beaty, Mary	3	1840–1857	19	30
Bell, Edward M.	3	1840–1857	19	32
Bell, George	1	1787–1819	4	5
Bell, John	1	1787–1819	7	3
Bell, Thomas	1	1787–1819	2	7
Bell, Thomas	3	1840–1857	19	34
Bell, Vincent H.	3	1840–1857	19	36
Bell, William (Sr.)	2	1820–1839	10	5
Belton, Jonathan(Merchant)	1	1787–1819	5	18
Belton, Sarah	1	1787–1819	5	18

Bennet, Sarah-	1	1787-1819	2	9
Berry, William	2	1820-1859	8	5
Bishop, Patarac	1	1787-1819	5	20
Blain, James	2	1820-1859	15	4
Blain, Mary	2	1820-1859	14	12
Blair, Rachel	3	1840-1857	19	37
Boney, Jacob	1	1787-1819	2	10
Bonner, John (Sr.)	2	1820-1859	8	7
Boulware, Allben	3	1840-1857	19	38
Boulware, Musco (Sr.)	2	1820-1859	10	8
Boulware, Muscoe (Planter)	2	1820-1859	15	6
Boulware, Nancy	2	1820-1859	11	9
Boulware, Reubin P.	2	1820-1859	10	15
Boulware, Thomas	2	1820-1859	18	3
Boulware, William R.A.	2	1820-1859	15	9
Boyd, Agness	2	1820-1859	12	1
Boyd, Andrew	2	1850-1859	9	4
Boyd, Archibald	3	1840-1857	19	41
Boyd, Nancy	5	1840-1857	19	42
Boyd, Robert	2	1820-1859	10	16
Boyd, Robert	3	1840-1857	19	45
Boyd, Robert	3	1840-1857	19	48
Boyd, Sarah	3	1840-1857	19	50
Bradford, Mary	3	1840-1857	19	51
Brannan, Elender	1	1787-1819	7	5
Brice, John	1	1787-1819	7	6
Brice, William (Sr.)	3	1840-1857	19	52
Briggs, Thomas	2	1820-1859	18	12
Briggs, Frederick	1	1787-1819	1	6
Brison, Robert	3	1840-1857	19	54
Broom, John	3	1840-1857	19	56
Broom, William	2	1820-1859	10	18
Brown, Jacob	1	1787-1819	1	8
Brown, James(Bricklayer)	2	1820-1859	8	9
Brown, Jemima	2	1820-1859	18	14
Brown, Robert	1	1787-1819	2	11
Brown, Thomas	2	1820-1859	8	12
Buchanan, Elizabeth	3	1840-1857	19	58
Buchanan, John	2	1820-1859	8	18
Buchanan, John R.	5	1840-1857	19	60
Buchanan, Sarah	2	1820-1859	9	6
Burns, Dennis (Sr.)	1	1787-1819	2	15
Cafsity, Peter	1	1787-1819	2	15
Caldwell, Jane S.	3	1840-1857	19	65
Caldwell, Joseph	3	1840-1857	19	69
Caldwell, Samuel	1	1787-1819	7	8
Calhoun, Alexander	2	1820-1859	9	8
Cameron, Andrew	1	1787-1819	5	22
Cameron, James	2	1820-1859	15	15
Cameron, John	1	1787-1819	7	10
Cameron, Joseph	1	1787-1819	2	17
Carden, Larkin	1	1787-1819	1	9
Cassity, Peter	1	1787-1819	2	15
Castles, Anna	3	1840-1857	19	71
Castles, John	2	1820-1859	12	5
Cato, William	2	1820-1859	15	16

Chapman, William (Sr.)	3	1840-1857	19	73
Chappell, John T.	3	1840-1857	19	72
Chappell, Laban (Sr.)(Planter)	2	1820-1839	12	6
Clarke, Elisabeth A.	3	1840-1857	19	77
Clarke, Martha	3	1840-1857	19	80
Cloud, Joseph	3	1840-1857	19	82
Cloud, Martha	3	1840-1857	19	81
Cloud, William	1	1787-1819	6	24
Cochran, William	1	1787-1819	5	26
Cockral, Moses	1	1787-1819	2	20
Coleman, Charles	1	1787-1819	1	10
Coleman, Charles (Sr.)	3	1840-1857	19	85
Coleman, J. A. J.	3	1840-1857	19	91
Coleman, Robert (Farmer)	1	1787-1819	2	22
Coleman, Robert	1	1787-1819	5	27
Colhoun, James	1	1787-1819	2	24
Colhoun, William	1	1787-1819	2	26
Collins, Daniel	1	1787-1819	6	7
Collins, Moses(Haberdasher)	1	1787-1819	2	28
Conner, Honour	2	1820-1839	13	19
Cook, Esther	1	1787-1819	2	29
Cook, Nathan	3	1840-1857	19	95
Cork, John	1	1787-1819	2	51
Cork, John	3	1840-1857	19	96
Cork, Samuel	3	1840-1857	19	98
Cork, William	3	1840-1857	19	92
Craig, James D.	3	1840-1857	19	100
Crankfield, Littleton	3	1840-1857	19	102
Crawford, Andrew	3	1840-1857	19	105
Cross, Samuell	1	1787-1819	7	13
Crumpton, Alexander	2	1820-1839	12	10
Crumpton, Zachariah	3	1840-1857	19	110
Cummings, Joseph	3	1840-1857	19	112
Curry, Stafford (Sr.)	1	1787-1819	6	9
Crupton, Henry	1	1787-1819	5	29
Davis, Henry M.	3	1840-1857	19	114
Davis, James	2	1820-1839	8	21
Day, Zachariah	3	1840-1857	19	115
Delleney, Isabella	2	1820-1839	18	16
Dickson, James	2	1820-1839	8	24
Dickson, Thomas	2	1820-1839	10	22
Diseker, William	2	1820-1839	10	23
Dods, John	1	1787-1819	1	12
Dods, John	1	1787-1819	5	30
Dods, Joseph	1	1787-1819	2	33
Douglass, Charles B.	3	1840-1857	19	117
Dove, Benjamin	2	1820-1839	12	13
Dove, Benjamin (Sr.)	3	1840-1857	19	120
Dubose, Martha	3	1840-1857	19	121
Dubose, Robert H.	2	1820-1839	13	21
Dubose, Samuel (Jr.)	3	1840-1857	19	123
Dunn, Benjamin	2	1820-1839	10	24
Duntze, Gerard	1	1787-1819	5	51
Durham, Charnel	2	1820-1839	17	1
Durham, Nancy	3	1840-1857	19	127
Dye, John	3	1840-1857	19	129

Edrington, Francis (Sr.)	2	1820-1859	9	9
Edrington, Henry	2	1820-1859	11	15
Edwards Vincint A.	2	1820-1859	9	11
Elder, James	3	1840-1857	19	150
Elliott, David A.	3	1840-1857	19	152
Elliott, Francis	2	1820-1859	10	26
Elliott, William Reid	3	1840-1857	19	154
Ellison, Robert	1	1787-1819	5	35
Ellison, William (Planter)	2	1820-1859	14	14
Emerson, Sarah (Widow)	3	1840-1857	19	156
Emerson, William T.	1	1787-1819	7	14
Ervin, Timothy (Planter)	2	1820-1859	8	26
Estes, William	3	1840-1857	19	157
Evans, David	1	1787-1819	2	34
Evans, David Read	3	1840-1857	19	159
Evans, Joseph H.	3	1840-1857	19	145
Ewing, William (Planter)	1	1787-1819	4	7
Ewings, Margaret	3	1840-1857	19	147
Fearys, William	1	1787-1819	5	36
Feaster, Andrew (Jr.)	1	1787-1819	5	39
Feaster, Andrew (Sr.)	1	1820-1859	8	27
Feaster, Jacob (Sr.)	3	1840-1857	19	148
Feaster, John	3	1840-1857	19	150
Fellows, Mathias	1	1787-1819	1	14
Ferguson, Abraham	2	1820-1859	9	12
Foote, John (Sr.)	1	1787-1819	5	40
Ford, Gardener	1	1787-1819	5	42
Foster, Robert	2	1820-1859	10	29
Fraser, William	1	1787-1819	2	35
Frazier, Thomas	3	1840-1857	19	156
Free, James	1	1787-1819	5	43
Free, William	3	1840-1857	19	157
Freeman, Elisabeth	3	1840-1857	19	159
Furgerson, Joseph	1	1787-1819	7	15
Fundenburgh, Henry	1	1787-1819	2	37
Funderburg, Mary	1	1787-1819	7	16
Gaither, Jerimiah	3	1840-1857	19	160
Gaither, Richard	2	1820-1859	10	31
Gamble, Hugh	1	1787-1819	2	39
Gamble, James	1	1787-1819	6	12
Gamble, Samuel	1	1787-1819	2	41
Gibson, Henry	3	1840-1857	19	163
Gibson, Jacob	1	1787-1819	2	43
Gibson, Jacob	3	1840-1857	19	171
Gibson, Minor	3	1840-1857	19	176
Gibson, Silas (Farmer)	3	1840-1857	19	178
Gibson, Stephen	2	1820-1859	14	16
Gibson, William	3	1840-1857	19	180
Gilliam, Jordain	3	1840-1857	19	182
Gladden, Jesse	2	1820-1859	8	29
Gladen, Samuel	1	1787-1819	3	1
Gladney, Hugh	3	1840-1857	19	183
Gladney, Jane	2	1820-1859	14	18
Gladney, Richard (Planter)	2	1820-1859	13	22
Gladney, Richard	3	1840-1857	19	185
Gladney, Thomas	2	1820-1859	8	32

Glazier, Elizabeth	3	1840-1857	19	189
Glazier, John	2	1820-1839	13	24
Glover, John	3	1840-1857	19	188
Gofa, Aaron	1	1787-1819	5	44
Going, Henry	1	1787-1819	5	46
Goodwyn, Lucy Ann	3	1840-1857	19	190
Gosa, Aaron, see -Gofa, Aaron				
Gowens, Daniel	2	1820-1839	10	34
Grafton, Mary	2	1820-1839	17	4
Graves, James	1	1787-1819	1	15
Gray, Stephen	3	1840-1857	19	195
Gregg, John (Blacksmith)	1	1787-1819	7	18
Griffin, Rachel	3	1840-1857	19	196
Grissim, Samuel W.	3	1840-1857	19	199
Grubbs, Enoch (Sr.)	2	1820-1839	13	26
Gwin, John (Sr.)	2	1820-1839	8	35
Haigood, Lewis,(Planter)	1	1787-1819	6	13
Haigood, William (Planter)	2	1820-1839	8	37
Hall, Anne	2	1820-1839	14	21
Hall, John	2	1820-1839	13	30
Hall, Martha	3	1840-1857	19	200
Hall, Thomas	3	1840-1857	19	202
Hall, Zachariah	2	1820-1839	12	14
Hamilton, David	2	1820-1839	18	17
Hamilton, Robert	3	1840-1857	19	205
Hamilton, William	3	1840-1857	19	207
Hanna, Robert	1	1787-1819	5	48
Hardage, James	1	1787-1819	2	46
Harrson, John	1	1787-1819	7	20
Harmon, Elisabeth	1	1787-1819	5	50
Harper, James	3	1840-1857	19	209
Harris, James	2	1820-1839	17	5
Harrison, Benjamin	3	1840-1857	19	211
Harrison, David	3	1840-1857	19	213
Harrison, Jonathan	3	1840-1857	19	215
Harrison, Joshua(Planter)	1	1787-1819	5	51
Harrison, Mary (Widow)	2	1820-1839	8	39
Harrison, Reuben	2	1820-1839	14	23
Harrison, William H.	2	1820-1839	11	15
Harrison, Willoughby	2	1820-1839	10	38
Hartin, Jacob	2	1820-1839	10	40
Harvey, James	1	1787-1819	5	54
Harvey, James	3	1840-1857	19	217
Hatcher, William	1	1787-1819	6	16
Havis, Jesse	2	1820-1839	10	42
Havis, John (Planter)	1	1787-1819	5	55
Hawthorn, Adam (Sr.)	1	1787-1819	5	57
Hawthorn, Adam	2	1820- 1839	10	46
Haygood, Elisha	2	1820-1839	10	48
Haygood, Henry	1	1787-1819	7	23
Hays, Ma thew	1	1787-1819	2	47
Hendrix, Elias	1	1787-1819	7	26
Hendrix, James	2	1820-1839	8	40
Henson, Bartlet	1	1787-1819	4	9
Henson, Obediah	1	1787-1819	5	61

Henson, Robert	2	1820-1839	8	42
Herron, William A.	3	1840-1857	19	219
Hill, Richard	1	1787-1819	5	59
Hill, William	1	1787-1819	1	17
Hindman, James	2	1820-1839	14	25
Hodge, James	2	1820-1839	10	52
Holles, Moses	1	1787-1819	2	49
Hollis, Berrey	1	1787-1819	5	62
Hollis, Burrel	2	1820-1839	11	17
Hollis, Elizabeth	3	1840-1857	19	221
Holmes, William	1	1787-1819	2	51
Hood, Robert	2	1820-1839	9	15
Hornsby, Leonard	1	1787-1819	1	18
Housch, Jacob	1	1787-1819	7	24
Huffman, Danl (Sr.)	2	1820-1839	12	16
Husey, Iacke	1	1787-1819	4	10
Hutchinson, John (Sr.)	3	1840-1857	19	223
Hutchinson, Robert	2	1820-1839	10	54
James, Charnal (Planter)	3	1840-1857	19	225
James, John	3	1840-1857	19	227
James, William T.	2	1820-1839	18	19
Jeffers, Ocborne V.	2	1820-1839	13	51
Johnston, Elizabeth	3	1840-1857	19	228
Johnston, James	1	1787-1819	2	52
Johnston, Samuel	2	1820-1839	10	57
Johnston, Samuel	3	1840-1857	19	230
Johnston, William	3	1840-1857	19	257
Jones, Darling	2	1820-1839	12	18
Jones, Elijah	2	1820-1839	8	44
Jones, Elisha	3	1840-1857	19	239
Jones, Henry	1	1787-1819	19	239
Jones, Henry	1	1787-1819	5	64
Jones, John	2	1820-1839	8	52
Jones, Mary	2	1820-1839	13	33
Jones, Ralph	1	1787-1819	7	28
Jones, Ralph	3	1840-1857	19	243
Jones, William	3	1840-1857	19	245
Jonston, Nancy	2	1820-1839	10	55
Judge, Hillard	2	1820-1839	8	54
Kelly, Nehimiah	3	1840-1857	19	249
Kennedy, Alexander (Sr.)	2	1820-1839	10	60
Kennedy, Henry	3	1840-1857	19	250
Kennedy, John	3	1840-1857	19	253
Kennedy, William(Planter)	1	1787-1819	7	51
Kerr, Joseph	2	1820-1839	8	58
Kiernagham, William	3	1840-1857	19	256
Killpatrick, Leonard	2	1820-1839	8	60
Killpatrick, Robert	3	1840-1857	19	258
Killpatrick, Robert	3	1840-1857	19	260
Killpatrick, Thomas (Sr.)	3	1840-1857	19	262
Kilpatrick, John (Sr.)	2	1820-1839	9	18
Kincaid, Alexander	2	1820-1839	14	27
Kincaid, James (Planter)	1	1787-1819	4	12
Kincaid, Mary (Sr.)	2	1820-1839	12	26

Kincaid, William (Planter)	2	1820-1839	14	30
Kirkland, Constance	3	1840-1857	19	265
Kirkland, Francis	1	1787-1819	2	54
Kirkland, John D.	2	1820-1839	11	19
Kirkland, Mary	2	1820-1839	8	61
Kirkland, William (Planter)	1	1787-1819	5	65
Kirkpatrick, Jean	3	1840-1857	19	267
Knighton, Moses	1	1787-1819	2	55
Knighton, Richard R.(Plant)	1	1787-1819	7	54
Knighton, Thomas	2	1820-1839	10	63
Laughlin, Charles	3	1840-1857	19	268
Lavender, David	2	1820-1839	13	55
Lavender, Jamima	3	1840-1857	19	271
Lavender, Lucy (Widow)	3	1840-1857	19	273
Leggo, M.A.M.	3	1840-1857	19	276
Leitner, Ann Christena	3	1840-1857	19	284
Lemley, Peter (Planter)	1	1787-1819	2	56
Lewey, George	1	1787-1819	2	57
Lewis, Frances	1	1787-1819	5	68
Lewis, John	1	1787-1819	1	19
Lewis, William	3	1840-1857	19	285
Lightner, John	1	1787-1819	4	15
Lightner, Mary	3	1840-1857	19	288
Littlejohn, Marcellus	1	1787-1819	2	59
Long, David (Sr.)	1	1787-1819	7	55
Long, Elizabeth	3	1840-1857	19	289
Long, James (Sr.)	1	1787-1819	7	57
Long, John (Sr.)	2	1820-1839	10	65
Lowe, Isaac	1	1787-1819	1	20
Lowery, Agnes	1	1787-1819	7	59
McBride, Henry	2	1820-1839	12	59
McBride, Robert	1	1787-1819	2	65
McCain, Alexander (Sr.)	1	1787-1819	7	47
McCall, Edwin L.	1	1787-1819	5	81
McCants, John	1	1787-1819	6	25
McCants, Martha C.	3	1840-1857	19	328
McCants, Robert	1	1787-1819	7	49
McClurken, John	1	1787-1819	2	67
McConnel, Mary	3	1840-1857	19	329
McCormick, Charles	3	1840-1857	19	330
McCormick, Hugh	3	1840-1857	19	331
McCreight, David (Planter)	1	1787-1819	2	70-a
McCreight, James	1	1787-1819	6	30
McCreight, William	1	1787-1819	1	26
McCrory, John	1	1787-1819	5	83
McCrory, John	3	1840-1857	19	333
McCrory, Molly Peggy	3	1840-1857	19	336
McCulloch, John	1	1787-1819	2	69
McCullough, Elizabeth	3	1840-1857	19	337
McCullough, Thomas	3	1840-1857	19	339
McDowell, Alex.	1	1787-1819	2	73
McDowell, Alexander	2	1820-1839	11	28
McDowell, James	1	1787-1819	6	27
McFadden, Anne	1	1787-1819	2	74
McGill, Andrew	1	1787-1819	6	29

McGomery, Hugh (Sr.)	2	1820-1859	10	72
McGraw, Benjamin	2	1820-1859	14	35
McGraw, Edward	2	1820-1859	15	40
McGraw, Enoch	2	1820-1859	12	40
McKane, Jane	2	1820-1859	10	74
McKee, Samuel	1	1787-1819	5	85
McKell, William (Planter)	2	1820-1859	8	69
McKemie, Johnston	2	1820-1859	8	72
McMaster, Hugh	1	1787-1819	1	24
McMorries, Elizabeth	2	1820-1859	10	76
McMorris, William	1	1787-1819	4	22
McMorris, William	2	1820-1859	10	78
McMullen, Samuel	3	1840-1857	19	342
McMullon, John	1	1787-1819	2	76
McNeill, John	3	1840-1857	19	344
McQuiston, William	1	1787-1819	3	3
McVea, John	2	1820-1859	18	21
Mabry, Daniel	1	1787-1819	7	41
Mabry, Mary	1	1787-1819	5	70
Maloney, John	2	1820-1859	11	21
Mann, James	1	1787-1819	7	43
Mann, James	3	1840-1857	19	290
Mann, Thomas (Sr.)	3	1840-1857	19	292
Marple, Northup	1	1787-1819	4	17
Marple, Thomas	1	1787-1819	1	21
Marshall, Robert	2	1820-1839	11	22
Martin, George	1	1787-1819	2	61
Martin, Margaret E.	3	1840-1857	19	294
Martin, Robert (Sr.)	1	1787-1819	6	17
Martin, Robert (Sr.)	2	1820-1839	11	24
Martin, Robert	3	1840-1857	19	296
Mason, Mary	2	1820-1859	9	19
Mason, Washington	2	1820-1859	12	28
Masters, John	2	1820-1859	17	6
Mayo, John	1	1787-1819	7	45
Mayo, Richard G.	3	1840-1857	19	298
Meador, John (Sr.)(Farmer)	2	1820-1839	14	33
Meador, M. P.	3	1840-1857	19	301
Means, David H.	3	1840-1857	19	302
Means, Edward	3	1840-1857	19	304
Means, John	1	1787-1819	5	72
Means, Robert	2	1820-1859	11	26
Means, Thomas	2	1820-1859	12	30
Means, Thomas I. (J)	3	1840-1857	19	306
Meredith, Thomas (Sr.)	1	1787-1819	6	20
Mickle, Elisabeth	1	1787-1819	6	23
Mickle, John	2	1820-1859	13	37
Mickle, Jonathan	3	1840-1857	19	308
Mickle, Thomas	1	1787-1819	2	65
Millar, John (Planter)	1	1787-1819	4	18
Miller, Abraham	2	1820-1859	8	63
Miller, Alex	1	1787-1819	1	23
Miller, Jane	2	1820-1859	13	39
Milling, Hugh	2	1820-1859	17	7
Milling, Robert	2	1820-1859	12	36

Milling, Sarah	3	1840-1857	19	309
Mills, Rachel Timmons	2	1820-1839	10	67
Mobley, Samuel (Sr.)	1	1787-1819	4	20
Mobley, Samuel	3	1840-1857	19	311
Mobley, Thomas (Farmer)	1	1787-1819	5	76
Mobley, William M.	3	1840-1857	19	313
Montgomery, Charles	2	1820-1839	8	65
Montgomery, David (Farmer)	1	1787-1819	5	78
Montgomery, Hugh (Sr.)	1	1787-1819	5	80
Montgomery, Nancy	3	1840-1857	19	315
Moore, Henry	3	1840-1857	19	317
Mooty, Mary	2	1820-1839	17	10
Morgan, Nancy	3	1840-1857	19	324
Morris, John (Sr.)	2	1820-1839	8	67
Mott, John W.	3	1840-1857	19	325
Mundle, William	3	1840-1857	19	326
Muse, Thomas (Sr.)	2	1820-1839	10	70
Neal, Samuel	1	1787-1819	1	28
Neeley, Richard	1	1787-1819	2	78
Neely, James	2	1820-1839	10	81
Neil, James (Planter)	3	1840-1857	19	345
Nelson, James (Sr.)	2	1820-1839	14	38
Nettles, Zachariah (Sr.)	2	1820-1839	8	75
Newton, James (Sr.)	1	1787-1819	7	51
Noakes, Richard	3	1840-1857	19	347
ONeale, Mary Ann	3	1840-1857	19	348
Osborne, William (Planter)	3	1840-1857	19	349
Owen, Benjamin	1	1787-1819	5	87
Owen, Benjamin (Farmer)	1	1787-1819	7	52
Owen, Elisheba	2	1820-1839	10	83
Owens, Samuel	1	1787-1819	7	56
Owens, Thomas (Sr.)	3	1840-1857	19	351
Owens, Thomas	1	1787-1819	1	30
Paul, Arsbdd	1	1787-1819	4	24
Paul, James	1	1787-1819	2	80
Paul, William	2	1820-1839	8	76
Pearson, John(Sr.)(Plant.)	1	1787-1819	7	59
Pearson, Mary	1	1787-1819	3	5
Peay, Austin F.	3	1840-1857	19	353
Peay, George	1	1787-1819	1	32
Peay, Nicholas	1	1787-1819	6	51
Peay, Nicholas (Planter)	3	1840-1857	19	360
Perry, Hugh A.	3	1840-1857	19	361
Perry, Isaac	3	1840-1857	19	365
Pettipool, Ephriam(Plant.)	1	1787-1819	2	82
Phillips, Anna (Widow)	1	1787-1819	6	54
Phillips, Robert	1	1787-1819	1	55
Phillips, Smith	2	1820-1839	17	12
Phillips, William	1	1787-1819	2	84
Picket, John (Sr.)	2	1820-1839	8	79
Picket, John	2	1820-1839	8	82
Pickett, Francis	2	1820-1839	10	84
Pickett, John B. (Jr.)	3	1840-1857	19	367
Pickett, Reub. L.	2	1820-1839	9	22
Pickett, Shepherd	1	1787-1819	6	56

Pickett, William R.	3	1840-1857	19	571
Player, Joshua(Planter)	2	1820-1839	14	40
Polley, Catherine	3	1840-1857	19	572
Polley, Thomas	1	1787-1819	6	37
Porter, James	1	1787-1819	2	86
Powel, Dorcas	2	1820-1839	14	45
Powell, Caleb	2	1820-1839	10	86
Proctor, Samuel	2	1820-1839	10	89
Pullig, John	2	1820-1839	14	46
Quigley, Robert	3	1840-1857	19-	374
Rabb, Elizabeth	2	1820-1839	9	23
Rabb, James	1	1787-1819	6	39
Rabb, John (Planter)	3	1840-1857	19	376
Rabb, Robert	1	1787-1819	7	66
Rabb, Thomas A	3	1840-1857	19	379
Rains, Anthony	3	1840-1857	19	382
Rains, John	2	1820-1839	8	84
Rawls, Thomas W.	3	1840-1857	19	385
Ray, Thomas W.	2	1820-1839	13	42
Richardson, Samuel	1	1787-1819	4	25
Richardson, William(Plant)	1	1787-1819	7	69
Rives, William	3	1840-1857	19	387
Roberts, Nicholas	3	1840-1857	19	388
Robertson, Alexander	1	1787-1819	2	88
Robertson, Ann	1	1787-1819	6	41
Robertson, Benoni	3	1840-1857	19	390
Robertson, Hannah	1	1787-1819	5	88
Robertson, Henry	1	1787-1819	1	34-A
Robertson, James	3	1840-1857	19	395
Robertson, James O.	3	1840-1857	19	397
Robertson, William (Sr.)	2	1820-1839	9	25
Robinson, Alexander (Sr.)	2	1820-1839	8	87
Robinson, James	1	1787-1819	4	26
Robinson, John A.	2	1820-1839	10	90
Robinson, Margaret	1	1787-1819	2	90a
Robinson, Martha	2	1820-1839	18	23
Robinson, Samuel	3	1840-1857	19	399
Rochell, Helen	2	1820-1839	12	42
Rodman, Hugh	2	1820-1839	10	92
Rogers, James (Rev.)	2	1820-1839	13	43
Rogers, John	1	1787-1819	1	35
Rosborough, James	3	1840-1857	19	402
Rosborough, John	3	1840-1857	19	407
Rosborough, John A.	3	1840-1857	19	305
Rosborough, William Q.	1	1787-1819	5	90
Roseborough, Alexander	2	1820-1839	8	89
Ross, Abner	2	1820-1839	12	44
Routledg, Thomas	1	1787-1819	1	36
Row, James	2	1820-1839	18	25
Rowe, David	2	1820-1839	17	15
Ruff, Daniel	2	1820-1839	12	50
Ruff, Elizabeth	3	1840-1857	19	410
Rugeley, Henry	1	1787-1819	2	91
Russel, James	1	1787-1819	5	93

Sanders, Nathan	1	1787-1819	2	94
Sanders, Washington	3	1840-1857	19	413
Scott, George (Planter)	1	1787-1819	1	37
Seglar, George (Sr.)	2	1820-1839	8	91
Seigler, George (Sr.)	1	1787-1819	5	95
Seigler, John W.(School teacher)	3	1840-1857	19	414
Shannon, Thomas	1	1787-1819	6	45
Shaver, Philip	1	1787-1819	2	95
Shedd, George	3	1840-1857	19	415
Shelton, David	2	1820-1839	8	93
Simmons, John	2	1820-1839	17	19
Simonton, John (Sr.)	3	1840-1857	19	420
Simpson, William	3	1840-1857	19	423
Sloan, John	3	1840-1857	19	425
Smart, Sarah	3	1840-1857	19	427
Smith, Agnes	3	1840-1857	19	429
Smith, Jane M.	3	1840-1857	19	432
Smith, John	2	1820-1839	14	47
Smith, Leah (Planter)	3	1840-1857	19	434
Smith, Mary	1	1787-1819	7	71
Smith, Minor	2	1820-1839	18	27
Starke, John A.(Planter)	2	1820-1839	10	94
Starke, Reuben	1	1787-1819	5	97
Starke, Thomas	1	1787-1819	5	100
Starns, Peter	1	1787-1819	1	38
Steel, James (Sr.)	2	1820-1839	10	97
Steel, Thomas	1	1787-1819	6	45
Sterling, John	3	1840-1857	19	437
Stevenson, Hugh	2	1820-1839	17	17
Stevenson, John	1	1787-1819	5	102
Stewart, Alexander	1	1787-1819	6	47
Stone, Samuel	3	1840-1857	19	442
Stradford, Thomas C.	2	1820-1839	8	95
Strain, James	1	1787-1819	7	72
Strother, Sarah	3	1840-1857	19	443
Summercle, Jacob	2	1820-1839	12	52
Swan, James (Sr.)	3	1840-1857	19	445
Swan, Jennet	3	1840-1857	19	447
Swatz, John P.	1	1787-1819	7	73
Sweat, John	1	1787-1819	7	74
Taylor, Jerimiah	3	1840-1857	19	448
Taylor, Leonard	1	1787-1819	6	49
Thompson, Alexander	3	1840-1857	19	450
Thompson, Gan	3	1840-1857	19	452
Thompson, John	1	1787-1819	4	28
Thompson, Nathaniel	2	1820-1839	11	29
Thomoson, Robert	2	1820-1839	9	26
Thompson, Robert	2	1820-1839	17	21
Thompson, William(Planter)	3	1840-1857	19	433
Tidewell, Robert	1	1787-1819	5	103
Tinkler, Martha	3	1840-1857	19	455
Trapp, Zachariah(Planter)	3	1840-1857	19	456
Turner, John	1	1787-1819	5	105
Turnipseed, Katherine	2	1820-1839	10	98
Turnipseed, Mara Barbara	2	1820-1839	8	96
Veal, Thomas (Printer)	2	1820-1839	10	100
Veale, Elizabeth(Widow)	2	1820-1839	14	48

Wages, Benjamin	3	1840-1857	19	**450**
Wages, William	2	1820-1839	9	29
Walker, Drury	3	1840-1857	19	461
Walker, Henry	1	1787-1819	4	30
Walling, John	3	1840-1857	19	463
Waring, John M.	3	1840-1857	19	465
Watson, John	1	1787-1819	6	52
Watson, William Alex.	2	1820-1839	11	31
Watt, John (planter)	3	1840-1857	19	466
Watt, William (Sr.)	3	1840-1857	19	468
Waugh, Samuel	1	1787-1819	2	97
Webb, James	2	1820-1839	8	98
Weir, David	2	1820-1839	8	102
Weir, Jane	3	1840-1857	19	471
Weir, John	1	1787-1819	7	75
Weir, Salley	2	1820-1839	12	53
Weldon, Martha	3	1840-1857	19	475
Weldon, Samuel (Farmer)	2	1820-1839	12	55
Weldon, William(Blacksmith)	2	1820-1839	8	104
Wells, John	3	1840-1857	19	477
Whittaker, Willis	2	1820-1839	13	46
Whitted, William	1	1787-1819	2	99
Widner, Jacob	2	1820-1839	8	106
Wier, David	1	1787-1819	2	101
Wiley, John	3	1840-1857	19	479
Willian, Reason	1	1787-1819	7	77
Williams, John	1	1787-1819	5	111
Williams, John	2	1820-1839	18	29
Williamson, Roling	2	1820-1839	8	107
Willingham, Aves	1	1787-1819	2	103
Willingham, Joseph	3	1840-1857	19	482
Wilmore, Reuben	2	1820-1839	14	54
Wilson, David	2	1820-1839	11	33
Wilson, Jefferson	3	1840-1857	19	484
Wilson, Jesse	2	1820-1839	12	57
Wilson, John	1	1787-1819	3	8
Wilson, William	1	1787-1819	6	54
Wirick, Nicholas	2	1820-1839	14	50
Woodward, Easter	1	1787-1819	7	79
Woodward, Elizabeth	1	1787-1819	4	32
Woodward, Henry (Planter)	1	1787-1819	4	34
Woodward, John	1	1787-1819	7	81
Woodward, John	2	1820-1839	8	109
Woodward, John	2	1820-1839	12	59
Woodward, Margaret	2	1820-1839	13	49
Woodward, O. M.	3	1840-1857	19	488
Woodward, Robert	1	1787-1819	5	113
Woodward, William T.	3	1840-1857	19	490
Wooten, Aaron (Sr.)	1	1787-1819	6	55
Wrenchley, John	2	1820-1839	12	61
Wright, William	1	1787-1819	2	105
Yarboro, Nancy (Widow)	3	1840-1857	19	493
Yarborough, Charles	1	1787-1819	6	57
Yarborough, John (Sr.)	1	1787-1819	7	92

Yarborough, Mary	3	1840-1857	19	497
Yarborough, Thomas	3	1840-1857	19	499
Yarborough, Thos. Griggs	1	1787-1819	3	12
Yarbrough, Henry	3	1840-1857	19	495
Yongue, Elisabeth(Widow)	3	1840-1857	19	501
Yongue, Rebecca	3	1840-1857	19	503
Yongue, Rev. Samuel Whorer	2	1820-1839	13	50
Yongue, William	3	1840-1857	19	506
Young, Hugh (Sr.)	1	1787-1819	5	114
Young, John	1	1787-1819	1	40
Young, Robert	3	1840-1857	19	507

Copied by:

/s/ Mrs. John D. Rogers

INDEX

TO

GREENVILLE COUNTY WILLS

VOLUME NO. 1
1787-1840

VOLUME NO. 2
1840-1853

This index is compiled from W.P.A. copies of
wills filed in the COUNTY PROBATE COURTS.
The volumes indexed are a part of the
South Carolina Collection of the
University of South Carolina
Library.

Columbia, S.C.
1939

Name	Vol.	Date	Section	Page
Adams, James	1	1787-1840	B	55
Alexander, James	1	1787-1840	B	219
Allan, George	2	1840-1853	C	5
Allen, Charles	1	1787-1840	B	9
Anderson, John	1	1787-1840	B	223
Arnold, Benjamin (Farmer)	1	1787-1840	A	37
Ashmore, James	2	1840-1853	C	197
Atkinson, Henry	1	1787-1840	B	2
Austin, Walter	2	1840-1853	C	166
Austin, William	2	1840-1853	C	3
Avary, Charles (Sr.)	1	1787-1840	B	72
Avery, William	2	1840-1853	C	114
Ayres, John	1	1787-1840	A	56
Bain, George (Sr.)	2	1840-1853	C	162
Barrett, Arthur	2	1840-1853	A	99
Barrett, Reubin	1	1787-1840	A	99
Barton, David	1	1787-1840	B	232
Barton, Shopleigh	2	1840-1853	C	202
Bates, John	1	1787-1840	B	17
Bates, William	2	1840-1853	C	207
Benson, Charles	1	1787-1840	B	254
Benson, Elizabeth	1	1787-1840	A	87
Benson, Joseph	2	1840-1853	C	19
Benson, Prue	1	1787-1840	B	15
Benson, Thomas	2	1840-1853	C	60
Benson, Willis	2	1840-1853	C	293
Berry, Hudson	1	1787-1840	B	259
Blasingame, James	1	1787-1840	B	11
Blasingame, J.W.M. (Planter)	1	1787-1840	B	198
Blyth, William (Sr.)	1	1787-1840	B	243
Boling, Elliott	2	1840-1853	C	97
Boling, Tully	2	1840-1853	C	100
Boswell, Benjamin	1	1787-1840	B	90
Boyd, T. Hugh	1	1787-1840	B	80
Bradford, Philemon	1	1787-1840	B	49
Bradley, Abraham	1	1787-1840	B	40
Bradley, Tidence	2	1840-1853	C	169
Brady, Aquila Q.	1	1787-1840	B	101
Brasher, Thomas	1	1787-1840	A	6
Brasher, Thomas	2	1840-1853	C	13
Bridges, Benjamin (Farmer)	1	1787-1840	B	65
Bridges, Edmund	2	1840-1853	C	201
Bridges, Lucy Ann	1	1787-1840	B	197
Brock, David	1	1787-1840	B	256
Brock, Henry	2	1840-1853	C	131
Brockman, Henry	1	1787-1840	B	164
Brockman, James H.	2	1840-1853	C	117
Brooks, George	1	1787-1853	B	74
Brown, William (Sr.)	1	1787-1853	B	39
Bruce, Joel	1	1787-1853	B	218
Brummett, Thomas	2	1840-1853	C	297
Bryson, Clarissa	2	1840-1853	C	249
Burns, Laird (Rev.)	1	1787-1840	B	7
Bulter, Anderson	1	1787-1840	B	16

Callahan, Gersham	1	1787-1840	B	200
Camp, Oliver G.	1	1787-1840	B	253
Camon, Henry	2	1840-1853	C	137
Carter, Jesse	2	1840-1853	C	20
Celay, Wilson K.	2	1840-1853	C	247
Chandler, Joel	1	1787-1853	A	33
Chandler, William	1	1787-1840	B	5
Charles, John	2	1840-1853	C	181
Chew, John Drury	2	1840-1853	C	22
Chick,Burwell (Planter)	2	1840-1853	C	147
Choice, William (Sr.)	2	1840-1853	C	120
Clardy, Elliott	2	1840-1853	C	145
Cleveland, Jeremiah (Sr.)	2	1840-1853	C	125
Cobb, Ransom	1	1787-1840	B	195
Cochram, Hezakiah	2	1840-1853	C	130
Cochram, John	1	1787-1853	B	139
Collins, Ezekiah	2	1840-1853	C	28
Collins, John	1	1787-1840	A	16
Cook, Jediah	2	1840-1853	C	225
Cook, Nancy	1	1787-1840	B	119
Cooley, Jacob (Jr.)	1	1787-1840	B	69
Cooley, Jacob	1	1787-1840	A	96
Couch, Benjamin	2	1840-1853	C	129
Cox, Barsheba	2	1840-1853	C	266
Cox, James E.	2	1840-1853	C	295
Cox, John	1	1787-1840	B	95
Crain, Judith	1	1787-1840	A	11
Crain, William	2	1840-1853	C	33
Crane, Judith, see - - - - - - - - - - - - - - -			Crain, Judith	
Crayton, Mary T.	1	1787-1840	B	131
Crayton, Samuel	1	1787-1840	B	97
Crayton, Thomas	1	1787-1840	B	46
Creemer, Absolam	2	1840-1853	C	87
Croft, Edward	2	1840-1853	C	236
Croft, Frederick	2	1840-1853	C	29
Curby, Francis, see - - - - - - - - - - - - - -			Kirby, Francis	
Cureton, Abner H.	2	1840-1853	C	204
Cureton, Mary A.	2	1840-1853	C	243
Dacus, Nathaniel (Sr.)	1	1787-1840	B	194
Dacus, William (Sr.)	1	1787-1840	B	214
Darrach, Hugh	1	1787-1840	A	77
Darrough, Esther	1	1787-1840	B	206
Darrough, Peggy	1	1787-1840	B	135
Daugherty, William	1	1787-1840	B	216
Davis, Henry H.	1	1787-1840	B	217
Davis, Jonathan	2	1840-1853	C	16
Davis, Paskal	2	1840-1853	C	43
Davis, Zerah	1	1787-1840	B	162
Devenport, Joseph	2	1840-1853	C	31
Devenport, William	2	1840-1853	C	54
Deweese, Jonathan	2	1840-1853	C	198
Dill, John	1	1787-1840	A	52
Dill, Stephen	2	1840-1853	C	47
Dougherty, William	1	1787-1840	B	216
Dozier, Richard M.	1	1787-1840	B	136
Duncan, Elizabeth	2	1840-1853	C	206
Duncan, Sally	1	1787-1840	B	96

Dunham, Benajah.	2	1840-1853	C	287
Dunn, Benjamin	1	1787-1840	A	117
Dyer, Samuel	1	1787-1840	B	57
Earle, Ann	2	1840-1853	C	281
Earle, Elias T.	1	1787-1840	B	193
Earle, George Washington	1	1787-1840	B	20
Edwards, J ohn	1	1787-1840	A	42
Edwards, Joseph (Sr.)	1	1787-1840	B	252
Edwards, Sally	1	1787-1840	A	54
Edwards, Thomas	1	1787-1840	B	147
Evans, Philip	2	1840-1853	C	189
Ferguson, Thomas	1	1787-1840	B	27
Ferguson, Robert	2	1840-1853	C	215
Ferguson, Thomas, see - - - - - - - - - - - - - - -			Ferguson, Thomas	
Few, William (Jr.)	2	1840-1853	C	168
Fisher, John	2	1840-1853	C	88
Fisher, Nicholas (Sr.)	1	1787-1840	A	12
Ford, Daniel	1	1787-1840	B	204
Ford, John	1	1787-1840	A	22
Ford, Mary	1	1787-1840	A	18
Ford, Stephen	1	1787-1840	B	128
Forrest, Jeremiah	1	1787-1840	B	127
Forrester, James	1	1787-1840	A	10
Foster, John	1	1787-1840	A	1
Foster, Robert	1	1787-1840	B	104
Fowler, Archibald	1	1787-1840	B	265
Gaines, Silas	1	1787-1840	B	250
Gantt, Richard	2	1840-1853	C	223
Gantt, Susannah Matilda	1	1787-1840	B	236
Garrett, John	2	1840-1853	C	209
Garrett, Sarah	2	1840-1853	C	246
Gaston, Elizabeth	1	1787-1840	B	61
Gaston, William	1	1787-1840	A	66
Goodlett, David	1	1787-1840	A	101
Goodlett, Hiram	1	1787-1840	A	98
Goodlett, James	2	1840-1853	C	79
Goodlett, John H.	1	1787-1840	B	130
Goodlett, Robert	1	1787-1840	A	121
Goodlett, William	1	1787-1840	B	201
Gosmell, Joshua	2	1840-1853	C	248
Grace, Joel E.	1	1787-1840	A	86
Green, Elisha	2	1840-1853	C	183
Green, Elizabeth	1	1787-1840	B	75
Green, George	2	1840-1853	C	254
Green, Samuel M.	1	1787-1840	B	176
Greer, Betsy	2	1840-1853	C	271
Griffin, Horatio	1	1787-1840	B	14
Hale, Henry	1	1787-1840	B	140
Hale, Merry	1	1787-1840	B	110
Hamilton, Ann	2	1840-1853	C	8
Hammett, Jonathan	2	1840-1853	C	217
Harrison, John	1	1787-1840	A	31
Harrison, John	1	1787-1840	A	69
Harrison, Susannah	2	1840-1853	C	153
Hawkins, Eaton	1	1787-1840	A	67

Hawkins, Frederick	1	1787-1840	B	1
Hawkins, Jesse	2	1840-1853	C	291
Hawkins, Joshua	1	1787-1840	A	41
Hawkins, Pinkeny	2	1840-1853	C	195
Hawkins, Pinkington	1	1787-1840	B	239
Headden, Robert	2	1840-1853	C	116
Henderson, Exekiah	2	1840-1853	C	143
Henson, John (Sr.)	2	1840-1853	C	231
Hethcock, Isaac	1	1787-1840	A	107
Hietts, William	2	1840-1853	C	34
Hightower, Elizabeth	2	1840-1853	C	241
H ightower, Jane	2	1840-1853	C	241
Hill, Samuel B.	2	1840-1853	C	158
Hitt, Peter	1	1787-1840	B	241
Holcombe, John	2	1840-1853	C	172
Holeman, Richard	1	1787-1840	B	52
Holland, Milly	2	1840-1853	C	230
Holloway, Silas	2	1840-1853	C	156
Holloway, Stephen M.	2	1840-1853	C	89
Hopkins, John	1	1787-1840	B	237
Hornbuckle, Lydia	2	1840-1853	C	227
Hornsby, Eleanor	1	1787-1840	B	88
Howard, Edward	1	1787-1840	A	44
Howard, John	1	1787-1840	A	126
Howard, Samuel	2	1840-1853	C	284
Hudson, Elizabeth	1	1787-1840	B	118
Hudson, Pleasant	2	1840-1853	C	9
Huff, Philemon	2	1840-1853	C	81
Hunt, William	1	1787-1840	A	28
Jackson, Elizabeth	1	1787-1840	A	51
Jackson, William	1	1787-1840	B	205
James, Joseph	1	1787-1840	B	41
Jenkins, Micajah	1	1787-1840	A	71
Jenkins, Nancy	1	1787-1840	B	13
Jenkins, Owen	2	1840-1853	C	279
Jenkins, Rolly	2	1840-1853	C	277
Johnson, Hannah	1	1787-1840	A	83
Jones, Solomon	2	1840-1853	C	105
Jones, William	1	1787-1840	B	38
Joyce, John H.	2	1840-1853	C	274
Kelly, John	1	1787-1840	B	242
Kelly, Samuel	1	1787-1840	A	129
Kemp, Richard	1	1787-1840	A	76
Kennedy, Adam M.	1	1787-1840	B	173
Kilgore, James (Sr.)	1	1787-1840	A	58
King, Edward	1	1787-1840	A	105
King, William	2	1840-1853	C	106
Kirby, Francis	1	1787-1840	A	39
Kytte, Jacob	2	1840-1853	C	63
Landrith, John	1	1787-1840	A	68
Langley, Carter	1	1787-1840	B	31
Langston, John	1	1787-1840	A	8
League, Jacob	1	1787-1840	B	142
Lee, Elizabeth B.	2	1840-1853	C	115
Lee, William	2	1840-1853	C	25
Lester, Archibald	1	1787-1840	B	85

Lewis, Marbill F.	1	1787-1840	B	191
Lister, David	1	1787-1840	B	159
Little, Frederick	1	1787-1840	A	93
Loftis, Lemuel	1	1787-1840	B	226
Loftis, Solomon (Sr.)	2	1840-1853	C	192
Long, Thomas (Sr.)	1	1787-1840	B	54
Loveless, Isaac (Sr.)	1	1787-1840	B	112
Loveless, James (Sr.)	2	1840-1853	C	135
Lynch, Ann	2	1840-1853	C	49
Lynch, William	1	1787-1840	B	26
McCay, J. MC. D.	2	1840-1853	C	45
McClanahan, William	1	1787-1840	A	26
McCoy, Susan	2	1840-1853	C	164
McCrary, Andrew	2	1840-1853	C	272
McCrary, James	1	1787-1840	A	114
McCreary, Andrew	1	1787-1840	B	121
McCullough, William	2	1840-1853	C	250
McDaniel, James	2	1840-1853	C	299
McDaniel, John	1	1787-1840	A	108
McDaniel, Keziah	2	1840-1853	C	152
McJunkin, Daniel	1	1787-1840	B	67
McJunkin, Samuel	2	1840-1853	C	23
McKinney, Alexander	1	1787-1840	B	227
McLeland, James	1	1787-1840	A	131
McMahan, William	2	1840-1853	C	200
McVicar, Adam	1	1787-1840	A	75
Machen, Henry	1	1787-1840	A	19
Machen, Henry (Sr.)	1	1787-1840	B	25
Machen, John	1	1787-1840	B	4
Mahaffey, J ohn	1	1787-1840	B	26
Marion, Mary Ann S.	2	1840-1853	C	85
Martin, George	1	1787-1840	A	123
Masters, Thomas	1	1787-1840	B	229
Mathers, William	1	1787-1840	A	97
Mayfield, John	2	1840-1853	C	244
Mayfield, Thomas	2	1840-1853	C	38
Mayrant, Caroline	2	1840-1853	C	53
Mears, Lavina	1	1787-1840	B	180
Mears, Thomas	1	1787-1840	B	30
Merrit, Milliner	1	1787-1840	B	129
Miller, Israel (Sr.)	1	1787-1840	B	187
Mitchel, Archibald	2	1840-1853	C	96
Mitchel, George (Sr.)	1	1787-1840	B	249
Moon, John	1	1787-1840	B	230
Monn, William	1	1787-1840	B	144
Moare, Charles	2	1840-1853	C	18
Moare, Samuel	1	1787-1840	B	141
Morgan, Isaac	1	1787-1840	A	14
Morton, David	2	1840-1853	C	170
Mosley, Samuel	1	1787-1840	B	71
Moss, John M.	2	1840-1853	C	294
Mosteller, David	2	1840-1853	C	41
Murrell, Robert	1	1787-1840	B	37

Nash, Edward	1	1787–1840	B	154
Neely, Samuel	2	1840–1853	C	232
Nelson, Robert	1	1787–1840	A	53
Newby, Leroy	2	1840–1853	C	111
Nicoll, John	1	1787–1840	B	169
Oliver, John M.	2	1840–1853	C	14
Owens, William	1	1787–1840	A	103
Payne, Isaeah	1	1787–1840	A	111
Payne, James	2	1840–1853	C	52
Payne, Thomas	1	1787–1840	A	35
Peden, Alexander	2	1840–1853	C	32
Peden, John (Sr.)	1	1787–1840	A	48
Peden, John S.	2	1840–1853	C	229
Peden, William	1	1787–1840	A	109
Pickett, James	2	1840–1853	C	123
Pickett, Micajah	1	1787–1840	B	33
Pike, Lewis	1	1787–1840	A	128
Pool, John	1	1787–1840	B	212
Pool, Sally P.	2	1840–1853	C	257
Pool, Young P.	2	1840–1853	C	75
Poole, William (Planter)	2	1840–1853	C	193
Potts, Jonathan (Sr.)	2	1840–1853	C	1
Praytor, Middeton	1	1787–1840	A	80
Prince, Henry	1	1787–1840	B	186
Ranes, Henry	1	1787–1840	A	95
Rea, William (Sr.)	1	1787–1840	B	102
Rector, Lewis	1	1787–1840	B	114
Redman, William	1	1787–1840	B	153
Reese, Travace	1	1787–1840	A	92
Rice, Zenus	2	1840–1853	C	83
Richards, William	2	1840–1853	C	128
Roark, Hugh	1	1787–1840	B	44
Robbs, Susannah	2	1840–1853	C	78
Robbs, William (Farmer)	1	1787–1840	B	156
Roberts, Hardy	1	1787–1840	A	4
Roberts, John M.	2	1840–1853	C	179
Roberts, Samuel (Sr.)	2	1840–1853	C	73
Roe, James	1	1787–1840	B	81
Ross, Elizabeth	1	1787–1840	B	258
Ross, James	2	1840–1853	C	77
Rowland, Thomas (Farmer)	1	1787–1840	B	208
Rush, Mathias	2	1840–1853	C	265
Russell, Jesse	1	1787–1840	B	245
Russell, John	2	1840–1853	C	40
Sammons, John (Sr.)	1	1787–1840	A	78
Savage, Anthony	2	1840–1853	C	70
Scrugs, Richard	1	1787–1640	B	134
Seahorn, George	1	1787–1840	A	125
Sherrell, Philip	2	1840–1853	C	36
Ship, William (Farmer)	1	1787–1840	A	132
Shumate, Strother D.	1	1787–1840	B	171
Simmons, John	1	1787–1840	A	63
Sims, Drury	1	1787–1840	A	36
Sloan, Elizabeth D.	2	1840–1853	C	103
Smith, Abner	1	1787–1840	B	92

Smith, Abraham	2	1840-1853	C	141
Smith, Alexander	1	1787-1840	A	32
Smith, Elliot T.	2	1840-1853	C	59
Smith, Frances (Mrs.)	2	1840-1853	C	226
Smith, George	2	1840-1853	C	82
Smith, John S.	1	1787-1840	B	207
Smith, Joseph	2	1840-1853	C	269
Smith, Joseph	1	1787-1840	B	174
Smith, Nancy	2	1840-1853	C	160
Smith, Reuben	1	1787-1840	A	49
Smith, Thomas	1	1787-1840	B	251
Southerlin, Banister Wade	2	1840-1853	C	173
Sparks, Jesse	1	1787-1840	B	59
Spillers, George (Sr.)	1	1787-1840	B	172
Spriggs, Thomas	2	1840-1853	C	26
Springfield, Thomas	2	1840-1853	C	112
Stairley, George	1	1787-1840	B	189
Stennis, John	2	1840-1853	C	107
Stinnes, John, see - - - - - - - - - - - - - - - -			Stennis, John	
Stokes, Jeremiah (Jr.)	1	1787-1840	B	63
Stone, Banister	2	1840-1853	C	91
Stone, Johnathan	1	1787-1840	A	55
Stone, Mary	1	1787-1840	B	126
Styles, John L.	2	1840-1853	C	211
Styles, Samuel	2	1840-1853	C	65
Sullivan, Hewlett (Sr.)	1	1787-1840	B	177
Tarrant, Benjamin	1	1787-1840	A	122
Tarrant, John	1	1787-1840	A	34
Tarrant, Leonard (Sr.)	1	1787-1840	A	7
Taylor, Archibald	1	1787-1840	B	150
Taylor, John	1	1787-1840	B	83
Taylor, Peter	2	1840-1853	C	62
Thackston, William (Sr.)	1	1787-1840	A	113
Thomas, John	2	1840-1853	C	11
Thomas, William Davis	1	1787-1840	A	89
Thompson, John D.	1	1787-1840	B	108
Thompson, Jonathan, see - - - - - - - - - - - - -			Tomson, Jonathan	
Thompson, Joshua	2	1840-1853	C	139
Thompson, Josiah	1	1787-1840	A	73
Thruston, Richard	2	1840-1853	C	69
Thruston, William	1	1787-1840	B	106
Tinsley, James	2	1840-1853	C	98
Tomson, Jonathan	1	1787-1840	B	19
Townes, Rachel	2	1840-1853	C	220
Townsend, Benjamin (Sr.)	1	1787-1840	B	77
Turner, William G. (Sr.)	1	1787-1840	A	94
Vaughn, David	2	1840-1853	C	251
Vaughn, James	2	1840-1853	C	233
Vaughan, John	1	1787-1840	B	246
Vickers, Alexander	1	1787-1840	B	167
Vickers, Martha	2	1840-1853	C	216
Vinson, Ezekiel (Farmer)	1	1787-1840	A	119
Waddell, Nathan	2	1840-1853	C	234
Waddill, Charles	1	1787-1840	A	57

Waddill, Edmund	2	1840-1853	C	212
Waldrop, John	2	1840-1853	C	44
Walker, Samuel (Sr.)	1	1787-1840	B	116
Walker, Sylvannus	1	1787-1840	A	85
Wasson, John	2	1840-1853	C	218
Watson, Edward (Jr.)	2	1840-1853	C	6
Watson, Edward (Sr.)	2	1840-1853	C	7
Welch, Daniel	1	1787-1840	B	247
Welch, William	1	1787-1840	A	116
Wells, Samuel	1	1787-1840	A	40
West, Isaac (Sr.)	1	1787-1840	B	133
Westmoreland, Rachel	2	1840-1853	C	155
Wheeler, William (Sr.)	2	1840-1853	C	177
Whitlock, Harrison	1	1787-1840	B	181
Wickliffe, Frankie	1	1787-1840	B	28
Wickliffe, Isaac	1	1787-1840	A	17
Williams, Samuel	2	1840-1853	C	258
Williams, Thomas B.	2	1840-1853	C	267
Williamson, William	1	1787-1840	B	123
Wolf, George	1	1787-1840	A	64
Woodside, James	1	1787-1840	B	185
Wright, Asa	1	1787-1840	B	234
Wynne, Matthew	1	1787-1840	A	46
Yeargin, Andrew	1	1787-1840	A	133
Yeargin, Devereaux	2	1840-1853	C	174
Yeargin, Oney	1	1787-1840	A	88
Young, John (Sr.)	1	1787-1840	A	13
Young, John	1	1787-1840	A	182
Young, William	1	1787-1840	B	93

Copied by:

/s/ Mrs. John D. Rogers

Mrs. John D. Rogers

INDEX TO

HORRY COUNTY WILLS

VOLUME NO. 1

1799-1853

This index is compiled from W.P.A. copies of
wills filed in the COUNTY PROBATE COURTS.
The volumes indexed are a part of
the South Carolina Collection of
the University of South Carolina
Library.

Columbia, S. C.
1939

Name	Vol.	Date	Section	Page
Alford, Arthur	1	1799-1853	A	47
Anderson, David	1	1799-1853	C	18
Anderson, Henry(Planter)	1	1799-1853	C	37
Anderson, Robert (Planter)	1	1799-1853	Wills from files	1
Atwater, Joseph A.	1	1799-1853	Wills from files	3
Beaty, Thomas A.	1	1799-1853	C	41
Bellemee, John	1	1799-1853	A	25
Befsent, James	1	1799-1853	A	57
Bessent, James, see				Befsent, James
Blanton, Moses	1	1799-1853	C	2
Brovard, John B.	1	1799-1853	A	50
Brunson, John	1	1799-1853	C	47
Bryan, Wm. A.D.	1	1799-1853	A	77
Bryan, Wm. D.	1	1799-1853	Wills from files	4
Cannon, Redden (Planter)	1	1799-1853	A	6
Carrel, William	1	1799-1853	C	1
Clardy, Michael	1	1799-1853	Wills from files	6
Conner, Sarah	1	1799-1853	C	35
Cox, John	1	1799-1853	A	85
Cox, Joseph (Planter)	1	1799-1853	A	16
Cox, Josiah	1	1799-1853	A	39
Daniels, Robert	1	1799-1853	Wills from files	8
Dawsey, Samuel	1	1799-1853	Wills from files	10
Dewitt, Jesse G.	1	1799-1853	C	3
Dewitt, Joseph (Jr.)	1	1799-1853	A	15
Dewitt, Martha R.	1	1799-1853	C	8
Durant, Bethel (Planter)	1	1799-1853	A	29
Durant, Henry (Planter)	1	1799-1853	A	80
Durant, John	1	1799-1853	C	16
Durant, Thomas	1	1799-1853	A	43
Edge, William	1	1799-1853	C	28
Elks, James	1	1799-1853	Wills from files	12
Foley, John	1	1799-1853	Wills from files	14
Forbes, John W.	1	1799-1853	B	2
Foxworth, Samuel	1	1799-1853	Wills from files	16
Gause, Benjamin (Sr.)	1	1799-1853	A	18
Gause, Bryan W.	1	1799-1853	Wills from files	18
Gause, John J.	1	1799-1853	A	23
Gore, William (Sr.)	1	1799-1853	A	52
Graham, Elizabeth	1	1799-1853	C	21
Graham, John (Sr.)	1	1799-1853	Wills from files	21
Graham, William (Sr.)	1	1799-1853	A	10
Grainger, John (Sr.)	1	1799-1853	Wills from files	23
Grainger, John	1	1799-1853	A	35
Grainger, Samuel	1	1799-1853	Wills from files	25
Grainger, Thomas	1	1799-1853	Wills from files	27
Hardee, Isaac	1	1799-1853	C	45
Hardee, Joseph	1	1799-1853	A	62

Hardy, John	1	1799-1853	Wills from files	29
Harrelson, Josiah	1	1799-1853	A	8
Harrelson, Moses	1	1799-1853	A	58
Hemingway, Thomas	1	1799-1853	B	5
Hemingway, Thomas	1	1799-1853	C	12
Herick, John	1	1799-1853	A	60
Herl, William	1	1799-1853	C	14
Herrelson, Josiah, see - - - - - - - - - - - - - - - - - - Harrelson, Josiah				
Hucks, David	1	1799-1853	B	9
Hughs, Cadar	1	1799-1853	C	23
Johnson, Joseph (Sr.)	1	1799-1853	A	65
Johnston, William (Planter)	1	1799-1853	A	92
Jordan, Henry D.	1	1799-1853	C	30
Jordan, William (Farmer)	1	1799-1853	A	32
Jordon, Robert	1	1799-1853	Wills from files	31
Jordon, William (Sr.)	1	1799-1853	Wills from files	34
Keyes, Peabody	1	1799-1853	A	1
King, Thomas (Planter)	1	1799-1853	Wills from files	36
Lawrimore, Robert (Sr.)	1	1799-1853	A	82
Lee, Noah	1	1799-1853	A	44
Lewis, Charles	1	1799-1853	C	4
Lewis, Daniel H.	1	1799-1853	Wills from files	38
Lewis, Josiah O.	1	1799-1853	A	66
Lewis, Rachel	1	1799-1853	Wills from files	40
Lewis, William	1	1799-1853	Wills from files	42
Lewis, William Henry	1	1799-1853	Wills from files	45
Livingston, Thomas	1	1799-1853	Wills from files	46
Livingston, Thomas	1	1799-1853	A	55
Lorimore, Robert (Sr.)	1	1799-1853	A	82
Lowe, William	1	1799-1853	A	81
Lowremore, Robert (Sr.)	1	1799-1853	Wills from files	48
McCracken, Robert	1	1799-1853	C	6
McKelduff, Dabid	1	1799-1853	Wills from files	51
McKilroey, Mary	1	1799-1853	A	33
McQueen, Daniel (Sr.)	1	1799-1853	Wills from files	53
McQueen, William	1	1799-1853	C	33
Milliken, Charity	1	1799-1853	B	1
Nicholson, Peter (Planter)	1	1799-1853	Wills from files	55
Norman, Samuel N.	1	1799-1853	C	20
Norton, William (Sr.)	1	1799-1853	Wills from files	57
Oliver, William	1	1799-1853	A	4
Parker, William	1	1799-1853	Wills from files	59
Phips, William	1	1799-1853	Wills from files	60
Pinner, Arthur	1	1799-1853	Wills from files	61
Pipkin, Daniel (Planter)	1	1799-1853	A	12
Pitman, Joel	1	1799-1853	Wills from files	63
Prince, Nicholas	1	1799-1853	A	90

Rabon, William	1	1799-1853	C	43
Ready, Thomas	1	1799-1853	Wills from files	64
Reaves, Mark (Sr.)	1	1799-1853	B	3
Rogers, John (Sr.)	1	1799-1853	A	37
Rogers, John (Jr.)	1	1799-1853	Wills from files	66
Sarvis, John	1	1799-1853	A	73
Singleton, John (Planter)	1	1799-1853	A	13
Singleton, Richard	1	1799-1853	Wills from files	69
Skipper, Abraham	1	1799-1853	A	64
Smith, Thomas	1	1799-1853	A	3
Snow, William	1	1799-1853	Wills from files	71
Stevenson, Benjamin(Planter)	1	1799-1853	A	48
Strickland, Matthew	1	1799-1853	C	9
Tilman, Josiah	1	1799-1853	Wills from files	74
Tindal, John (Sr.)	1	1799-1853	A	21
Vaught, Matthias (Sr.)	1	1799-1853	A	68
Vereen, Charles W.(Planter)	1	1799-1853	A	72
Vereen, Charles	1	1799-1853	Wills from files	76
Vereen, Hester	1	1799-1853	A	70
Vereen, John E.	1	1799-1853	A	86
Vereen, William (Jr.)	1	1799-1853	Wills from files	79
Waller, William (Planter)	1	1799-1853	Wills from files	81
West, Robert	1	1799-1853	A	40
Whitman, William(Planter)	1	1799-1853	A	51
Williams, Jacob (Planter)	1	1799-1853	A	28
Woodward, James (Sr.)	1	1799-1853	B	7

Copied by:

/s/   Mrs. John D. Rogers

INDEX

TO

KERSHAW COUNTY WILLS.

VOLUME NO. 1
1770-1841

VOLUME NO. 2
1775-1839

VOLUME NO. 3
1823-1853

This index is compiled from W.P.A. copies of
wills filed in the COUNTY PROBATE COURTS.
The volumes indexed are a part of the
South Carolina Collection of the
University of South Carolina
Library.

Columbia, S.C.
1939

Name	Vol.	Date	Section	Page
Abbot, John	1	1770-1841	C	67
Adams, Dinah	1	1770-1841	C	73
Adams, William	2	1775-1839	C	12
Adamson, John (Planter)	2	1775-1839	G	4
Alexander, Margaret	1	1770-1841	C	74
Alexander, Rebekah	1	1770-1841	C-	70
Alexander, Rebekah	1	1770-1841	C	72
Ancrum, William (Planter)	3	1823-1853	L	37
Anderson, David (Planter)	1	1770-1841	A-1	89
Anderson, Edward H. (Dr.)	3	1823-1853	A	52
Archer, James	1	1770-1841	A-1	236
Arrant, Conrod	1	1770-1841	A-1	223
Atkins, John	1	1770-1841	A-1	47
Atkinson, James	1	1770-1841	A-1	219
Austin, Drewry	1	1770-1841	A-1	32
Bagnall, Ebenzer	1	1770-1841	A-1	204
Baldwin, Susannah	3	1823-1853	Q	1
Ballard, Rebecca	3	1823-1853	A	85
Barber, Agness	1	1770-1841	A-1	130
Barber, Charles	2	1775-1839	C	10
Barber, Margaret	2	1775-1839	G	2
Barkey, James	1	1770-1841	C	83
Barnet, Humphrey	1	1770-1841	C	2
Barnet, Michel	1	1770-1841	A-1	238
Barnet, William	1	1770-1841	A-1	152
Baskin, James	3	1823-1853	A	170
Baskin, Joseph	3	1823-1853	A	48
Bass, Elijah (Planter)	3	1823-1853	A	190
Bass, Molly	2	1775-1839	O	9
Beckham, William (Sr.)	1	1770-1841	Wills not recorded	12
Belk, Isabella Jane	3	1823-1853	A	173
Belk, William	2	1775-1839	C	29
Belton, John	1	1770-1841	C	80
Belton, Samuel (Planter)	1	1770-1841	C	51
Belton, Samuel (Jr.)	1	1770-1841	C	44
Benbow, Richard (Planter)	1	1770-1841	A-1	75
Berry, Thomas	3	1823-1853	A	67
Bethany, William (Jr.)	1	1770-1841	C	87
Bethany, William (Sr.)	2	1775-1839	C	18
Biggart, James	3	1823-1853	A	201
Bishop, Nicholas(Shoemaker)	1	1770-1841	Wills not recorded	9
Bliss, Henry	1	1770-1841	A-1	137
Bond, Moses	1	1770-1841	A-1	63
Boothe, William (Planter)	1	1770-1841	A-1	139
Bowdon, Arthur	2	1775-1839	C	11
Bowen, John A.	3	1823-1853	A	206
Boykin, Burwell	1	1770-1841	A-1	245
Boykin, John (Planter)	3	1823-1853	A	224
Boykin, Lemuel (Planter)	3	1823-1853	A	165
Boykin, Samuel	1	1770-1841	C	10
Bracey, Elizabeth	1	1770-1841	Wills not recorded	13
Bracey, Thomas	2	1775-1839	K	22
Bradley, Samuel	1	1770-1841	A-1	114

Bradley, Solomon	2	1775-1839	K	15
Bradshaw, Thomas	1	1770-1841	C	81
Branen, John	3	1823-1853	A	121
Branom, Andrew	3	1823-1853	A	145
Breaker, Susan	3	1823-1853	Q	3
Brevard, Joseph	1	1770-1841	A-1	250
Brewer, William	3	1823-1853	A	97
Bridges, Thomas (Planter)	1	1770-1841	A-1	10
Brisbane, Mary	1	1770-1841	A-1	242
Britt, Elizabeth	2	1775-1839	O	8
Britt, Richard	2	1775-1839	O	8
Bronson, Mary	2	1775-1839	O	1
Bronson, Stephen	1	1770-1841	A-1	240
Broom, Thomas	1	1770-1841	C	68
Brown, Ann	3	1823-1853	A	24
Brown, George	1	1770-1841	Wills not recorded	17
Brown, James	2	1775-1839	O	7
Brown, James	3	1823-1853	A	6
Brown, John N.	1	1770-1841	A-1	83
Brown, Mary	2	1775-1839	G	3
Brown, Sarah M.	1	1770-1841	C	79
Brown, William	1	1770-1841	A-1	110
Bryant, Lewis Franklin	1	1770-1841	C	36
Bunckley, Jonathan	1	1770-1841	Wills not recorded	15
Burfby, Jacob	1	1770-1641	A-1	181
Burgess, John (Sr.)	3	1823-1853	L	20
Burgess, Timothy(Sr.)	1	1770-1841	C	85
Burns, Leard	1	1770-1841	A-1	66
Bursby, Jacob, see - Burfby, Jacob				
Buser, George (Planter)	1	1770-1841	A-1	44
Cain, Dempsey	1	1770-1841	C	89
Campbell, Alexander(Plant.)	1	1770-1841	A-1	94
Campbell,Drury	1	1770-1841	C	38
Cantey, John	3	1823-1853	A	192
Cantey, Joseph	1	1770-1841	A-1	1
Cantey, Zachariah	2	1775-1839	I	28
Carter, Benj.	3	1823-1853	N	13
Carter, Henry (Planter)	1	1770-1841	A-1	193
Carter, Jacob	2	1775-1839	N-1	7
Caskey, John (Planter)	1	1770-1841	A -1	227
Cason, Cannon	2	1775-1839	N-1	5
Cassity, Thomas (Planter)	2	1775-1839	N-1	1
Center, Nathan	1	1770-1841	Wills not recorded	7
Champion, Jacob	2	1775-1839	O	12
Champion, John Lloyd	1	1770-1841	C	53
Chappell, Henry	1	1770-1841	A-1	34
Chapple, Elizabeth	2	1775-1839	N-1	4
Cherry, Jacob	2	1775-1839	K	3
Chesnut, John (Planter)	1	1770-1841	A-1	257
Chesnut, Ellen	3	1823-1853	A	152
Chesnut, John	3	1823-1853	Q	9
Clanton, John (Sr.)	3	1823-1853	A	40
Clanton, Richard	1	1770-1841	C	28
Clemmons, William (Planter)	1	1770-1841	A-1	189
Coates, Sion	2	1775-1839	O	16

Coates, William	1	1770-1841	A-1	68
Colder, Peter	1	1770-1841	C	91
Collins, Elizabeth	1	1770-1841	C	90
Collins, Lewis	1	1770-1841	Wills not recorded	5
Collins, Lewis	2	1775-1839	C	27
Collins, Reuben	2	1775-1839	O	11
Collins, William	1	1770-1841	C	9
Colquhoun, Robert	1	1770-1841	A-1	254
Commander, Samuel (Planter)	1	1770-1841	A-1	77
Conway, Bonds (Negro)	3	1823-1853	A	36
Conyers, James (Jr.)	1	1770-1841	A-1	37
Conyers, James (Planter)	1	1770-1841	A-1	106
Cook, Henry Baines	3	1823-1853	A	54
Cook, John	1	1770-1841	A-1	160
Cook,William(Bricklayer)	3	1823-1853	L	27
Coopley,Elizabeth(Planter)	1	1770-1841	A-1	162
Cornelius, Roland	3	1823-1853	A	14
Colton, Joab	3	1823-1853	A	197
Cousart, Richard	1	1770-1841	A-1	45
Craig, John	1	1770-1841	A-1	209
Crawford, James	1	1770-1841	Wills not recorded	6
Croft, Henry (Tailor)	1	1770-1841	Wills not recorded	42
Cunningham, Arthur	3	1823-1853	L	34
Cunningham, Elizabeth	3	1823-1853	A	44
Cunningham, Joseph (Plant)	3	1823-1853	A	129
Daniel, William (Planter)	3	1823-1853	N	10
Daughtery, Rhoda	2	1775-1839	I	23
Davis, Amos	1	1770-1841	A-1	215
Davis, Ann	2	1775-1839	N-1	16
Davis, Edward	1	1770-1841	Wills not recorded	3
Davis, John	1	1770-1841	A-1	176
Davis, Mary J.	3	1823-1853	A	195
Davis, Rachel	1	1770-1841	C	99
Davis, Richard	1	1770-1841	Wills not recorded	11
Debrhul, Patience	3	1823-1853	A	62
DeLeon, Abraham(Physician)	3	1823-1853	A	94
DeLeon, Hannah	2	1775-1839	N-1	18
Deveaux, Isreal D.(Phys.)	1	1770-1841	C	95
Dickinson, James,(Planter)	3	1823-1853	A	93
Dinkins, Thomas	1	1770-1841	C	92
Dixon, John	1	1770-1841	C	101
Dixon, Thomas	1	1770-1841	C	97
Dixon, Tilman L.	3	1823-1853	A	159
Donnom, Jane	2	1775-1839	N-1	14
Doughtery, John	1	1770-1841	C	39
Dougherty, Samuel	2	1775-1839	G	1
Dougherty, John, see - - - - - - - - - - - - - - - - - - Doughtery, John
Douglas, James	1	1770-1841	C	41
Douglas, James K.	3	1823-1853	A	209
Drakeford, John (Sr.)	3	1823-1853	A	200
Drakeford, Richard	3	1823-1853	N	1
DuBose, Isaac	1	1770-1841	Wills not recorded	43
Duke, Robert	1	1770-1841	A-1	124
Duncan, James	1	1770-1841	A-1	39
Duncan, Patrick	1	1770-1841	A-1	22
Dunlap, James	1	1770-1841	Wills not recorded	1
Duren, George	2	1775-1839	C	34
Dye, John	1	1770-1841	C	55
Dye, Thomas	3	1823-1853	A	146

Edwards, Will	1	1770-1841	A-1	96
Egleton, Mary	1	1770-1841	Wills not recorded	41
Elkins, Robert	2	1775-1839	C	56
Elliott, Thomas	1	1770-1841	A-1	54
English, James (Planter)	3	1825-1855	L	17
English, John	2	1775-1839	C-1	1.
English, John	1	1770-1841	C	103
English, Joshua	1	1770-1841	C	51
English, Thomas	2	1775-1839	N-1	20
Evans, Barwell	1	1770-1841	Wills not recorded	40
Evans, Howell	3	1825-1855	A	128
Evans, Jacob	1	1770-1841	C	23
Evans, John	1	1770-1841	C	105
Evans, Sarah	2	1775-1839	G	13
Fisher, Mariah	2	1775-1839	O	20
Flake, Thomas	2	1775-1839	C	58
Folmer, Ignatius	3	1825-1855	L	14
Forgueson, William	1	1770-1841	Wills not recorded	49
Fortune, Anne	1	1770-1841	A-1	98
Fortune, John	1	1770-1841	A-1	15.
Franklin, Susanna	2	1775-1839	O	21
Frierson, J.James(Plant.)	1	1770-1841	A-1	8
Furman, Wood	1	1770-1841	A-1	16
Galman, Henry	1	1770-1841	A-1	31
Gardner, John	1	1770-1841	A-1	73
Gardner, Mary	2	1775-1839	N-1	13
Gardner, Mary	2	1775-1839	O	22
Gaskin, Tillitha	3	1825-1855	A	5
Gaskins, Ezekel	2	1775-1839	C	6
Gaulden, John	1	1770-1841	A-1	4
Gee, John	1	1770-1841	A-1	156
Geno, Taussaint	2	1775-1839	D-1	1
George, David	2	1775-1839	D-1	4
George, David	3	1825-1855	Q	4
Ghent, Charles	1	1770-1841	A-1	51
Gibson, Mary	2	1775-1839	N-1	26
Gibson, Roger (Planter)	1	1770-1841	A-1	182
Gibson, Roger	1	1770-1841	C	50
Gill, John	2	1775-1839	C	13
Gilman, Ann	3	1825-1855	A	64
Gindrat, Abraham	1	1770-1841	A-1	167
Goffe, Gates (Planter)	3	1825-1855	A	157
Gooch, Buley G.(Planter)	2	1775-1839	D-1	2
Goodall, Alexander	1	1770-1841	Wills not recorded	50
Goodwin, John	2	1775-1839	D-1	6
Goodwyn, Francis	1	1770-1841	A-1	168
Goodwyn, Howell	1	1770-1841	A-1	173
Goodwyn, Robert	1	1770-1841	A-1	170
Goodwyn, Uriah	1	1770-1841	A-1	229
Goodwyn, William (Sr.)	1	1770-1841	A-1	92
Gore, James	1	1770-1841	A-1	128
Gosse, Gates, see - Goffe, Gates				
Graham, Dency	3	1825-1855	A	61
Graves, John	1	1770-1841	A-1	64
Griffen, Jonas	1	1770-1841	A-1	191
Griffith, Elizabeth	2	1775-1839	C	25

Guphill, William	2	1775-1839	G	15
Haile, Benjamin (Planter)	1	1770-1841	Wills not recorded	18
Haile, Benjamin (Planter)	1	1770-1841	Wills not recorded	27
Haile, Benjamin (Planter)	3	1823-1853	A	99
Hall, John	1	1770-1841	A-1	108
Hall, John (Planter)	3	1823-1853	A	181
Hammond, Francis	3	1823-1853	Q	7
Hammond, Samuel	2	1775-1839	D-1	8
Hancock, George	2	1775-1839	N-1	22
Harris, James Mortimer(Pl.)	1	1770-1841	A-1	5
Harris, Joseph	1	1770-1841	Wills not recorded	56
Hawthorne, John	1	1770-1841	A-1	100
Hay, William	1	1770-1841	A-1	81
Henderson, Nathinal	1	1770-1841	A-1	150
Hermon, Andrew	1	1770-1841	A-1	178
Hinson, Phillip	1	1770-1841	A-1	148
Hogan, Lewis	3	1823-1853	A	69
Holland, Martha	3	1823-1853	A	148
Holley, Richard (Farmer)	3	1823-1853	L	15
Holleyman, Herman (Sr.)	3	1823-1853	A	110
Hood, William	2	1775-1839	N	8
Horn, Henry	1	1770-1841	I	22
Howard, Joseph	1	1770-1841	A-1	186
Howell, William	1	1770-1841	A-1	41
Huey, Hercules	1	1770-1841	Wills not recorded	55
Huff, Joseph	3	1823-1853	A	150
Hughey, Hercules, see - - - - - - - - - - - - - - - - - - Huey, Hercules				
Hunter, Henry	1	1770-1841	A	164
Hutchinson, William	2	1775-1839	D-1	9
Hyot, Charles	1	1770-1841	Wills not recorded	52
Ingram, Chas. (Minister)	3	1823-1853	N	3
James, John (Planter)	1	1770-1841	A-1	134
James, Sherwood (Planter)	1	1770-1841	A-1	70
Jenkins, James	3	1823-1853	A	89
Jenkins, Thomas William	1	1770-1841	A-1	213
Jones, John	2	1775-1839	D-1	10
Jones, John (Carpenter)	2	1775-1839	N-1	25
Jones, John L.	3	1823-1853	A	45
Jones, Leroy	3	1823-1853	A	1
Jones, Nathaniel	3	1823-1853	A	71
Jones, Samuel	3	1823-1853	A	75
Kelley, James (Farmer)	1	1770-1841	A-1	174
Kennedy, James	2	1775-1839	N-1	23
Kent, Henry	2	1775-1839	D-1	13
Kershaw, Ely	2	1775-1839	D-1	11
Kershaw, George	2	1775-1839	D-1	12
Kershaw, James	2	1775-1839	G	17
Kershaw, John	2	1775-1839	O	28
Kershaw, Joseph	1	1770-1841	C	13
Kershaw, Lydia A.	2	1775-1839	O	3
Kershaw, Mary	3	1823-1853	A	95
Kershaw, Samuel Geoffrey	1	1770-1841	Wills not recorded	54
Kilgore, James L.	3	1823-1853	A	123
Kimball, Benjamine (Sr.)	1	1770-1841	A-1	26

130

King, John	1	1770-1841	A-1	87
King, Nathaniel(Planter)	1	1770-1841	A-1	184
Kirkland, Daniel	2	1775-1839	O	24
Kirkland, Joseph	3	1823-1853	A	115
Kirkpatrick, James	1	1770-1841	A-1	225
Knox, Isaac	2	1775-1839	C	39
Lang, James W.	3	1823-1853	A	3
Larney, Thomas	1	1770-1841	A-1	146
Lee, John (Farmer)	1	1770-1841	Wills not recorded	59
Leigh, Rachael	3	1823-1853	A	107
Levy, Samuel (Merchat)	1	1770-1841	C	63
Levy, Sarah	3	1823-1853	A	19
Lewellin, Lyson	2	1775-1839	O	4
Little, Daniel	2	1775-1839	D-1	14
Livingston, James	1	1770-1841	A-1	195
Lockhart, Joseph (Sr.)	2	1775-1841	O	28
Logan, David	2	1775-1839	O	31
Long, Darret	1	1770-1841	C	12
Long, Isaac	1	1770-1841	C	46
Love, Margaret	2	1775-1839	O	30
Love, Robert (Planter)	1	1770-1841	Wills not recorded	62
Lovett, Ann Elizabeth	3	1823-1853	A	189
Lowrey, Rebecca	3	1823-1853	A	42
Lucius, Phillips, I.	3	1823-1853	A	57
Luyten, William	1	1770-1841	Wills not recorded	37
McAdams, Hiram A.	2	1775-1839	O	40
McCallom, Henry(Planter)	2	1775-1839	N-1	29
McCaskill, Peter	3	1823-1853	A	212
McClelland, John	3	1823-1853	A	180
McClester, Hugh	2	1775-1839	D-1	16
McClure, John	3	1823-1853	A	50
McCarkle, William	1	1770-1841	A-1	151
McDill, Nathaniel	1	1770-1814	Wills not recorded	67
McDowell, Hugh	2	1775-1839	D-1	20
McDowell, W.D.	3	1823-1853	A	179
McFee, Archibald	2	1775-1839	D-1	22
McGraw, Edward (Sr.)	1	1770-1841	Wills not recorded	77
McInnis, Donald	2	1775-1839	K	16
McKain, James R.(Druggist)	3	1823-1853	A	127
McKain, William	3	1823-1853	A	175
McKee, Elsey	1	1770-1841	N-1	30
McKee, John (Planter)	1	1770-1841	Wills not recorded	76
McKee, Samuel	2	1775-1839	G	21
McKewn, James	1	1770-1841	A-1	112
McKinney, William	1	1770-1841	A-1	102
McLean, Daniel (Planter)	1	1770-1841	Wills not recorded	74
McLeod, Alexander	2	1775-1839	K	9
McLeaod, Daniel	3	1823-1853	L	12
McLeod, Daniel, see - - - - - - - - - - - - - - - - - - - McLeaod, Daniel				
MacNair, Elizabeth	2	1775-1839	O	38
McNeill, John	1	1770-1841	Wills not recorded	79
McNies, John	1	1770-1841	Wills not recorded	73
McRa, Duncan (Planter)	3	1823-1853	L	1
McRa, Mary	3	1823-1853	A	26
McRa, Powell, (Planter)	3	1823-1853	A	82

McSween, Finlay	2	1775-1859	O	56
McWillies, Adam	3	1825-1853	L	23
Marion, John	1	1770-1841	A-1	179
Marsh, John (Planter)	2	1775-1859	O	35
Marshall, Charity	2	1775-1859	P	1
Marshall, James (Planter)	2	1775-1859	C	8
Marshall, Tamer	2	1775-1859	O	53
Martin, James	1	1770-1841	Wills not recorded	64
Martin, James	1	1770-1841	Wills not recorded	65
Martin, Samuel	2	1775-1859	D-1	27
Martin, Sarah	2	1775-1859	I	29
Martin, Susanna	2	1775-1859	C	52
Massey, Arthur	2	1775-1859	D-1	18
Mathis, Samuel	2	1775-1859	K	4
Mayhew, Ezekiel	3	1825-1853	N-1	28
Merryman, Joshua	2	1775-1859	A	72
Newboarn, John	2	1775-1859	D-1	25
Miller, James	1	1770-1841	C	16
Miller, Samuel	1	1770-1841	A-1	2
Millwee, William	1	1770-1841	A-1	152
Mixon, William	1	1770-1841	Wills not recorded	68
Moody, Solomon	1	1770-1841	Wills not recorded	71
Moore, Israll (Sr.)	1	1770-1841	Wills not recorded	57
Moore, John	1	1770-1841	Wills not recorded	72
Moseley, Reddick (Sr.)	3	1825-1853	A	160
Motley, Apple	3	1825-1853	N	6
Murchison, Margarett	3	1825-1853	A	84
Murphy, Joseph (Planter)	3	1825-1853	A	215
Nance, Peter, see - Vance, Peter				
Naudin, John	2	1775-1839	G	20
Neeley, William	1	1770-1841	A-1	56
Neilson, Samuel	1	1770-1841	A-1	158
Neteles, William	2	1775-1839	D-1	30
Newton, Jeane	1	1770-1841	A-1	141
Nixon, John (Sr.)	1	1770-1841	C	60
Norris, William (Sr.)	1	1770-1841	C	1
Nutt, Elizabeth	2	1775-1859	D-1	29
O'Cain, Louisa	2	1775-1859	D-1	32
O'Daniel, William (Sr.)	1	1770-1841	C	56
O'Neal, Presslar	2	1775-1859	G	23
Owen, Thomas	1	1770-1841	A-1	231
Owings, Archibald	2	1775-1859	K	23
Parish, Edward	2	1775-1859	I	26
Parker, William	1	1770-1841	Wills not recorded	80
Parker, Wm.D.(Cab-maker)	2	1775-1859	C	43
Parkins, Benjamin (Sr.)	3	1825-1853	A	7
Patterson, Joseph	3	1825-1853	A	75
Patton, Mathew	1	1770-1841	A-1	128
Pearson, William(Planter)	1	1770-1841	A-1	29
Peary, Benjamin(Planter	1	1770-1841	Wills not recorded	89
Peay, John	3	1825-1853	Q	19
Pegan, Alexander	1	1770-1841	A-1	48
Perkins, Benjamin, see - - - - - - - - - - - - - - - - - Parkins, Benjamin				

Perkins, Wm.(Ship-Carpent.)	1	1770-1841	Wills not recorded	82
Perry, Benjamin(Planter)	1	1770-1841	Wills not recorded	91
Perry, Jacob	1	1770-1841	A-1	85
Perry, Jacob	2	1775-1839	C	41
Perry, James	2	1775-1839	D-1	33
Perry, James	2	1775-1839	D-1	58
Perry, Josiah	2	1775-1839	C	3
Perry, Lemuel	1	1770-1841	C	5
Peters, Solomon	1	1770-1841	Wills not recorded	83
Pettaway, Sterling	1	1770-1841	C	19
Petty, Luke	1	1770-1841	A-1	166
Phillips, John (Planter)	1	1770-1841	A-1	52
Pickett, James	1	1770-1841	A-1	50
Pierce, James (Planter)	2	1775-1839	D-1	35
Platt, John	1	1770-1841	C	4
Plunket, John	2	1775-1839	D-1	36
Porter, Nathaniel	1	1770-1841	A-1	97
Quin, Daniel O.	2	1775-1839	K	11
Ragan, William	1	1770-1841	A-1	233
Raley, Charles	2	1775-1839	D-1	46
Ray, James	2	1775-1839	G	26
Reed, Nancy	3	1823-1853	A	38
Rees, Edwin (Planter)	2	1775-1841	N-1	32
Rembert, William	2	1775-1839	D-1	49
Rhodes, Catherine	2	1775-1839	D	2
Richardson, George	2	1775-1859	D-1	44
Richardson, Richard	2	1775-1839	N-1	36
Richardson, Thomas (Sr.)	1	1770-1841	Wills not recorded	84
Richardson, William	1	1770-1841	A-1	202
Riddle, James	2	1775-1839	O	5
Riddle, John	1	1770-1841	A-1	197
Rives, William	1	1770-1841	A-1	58
Roach, Ann	2	1775-1839	D	3
Robinson, Alexander	1	1770-1841	A-1	118
Robinson, Frances	2	1775-1839	G	24
Robinson, John	2	1775-1839	D-1	42
Rochelle, Margaret	3	1823-1853	A	89
Rochelle, Lodowick	2	1775-1839	D-1	39
Rochelle, Margaret	3	1823-1853	A	91
Rodgers, William	1	1770-1841	A-1	104
Rollo, William	2	1775-1839	C	5
Roy, William	1	1770-1841	C	58
Rush, Fredreck(Planter)	1	1770-1841	A-1	211
Rush, Peter W.	3	1823-1853	A	162
Russell, Samuel (Planter)	2	1775-1839	N-1	34
Russell, William	2	1775-1839	D-1	51
Rutledge, Edward	2	1775-1839	D-1	48
Rutledge, John (Planter)	1	1770-1841	C	65
Rutledge, John (Planter)	2	1775-1839	D-1	50
Sadler, John	1	1770-1841	A-1	122
Salmond, William	2	1775-1839	D-1	58
Sanders, George (Sr.)	2	1775-1839	I	5
Sanders, Josiah (Planter)	2	1775-1839	O	42
Scheurer, Elizbaeth	1	1770-1841	Wills not recorded	88

Scoldfield, Phillip (Plant)	1	1770-1841	A-1	221
Scott, John	2	1775-1841	C-1	2
Scott, William	1	1770-1841	C	48
Seals, Anthony	2	1775-1839	D	4
Segars, Burwell	1	1770-1841	Wills not recorded	101
Shropshire, Elizabeth	3	1823-1853	A	11
Shropshire, James (Sr.)	2	1775-1839	I	1
Simpson, William	1	1770-1841	Wills not recorded	86
Sloan, William (Planter)	1	1770-1841	C	21
Smith, Catharine	1	1770-1841	C	59
Smith, James	1	1770-1841	C	34
Smith, Thomas (Planter)	3	1823-1855	A	223
Smyrl, Elizabeth	2	1775-1839	G	27
Smyrl, Thomas (Sr.)	2	1775-1839	D-1	55
Smyth, Samuel	2	1775-1839	G	30
Sowell, Warley (Planter)	2	1775-1839	I	24
Sparling, Charles, see - - - - - - - - - - - - - -			Spradling, Charles	
Spears, Nancy	2	1775-1839	G	29
Spradley, Dillard	2	1775-1839	D	1
Spradling, Charles	1	1770-1841	D	121
Stallings, John	1	1770-1841	A-1	60
Starke, Douglas	1	1770-1841	Wills not recorded	94
Starke, Turner	2	1775-1839	D-1	53
Stephens, Mark	2	1775-1839	D-1	59
Stewart, Alexander	2	1775-1839	D-1	57
Stewart, Robert	1	1770-1841	A-1	198
Stewart, William	1	1770-1841	Wills not recorded	97
Stokes, Rebekah	2	1775-1839	K	13
Stradford, John	3	1823-1853	A	46
Stradford, Richard	2	1775-1839	C	23
Stripling, Thomas	2	1775-1839	D-1	54
Strong, Charles	1	1770-1841	A-1	206
Stuart, William, see - - - - - - - - - - - - - - - -			Stewart, William	
Sutton, Jasper	1	1770-1841	C	25
Swelley, John (Jr.)	2	1775-1839	G	33
Tamson, Adam	2	1775-1839	I	14
Tate, Elizabeth	2	1775-1839	I	31
Tate, William	1	1770-1841	C	20
Taylor, Ann	3	1823-1853	A	56
Taylor, George	2	1775-1839	N-1	43
Taylor, John (Planter)	1	1770-1841	Wills not recorded	99
Thomas, Jane	2	1775-1839	N-1	42
Thomas, Richard	2	1775-1839	N-1	40
Thompson, Pricilla	3	1823-1853	A	59
Thomson, William	2	1775-1839	C	20
Tharn, John	1	1770-1841	Wills not recorded	103
Thornton, Joseph	2	1775-1839	I	18
Thurtle, Hannah	2	1775-1839	I	20
Tiller, James	3	1823-1853	A	187
Tiller, William	2	1775-1839	I	12
Tillman, James T.	3	1823-1853	A	13
Tillman, Jesse	2	1775-1839	D-1	62
Tomson, Peter	2	1775-1839	D-1	61
Trantham, James	1	1770-1841	Wills not recorded	105
Trantham, John	2	1775-1839	C	21
Trantham, John	2	1775-1839	I	16
Trusdel, John	3	1823-1853	A	184

Tucker, Wood (Sr.)	1	1770-1841	A-1	79
Turley, Elizabeth	1	1770-1841	Wills not recorded	108
Turley, James	2	1775-1839	G	34
Turley, Peter	2	1775-1839	C	1
Turner, George (Planter)	2	1775-1839	N-1	44
Turnipseed, Beat (Planter)	2	1775-1839	N-1	53
Valendigham, Dawson	1	1770-1841	C	42
Vance, Peter	1	1770-1841	A-1	28
Vaughan, Willie	2	1775-1839	I	10
Vaughn, Thomas	1	1770-1841	C	43
Wages, Susannah	3	1823-1853	A	120
Wages, William	3	1823-1853	A	120
Wallace, James	1	1770-1841	Wills not recorded	104
Walling, Daniel	1	1770-1841	Wills not recorded	114
Walters, John	1	1770-1841	C	30
Watson, Ann	2	1775-1839	K	1
Watson, Archibald (Planter)	2	1775-1839	D-1	65
Watson, David	1	1770-1841	A-1	217
Watson, Edward	2	1775-1839	G	36
Welsh, William	1	1770-1839	C	33
Whitaker, James	2	1775-1839	N-1	48
Whitaker, Lemuel	2	1775-1839	N-1	50
Whitaker, Thomas	2	1775-1839	I	7
White, Joseph	1	1770-1841	A-1	154
Williams, John (Planter)	1	1770-1841	C	7
*Williams, John	2	1775-1839	N-1	7
Williams, Nancy	1	1770-1841	A	158
Williams, Nancy (Widow)	3	1823-1853	Wills not recorded	111
Williams, Nathan (Planter)	2	1775-1839	A	17
Williams, Robert	2	1775-1839	N-1	52
Willson, William	1	1770-1841	K	18
Wilson, David	1	1770-1841	A-1	230
Winn, John (Planter)	1	1770-1841	A-1	119
Wood, John	1	1770-1841	A-1	13
Woodward, Moses	2	1775-1839	D-1	24
Woodward, Thomas (Farmer)	2	1775-1839	N-1	64
Wyche, Drury	1	1770-1841	A-1	46
Wyly, Dinah	1	1770-1841	C	143
* Wyly, William	1	1770-1841	A-1	200
Williams, John	3	1823-1853	N-1	11
Young, Archibald	3	1823-1853	A	204
Young, Jane D.	3	1823-1853	A	177

Copied by:

/s/ Mrs. John D. Rogers
Mrs. John D. Rogers

INDEX

TO

LAURENS COUNTY WILLS.

VOLUME NO. 1
1766-1825

VOLUME NO. 2
1825-1853

This index is compiled from W.P.A. copies of
wills filed in the COUNTY PROBATE COURTS.
The volumes indexed are a part of the
South Carolina Collection of the
University of South Carolina
Library.

Columbia, S.C.
1939

Name	Vol.	Date	Section	Page
Abbeth, Daniel	1	1766-1802	A	154
Abbott, Daniel, see — — — — — — — — — — — — —			Abbeth, Daniel	
Abercrombie, Alexander	2	1825-1853	F	135
Abercrombie, Alexander	2	1825-1853	A	309
Abercrombie, Calvin	2	1825-1853	A	165
Abercrombie, James	1	1818-1830	E	23
Abrams, Martha	2	1825-1853	A	45
Adair, Hannah	2	1825-1853	F	38
Adair, Joseph	1	1766-1802	A	21
Adair, Joseph	1	1810-1818	D-1	30
Akins, Lewis	1	1766-1802	A	41
Allison, James	1	1766-1802	A	11
Allison, Robert	1	1766-1802	A	55
Anderson, Phillip	1	1810-1818	D-1	42
Armstrong, John	2	1825-1853	A	78
Armstrong, Joseph	1	1766-1802	A	39
Arnall, Joshua, see — — — — — — — — — — — — —			Arnold, James	
Arnold, Hendrick	1	1766-1802	A	85
Arnold, Joshua	1	1766-1802	A	36
Arnold, Zachariah	2	1825-1853	F	80
Atkinson, Henry	1	1766-1802	A	115
Atwood, James	1	1810-1818	D-1	74
Austin, Alexander (Sr.)	2	1825-1853	F	42
Austin, James	2	1825-1853	F	155
Austin, Samuel	2	1825-1853	F	44
Avery, Joseph	2	1825-1853	A	180
Babb, Sampson	2	1825-1853	A	222
Backman, John	1	1766-1802	A	149
Bailey, James	2	1825-1853	F	29
Bailey, William	1	1766-1802	A	49
Ball, George	1	1810-1818	D-1	104
Ball, Jeremiah	2	1825-1853	A	256
Ball, John	1	1818-1830	E	135
Ball, Martin	2	1825-1853	F	67
Ball, William	1	1802-1809	C-1	52
Barksdale, Nathan	1	1810-1818	D-1	24
Barksdale, John	2	1825-1853	F	113
Baugh, William	1	1766-1802	A	25
Beasly, Thomas	2	1825-1853	F	151
Bell, Adam	1	1802-1809	C-1	56
Bell, James	1	1818-1830	E	117
Bennett, Richard	1	1818-1830	E	59
Blackwell, Richard	2	1825-1853	F	162
Blakely, William (Sr.)	2	1825-1853	A	150
Bobo, Absolum	1	1810-1818	D-1	44
Bobo, E. M. (Dr.)	2	1825-1853	A	306
Bockman, John, see — — — — — — — — — — — — —			Backman, John	
Boling, Samuel	1	1802-1809	C-1	99
Bolling, Thornberry, see — — — — — — — — — — —			Bowling, Thornberry	
Bolt, Robert	1	1766-1802	A	89
Bonds, James	1	1818-1830	E	34
Borockman, John, see — — — — — — — — — — — — —			Backman, John	

Name		Dates		Vol/Page
Bouland, John	1	1818-1830	E	28
Bourland, William, see - - - - - - - - - - - -			Bowland, William	
Bowland, Henry B.	2	1825-1853	F	131
Bowland, William	1	1802-1809	C-1	25
Bowlin, Martha	2	1825-1853	A	5
Bowling, Thornberry	2	1825-1853	F	52
Box, John	1	1818-1830	E	47
Boyce, Drury	2	1825-1853	F	119
Boyce, John	2	1825-1853	A	70
Boyd, Isabelle	2	1825-1853	A	210
Boyd, Margaret	2	1825-1853	A	307
Braden, David	1	1818-1830	E	81
Brady, Charles	1	1802-1809	C-1	50
Bramlett, Nathan	2	1825-1853	A	20
Breazeale, Enoch	2	1825-1853	F	24
Breazeale, Rutha	2	1825-1853	F	156
Brockman, John, see - - - - - - - - - - - - - -			Backman, John	
Brown, Benjamin	2	1825-1853	A	152
Brown, James	1	1818-1830	E	90
Brown, Rodger	2	1825-1853	F	9
Brown, William (Sr.)	1	1810-1818	D-1	127
Brownlee, Esther	2	1825-1853	F	83
Bryson, John	1	1802-1809	C-1	29
Bryson, William	1	1802-1809	C-1	88
Bryson, William	1	1810-1818	D-1	121
Burgess, Joel	1	1802-1809	C-1	10
Burnside, Ann Jane	2	1825-1853	F	75
Burnside, Elizabeth	2	1825-1853	F	79
Burnside, James (Sr.)	1	1766-1802	A	107
Burnside, James	1	1802-1809	C-1	12
Burnside, Martha	2	1825-1853	F	76
Burnside, Thomas	2	1825-1853	F	27
Burnside, William	2	1825-1853	F	12
Burton, John	2	1825-1853	A	308
Burton, Thomas	1	1802-1809	C-1	1
Burton, Thomas	1	1825-1853	F	100
Byrd, Benjamin	2	1825-1853	F	132
Byrd, Elizabeth	2	1825-1853	A	84
Cabaness, Aimy	1	1818-1830	E	102
Cabaness, Elizabeth	1	1818-1830	E	104
Caldwell, James	2	1825-1853	F	53
Campbell, Angus	1	1802-1809	C-1	116
Campbell, John N.	2	1825-1853	A	153
Cargile, William	2	1825-1853	A	50
Carlisle, Coleman	1	1818-1830	E	130
Carter, John	1	1766-1802	A	109
Carter, John	1	1810-1818	D-1	34
Carter, Robert	2	1825-1853	F	3
Carter, William	2	1825-1853	A	131
Carson, Mary	1	1818-1830	E	46
Chandler, John	1	1818-1830	E	79
Charles, John	1	1802-1809	C-1	98
Cheek, Ellis	2	1825-1853	A	189
Cheek, Willis	2	1825-1853	A	234
Cheek, Willis D.	2	1825-1853	A	186
Childress, Richard	2	1825-1853	F	118
Clardy, James (Sr.)	2	1825-1853	A	74
Clardy, Jesse E.	2	1825-1853	A	62

Coker, Drury	2	1825-1853	F	122
Coker, Joseph	1	1766-1802	A	59
Coleman, Absolum	1	1810-1818	D-1	53
Coley, Charles	1	1818-1830	F	2
Cook, Abraham	2	1825-1853	A	31
Cook, G eorge	2	1825-1853	A	123
Cook, James	1	1810-1818	D-1	93
Cook, John	2	1825-1853	A	35
Cook, William	2	1825-1853	A	268
Couch, Isaac	2	1825-1853	F	138
Cracker, James	1	1818-1830	E	84
Crage, Elanor	1	1766-1802	A	66
Crage, James	1	1810-1818	D-1	38
Craig, Elanor, see - - - - - - - - - - - - - -			Crage, Elanor	
Craig, James, see - - - - - - - - - - - - - - -			Crage, James	
Craig, John	2	1825-1853	A	59
Craig, William	1	1818-1830	E	133
Crawford, John	2	1825-1853	F	39
Creece, John (Dr.)	1	1810-1818	D-1	13
Croson, Thomas	1	1766-1802	A	134
Cunningham, John	1	1766-1802	A	18
Cunningham, John	1	1810-1818	D-1	52
Cunningham, John	2	1825-1853	F	159
Cunningham, John D.	2	1825-1853	F	178
Cunningham, Patrick	1	1766-1802	A	93
Cunningham, Sally	2	1825-1853	A	259
Cunningham, Thomas	1	1802-1809	C-1	63
Cunningham, William	1	1818-1830	F	86
Cureton, David	2	1825-1853	A	164
Cureton, John	1	1802-1809	C-1	7
Dalrymple, Anna	2	1825-1853	A	293
Dalrymple, John G.	2	1825-1853	A	42
Dandy, Daniel	2	1825-1853	F	96
Danday, Thomas (Sr.)	1	1766-1802	A	127
Danday, William, see - - - - - - - - - - - - -			Dendy, William	
Darrah, James, see - - - - - - - - - - - - - -			Dorrch, James	
Davenport, John	1	1802-1809	C-1	86
Davenport, Thomas	1	1810-1818	D-1	86
Davis, John	2	1825-1853	F	141
Day, Jemimah	2	1825-1853	A	209
Day, Phillip	1	1766-1802	A	78
Dean, Easter	2	1825-1853	A	89
Dendy, Daniel, see - - - - - - - - - - - - - -			Dandy, William	
Dendy, John	2	1825-1853	A	140
Dendy, William	1	1766-1802	A	157
Devenport, John, see - - - - - - - - - - - - -			Davenport, John	
Dial, Hastings	1	1802-1809	C-1	114
Dial, Martin	2	1825-1853	A	54
Dial, Rebecca	1	1818-1830	E	140
Dillard, Ann	1	1818-1830	E	71
Dillard, George	2	1825-1853	A	136
Dollar, Sarah	2	1825-1853	A	17
Donahoe, John	1	1766-1802	A	163
Dorrah, James	1	1818-1830	E	38
Dorrch, James	2	1825-1853	A	18
Dorrch, James	2	1825-1853	A	300
Downs, Johnathan	:	1818-1830	E	6
Downs, Joseph	1	1818-1830	E	15

Downs, Sarah	2	1825-1853	A	86
Drew, William	1	1766-1802	A	1
Duncan, James	2	1825-1853	F	69
Duckett, Sarah	2	1825-1853	F	166
Dunlap, David	1	1802-1809	C-1	84
Dunlap, Samuel	1	1766-1802	A	43
Eagerton, Charles	2	1825-1853	A	159
Eakins, Lewis	1	1766-1802	A	57
East, Josiah	1	1818-1830	E	127
East, Shadrick	1	1766-1802	A	64
Evans, John	1	1802-1809	C-1	42
Fairburn, Alexander	1	1766-1802	A	114
Farley, Mary	1	1818-1830	E	45
Farrow, John	2	1825-1853	A	40
Farrow, Patillo	2	1825-1853	A	175
Farrow, Thomas F.	2	1825-1853	A	261
Felts, John (Sr.)	2	1825-1853	A	241
Ferguson, Nehemiah	1	1766-1802	A	20
Ferguson, Richard	1	1802-1809	C-1	96
Fillson, Alexander	2	1825-1853	A	23
Finley, John	2	1825-1853	A	227
Finley, Paul	2	1825-1853	A	48
Finney, John	1	1818-1830	E	136
Forguson, Nehimiah, see - - - - - - - - - - - -			Ferguson, Nehimiah	
Forgy, Peggy	2	1825-1853	F	84
Foshee, Benjamin	1	1818-1830	E	115
Fowler, John	1	1776-1802	A	34
Fowler, John	2	1825-1853	A	185
Fowler, Josiah	1	1810-1818	D-1	107
Fowler, Nathan	2	1825-1853	F	55
Fowler, Richard	1	1766-1802	A	42
Fowler, William	1	1802-1809	C-1	20
Franklin, Mathew	1	1818-1830	E	75
Franks, Joshua	2	1825-1853	A	171
Fuller, Avent	2	1825-1853	A	14
Fuller, Henry	1	1810-1818	D-1	49
Fuller, John	2	1825-1853	A	47
Fuller, Soloman	1	1818-1830	E	67
Fuller, Solomon	2	1825-1853	A	100
Funk, George	2	1825-1853	A	72
Gamble, James	1	1766-1802	A	136
Gamble, James	1	1810-1818	D-1	32
Garlington, Edwin	1	1818-1830	E	1 7
Garner, Thomas	1	1766-1802	A	45
Garnett, Ambrose G.	2	1825-1853	A	3
Garrett, Hannah	1	1818-1830	E	60
Garrett, Jessee (Sr.)	2	1825-1853	A	243
Garrett, John	1	1802-1809	C-1	66
Garrett, Silas	1	1802-1809	C-1	39
Garrott, Edward	1	1766-1802	A	75
Gary, Charles	1	1802-1809	C-1	65
Gary, David	2	1825-1853	F	167
Gary, Newman	2	1825-1853	A	190
Gilbert, William	1	1818-1830	E	82
Gilbert, William	2	1825-1853	A	44
Glenn, Alexander	2	1825-1853	F	18

Glenn, David	1	1818-1830	E	63
Glenn, James	1	1810-1818	D-1	88
Glenn, Jeremiah	1	1802-1809	C-1	111
Glenn, Rueben	1	1802-1809	C-1	103
Goff, Hugh	1	1818-1830	E	94
Golding, Anthony	1	1766-1802	A	151
Golding, Anthony F.	2	1825-1853	A	301
Golding, Temperance	2	1825-1853	A	125
Goodgoins, Joseph	2	1825-1853	A	7
Goodman, Duke	2	1825-1853	A	224
Goodman, Samuel (Sr.)	2	1825-1853	A	126
Goodman, Samuel (Sr.)	2	1825-1853	F	124
Goodman, William	1	1766-1802	A	72
Gordan, Ann I.	2	1825-1853	F	14
Gordan, Jane	2	1825-1853	F	164
Grant, Isaac	2	1825-1853	F	165
Grant, John	2	1825-1853	A	230
Gray, Isaac	2	1825-1853	F	103
Gray, James	1	1766-1802	A	142
Green, James	1	1818-1830	E	1
Green, William	1	1818-1830	E	129
Green, William	2	1825-1853	A	217
Green, Zachariah	1	1766-1802	A	63
Griffin, Anthony	1	1766-1802	A	105
Griffin, Anthony	2	1825-1853	A	207
Griffin, Richard	1	1802-1809	C-1	58
Griffin, Richard (Sr.)	1	1802-1809	C-1	60
Griffin, William (Sr.)	1	1766-1802	A	50
Grisel, John	1	1810-1818	D-1	5
Hairston, Peter	2	1825-1853	A	214
Hall, William	1	1766-1802	A	117
Hall, William	1	1818-1830	E	49
Hambleton, Robert	1	1810-1818	D-1	17
Hamilton, Andrew	2	1825-1853	A	188
Hamilton, Jane	2	1825-1853	A	8
Hamilton, Jane	2	1825-1853	A	82
Hammond, Joseph	1	1810-1818	D-1	124
Hammond, Peter	1	1810-1818	D-1	78
Hancock, William	1	1802-1809	C-1	44
Hand, Robert (Sr.)	2	1825-1853	A	12
Harding, William	1	1802-1809	C-1	109
Harlen, Aron	1	1802-1809	C-1	78
Hathorn, James	1	1810-1818	D-1	117
Hazlet, Guzzlet	1	1810-1818	D-1	84
Hellams, William	1	1766-1802	A	9
Henderson, Ann	1	1766-1802	A	161
Henderson, Mildred A.	2	1825-1853	A	146
Henderson, Samuel	1	1810-1818	D-1	111
Hendrick, Margaret	1	1766-1802	A	95
Hewit, Charles	1	1810-1818	D-1	76
Hill, Elender	2	1825-1853	F	94
Hill, Silas	2	1825-1853	A	117
Hill, Thomas	1	1818-1830	E	44
Hinton, Robert	1	1766-1802	A	103
Hitt, Elizabeth S.	2	1825-1853	A	218
Hitt, Henry	2	1825-1853	F	111
Holcombe, Casea	2	1825-1853	A	63
Holcombe, Richard	1	1766-1802	A	77

Holder, Jessie	1	1766-1802	A	118
Holland, Jane	2	1825-1853	F	117
*Holland, Regin	1	1802-1809	C-1	5
Holt, Sarah	2	1825-1853	A	61
Hood, Robert	1	1766-1802	A	120
Hopkins, Solomon	1	1810-1818	D-1	56
Hopper, William	2	1825-1853	F	127
Horton, Enas	1	1818-1830	E	36
Houlditch, William	1	1802-1809	C-1	22
Hughes, Aron	1	1802-1809	C-1	73
Hunter, Andrew	1	1766-1802	A	83
Hunter, John (Sr.)	1	1802-1809	C-1	13
Hunter, John	1	1818-1830	E	9
Hunter, Laughlin	1	1802-1809	C-1	9
Hunter, Mathew	1	1810-1818	D-1	39
Hunter, Mathew (Sr.)	1	1810-1818	D-1	61
Hunter, Mathew (Sr.)	1	1818-1830	E	89
Hunter, Robert	1	1818-1830	E	50
Hunter, Thomas	1	1818-1830	E	122
Hunter, William	1	1766-1802	A	166
*Hutcheson, William (Sr.)	1	1802-1809	C-1	41
*Holliday, William	2	1825-1853	F	32
Irby, William	2	1825-1853	F	73
Janney, John, see - - - - - - - - - - - - - - -			Tanney, John	
Johnson, Abraham	2	1825-1853	F	88
Johnson, George	2	1825-1853	A	162
Johnson, Jabez	2	1825-1853	A	65
Johnson, John	1	1766-1802	A	70
Johnson, John	2	1825-1853	A	110
Johnson, Mathew	1	1818-1830	E	41
Johnston, Abner	2	1825-1853	F	46
Johnston, Thomas	1	1810-1818	D-1	35
Johnston, William	1	1766-1802	A	111
Jones, Abner	2	1825-1853	A	248
Jones, Elizabeth	1	1802-1809	C-1	107
Jones, James	1	1802-1809	C-1	34
Jones, John	1	1810-1818	D-1	7
Jones, Joseph	2	1825-1853	F	23
Jones, Joseph	2	1825-1853	F	140
Keirk, James, see - - - - - - - - - - - - - -			Kirk, James	
Kellett, Joseph	1	1766-1802	A	4
Kellett, William	1	1766-1802	A	81
Kern, Elizabeth	2	1825-1853	F	187
Kevil, Thomas	1	1810-1818	D-1	40
Kierk, James, see - - - - - - - - - - - - - -			Kirk, James	
Kinard, Martin	2	1825-1853	A	276
Kinmon, James	1	1810-1818	D-1	129
Kirk, James	1	1766-1802	A	129
Kirkpatrick, Alexander	2	1825-1853	F	173
Knight, Ephriam	2	1825-1853	F	28
Langston, Soloman	1	1818-1830	E	142
Leake, Jeremiah	2	1825-1853	A	262
Leake, William	1	1810-1818	D-1	81
Leek, George	1	1818-1830	E	25
Leeman, Samuel	1	1818-1830	E	65

Leonard, John	1	1818-1830	E	92
Lewis, Elimor	1	1766-1802	A	27
Ligon, Susana	2	1825-1853	F	59
Ligon, William	2	1825-1853	A	204
Lindley, Thomas	1	1810-1818	D-1	1
Little, Charles (Planter)	2	1825-1853	F	146
Little, David	1	1810-1818	D-1	27
Little, David	2	1825-1853	A	229
Little, James	1	1802-1809	C-1	94
Logan, David	1	1766-1802	A	14
Long, Elizabeth	2	1825-1853	F	149
Long, Robert	1	1818-1830	E	147
Lowe, William (Sr.)	2	1825-1853	A	37
McCain, James	1	1766-1802	A	3
McCarley, Thomas	2	1825-1853	A	10
McCellar, Bridget	1	1810-1818	D-1	116
McClintock, John	1	1802-1809	C-1	19
McClure, William	1	1818-1830	E	70
McClurken, James	2	1825-1853	F	129
McConehy, Samuel	1	1818-1830	E	4
McCrady, William	2	1825-1853	F	19
McCrary, George	2	1825-1853	A	138
McCrary, Thomas	1	1766-1802	A	61
McCurley, John	2	1825-1853	F	5
McDaniel, Archibald	2	1825-1853	F	1
McDowell, Benjamin	1	1766-1802	A	31
McDowell, James	1	1810-1818	D-1	50
McDowell, James	2	1825-1853	A	270
McGin, Daniel	1	1802-1809	C-1	71
McGown, John	2	1825-1853	F	184
McGowing, Mary	2	1825-1853	F	108
McKelvey, John (Planter)	2	1825-1853	F	40
McKitrick, George	2	1825-1853	A	91
McKnight, Andrew (Sr.)	1	1766-1802	A	16
McMurtry, William	1	1802-1809	C-1	90
McNeer, Robert	2	1825-1853	A	1
McNees, Sally	2	1825-1853	A	253
McTeer, Frances	1	1802-1809	C-1	23
McTeer, William	1	1766-1802	A	133
McWilliams, Alexander	1	1810-1818	D-1	33
McWillians, Samuel	2	1825-1853	A	102
Madden, George	2	1825-1853	A	97
Madden, John	1	1766-1802	A	87
Madden, William	2	1825-1853	A	173
Mahaffey, Hugh	2	1825-1853	A	158
Mahaffey, Martin (Sr.)	1	1766-1802	A	58
Mahaffey, Nancy	2	1825-1853	F	170
Manley, John	1	1802-1809	C-1	101
Manley, William	1	1766-1802	A	139
Martin, David	2	1825-1853	A	114
Martin, Edward	2	1825-1853	A	133
Martin, Mary	2	1825-1853	A	119
Martin, Reuben	1	1810-1818	D-1	19
Mason, David	2	1825-1853	F	90
Mathews, John	2	1825-1853	F	17
Mayers, John	2	1825-1853	F	86
Mayhon, Joseph	1	1818-1830	E	13

Meadors, James	1	1802-1809	C-1	36
Meadows, Mary	2	1825-1853	F	56
Meadows, Reuben	2	1825-1853	F	92
Meadows, Susana	2	1825-1853	E	20
Medley, Edward	1	1818-1830	E	69
Meek, John	1	1802-1809	C-1	17
Meredith, Henry	2	1825-1853	A	67
Middleton, Ainsworth	1	1766-1802	A	79
Middleton, Jane	2	1825-1853	F	48
Milam, John	2	1825-1853	A	299
Miller, Hance	1	1766-1802	A	6
Miller, John	2	1825-1853	A	142
Miller, Martin	2	1825-1853	F	61
Miller, Sarah	2	1825-1853	F	71
Millwee, William	1	1766-1802	A	7
Milner, Richard	1	1810-1818	D-1	18
Mims, John	2	1825-1853	F	168
Mitchell, Judith	2	1825-1853	F	26
Mitchell, William	1	1802-1809	C-1	76
Moats, Johnathan, see - - - - - - - - - - - -			Motes, Johnathan	
Monro, John	1	1818-1830	E	57
Monroe, Jane	2	1825-1853	A	154
Monroe, Larkin S.	2	1825-1853	A	178
Montgomery, James	1	1766-1802	A	53
Moore, James	1	1802-1809	C-1	62
Morrison, Alexander	1	1810-1818	D-1	82
Mosely, George (Sr.)	1	1818-1830	E	111
Motes, Jessee (Sr.)	2	1825-1853	F	51
Motes, Johnathan	2	1825-1853	A	121
Munford, Hugh	1	1802-1809	C-1	77
Musgrove, Edward	1	1766-1802	A	32
Neil, Hugh, see - - - - - - - - - - - - - - -			Oneall, Hugh	
Neely, George	1	1766-1802	A	68
Neely, James (Sr.)	2	1825-1853	F	157
Neely, Joseph	2	1825-1853	F	99
Neely, Nancy	2	1825-1853	A	170
Nesbett, Samuel	1	1818-1830	E	120
Newport, Jane	1	1810-1818	D-1	48
Nichols, Nathaniel	1	1802-1809	C-1	31
Nickel, Chartis	2	1825-1853	F	21
Nickels, John (Dr.)	2	1825-1853	A	196
Nickels, Nathaniel, see - - - - - - - - - - -			Nichols, Nathaniel	
Norris, Thomas	2	1825-1853	F	175
Nugent, William	2	1825-1853	A	55
O'Dell, John	2	1825-1853	F	101
O'Dell, Rachel	2	1825-1853	A	112
ONeal, Ann Jane	1	1802-1809	D-1	135
ONeal, John	1	1802-1809	C-1	45
Oneall, Hugh	1	1766-1802	A	144
Osborne, Daniel	2	1825-1853	F	7
Osborne, John	2	1825-1853	A	148
Osborne, William	1	1810-1818	D-1	105
Overly, Meshack	1	1810-1818	D-1	89
Owens, Daniel	1	1810-1818	D-1	9
Owens, John	1	1802-1809	C-1	81
Owens, John	1	1810-1818	D-1	112
Owing, Pressley	2	1825-1853	A	113

, Rachel	2	1825-1853	A	4
, Richard	2	1825-1853	F	193
~~Owings~~, Richard M.	1	1810-1818	D-1	80
Owings, Thomas	1	1766-1802	A	137
Page, John	1	1802-1809	C-1	27
Park, Agnes	2	1825-1853	A	107
Park, Andrew	1	1802-1809	C-1	118
Park, James	1	1818-1830	E	144
Parks, Charles (Sr.)	2	1825-1853	F	186
Pasley, Robert	1	1810-1818	D-1	133
Patterson, Joseph	1	1818-1818	E	109
Pearson, Joel O.	2	1825-1853	F	105
Perrett, Alfred	2	1825-1853	A	99
Peterson, James	1	1766-1802	A	132
Pinson, Aaron	1	1766-1802	A	97
Pinson, John (Planter)	1	1810-1818	D-1	11
Pinson, M. D.	2	1825-1853	A	212
Pinson, Marmeduke	1	1818-1830	E	42
Pitts, Milton	2	1825-1853	A	105
Pollard, William	1	1810-1818	D-1	119
Pollock, James	1	1766-1802	A	73
Pool, Elizabeth	2	1825-1853	A	192
Potter, Thomas G.	2	1825-1853	A	266
Powell, Samuel	1	1818-1830	E	119
Powell, Thomas (Sr.)	2	1825-1853	F	190
Powell, William	1	1810-1818	D-1	102
Prater, Ann	2	1825-1853	F	194
Prather, Josiah	1	1818-1830	E	100
Prather, William	1	1766-1802	A	13
Puckett, James	1	1766-1802	A	125
Pugh, John	1	1810-1818	D-1	55
Pugh, Richard	1	1766-1802	A	90
Pyles, Abner	2	1825-1853	A	156
Pyles, Hewlitt	2	1825-1853	A	24
Ragadale, Edmond	2	1825-1853	A	257
Reafs, Nancy	1	1802-1809	C-1	104
Reed, David	1	1810-1818	D-1	70
Reed, Mary	2	1825-1853	F	137
Reeder, Simon	1	1818-1830	E	98
Rees, Nancy, see - - - - - - - - - - - - - - -			Reafs, Nancy	
Richey, John (Sr.)	1	1766-1802	A	23
Richey, John (Sr.)	1	1818-1830	E	19
Riddle, John	2	1825-1853	A	272
Ritchey, John, see - - - - - - - - - - - - - -			Richey, John	
Roberson, John	1	1766-1802	A	164
Roberts, Jacob	1	1802-1809	C-1	68
Roberts, James	1	1766-1802	A	147
Roberts, James	1	1810-1818	D-1	92
Robertson, Manoah	2	1825-1853	A	109
Robertson, Manoah	2	1825-1853	A	109
Robirson, William	1	1810-1818	D-1	15
Rodgers, Andrew	1	1818-1830	E	62
Rodgers, John	2	1825-1853	F	63
Rodgers, Sara	2	1825-1853	F	161
Rook, William (Sr.)	2	1825-1853	A	203
Ross, Catherine	2	1825-1853	F	31
Rowland, Christopher	1	1766-1802	A	92
Rowland, Henery B.	2	1825-1853	F	131

Runnold, Joseph	1	1810–1818	D-1	96
Rusing, Aquilla	1	1802–1809	C-1	49
Rutledge, William	1	1818–1830	E	77
Rutledge, William	1	1818–1830	E	87
Saddler, John	1	1818–1830	E	21
Satterwhite, Mary	1	1818–1830	E	128
Saxon, Charles	1	1810–1818	D-1	97
Saxon, Hugh	2	1825–1853	A	219
Seurlock, Ann	1	1766–1802	A	99
Seillion, Hugh (Farmer)	1	1810–1818	D-1	91
Shea, Patrick P.	1	1818–1818	D-1	120
Shears, Jude	2	1825–1853	F	114
Simmons, Charles	1	1766–1802	A	47
Simmons, Elizabeth	1	1818–1830	E	96
Simpson, Alexander	1	1810–1818	D-1	46
Simpson, John (Merchant)	1	1810–1818	D-1	63
Simpson, John	2	1825–1853	A	177
Sims, Charles	1	1810–1818	D-1	37
Sims, Francis	2	1825–1853	A	201
Sims, William	1	1802–1809	C-1	53
Smith, Drury	1	1766–1802	A	113
Smith, John	1	1810–1818	D-1	87
Smith, Lucy	2	1825–1853	F	97
Smith, Robert	1	1810–1818	D-1	131
Smith, Willimm R.	2	1825–1853	A	298
South, William	2	1825–1853	A	76
Speirs, William (Sr.)	2	1825–1853	A	169
Starnes, Ann	1	1802–1809	C-1	3
Starnes, Ebenezer	1	1766–1802	A	29
Starnes, Mary Ann	2	1825–1853	A	295
Stevens, John	1	1766–1802	A	67
Stewart, Francis	2	1825–1853	A	129
Stimson, Enos	1	1766–1802	A	138
Stone, John	1	1766–1802	A	131
Stone, John	2	1825–1853	F	49
Strain, David	2	1825–1853	F	139
Strain, James	1	1810–1818	D-1	29
Stwart, John	1	1802–1809	C-1	70
Sula, William	2	1825–1853	A	11
Sullivan, Joseph	2	1825–1853	A	181
Sutherland, Joshua	1	1766–1802	A	159
Swan, Timothy	1	1810–1818	D-1	99
Swindler, Michael	1	1810–1818	D-1	59
Tanney, John	1	1766–1802	A	122
Taylor, Alexander	1	1818–1830	E	73
Taylor, James	2	1825–1853	A	57
Taylor, John	1	1818–1830	E	8
Taylor, John	2	1825–1853	F	177
Taylor, Margarett	2	1825–1853	F	106
Taylor, Martha	2	1825–1853	A	56
Taylor, Robert	2	1825–1853	A	216
Taylor, Robert	2	1825–1853	A	223
Taylor, Samuel	2	1825–1853	A	26
Teague, Elijah (Sr.)	2	1825–1853	F	15
Teague, Joshua	1	1802–1809	C-1	92
Templeton, David (Sr.)	1	1810–1818	D-1	114

Thomas, Isaac	1	1802-1809	C-1	47
Thomason, Nancy	2	1825-1853	A	274
Thompson, Henry	2	1825-1853	F	185
Thompson, William	2	1825-1853	A	2
Thompson, see, also, - - - - - - - - - - - - -			Tompson	
Threett, Sarah	1	1818-1830	E	18
Tinsley, Abraham	1	1810-1818	D-1	3
Tinsley, Cornelius	1	1810-1818	D-1	125
Tinsley, Zachariah	2	1825-1853	F	115
Todd, Andrew	2	1825-1853	A	43
Todd, John	1	1818-1830	E	56
Todd, Patrick	2	1825-1853	A	231
Todd, Samuel	1	1818-1830	E	137
Todd, S. T. H.	2	1825-1853	A	93
Tompson, William	2	1825-1853	F	57
Tompson, William	2	1825-1853	F	58
Tompson, see, also, - - - - - - - - - - - - -			Thompson	
Tucker, Lavena	2	1825-1853	A	283
Turk, Mary	1	1766-1802	A	123
Turk, Rachel	1	1766-1802	A	101
Underwood, James	1	1818-1830	E	106
Vance, Mary	2	1825-1853	A	15
Vaughan, Claiborn	1	1818-1830	E	14
Vaughan, Walter P.	2	1825-1853	F	72
Walker, Elizabeth M.	2	1825-1853	A	68
Walker, Ketural	2	1825-1853	A	106
Walker, Moses	1	1766-1802	A	38
Watkins, Charles	1	1810-1818	D-1	128
Watts, James	2	1825-1853	A	52
Watts, John	1	1810-1818	D-1	21
Watts, Nancy C.	2	1825-1853	A	103
Wells, Aron	1	1802-1809	C-1	74
Wells, Elsha	1	1818-1830	E	27
Wesson, John	1	1802-1809	C-1	48
White, James	1	1810-1818	D-1	113
Whitehead, William	1	1802-1809	C-1	55
Whitmore, Joseph	1	1802-1809	C-1	37
Whitten, John	2	1825-1853	F	148
Whitworth, Cinthea	2	1825-1853	A	167
Wilks, Whitehead	2	1825-1853	A	194
Willard, John	1	1810-1818	D-1	101
Williams, David	2	1825-1853	A	245
Williams, James A.	1	1810-1818	D-1	71
Williams, Mary	2	1825-1853	F	65
Williamson, Agnes	2	1825-1853	A	144
Williamson, Elisha	2	1825-1853	A	237
Williamson, Jane	2	1825-1853	A	46
Witson, Benjamin	1	1810-1818	D-1	57
Witson, Charles	1	1818-1830	E	32
Witson, John	1	1766-1802	A	141
Witson, John	2	1825-1853	F	13
Wolf, George	1	1810-1818	D-1	75
Wolff, John F.	1	1818-1830	E	52
Wolff, Mary	2	1825-1853	A	95
Wood, Joseph	1	1810-1818	D-1	123
Word, Robert	2	1825-1853	F	109

Wright, Samuel	1	1802-1809	C-1	105
Young, Abner	2	1825-1853	F	180
Young, George (Sr.)	2	1825-1853	F	182
Young, James	1	1766-1802	A	100
Young, James	1	1802-1809	C-1	87
Young, James	1	1818-1830	F	124
Young, Joseph	2	1825-1853	F	77
Young, Robert	1	1818-1830	E	131
Young, William	2	1825-1853	F	34

Copied by:

/s/   Mrs. John D. Rogers

Mrs. John D. Rogers

INDEX TO

MARION COUNTY WILLS

VOLUME NO. 1
1796-1855

This index is compiled from W.P.A. copies of
wills filed in the COUNTY PROBATE COURTS.
The volumes indexed are a part of the
South Carolina Collection of the
University of South Carolina
Library.

Columbia, S. C.
1939

Name	Vol.	Date	Page
Allen, Bennet	1	1796-1855	146
Allen, Mathew	1	1796-1855	177
Anderson, Silas S.	2	1796-1855	75
Arrington, Benjamin (Sr.)	1	1796-1855	66
Avant, Abraham	1	1796-1855	181
Avant, Ebenezer, see -			Avant, Abraham
Ayres, Darius	1	1796-1855	316
Baker, John	2	1796-1855	140
Bailey, William, see - - - - - - - - - - - - - - - - - - -			Baley, William
Baley, William	1	1796-1855	309
Ballard, Benjamin Port	1	1796-1855	45
Ballard, Rachel	1	1796-1855	47
Barnes, Elias	2	1796-1855	8
Barrows, Benjamin P. (Planter)	1	1796-1855	45
Bartell, Mary	1	1796-1855	256
Bartell, Philip	2	1796-1855	94
Bass, Right	1	1796-1855	137
Bass, Wright, see -			Bass, Right
Beckwith, Henry	1	1796-1855	153
Bellune, James C.	1	1796-1855	293
Benson, John	1	1796-1855	266
Berry, Eli	1	1796-1855	304
Bethea, John	1	1796-1855	163
Bethea, Phillip	1	1796-1855	102
Bethea, William	1	1796-1855	202
Bethea, William	1	1796-1855	317
Bigham, James	1	1796-1855	108
Bigham, John	2	1796-1855	19
Bird, Arthur	1	1796-1855	289
Bird, Elisabeth	2	1796-1855	52
Broddy, Martha	2	1796-1855	129
Britton, Stephen (Planter)	1	1796-1855	87
Britton, William	1	1796-1855	11
Brown, Ann	2	1796-1855	9
Brown, Edward	1	1796-1855	298
Brown, Jeremiah	1	1796-1855	218
Brown, Samuel	1	1796-1855	39
Bryant, Jesse	1	1796-1855	213
Burch, Joseph	1	1796-1855	13
Burkett, Thomas	1	1796-1855	170
Burnett, John	1	1796-1855	100
Burnett, John	1	1796-1855	133
Campbell, Apsley	2	1796-1855	137
Campbell, James	1	1796-1855	267
Campbell, Peter	1	1796-1855	214
Carter, Josiah	1	1796-1855	71
Carter, Stephen	1	1796-1855	210
Clark, Joseph (Planter)	1	1796-1855	311
Coleman, John	2	1796-1855	143
Collins, J onah	2	1796-1855	142
Cooper, Elizabeth S.	2	1796-1855	84
Coward, John	1	1796-1855	287

Coward, Wilson	2	1796-1855	101
Cox, Ann	2	1796-1855	82
Cox, Herbert	2	1796-1855	105
Coxe, Judith	1	1796-1855	139
Crawford, James	1	1796-1855	120
Crawford, James	1	1796-1855	166
Crawford, James G.	2	1796-1855	46
Creel, James	1	1796-1855	207
Cribb, John C.	2	1796-1855	109
Daniel, Ezekiel	2	1796-1855	71
Davis, Benjamin	1	1796-1855	29
Davis, Francis	1	1796-1855	295
Davis, Hannah	1	1796-1855	272
Davis, James (Planter)	1	1796-1855	224
Davis, Joseph	1	1796-1855	258
Davis, Phillip F. (Planter)	1	1796-1855	271
Davis, William	1	1796-1855	246
Davis, William	1	1796-1855	270
Dees, Arthur	1	1796-1855	275
Dees, Malakiah	1	1796-1855	239
Dennis, Joshua	1	1796-1855	234
Dew, Christopher (Sr.)	1	1796-1855	182
Dewitt, Thomas	1	1796-1855	75
Donnelly, Ann W.	2	1796-1855	33
Doudge, Tully (Planter)	1	1796-1855	44
Dozer, John	1	1796-1855	51
Dozier, Ann	1	1796-1855	157
Dozier, Leonard	1	1796-1855	73
Dozier, Tully	1	1796-1855	44
Drew, Thomas	1	1796-1855	98
Edwards, Samuel	1	1796-1855	105
Evans, Nathan	1	1796-1855	69
Exum, Benjamin	1	1796-1855	208
Exum, Richard	1	1796-1855	242
Exum, William	1	1796-1855	273
Finklea, John (Jr.)	1	1796-1855	125
Flowers, Nathan	1	1796-1855	257
Ford, Preserved	1	1796-1855	221
Fore, Joel	2	1796-1855	158
Fore, Judith	1	1796-1855	176
Foxworth, James	1	1796-1855	7
Foxworth, Job	1	1796-1855	59
Foxworth, Mary	2	1796-1855	10
Gaddy, Allen	2	1796-1855	146
Gaddy, Ithamar	2	1796-1855	103
Gaddy, William	2	1796-1855	96
Gasque, Henry	2	1796-1855	126
Gibson, John C.	2	1796-1855	100
Gibson, Jordan (Farmer)	1	1796-1855	4
Godbold, Thomas	1	1796-1855	141
Godbold, Thomas	1	1796-1855	296
Gordon, Roger	2	1796-1855	92
Gourley, Joseph	1	1796-1855	253

ives, John	1	1796-1855	54
aves, Joseph	1	1796-1855	225
Greaves, William Henry	1	1796-1855	291
Greaves, John	1	1796-1855	54
Gregg, James	1	1796-1855	21
Gregg, John	1	1796-1855	312
Gregg, Joseph	1	1796-1855	160
Gregg, Mary	2	1796-1855	125
Gregg, Richard (Planter)	1	1796-1855	94
Gregg, Richard	1	1796-1855	288
Gregg, William	1	1796-1855	6
Gregg, William (Sr.)	1	1796-1855	112
Grice, James	1	1796-1855	310
Grice, William	1	1796-1855	152
Griggs, William (Planter)	1	1796-1855	6
Harllee, Thomas (Sr.)	1	1796-1855	191
Harralson, Benjamin (Sr.)	1	1796-1855	23
Harrell, James	1	1796-1855	180
Harrell, Lewis	1	1796-1855	196
Harrelson, Jeremiah	1	1796-1855	274
Harrelson, Jeremiah	1	1796-1855	274
Harrelson, Lewis	1	1796-1855	277
Haselden, William	1	1796-1855	79
Hatchell, John	2	1796-1855	151
Hays, Benjamin	1	1796-1855	264
Henagan, B. K.	2	1796-1855	148
Herring, Arthur	2	1796-1855	50
Hinds, Asia	2	1796-1855	139
Hinds, Restor	2	1796-1855	62
Hinds, Richard (Planter)	1	1796-1855	122
Hodges, Moses (Sr.)	1	1796-1855	278
Hodges, Richard	1	1796-1855	118
Hodges, Samuel (Dr.)	2	1796-1855	1
Holland, James	1	1796-1855	275
Hooks, Dempcy	1	1796-1855	58
Howard, Richard	1	1796-1855	229
Hudson, James	1	1796-1855	77
Hyman, Eaton	1	1796-1855	140
Jackson, Owen	2	1796-1855	145
Johnson, Andrew F. (Atty.)	1	1796-1855	283
Johnson, Andrew F. (Atty.)	1	1796-1855	285
Johnson, James C.	1	1796-1855	135
Jolly, Joseph	1	1796-1855	37
Jolly, Joseph A.	2	1796-1855	112
Jones, Bryant	2	1796-1855	90
Jones, David	1	1796-1855	315
Jones, Frederick	1	1796-1855	147
Jordon, John	1	1796-1855	155
Keen, James	1	1796-1855	119
Keith, Sariann	1	1796-1855	107
Kerby, Archibald	2	1796-1855	31
Kiff, James	1	1796-1855	119
Kilburn, Samuel (Dr.)	1	1796-1855	76
Kirby, Archibald D. J.	2	1796-1855	31
Kirton, Philip (Sr.)	1	1796-1855	302

Lewis, James	1	1796-1855	132
Lewis, Jonathan	2	1796-1855	64
MacArthur, Peter	1	1796-1855	235
McBride, Francis	1	1796-1855	255
McCall, Nathaniel S.	2	1796-1855	53
McInnis, Daniel	2	1796-1855	88
McInnis, Malcolm	2	1796-1855	49
McInnis, Neill	1	1796-1855	233
McIntyre, Alexander	2	1796-1855	98
McKay, Donald	1	1796-1855	245
McKay, Flora	1	1796-1855	237
McKimmon, Alexander	2	1796-1855	21
McKinsey, John	1	1796-1855	305
MacLellan, Angus	1	1796-1855	188
McLeod, John B.	1	1796-1855	223
McPherson, Celia	1	1796-1855	280
McQueen, Neal	1	1796-1855	281
McRae, John T. (Sr.)	2	1796-1855	80
MacSwain, Malcolm	1	1796-1855	49
McWhite, Elizabeth	2	1796-1855	40
McWhite, Lewis	2	1796-1855	85
Manning, John	2	1796-1855	73
Manning, Sarah	1	1796-1855	308
Maree, David	1	1796-1855	93
Maree, Penelope	1	1796-1855	279
Martin, Aaron (Sr.)	2	1796-1855	15
Martin, James	1	1796-1855	43
Meggs, John	2	1796-1855	152
Melton, Peter	1	1796-1855	168
Miers, Daniel, see -			Myers, Daniel
Miles, David	2	1796-1855	77
Moody, James	2	1796-1855	110
Moore, Redding	2	1796-1855	66
Moree, David	1	1796-1855	93
Morree, Penelope	1	1796-1855	279
Munnerlyn, Ann	2	1796-1855	60
Myers, Daniel	1	1796-1855	26
Napper, Robert	1	1796-1855	230
O'Cain, William	1	1796-1855	219
Owens, David	1	1796-1855	35
Owens, Edward	1	1796-1855	1
Owens, Ruth	1	1796-1855	41
Owens, Solomon	2	1796-1855	35
Page, Joseph	1	1796-1855	124
Paisley, John (Planter)	1	1796-1855	205
Palmer, David	2	1796-1855	27
Perrit, Joseph	2	1796-1855	11
Phillips, Ann	2	1796-1855	86
Pitman, Amy	2	1796-1855	51
Port, Frances	1	1796-1855	83
Porter, Abijah	1	1796-1855	171

Porter, Charity	2	1796-1855	42
Poston, Ely	2	1796-1855	30
Pritchett, Simon	1	1796-1855	130
Reynolds, Dreadzell	1	1796-1855	64
Rice, John	1	1796-1855	300
Richardson, John	2	1796-1855	25
Roberts, Kezia	1	1796-1855	209
Rogers, Dew	2	1796-1855	116
Rogers, Eli	1	1796-1855	186
Rogers, Lot	1	1796-1855	211
Rogers, Patience	1	1796-1855	174
Rogers, William S.	2	1796-1855	72
Roper, John	2	1796-1855	13
Rowell, William	2	1796-1855	123
Rozar, William	1	1796-1855	173
Rozier, William, see - - - - - - - - - - -		Rozar, William	
Runnals, Dreadzel	1	1796-1855	64
Salmon, Desdamona	2	1796-1855	156
Scarborough, Richard J.	2	1796-1855	136
Shackelford, Francis(Plant.)	1	1796-1855	144
Shackelford, Stephen	1	1796-1855	261
Shackelford, Stephen (Jr.)		1796-1855	286
Shields, James	2	1796-1855	68
Singletary, William G.	2	1796-1855	133
Smith, John	2	1796-1855	4
Smith, John	1	1796-1855	20
Smith, Moses (Planter)	2	1796-1855	38
Smith, William	1	1796-1855	68
Smith, William	2	1796-1855	121
Stackhouse, Celia	2	1796-1855	119
Stackhouse, Isaac	2	1796-1855	153
Stephenson, Elizabeth	1	1796-1855	249
Stephenson, Thomas	1	1796-1855	114
Stone, Austin (Sr.)	1	1796-1855	128
Stone, Daniel	1	1796-1855	243
Stone, Francis	2	1796-1855	17
Summerford, Joshua (Farmer)	1	1796-1855	89
Sweet, Anthony	1	1796-1855	90
Tart, Enos (Sr.)	1	1796-1855	17
Tart, John	1	1796-1855	247
Tart, Nathan J.	2	1796-1855	135
Tease, William	1	1796-1855	117
Thompson, James	1	1796-1855	216
Thompson, Lewis	1	1796-1855	150
Thompson, Stephen	1	1796-1855	126
Timmons, John (Sr.)	1	1796-1855	178
Townsend, William, see - - - - - - - - - -		Townson, William	
Townson, William	2	1796-1855	7
White, Daniel	1	1796-1855	110
White, Darling	1	1796-1855	306
Whittington, Nathaniel (Sr.)	2	1796-1855	108

Wiggins, Baker	1	1796-1855	198
Wiggins, Jesse	1	1796-1855	190
Wiggins, Lewis (Planter)	1	1796-1855	62
Williams, Henry (Sr.)	2	1796-1855	23
Wilson, Robert W.	1	1796-1855	232
Windham, Charles (Planter)	2	1796-1855	12
Witherspoon, John	1	1796-1855	32
Wood, John	1	1796-1855	56
Woodberry, Elizabeth	1	1796-1855	227
Woodberry, Richard	1	1796-1855	81
Woodberry, Richard	1	1796-1855	251
Yelventon, Jacob	1	1796-1855	9
Yelvington, Levi	2	1796-1855	61

Copied by:

/s/ Mrs. John D. Rogers

Mrs. John D. Rogers

INDEX

TO

MARLBORO COUNTY WILLS.

VOLUME NO. 1
1787-1853

This index is compiled from W.P.A. copies of
wills filed in the COUNTY PROBATE COURTS.
The volume indexed are a part of the
South Carolina Collection of the
University of South Carolina
Library.

Columbia, S. C.
1939

Name	Vol.	Date	Section	Page
Ammons, Joshua	1	1787-1853	A	245
Ammons, Thomas	1	1787-1853	A	185
Askew, John	1	1787-1853	A	269
Barrentine, Philip	1	1787-1853	A	379
Bedgegood,Malachi Nicholas	1	1787-1853	A	90
Bennett, William	1	1787-1853	A	103
Bethea, Jesse (Planter)	1	1787-1853	A	84
Billingsly, Catherine	1	1787-1853	A	339
Bingham, Thomas	1	1787-1853	A	45
Blair, Robert (Planter)	1	1787-1853	A	19
Bridges, William	1	1787-1863	A	333
Brigman, Isaac	1	1787-1853	A	82
Brown, Edmond (Planter)	1	1787-1853	A	164
Brown, William	1	1787-1853	A	176
Burn, Absolum	1	1787-1853	A	147
Campbell, John	1	1787-1853	A	314
Campbell, Robert (Capt.)	1	1787-1853	A	153
Carloss, Robertson	1	1787-1853	A	201
Cherry, George	1	1787-1853	A	36
Cochran, Thomas	1	1787-1853	A	133
Colquhoun, Archibald	1	1787-1853	A	219
Colquhoun, Margaret	1	1787-1853	A	61
Cook, James (Planter)	1	1787-1853	A	242
Corgill, Elizabeth	1	1787-1853	A	235
Corgill, Magnus	1	1787-1853	A	72
Cottingham, Charles (Planter)	1	1787-1853	A	183
Cottingham, Jonathan	1	1787-1853	A	186
Cottingham, Sarah	1	1787-1853	A	328
Council, Henry	1	1737-1853	A	282
Council, Jesse	1	1787-1853	A	48
Covington, Henry (Rev.)	1	1787-1853	A	409
Covington, John	1	1787-1853	A	29
Covington, John W.	1	1787-1853	A	74
Covington, Robert	1	1787-1853	A	127
Cranor, Moses	1	1787-1853	A	27
Crosland, Edward	1	1787-1853	A	94
Crosland, Edward	1	1787-1853	A	112
Crosland, Mary A.	1	1787-1853	A	286
David, Elizabeth	1	1787-1853	A	139
David, John H.	1	1787-1853	A	385
Davis, Mary B.	1	1787-1853	A	87
Dixon, Joseph	1	1787-1853	A	369
Douglas, Daniel	1	1787-1853	A	251
Douglas, John	1	1787-1853	A	202
Dunnam, William	1	1787-1853	A	131
Edwards, Mary	1	1787-1853	A	65

Elerbe, William F.	1	1787-1853	A	193
Evans, Elizabeth	1	1787-1853	A	161
Evans, John	1	1787-1853	A	135
Evans, Josiah	1	1787-1853	A	15
Evans, William	1	1787-1853	A	270
Faegin, William G.	1	1787-1853	A	377
Furniss, James (Planter)	1	1787-1853	A	321
Furniss, William	1	1787-1853	A	59
Fuller, Shadrack	1	1787-1853	A	38
Gay, Josiah	1	1787-1853	A	209
Gordon, Mary	1	1787-1853	A	34
Crant, Elizabeth	1	1787-1853	A	394
Hardwick, William (Planter)	1	1787-1853	A	6
Harrington, Eleanor W.	1	1787-1853	A	294
Harrington, James A.	1	1787-1853	A	250
Harrington, Rosanna	1	1787-1853	A	221
Harry, David	1	1787-1853	A	137
Henagan, Barnabas	1	1787-1853	A	191
Henagan, Elizabeth	1	1787-1853	A	364
Hicks, George	1	1787-1853	A	24
Hill, James B.	1	1787-1853	A	152
Hodges, George (Capt.)	1	1787-1853	A	354
Hodges, Henry	1	1787-1853	A	129
Hodges, Sion	1	1787-1853	A	123
Hubbard, John	1	1787-1853	A	336
Huckaby, Thomas	1	1787-1853	A	199
Huggins, Elizabeth	1	1787-1853	A	318
Ivey, James	1	1787-1853	A	162
Ivey, Joseph	1	1787-1853	A	396
James, Thomas A.	1	1787-1853	A	42
John, Jesse	1	1787-1853	A	272
Johnson, Tobius	1	1787-1853	A	365
Joyce, M ichael	1	1787-1853	A	367
Lee, Mason	1	1787-1853	A	101
Leget, James (Sr.)	1	1787-1853	A	283
Lezinby, Stephen	1	1787-1853	A	198
Lide, John	1	1787-1853	A	97
Lide, Thomas (Col.)	1	1787-1853	A	1
Lister, Joseph	1	1787-1853	A	32
Lizenby, Stevin, see - - - - - - - - - - - - -			Lezinby, Stephen	
McColl, David	1	1787-1853	A	76
McColl, Duncan	1	1787-1853	A	64
McColl, Duncan	1	1787-1853	A	148

McColl, Duncan	1	1787-1853	A	347
McColl, Mary	1	1787-1853	A	216
McDaniel, Joseph (Sr.)	1	1787-1853	A	50
McDearmid, Donald	1	1787-1853	A	239
McFarlan, John (Merchant)	1	1787-1853	A	205
McFarlan, Rebecca	1	1787-1853	A	253
McGill, Archibald D.	1	1787-1853	A	378
McIntyre, Archibald	1	1787-1853	A	259
McIntyre, Daniel (Jr.)	1	1787-1853	A	289
McIntyre, Daniel	1	1787-1853	A	338
McKay, John	1	1787-1853	A	224
McKay, Mary	1	1787-1853	A	249
McKay, Sarah	1	1787-1853	A	315
McLaurin, Hugh	1	1787-1853	A	285
McLeod, Elizabeth	1	1787-1853	A	231
McLeod, Isabel	1	1787-1853	A	231
McLucas, John	1	1787-1853	A	237
McLucas, Mary	1	1787-1853	A	383
McLucas, Nancy	1	1787-1853	A	256
McRae, Alexander	1	1787-1853	A	177
McRae, Christian	1	1787-1853	A	389
McRae, Duncan D.	1	1787-1853	A	401
McRae, Roderick (Sr.)	1	1787-1853	A	349
Macy, Joseph (Planter)	1	1787-1853	A	78
Mandeville, Daird	1	1787-1853	A	210
Manship, Aaron	1	1787-1853	A	30
Marlow, James	1	1787-1853	A	70
Maxwell, Joseph	1	1787-1853	A	66
Meekins, Jonathan	1	1787-1853	A	232
Miller, Abner (Planter)	1	1787-1853	A	57
Moor, Frances	1	1787-1853	A	330
Murdock, John	1	1787-1853	A	291
Murdock, John (Jr.)	1	1787-1853	A	298
Neavel, Isaac	1	1787-1853	A	40
Neavel, Rhoda	1	1787-1853	A	150
Neavel, William	1	1787-1853	A	120
Newton, Giles (Planter)	1	1787-1853	A	68
Newton, James (Sr.)	1	1787-1853	A	267
Newton, Pleasant	1	1787-1853	A	407
Parker, Nancy	1	1787-1853	A	384
Parker, Stephen	1	1787-1853	A	168
Pearson, Moses	1	1787-1853	A	43
Pegues, Claudius (Planter)	1	1787-1853	A	8
Pegues, William	1	1787-1853	A	398
Peterkin, Alexander	1	1787-1853	A	228
Peterkin, Elizabeth	1	1787-1853	A	248
Peterkin, James	1	1787-1853	A	372
Peterkin, Jesse	1	1787-1853	A	301
Pledger, William	1	1787-1853	A	188
Pouncey, Anthony (Blanter)	1	1787-1853	A	92
Pouncey, Anthony (Planter)	1	1787-1853	A	106

Pouncey, James (Sr.)	1	1787-1853	A	316
Purnell, Robert (Planter)	1	1787-1853	A	178
Quick, Aquilla (Planter)	1	1787-1853	A	116
Quick, Elisabeth	1	1787-1853	A	241
Quick, George	1	1787-1853	A	218
Quick, Jesse	1	1787-1853	A	303
Quick, Levy	1	1787-1853	A	47
Quick, Sarah	1	1787-1853	A	362
Quick, Thomas	1	1787-1853	A	141
Robertson, Drury	1	1787-1853	A	171
Robeson, Luke	1	1787-1853	A	114
Rogers, Ann S.	1	1787-1853	A	392
Smith, Simon	1	1787-1853	A	390
Smith, William	1	1787-1853	A	107
Stewart, David	1	1787-1853	A	80
Stewart, Donald	1	1787-1853	A	170
Stroud, Elizabeth	1	1787-1853	A	17
Stubbs, Lewis (Sr.)	1	1787-1853	A	304
Stubbs, Thomas (Sr.)	1	1787-1853	A	324
Stubbs, William (Sr.)	1	1787-1853	A	263
Thomas, Caroline	1	1787-1853	A	335
Thomas, Celia	1	1787-1853	A	320
Thomas, Nathan	1	1787-1853	A	290
Thomas, Philip	1	1787-1853	A	262
Thomas, William (Planter)	1	1787-1853	A	274
Thompson, Hugh	1	1787-1853	A	71
Turner, Thomas	1	1787-1853	A	175
Turner, William	1	1787-1853	A	176
Weatherly, Isiah	1	1787-1853	A	329
Weatherly, Job	1	1787-1853	A	214
Whittington, Elizabeth	1	1787-1853	A	62
Whittington, Francis	1	1787-1853	A	118
Wiggins, Sion (Sr.)	1	1787-1853	A	256
Williams, Ann J.	1	1787-1853	A	230
Williams, Mary	1	1787-1853	A	207
Wilson, John (Planter)	1	1787-1853	A	108
Windham, John	1	1787-1853	A	55
Winds, Samuel	1	1787-1853	A	166
Winfield, Joel	1	1787-1853	A	52
Wright, Sarah	1	1787-1853	A	125

Copied by:

/s/   Mrs. John D. Rogers

Mrs. John D. Rogers

INDEX

TO

NEWBERRY COUNTY WILLS.

VOLUME NO. 1
1776-1814

VOLUME NO. 2
1805-1826

VOLUME NO. 3
1823-1840

VOLUME NO. 4
1840-1858

This index is compiled from W.P.A. copies of
Wills filed in the COUNTY PROBATE COURTS.
The volumes indexed are a part of the
South Carolina Collection of the
University of South Carolina
Library.

Columbia, S.C.
1939

Name	Vol.	Date	Section	Page
Abrams, James (Farmer)	4	1840-1858	1	243
Abrams, Mary	3	1823-1840	Loose Will	10
Adams, George	1	1776-1814	D	45
Adams, William	2	1805-1826	F	11
Adams, William	3	1823-1840	L	178
Adkinson, Thomas	3	1823-1840	L	96
Akin, George (Farmer)	2	1805-1826	G	1
Alewine, Thomas	4	1840-1858	2	164
Allen, William	2	1805-1826	E	1
A mos, Clough S.	3	1823-1840	M	86
Anderson, Elizabeth	4	1840-1858	1	263
Anderson, James	3	1823-1840	L	47
Anderson, Jane	4	1840-1858	1	2 49
Anderson, Richard	4	1840-1858	1	134
Anderson, William (Sr.)	1	1776-1814	D	24
Anderson, William	4	1840-1858	1	46
Anderson, William	4	1840-1858	2	314
Andrews, Ephraim	2	1805-1826	I	5
Arnold, John	1	1776-1814	B	51
Ashford, George (Planter)	2	1805-1826	G	3
Ashford, Michael	2	1805-1826	I	22
Atkinson, John (Sr.)	1	1776-1814	B	61
Aubrey, George	2	1805-1826	Loose Will	2
Aull, Harmon	4	1840-1858	2	76
Aulton, James	1	1776-1814	B	55
Babb, Francis	4	1840-1858	2	90
Babb, Mercer	1	1776-1814	B	35
Baird, James	1	1776-1814	B	56
Banskett, Thomas	4	1840-1858	1	55
Barre, Rebecca M.	4	1840-1858	2	8
Bartwisle, Richard	1	1776-1814	A	78
Basket, James	1	1776-1814	B	32
Basket, Daniel	2	1805-1826	H	5
Bates, George	1	1776-1814	D	27
Bates, Henry	2	1805-1826	H	9
Bates, Michael	1	1776-1814	C	40
Beard, John (Farmer)	1	1776-1814	D	29
Bedenbaugh, Adam (Sr.)	3	1823-1840	L	167
Bell, John	1	1776-1814	C	24
Beltz, Andrew	3	1823-1840	L	65
Bickley, John	2	1805-1826	Loose Will	72
Black, John	1	1776-1814	B	25
Blackburn, Stephen	3	1823-1840	L	176
Blackburn, William	2	1805-1826	G	16
Blair, James (Planter)	4	1840-1858	1	223
Blair, John	4	1840-1858	1	227
Blalock , John (Carpenter)	1	1776-1814	A	56
Boazman, David J.	3	1823-1840	L	99
Boazman, John	3	1823-1840	M	6
Bob, Francis	3	1823-1840	N	35
Bobo, John Edward	4	1840-1858	2	255
Bonds, Dudley	2	1805-1826	H	7

Bonds, Louisa C.	4	1840-1858	2	103
Bonds, Nancy (Sr.)	4	1840-1858	2	28
Bonds, Noah	2	1805-1826	H	10
Bonds, Richard (Farmer)	1	1776-1814	A	6
Boozer, David	4	1840-1858	2	6
Boozer, David	4	1840-1858	2	197
Boozer, Frederick	2	1805-1826	F	9
Boozer, Frederick	4	1840-1858	2	194
Boozer, Frederick (Planter)	4	1840-1858	2	258
Boozer, Henry	3	182 3-1840	M	81
Boozer, John	4	1840-1858	2	168
Boozer, Mary	4	1840-1858	2	238
Boulware, Robert R.	2	1805-1826	H	3
Boyce, James	2	1805-1826	E	71
Boyd, Elizabeth	3	1823-1840	Loose will	16
Boyd, Hugh	1	1776-1814	B	57
Boyd, John (Sr.)	3	1823-1840	L	31
Boyd, Matthew	3	1823-1840	M	20
Bradley, James	2	1805-1826	G	81
Braselman, Drusilla	3	1823-1840	M	78
Braselman, Peter (Planter)	2	1805-1826	H	12
Braselman, Thomas P.	3	1823-1840	M	87
Bridges, William	4	1840-1858	2	161
Brooks, David	1	1776-1814	B	59
Brooks, Elisha	1	1776-1814	D	51
Brooks, James	2	1805-1826	G	74
Brooks, Matthews	1	1776-1814	B	5
Brown, Nancy	4	1840-1858	Loose will	14
Brown, R. S.	4	1840-1858	1	11
Brown, Thomas	1	1776-1814	B	12
Browne, George	1	1776-1814	D	74
Buchanan, John (Sr.)	1	1776-1814	A	81
Buchanan, Lucy	4	1840-1858	1	18
Buchanan, Micajah	3	1823-1840	L	116
Bundrick, Agnes	2	1805-1826	H	62
Bundrick, Dav.	2	1805-1826	I	36
Bundrick, Sarah	4	1840-1858	1	19
Burton, Aaron	4	1840-1858	1	211
Burton, John G.	4	1840-1858	1	131
Burton, William (Sr.)	3	1823-1840	L	7
Burton, William	3	1823-1840	Loose will	37
Bushart, Anna Mary	1	1776-1814	A	73
Butler, Benjamin B.	3	1823-1840	L	135
Butler, Henry	2	1805-1826	H	1
Butler, Hetty	4	1840-1858	2	100
Butler, Robert	3	1823-1840	Loose will	9
Butler, William J.	4	1840-1858	1	258
Buzard, Anna Mary, see - - - - - - - - - - - - -			Bushart, Anna Mary	
Buzhardt, Jacob	2	1805-1826	F	69
Buzheart, Mary	3	1823-1840	L	61
Buzzard, Ann Margaret	2	1805-1826	F	70
Buzzard, Calvin S.	4	1840-1858	2	208
Buzzard, Jacob S.	4	1840-1858	2	234
Byerly, Casper (Sr.)	2	1805-1826	E	24
Caldwell, Elen	3	1823-1840	Loose will	3

Caldwell, James	3	1823-1840	Loose will	12
Caldwell, James (Planter)	4	1840-1858	1	230-A
Caldwell, John (Sr.)	1	1776-1814	A	140
Caldwell, John	4	1840-1858	1	125
Caldwell, John	4	1840-1858	2	36
Caldwell, John	4	1840-1858	2	163
Caldwell, Joseph	3	1823-1840	N	40
Caldwell, Nancy	4	1840-1858	2	121
Caldwell, Rebecka	2	1805-1826	G	10
Caldwell, Robert (Sr.)	2	1805-1826	G	7
Caldwell, Robert (Sr.)	2	1805-1826	I	7
Caldwell, Robert	4	1840-1858	2	178
Caldwell, Samuel	3	1823-1840	Loose will	20
Caldwell, William	2	1805-1826	Loose will	41
Calmes, George B.	4	1840-1858	L	93
Calmes, William (Sr.)	3	1823-1840	M	10
Camec, Tabitha	4	1840-1858	2	61
Campbell, Edmund F. (Capt.)	4	1840-1858	1	265
Campbell, Elizabeth (Widow)	2	1805-1826	G	32
Campbell, Joseph	1	1776-1814	A	58
Cannon, David (Sr.)	3	1823-1840	L	11
Cannon, Ephriam	1	1776-1814	D	31
Cannon, Essac	1	1776-1814	D	72
Cannon, John	3	1823-1840	N	52
Cannon, Richard S.	4	1840-1858	1	91
Cannon, Samuel (Planter)	1	1776-1814	A	65
Cannon, Samuel	4	1840-1858	1	261
Carmichael, Robert (Planter)	4	1840-1858	2	244
Carter, John	4	1840-1858	2	240
Carwile, John S.	4	1840-1858	2	81
Cate, Isiah	2	1805-1826	F	40
Cate, Thomas	2	1805-1826	F	73
Cate, Aaron	2	1805-1826	F	6
Chalmers, Alexander (Plant.)	1	1776-1814	A	118
Chalmers, Thomas B.	4	1840-1858	1	57
Chalmers, Wm. (Sr.)	3	1823-1840	M	1
Chambers, Thorogood	2	1805-1826	F	17
Chandler, James	1	1776-1814	D	76
Chandler, Jesse	2	1805-1826	H	68
Chapman, Abraham	1	1776-1814	D	65
Chapman, Giles (Sr.)	2	1805-1826	G	26
Chapman, Mary	4	1840-1858	1	95
Chapman, William (Sr.)	3	1823-1840	N	20
Chappell, John	4	1840-1858	2	204
Chappell, Thomas	2	1805-1826	E	26
Cheuning, Hulda	4	1840-1858	2	188
Chupp, Joseph	4	1840-1858	Loose will	21
Clapp, Joseph	2	1805-1826	Loose will	47
Clark, Catherine	4	1840-1858	2	262
Clark, George	3	1823-1840	M	15
Clark, Thomas (Weaver)	1	1776-1814	A	91
Clarke, John	1	1776-1814	A	109
Clary, John	4	1840-1858	2	97
Cleland, Robert	3	1823-1840	M	44
Cleland, Robert	4	1840-1858	2	180
Clinch, Andrew	4	1840-1858	2	94
Clinch, Andrew	4	1840-1858	2	179
Coat, Thomas (Farmer)	1	1776-1814	C	31

Coate, John	1	1776-1814	D	9
Coate, Mary	3	1823-1840	M	90
Coate, Sarah Anne	3	1823-1840	N	30
Coate, William	2	1805-1826	1	13
Coats, Ann	2	1805-1826	G	9
Coats, John	2	1805-1826	E	11
Coats, Wright	2	1805-1826	G	5
Cobb, Howell,	2	1805-1826	E	23
Cockerill, Sanford	2	1805-1826	G	64
Cohe, Joseph	1	1776-1814	D	69
Cole, Jeanor	2	1805-1826	I	29
Cole, John (Sr.)	2	1805-1826	E	3
Colyer, Benjamin	1	1776-1814	B	14
Conway, Edwin	1	1776-1814	C	72
Conwell, Joseph	2	1805-1826	Loose will	33
Conwill, Sophia	4	1840-1858	1	170
Cooper, Elizabeth	3	1823-1840	Loose will	14
Cooper, William	1	1776-1814	C	29
Coppock, Isaac	2	1805-1826	F	66
Coppock, John (Jr.)	1	1776-1814	C	42
Coppock, Joseph	1	1776-1814	C	58
Coppock, Joseph	2	1805-1826	G	66
Coppock, Martha	1	1776-1814	B	10
Counts, Catherine	2	1805-1826	F	64
Counts, Henry	2	1805-1826	E	50
Counts, Henry	2	1805-1826	F	67
Counts, Jacob	2	1805-1826	F	13
Counts, John	3	1823-1840	N	25
Counts, John	4	1840-1858	1	196
Cox, Allen	3	1823-1830	Loose will	22
Cox, Cornelius	1	1776-1814	A	44
Cox, David	1	1776-1814	A	128
Cox, William	1	1776-1814	D	80
Creighton, Hugh	1	1776-1814	A	104
Crenshaw, Archibald	2	1805-1826	F	68
Crenshaw, Charles	2	1805-1826	Loose will	7
Cromer, Christina	4	1840-1858	1	202
Cromer, David (Sr.)	4	1840-1858	2	269
Cromer, Frederick (Planter)	1	1776-1814	B	49
Cromer, George (Sr.)	2	1805-1826	Loose will	39
Cromer, Hannah	4	1840-1858	1	16
Cromer, John F.	4	1840-1858	2	209
Cromer, John Michael(Planter)	2	1805-1826	F	2
Cromer, Mathais	3	1823-1840	Loose will	11
Cromer, Michael	4	1840-1858	1	152
Crommer, Jacob	3	1823-1840	L	94
Crooks, Jane	4	1840-1858	2	236
Crooks, John	4	1840-1858	1	41
Crosson, David A	3	1823-1840	L	149
Crosson, Jane	4	1840-1858	Loose will	12
Crosswhite, Jacob	3	1823-1840	L	54
Crosswhite, William	3	1823-1840	L	156
Crow, Charles (Sr.)	1	1776-1814	C	58
Crow, Sarah	3	1823-1840	L	148
Crumly, John	1	1776-1814	A	102
Cruston, Hannah	2	1805-1826	G	82
Cruston, Thomas T.	3	1823-1840	L	49

Dalrymple, John	1	1776-1814	B	45
Dalrymple, Thomas	4	1840-1858	1	144
Dalrymple, Thomas W.	4	1840-1858	2	191
Darby, Elizabeth Wells	3	1823-1840	N	45
Darby, John	2	1805-1826	I	43
Daugherty, James (Sr.)	1	1776-1814	A	131
Davenport, Francis (Jr.)	1	1776-1814	B	41
Davenport, John Gillian	4	1840-1858	2	299
Davenport, Jonathan	4	1840-1858	1	52
Davenport, William	3	1823-1840	L	138
Davidson, John	4	1840-1858	1	205
Davidson, John B.	3	1823-1840	L	87
Davidson, Mary Ann	3	1823-1840	L	84
Davidson, Nathaniel	4	1840-1858	2	316
Davis, Mary	1	1776-1814	A	122
Davis, Reason	3	1823-1840	L	158
Davis, Thomas	4	1840-1858	1	59
Dawkins, George (Sr.)	1	1776-1814	A	28
Dawkins, Thomas H.	3	1823-1840	L	92
Dennis, Prudence	4	1840-1858	1	184
Derick, John	2	1805-1826	I	53
Desaker, Catherine	4	1840-1858	2	166
Devenport, Frances	1	1776-1814	D	8
Devenport, Francis (Jr.)	1	1776-1814	B	41
Devinport, Isaac	2	1805-1826	H	16
Devinport, Joseph	1	1776-1814	A	66
Devinport, William	2	1805-1826	H	14
Devlin, Mary	4	1840-1858	2	101
DeWalt, Daniel	1	1776-1814	A	35
DeWalt, Daniel	2	1805-1826	E	37
DeWalt, Daniel	4	1840-1858	2	113
DeWalt, David	3	1823-1840	M	41
DeWalt, Peter	1	1776-1814	A	39
Dial, Jeremiah	2	1805-1826	H	18
Dickert, Michael (Sr.)	2	1805-1826	E	66
Dickson, Mourning	4	1840-1858	1	218
Dobbins, James	3	1823-1840	L	145
Dominick, George	4	1840-1858	1	35
Dominick, Henry (Sr.)	3	1823-1840	M	17
Dominick, Margaret	4	1840-1858	1	96
Dominick, Noah	3	1823-1840	Loose will	19
Downing, John W. (Planter)	4	1840-1858	1	204
Drenan, Robert	1	1776-1814	C	78
Duncan, Amos	2	1805-1826	E	52
Duncan, James	2	1805-1826	F	75
Duncan, Robert	2	1805-1826	H	20
Duckett, Jacob	4	1840-1858	1	192
Duckett, James W.	4	1840-1858	2	265
Duckett, Thomas (Sr.)	2	1805-1826	I	37
Duckett, William (Farmer)	4	1840-1858	2	192
Dugan, George	3	1823-1840	L	53
Dugan, Nancy	4	1840-1858	2	151
Dugan, Robert	2	1805-1826	H	69
Dugan, Thomas	2	1805-1826	I	3
Dunkin, Amos, see - - - - - - - - - - - - - - - - - - - Duncan, Amos				
Dunkin, John	2	1805-1826	E	9
Dunlop, William	1	1776-1814	B	53

Dyson, Abram	3	1825–1840	M	38
Eastland, Thomas	2	1805–1826	F	18
Edens, Abraham	1	1776–1814	C	65
Edwards, Marey (Widow)	2	1805–1826	F	15
Egner, George	3	1825–1840	L	123
Eichleberger, John	3	1825–1840	L	58
Eichleberger, George	1	1776–1814	D	25
Eichleberger, George	1	1776–1814	Loose will	2
Elleman, John	1	1776–1814	D	57
Ellemon, Enos	1	1776–1814	A	22
Elmore, Ridgeway	1	1776–1814	D	20
Elmore, William (Planter)	1	1776–1814	A	87
Enlow, Margaret	4	1840–1858	1	175
Eppes, John	2	1805–1826	I	39
Epps, Daniel	3	1825–1840	M	37
Epps, George F.	4	1840–1858	1	172
Epps, William	4	1840–1858	1	84
Erskin, Margaret	4	1840–1858	1	75
Eutts, Jacob	2	1805–1826	Loose will	54
Eutts, Mary	4	1840–1858	2	224
Fair, William	4	1840–1858	2	41
Farrow, Christian	2	1805–1826	H	21
Farrow, William (Sr.)	1	1776–1814	A	85
Feagle, Laurens	4	1840–1858	1	188
Fear, Samuel	1	1776–1814	C	18
Felker, Jacob	2	1805–1826	C	75
Feller, John	1	1776–1814	C	13
Ferguson, George M.	3	1825–1840	M	58
Fike, George	2	1805–1826	H	57
Finch, Edward	2	1805–1826	I	25
Finlay, James (Planter)	1	1776–1814	A	126
Finlay, Anne (Widow)	1	1776–1814	C	56
Flenigan, Abrilla (Widow)	2	1805–1826	E	72
Floyd, Charles (Jr.)	4	1840–1858	1	187
Floyd, Elizabeth	3	1825–1840	M	24
Floyd, Jefferson	3	1825–1840	Loose will	41
Floyd, Nancy	4	1840–1858	2	199
Folk, John	4	1840–1858	1	120
Folk, John A.	4	1840–1858	2	159
Ford, James (Planter)	1	1776–1814	A	17
Fowler, Elijah	2	1805–1826	Loose will	1
Fowler, Richard	1	1776–1814	B	37
Frean, Thomas	4	1840–1858	2	289
Frey, Jacob	1	1776–1814	C	8
Frick, Thomas (Jr.)	2	1805–1826	Loose will	73
Gaines, Thomas	1	1776–1814	C	27
Galbreath, John	1	1776–1814	D	33
Gallman, George	2	1805–1826	Loose will	4
Gallman, Henry	4	1840–1858	1	139
Gallman, John P.	4	1840–1858	2	80
Gallman, Susannah	4	1840–1858	2	78
Galloway, John	4	1840–1858	1	25
Galloway, Peter	1	1776–1814	A	10
Garner, James (Planter)	4	1840–1858	1	63
Gary, Charles	1	1776–1814	D	77
Gary, David	2	1805–1826	E	73

Gary, Elizabeth	2	1805–1826	E	52
Gary, Elizabeth	4	1840–1858	1	124
Gary, Jacob	3	1823–1840	N	52
Gary, John (Jr.)	1	1776–1814	Loose will	1
Gary, John (Jr.)	1	1776–1814	A	40
Gary, John (Sr.)	2	1805–1826	E	49
Gary, Neomy	4	1840–1858	1	255
Gary, Thomas	1	1776–1814	B	23
Gary, Thomas	1	1776–1814	C	54
Gary, Thomas (Farmer)	2	1805–1826	G	58
Gary, William D.	3	1823–1840	L	132
Gaunt, Israel	1	1776–1814	C	6
Gauntt, Hannah (Widow)	2	1805–1826	Loose will	3
Gilbal, A.	4	1840–1858	1	44
Gilbert, Caleb	2	1805–1826	Loose will	5
Gilbreath, William	1	1776–1814	A	105
Gilder, James L.	4	1840–1858	2	124
Gillam, Jemima, see			Gilliam, Jemima	
Gillam, John	1	1776–1814	C	35
Gilliam, Frances (Planter)	4	1840–1858	Loose will	16
Gilliam, Jemima (Widow)	2	1805–1826	G	12
Gilliam, Robert	1	1776–1814	A	142
Gilliam, Robert	1	1776–1814	B	77
Gilliam, William	1	1776–1814	A	42
Gilliam, William (Planter)	2	1805–1826	I	9
Glasgow, James (Planter)	1	1776–1814	A	89
Glasgow, James	3	1823–1840	L	122
Glasgow, Mary	2	1805–1826	H	74
Glasgow, Mary	3	1823–1840	N	1
Glen, John O.	1	1776–1814	A	8
Glenn, David B.	3	1823–1840	M	3
Glenn, Naomi	4	1840–1858	1	90
Glenn, Rosanna	3	1823–1840	L	1
Goggans, George	2	1805–1826	F	1
Golden, William	4	1840–1858	2	293
Golding, Polly	4	1840–1858	Loose will	1
Golding, Reuben	3	1823–1840	L	110
Golding, Robert (Jr.)	2	1805–1826	I	48
Golding, Robert	3	1823–1840	L	74
Goodman, Timothy	1	1776–1814	C	63
Goodman, Walter	3	1823–1840	L	57
Gordan, Eli (Sr.)	4	1840–1858	1	199
Gordan, Jane	1	1776–1814	B	17
Gore, Edward	2	1805–1826	I	17
Goree, John	3	1823–1840	L	46
Goree, Martin	4	1840–1858	Loose will	4
Goree, Micajah	4	1840–1858	2	299
Gorey, John (Sr.)	1	1776–1814	A	116
Gorre, Daniel	1	1776–1814	C	51
Gorrie, William (Planter)	1	1776–1814	C	47
Grant, Isaac	2	1805–1826	Loose will	56
Grasty, Thomas	1	1776–1814	A	46
Gray, George	1	1776–1814	A	137
Gray, George (Sr.)	3	1823–1840	L	16
Gray, Jacob	1	1776–1814	A	79
Gray, Peter	4	1840–1858	1	114
Green, John	1	1776–1814	A	70
Green, Thomas	1	1776–1814	A	5
Gregg, Elizabeth (Widow)	2	1805–1826	G	68

Griffin, Anne	2	1805–1826	E	80
Griffin, Charles	2	1805–1826	H	53
Griffin, Christopher	3	1823–1840	L	125
Griffin, John	1	1776–1814	B	19
Griffin, John	2	1805–1826	E	76
Griffin, Reubin	3	1823–1840	L	69
Griffith, Isaac	4	1840–1958	1	13
Griffith, Joshua (Sr.)	1	1776–1814	B	18
Griffith, Joshua	2	1805–1826	E	16
Grigsby, John	2	1805–1826	G	57
Gruber, Mary Katherine	3	1823–1840	N	46
Hair, Mathais	2	1805–1826	F	78
Haire, Peter (Planter)	1	1776–1814	A	75
Haley, Thomas	4	1840–1858	Loose will	11
Halfacre, Henry	3	1823–1840	L	78
Halfacre, Jacob	1	1776–1814	A	133
Hall, Matthews	2	1805–1826	G	79
Hampton, Benjamin	2	1805–1826	H	32
Harbert, George	2	1805–1826	H	23
Hardy, John W.	2	1805–1826	H	29
Hardy, Thomas	2	1805–1826	H	76
Hardy, Thomas	2	1805–1826	Loose will	35
Harmon, David	4	1840–1858	1	128
Harmon, John (Planter)	1	1776–1814	A	96
Harmon, John	4	1840–1858	2	87
Harmon, William	1	1776–1814	D	58
Harmon, William	4	1840–1858	1	86
Harress, Abraham	2	1805–1826	G	50
Harris, Nathaniel	1	1776–1814	A	20
Harriss, Micajah	2	1805–1826	E	69
Harriss, Sarah	2	1805–1826	G	22
Hatcher, Seth	2	1805–1826	Loose will	10
Hatton, David	4	1840–1858	1	61
Hatton, John	4	1840–1858	Loose will	2
Hawkins, Mark	4	1840–1858	2	276
Hawkins, Peter (Sr.) (Planter)	1	1776–1814	C	48
Hayes, John	4	1840–1858	1	252
Haynie, Maximilian	2	1805–1826	E	78
Haynie, William	1	1776–1814	C	44
Hays, James (Farmer)	1	1776–1814	C	1
Heaton, Benjamin	1	1776–1814	A	63
Heller, Jacob	3	1823–1840	N	54
Henderson, David (Planter)	2	1805–1826	E	34
Henderson, David Watland	2	1805–1826	F	23
Henderson, John	2	1805–1826	F	21
Henderson, Mary	4	1840–1858	2	31
Henderson, Thomas H.	4	1840–1858	2	253
Henry, James	4	1840–1858	1	158
Henry, John	3	1823–1840	Loose will	8
Henry, Nancy	3	1823–1840	Loose will	24
Henry, William (Haberdasher)	1	1776–1814	B	4
Hentz, David	4	1840–1858	2	9
Herbert, Ann	2	1805–1826	I	42
Herbert, Walter	4	1840–1858	2	39
Herbert, William B.	3	1823–1840	N	43
Herndon, Benjamin (Sr.)	2	1805–1826	G	51
Hewet, Jacob	2	1805–1826	H	24

Higgins, Francis	2	1805-1826	I	18
Hilbarn, Levi	3	1825-1840	L	35
Hilburn, Israel	3	1825-1840	M	75
Hill, David	3	1825-1840	M	5
Hill, Joseph	3	1825-1840	N	56
Hinson, John K.	4	1840-1858	2	155
Hipp, George (Sr.)	4	1840-1858	2	156
Hipp, John	1	1776-1814	C	56
Hipp, John (Sr.)	4	1840-1858	1	255
Hodges, James	1	1776-1814	A	5
Hogg, Mildred T.	4	1840-1858	2	307
Hogg, Sarah	4	1840-1858	2	75
Hogg, Zachariah	2	1805-1826	H	27
Holloway, John	4	1840-1858	1	158
Hord, James	1	1776-1814	B	20
Hough, Martin	2	1805-1826	G	41
Howe, James	2	1805-1826	H	34
Hughens, Samuel	2	1805-1826	H	30
Hume, David	4	1840-1858	1	181
Hunt, Elizabeth	1	1776-1814	B	47
Hunter, James	2	1805-1826	F	25
Hunter, Joseph	4	1840-1858	1	258
Hunter, Nathan (Sr.)	3	1825-1840	L	66
Hunter, Nathan	4	1840-1858	2	147
Hunter, William	4	1840-1858	2	85
Huston, Mary (Widow)	2	1805-1826	E	64
Hutchinson, Alexander (Hatter)	1	1776-1814	C	52
Inman, Benjamin	1	1776-1814	B	69
Inman, Jehu	1	1776-1814	D	11
Inman, Joshua (Sr.)	2	1805-1826	H	35
Irby, Francis	1	1776-1814	B	59
James, John	1	1776-1814	D	63
Jay, William	1	1776-1814	B	26
Johnson, Aaron	4	1840-1858	2	105
Johnson, Daniel C.	3	1825-1840	Loose will	42
Johnson, Joseph	3	1825-1840	L	25
Johnston, Alexander (Plant.)	2	1805-1826	F	27
Johnston, John	1	1776-1814	B	29
Johnston, John (Sr.)(Plant.)	1	1776-1814	C	2
Johnston, John	1	1776-1814	C	59
Johnston, William (Planter)	1	1776-1814	D	13
Johnston, Winiford	2	1805-1826	H	36
Jones, John	4	1840-1858	2	153
Jones, Joseph	2	1805-1826	F	76
Jones, Joshua (Farmer)	1	1776-1814	D	43
Keer, John A.	3	1825-1840	L	134
Keller, Jacob	4	1840-1858	1	69
Kelley, John (Sr.)	2	1805-1826	G	45
Kelley, John	4	1840-1858	1	67
Kelley, Hannah	2	1805-1826	G	46
Kelley, John	1	1776-1814	A	61
Kelley, Joseph	1	1776-1814	B	7
Kelley, Mary	1	1776-1814	B	48
Kelley, Robert	4	1840-1858	1	33
Kelley, Samuel (Sr.)	1	1776-1814	Loose will	6
Kelley, William	1	1776-1814	B	40

Kenner, James L.	4	1840-1858	1	180
Kenner, Samuel E.	4	1840-1858	1	102
Kesler, Henry (Planter)	1	1776-1814	C	69
Kibler, Nancy (Widow)	3	1823-1840	M	59
Kibler, William	4	1840-1858	2	189
Kilgore, Rhoda W.	4	1840-1858	2	248
Kinard, Andrew	4	1840-1858	2	28
Kinard, George (Sr.)	3	1823-1840	Loose will	25
Kinard, George	4	1840-1858	1	182
Kinard, John (Planter)	1	1776-1814	D	70
Kinard, John Michael	4	1840-1858	1	71
Kinard, Martin (Sr.)	4	1840-1858	1	173
Kinard, Michael (Sr.)	3	1823-1840	N	54
King, Charles	1	1776-1814	A	57
King, Ethelred	2	1805-1826	I	44
Kirk, Rebecca (Widow)	3	1823-1840	M	73
Koon, David	4	1840-1858	2	157
Koon, George	4	1840-1858	1	259
Koon, George A.	2	1805-1826	H	50
Koon, Henry	2	1805-1826	F	29
Koon, John	4	1840-1858	1	207
Krommer, John Michael, see — — — — — — — — — — — Cromer, John Michael				
Lake, Elijah	2	1805-1826	Loose will	53
Lake, Elijah	4	1840-1858	2	3
Lake, Enoch	4	1840-1858	1	190
Lake, John	3	1823-1840	L	151
Lake, Thomas	2	1805-1826	Loose will	12
Lake, Thomas	4	1840-1858	2	144
Landers, Michael	1	1776-1814	D	7
Lane, Mary Ann (Widow)	1	1776-1814	A	120
Lane, Nancy	4	1840-1858	1	153
Langford, John	1	1776-1814	A	147
Langford, Polly	4	1840-1858	1	156
Lavender, David	3	1823-1840	L	9
Law, Jas.	3	1823-1840	M	54
Law, Martha	4	1840-1858	1	250
Law, Samuel (Jr.)	1	1776-1814	D	78
Law, Saml.	2	1805-1826	E	60
Leavell, James	2	1823-1840	H	37
Leavell, John	3	1823-1840	L	3
Leavell, Robert	1	1776-1814	B	21
Leitz, George	2	1805-1826	F	51
Lenam, Samuel	1	1776-1814	A	83
Lester, James (Sr.) (Farmer)	3	1823-1840	M	40
Lester, William R.	2	1805-1826	F	52
Lettener, John Volentine	1	1776-1814	C	74
Lever, George	3	1823-1840	L	90
Leverett, Temperance	2	1805-1826	Loose will	58
Levingston, Jacob	3	1823-1840	N	23
Lewis, Stephen	1	1776-1814	A	41
Liles, Ephraim (Planter)	2	1805-1826	G	59
Liles, Marcus	3	1823-1840	L	171
Liles, Ruth	2	1805-1826	F	54
Liles, Williamson	1	1776-1814	B	16
Lindsey, Benjamin	4	1840-1858	1	6
Lindsey, Edmond	2	1805-1826	G	23

Lindsay, James (Sr.)	1	1776-1814	B	67
Lindsey, James	4	1840-1858	1	29
Lindsey, John (Sr.)	1	1776-1814	A	14
Lindsey, John	4	1840-1858	2	247
Litsey, David B.	4	1840-1858	2	221
Litzey, David R.	4	1840-1858	2	34
Livingston, David	3	1823-1840	M	82
Livingston, John	4	1840-1858	1	80
Livingston, Miriam	4	1840-1858	1	256
Lofton, John (Sr.)	1	1776-1814	C	23
Lofton, Mary	4	1840-1858	2	22
Lofton, William	2	1805-1826	H	59
Lofton, William	4	1840-1858	1	214
Lomineck, Michael(Planter)	2	1805-1826	E	62
Lonam, Samuel	1	1776-1814	A	83
Long, Elizabeth (Widow)	2	1805-1826	F	33
Long, Elizabeth	4	1840-1858	2	154
Long, John Michael	3	1823-1840	M	22
Long, John Thomas	4	1840-1858	1	116
Long, Priscilla	3	1823-1840	L	166
Longshore, Robert	3	1823-1840	Loose will	21
Lyles, Ephriam	4	1840-1858	2	122
Lyles, Joicy	3	1823-1840	Loose will	35
Lyles, Mary	4	1840-1858	1	17
Lyles, Robert	4	1840-1858	1	177
Lynch, Elijah	4	1840-1858	1	50
McAdams, Robert	2	1805-1826	I	8
McCalla, Samuel	2	1805-1826	Loose will	50
McConnel, Andrew	4	1840-1858	1	167
McConnell, William	1	1776-1814	D	59
McConnell, William P.	4	1840-1858	2	317
McCrackin, Cyrus	4	1840-1858	2	59
McCrackin, Nancy	4	1840-1858	1	163
McCrackin, William	2	1805-1826	H	41
McCrakin, Thomas (Planter)	3	1823-1840	L	48
McGowen, Jane	3	1823-1840	M	19
McGraw, Mathew	4	1840-1858	Loose will	10
McKee, Elizabeth	4	1840-1858	2	294
McKee, Joseph	4	1840-1858	1	77
McKee, Robert (Planter)	3	1823-1840	L	89
McKennie, William	2	1805-1826	F	35
McKitrick, James	3	1823-1840	L	112
McLease, Andrew (Sr.)	1	1776-1814	A	107
McLemare, M. E.	4	1840-1858	1	5
McMaster, James	2	1805-1826	G	19
McMorries, John	2	1805-1826	I	20
Maffett, Robert (Sr.)	3	1823-1840	N	28
Malone, William	3	1823-1840	Loose will	1
Man, John	1	1776-1814	D	37
Man, Robert	1	1776-1814	A	16
Man, Susannah	1	1776-1814	C	25
Mangum, Anna	4	1840-1858	1	220
Manning, Levi	1	1776-1814	B	2
Marput, John	2	1805-1826	Loose will	60
Mars, Robert	2	1805-1826	E	59

Mars, William	4	1840-1858	2	311
Martin, David (Minister)	1	1776-1814	A	99
Martin, David	1	1776-1814	Loose will	7
Martin, George	3	1823-1840	Loose will	4
Martin, Patrick	2	1805-1826	H	40
Maxwell, Andrew	2	1805-1826	H	70
Maxwell, John	3	1823-1840	L	20
Maybin, Benjamin	4	1840-1858	2	63
Maybin, John	4	1840-1858	1	97
Meadows, James	2	1805-1826	Loose will	37
Miles, Samuel	1	1776-1814	D	47
Miles, Sarah	2	1805-1826	H	56
Miller, Nancy	4	1840-1858	1	101
Mills, Andrew	2	1805-1826	I	32
Mills, James	2	1805-1826	F	36
Mills, Sarah	3	1823-1840	M	88
Mitchel, Isaac	2	1805-1826	E	30
Montgomery, David	3	1823-1840	L	120
Montgomery, Sarah	4	1840-1858	2	196
Montgomery, William (Sr.)	1	1776-1814	C	17
Moon, Dalton Lark	3	1823-1840	N	8
Moon, Meredith William	3	1823-1840	L	107
Morgan, Elizabeth	3	1823-1840	M	45
Mounce, Robert	1	1776-1814	D	75
Murdock, Jefse	3	1823-1840	Loose will	27
Murphy, James	1	1776-1814	A	1
Myers, Isabel	2	1805-1826	F	37
Nabours, Nathan	3	1823-1840	N	3
Nance, Clement	4	1840-1858	1	88
Nance, Drayton	4	1840-1858	2	182
Nance, Erastus G.	4	1840-1858	2	139
Nance, Frederick (Sr.)	4	1840-1858	1	1
Nance, Robert	2	1805-1826	I	1
Nates, Jesse	4	1840-1858	1	237
Nealley, Robert	3	1823-1840	N	18
Nealley, George	2	1805-1826	G	43
Nealy, Robert	3	1823-1840	L	118
Neel, Benjamin (Sr.)(planter)	3	1823-1840	N	10
Newman, John	1	1776-1814	A	12
Newman, Samuel	1	1776-1814	D	17
Nichols, Elizabeth(Widow)	1	1776-1814	Loose will	4
Nichols, Solomon(Planter)	1	1776-1814	A	93
Noland, Aubrey (Planter)	2	1805-1826	Loose will	15
Noland, Sampson	3	1823-1840	L	77
O'Dell, Baruch	3	1823-1840	M	9
O'Neall, Mary (Sr.)	1	1776-1814	D	81
Oneall, Wm.	1	1776-1814	A	32
Owens, William	2	1805-1826	G	77
Oxner, Jacob (Sr.)	2	1805-1826	Loose will	13
Parmer, Isaac	1	1776-1814	A	24
Paterson, James	2	1805-1826	G	18
Patterson, Elanor	3	1823-1840	L	147
Patty, Margaret	1	1776-1814	D	3
Payne, James	4	1840-1858	Loose will	19
Payne, Richard	1	1776-1814	D	1

Name		Date		Page
Payne, Richard P	4	1840-1858	2	120
Payne, William	2	1823-1840	M	63
Paysinger, Elizabeth	4	1840-1858	2	267
Paysinger, John	4	1840-1858	1	107
Pearson, Benj.	1	1776-1814	A	30
Pearson, Enoch	1	1776-1814	A	52
Pearson, Samuel	1	1776-1814	A	47
Peaster, Adam	2	1805-1826	H	72
Peaster, Rachel	2	1805-1826	G	36
Pemberton, Isaiah	1	1776-1814	C	34
Pemberton, Richard	2	1805-1826	E	65
Phillips, Gabrial	2	1805-1826	E	14
Phillips, Robert	3	1823-1840	L	18
Pitts, Abner (Planter)	1	1776-1814	C	45
Pitts, Abner	4	1840-1858	2	32
Pitts, Caleb	2	1805-1826	F	44
Pitts, Calib	3	1823-1840	Loose will	28
Pitts, Cealy	2	1805-1826	Loose will	19
Pitts, Daniel(Sr.)(Plant)	2	1805-1826	Loose will	17
Pitts, David	4	1840-1858	2	170
Pitts, Hanah Kritter	3	1823-1840	L	25
Pitts, Henderson	3	1823-1840	Loose will	26
Pitts, Henry (Sr.)	1	1776-1814	D	5
Pitts, John	2	1805-1826	F	40
Pitts, John	2	1805-1826	H	60
Pitts, Jonathan	3	1823-1840	L	88
Pitts, Joseph	2	1805-1826	F	42
Pitts, Joseph	2	1805-1826	Loose will	21
Pitts, Joshua	2	1805-1826	I	38
Pitts, Thomas	3	1823-1840	Loose will	29
Pitts, William	3	1823-1840	Loose will	5
Plonket, Charles	1	1776-1814	C	76
Plonket, Charles	2	1805-1826	Loose will	44
Pool, Frances	2	1805-1826	E	48
Pool, William	1	1776-1814	B	1
Pool, William	1	1776-1814	Loose will	9
Pool, William Patty	2	1805-1826	F	39
Pope, Harriet	4	1840-1858	2	281
Pope, Jas. Alexander	4	1840-1858	2	66
Prater, Brice	2	1805-1826	Loose will	201
Pratt, Dorothy B.	4	1840-1858	2	131
Pratt, Thomas	3	1823-1840	M	47
Pratt, Thomas F.	3	1823-1840	M	51
Price, John (Farmer)	1	1776-1814	D	15
Price, Susanna	2	1805-1826	G	14
Prisock, Barbary	4	1840-1858	1	15
Proctor, John	2	1805-1826	I	31
Proctor, Samuel (Sr.)	1	1776-1814	A	110
Pugh, Azariah	1	1776-1814	A	101
Pugh, Sarah	4	1840-1858	2	250
Pushart, John	1	1776-1814	Loose will	12
Ramage, Lucy	4	1840-1858	1	231
Rane, Conrad	2	1805-1826	E	15
Reagan, Mary	2	1805-1826	F	49
Reagin, Phebe	3	1823-1840	L	164
Reagin, Rezin	2	1805-1826	I	49
Reagin, William	2	1805-1826	Loose will	74

Name		Date	Code	Page
Red, James	4	1840-1858	2	230
Reeder, Mary	4	1840-1858	2	149
Reeder, William	3	1823-1840	L	37
Rees, Jane	4	1840-1858	1	99
Reid, David (Sr.)	3	1823-1840	L	102
Reid, Elliott, D.	4	1840-1858	2	129
Reid, Jane	4	1840-1858	2	174
Reiney, Thomas (Sr.)	3	1823-1840	Loose will	31
Reitlehouver George(Plant.)	1	1776-1814	C	15
Renwick, Agnes	3	1823-1840	M	89
Renwick, Jane	4	1840-1858	1	205
Replogle, Jacob(Planter)	1	1776-1814	A	135
Richardson, John	1	1776-1814	B	52
Ridlehuber, John	4	1840-1858	2	19
Rikard, George	2	1805-1826	I	52
Rikard, Michael	4	1840-1858	1	161
Riley, Hanah	1	1776-1814	A	51
Riley, John	1	1776-1814	A	129
Riser, Martin	4	1840-1858	1	110
Robards, Barden Wise	3	1823-1840	L	73
Roberts, Elizabeth	3	1823-1840	L	172
Robertson, John	3	1823-1840	L	140
Robinson, James	4	1840-1858	1	127
Ruble, Peter	1	1776-1814	A	59
Rudd, Daniel	4	1840-1858	2	172
Rudd, Fields	2	1805-1826	F	47
Rudd, John (Sr.)	3	1823-1840	L	103
Rudd, Mary Ann	4	1840-1858	1	31
Rudd, Robert	3	1823-1840	Loose will	33
Ruff, Christian (Sr.)	1	1776-1814	B	27
Ruff, George	1	1776-1814	Loose will	17
Ruff, Henry	3	1823-1840	N	49
Ruff, John	2	1805-1826	G	34
Ruff, Maria Elizabeth	4	1840-1858	1	245
Russel, Andrew	3	1823-1840	L	143
Rutherford, Robert(Sr.)	1	1776-1814	B	74
Rutherford, William	4	1840-1858	1	147
Rutherford, William	4	1840-1858	1	147
Ryhard, Annastasia(Widow)	2	1805-1826	Loose will	23
Satterwhite, Barlet (Sr.)	1	1776-1814	D	59
Satterwhite, John(Sr.)	1	1776-1814	D	41
Satterwhite, John (Sr.)	2	1805-1826	E	19
Satterwhite, Rebecca	2	1805-1826	Loose will	69
Schwartz, Mary Ann	3	1823-1840	N	38
Scott, Charles	2	1805-1826	F	53
Scott, Martha (Widow)	3	1823-1840	L	130
Scott, Mary	2	1805-1826	G	15
Scott, William	2	1805-1826	E	21
Setsler, Jacob	3	1823-1840	N	16
Seymore, Isaac (Sr.)	2	1805-1826	G	30
Sheely, Henry	3	1823-1840	L	63
Shell, John	2	1805-1826	H	44
Shell, Lemmon(Planter)	2	1805-1826	Loose will	26
Shell, Nancy (Widow)	2	1805-1826	G	20
Shell, Stephen	2	1805-1826	I	15
Sheppard, Honorias(Planter)	4	1840-1858	2	243

179

Sheppard, Honorias	4	1840-1858	2	285
Sheppard, Jennet	2	1805-1826	G	70
Shumpert, Jacob	4	1840-1858	1	58
Sibley, Joseph	2	1823-1840	L	53
Simpson, Perry J.	4	1840-1858	2	308
Sims, David (Sr.)	3	1823-1840	L	114
Sims, David G.	3	1823-1840	L	161
Sims, Matthew (Sr.)	1	1766-1814	A	123
Sims, Patrick Henry	2	1805-1826	H	66
Sims, Reubin	2	1805-1826	F	55
Single, Martin(Planter)	1	1776-1814	A	80
Single, Martin	4	1840-1858	2	212
Singley, Martin, see - - - - - - - - - - - - - - - - - Single, Martin				
Sitgreaves,Elizabeth J.	4	1840-1858	Loose will	17
Sligh, Andrew J.	4	1840-1858	2	251
Sligh, Charles F.	4	1840-1858	2	278
Sligh, David (Planter)	4	1840-1858	2	92
Sligh, Jacob (Sr.)	4	1840-1858	1	146
Sligh, Philip	2	1805-1826	H	48
Slike, Nicklys	1	1776-1814	A	68
Sloan, James J.	4	1840-1858	2	261
Sloan, Samuel	4	1840-1858	2	53
Smith, Esther (Widow)	2	1805-1826	G	84
Smith, Jared	3	1823-1840	L	19
Smith, Lawrence	1	1776-1814	B	31
Smith, Martha	4	1840-1858	1	150
Smith, Matthew	2	1805-1826	G	62
Smith, Susannah	3	1823-1840	L	165
Smith, William B.	4	1840-1858	2	232
Smyly, Dan	2	1805-1826	F	52
Smyth, James	1	1776-1814	D	54
Snith, Matthew	2	1805-1826	G	62
Sondley, Richard	3	1823-1840	L	105
Soulter, Martin(Planter)	1	1776-1814	C	67
Sparks, George	1	1776-1814	A	159
Speak, Sa ah	3	1823-1840	M	61
Speake, George	4	1840-1858	2	296
Speakman, William	1	1776-1814	A	55
Spearman, James	1	1776-1814	C	21
Spearman, John	4	1840-1858	1	129
Spearman, Thomas	1	1776-1814	Loose will	10
Spence, Elizabeth(Widow)	2	1805-1826	Loose will	25
Spence, Robert (Sr.)	2	1805-1826	F	84
Stabler, Moses	4	1840-1858	1	81
Stairley, Jacob	2	1805-1826	H	64
Steel, Anna	2	1805-1826	Loose will	70
Stephens, John	3	1823-1840	M	27
Stweard, Robert	1	1776-1814	D	36
Stewart, Daniel	4	1840-1858	2	176
Stewart, Isaac	4	1840-1858	1	254
Stewart, John	2	1805-1826	I	27
Stewart, Joshua	1	1776-1814	D	55
Stewart, Levinia	3	1823-1840	N	33
Stockman, Catherine	4	1840-1858	2	271
Stockman, Henry (Sr.)	3	1823-1840	L	71
Stone, David	4	1840-1858	2	4
Stone, Phebe	4	1840-1858	1	65
Stripling, William	2	1805-1826	F	50
Stuard, Robert	1	1776-1814	D	35

Suber, Andrew	5	1823-1840	N	51
Suber, Andrew	4	1840-1858	1	82
Suber, Conrad, see - - - - - - - - - - - - - - - - - - Zuber, Conrad				
Suber, David	4	1840-1858	2	89
Suber, Henry (Sr.)	4	1840-1858	2	127
Suber, Jacob (Sr.)	4	1840-1858	2	67
Suber, John	5	1823-1840	L	14
Suber, John	4	1840-1858	2	16
Suber, Martin	4	1840-1858	2	141
Suber, Micajah (Planter)	4	1840-1858	2	48
Suber, Michael	2	1805-1826	E	54
Suber, Michael	4	1840-1858	2	1
Suber, Rebeccah	5	1823-1840	Loose will	36
Suber, Solomon	5	1823-1840	M	70
Suber, Sophia Rebecca	5	1823-1840	L	68
Sumers, Wm.(Sr.)(Farmer)	2	1805-1826	I	23
Summer, Nichols	5	1823-1840	M	52
Summer, Hezekiah	2	1805-1826	I	34
Summer, John (Planter)	5	1823-1840	M	29
Summer, Joseph (Planter)	2	1805-1826	E	7
Summer, Rosannah	4	1840-1858	1	23
Swan, John (Planter)	2	1805-1826	E	68
Swindler, Jefse	4	1840-1858	2	134
Swittenberg, Geo. Michae˜	4	1840-1858	2	58
Taylor, Benjamin	2	1805-1826	F	58
Taylor, Jonathan(Farmer)	1	1776-1814	A	112
Taylor, Martin	2	1805-1826	Loose will	29
Taylor, William	1	1776-1814	A	45
Teacle, Nathaniel	4	1840-1858	2	56
Teague, Abraham	3	1823-1840	L	133
Teague, James	2	1805-1826	F	61
Thomas, Abel	2	1805-1826	Loose will	32
Thomas, Ann	2	1805-1826	Loose will	51
Thomas, David	3	1823-1840	M	66
Thomas, James	3	1823-1840	L	26
Thomas, John G.	4	1840-1858	1	164
Thomas, Mary	4	1840-1858	1	66
Thomas, Nancy	4	1840-1858	2	226
Thomas, Nehemiah	1	1776-1814	B	8
Thompson, Henry	4	1840-1858	2	14
Thompson, Henry	4	1840-1858	2	38
Tinney, Richard (Planter)	2	1805-1826	H	55
Tinney, William (Planter)	1	1776-1814	D	49
Tinsley, Elizabeth(Widow)	1	1776-1814	C	61
Tinsley, Rucker	2	1805-1826	Loose will	54
Toland, Mary (Jr.)	2	1805-1826	Loose will	28
Turner, Elizabeth (Widow)	2	1805-1826	E	41
Turner, Little Bery	3	1823-1840	L	127
Turner, Thomas (Planter)	1	1776-1814	B	42
Turner, Wm.	1	1776-1814	A	49
Thweatt, Edward	3	1823-1840	M	71
Vardman, William	1	1776-1814	B	72
Vaughan, Drury T.	4	1840-1858	1	140
Vaughan, Elizabeth	1	1776-1814	A	77
Vaughan, Nicholas	1	1776-1814	D	22
Vaun, John	1	1776-1814	A	19

Vicary, William	2	1805-1826	Loose will	67
Voss, Joseph	2	1805-1826	E	59
Wadlington, Ann B.	4	1840-1858	1	228
Wadlington, Dorothy R.	3	1823-1840	L	169
Wadlington, Edward	1	1776-1814	A	71
Wadlington, William	1	1776-1814	C	10
Waits, William (Sr.)	4	1840-1858	Loose will	5
Waldrop, Elijah	2	1805-1826	H	58
Waldrop, Elisha	2	1805-1826	E	18
Waldrop, James	1	1776-1814	B	65
Waldrop, John	1	1776-1814	A	94
Waldrop, Milly	4	1840-1858	1	159
Waldrop, Samuel	1	1776-1814	B	71
Walker, Jennet	1	1776-1814	A	84
Wallace, Beheathlin	4	1840-1858	2	274
Wallace, John (Sr.)	1	1776-1814	Loose will	15
Wallace, William	2	1805-1826	G	72
Wallern, Frederick Joseph	2	1805-1826	F	80
Waters, Philm. B.	2	1805-1826	E	74
Watkins, Catherine	3	1823-1840	M	84
Watson, Nancy	4	1840-1858	2	104
Watts, Jenetta Muir	3	1823-1840	L	51
Watts, Richard	2	1805-1826	E	46
Wedaman, Margaret	4	1840-1858	2	241
Weldeman, Peter	3	1823-1840	N	6
Welch, William	4	1840-1858	2	106
Wells, Abegail	2	1805-1826	Loose will	65
Wells, George	3	1823-1840	N	47
Wells, George	4	1840-1858	1	216
Wells, Horatio N.	3	1823-1840	M	68
Wells, Livingston	3	1823-1840	M	65
Wendle, Susannah -	2	1805-1826	Loose will	45
Werts, George Henry	4	1840-1858	1	20
Werts, John	4	1840-1858	1	38
West, Walter	2	1805-1826	Loose will	38
Wheeler, Barbara	4	1840-1858	1	79
Wheeler, George	3	1823-1840	L	179
Whipple, Israel	2	1805-1826	I	46
White, William	4	1840-1858	1	119
Whitmire, Phebe	3	1823-1840	M	85
Whitmire, William	4	1840-1858	1	27
Wicker, Henry	2	1805-1826	G	24
Wicker, Henry	2	1805-1826	Loose will	57
Wicker, John Adam	3	1823-1840	L	44
Wicker, Michael	4	1840-1858	2	305
Wicker, Simon	4	1840-1858	1	156
Wicker, Uriah	2	1805-1826	E	13
Wickert, Mathias (Jr.)	1	1776-1814	A	26
Wilkerson, John (Sr.)	1	1776-1814	A	115
Wilkinson, John See - - - - - - - - - - - - - - - - - - - Wilkerson, John				
Wilhelm, Peter	4	1840-1858	1	185
Williams, Casandre	3	1823-1840	Loose will	40
Williams, Daniel	2	1805-1826	I	50
Williams, Frances	4	1840-1858	1	235
Williams, Hopkin	2	1805-1826	Loose will	62
Williams, James	2	1805-1826	Loose will	68

Williams, James	3	1823-1840	L	173
Williams, Joseph	1	1776-1814	Loose will	13
Williams, Nathan	1	1776-1814	A	144
Williams, Providence	2	1805-1826	H	46
Williams, Thomas	2	1805-1826	F	4
Williams, Washington	3	1823-1840	L	80
Williamson, John	3	1823-1840	L	153
Wilmot, Thomas	2	1805-1826	Loose will	64
Wilson, Henry	1	1776-1814	A	114
Wilson, John	1	1776-1814	A	98
Wilson, John (Surgeon)	1	1776-1814	A	145
Wilson, John	2	1805-1826	H	75
Wilson, John	2	1805-1826	Loose will	48
Wilson, John	4	1840-1858	1	240
Wilson, Mary (Widow)	1	1776-1814	A	130
Wilson, Thomas	3	1823-1840	N	13
Wise, Elizabeth	4	1840-1858	2	228
Wise, John	4	1840-1858	2	272
Wood, John (Planter)	1	1876-1814	C	19
Worthington, Jacob A	4	1840-1858	1	105
Worthington, John	3	1823-1840	L	41
Worthington, Reuben C.	2	1805-1826	I	41
Wright, John (Sr.)	1	1776-1814	A	54
Wright, Nancy	4	1840-1858	2	211
Yeargan, John	2	1805-1826	F	63
Young, Harriet	4	1840-1858	1	54-A
Young, John T.	4	1840-1858	1	41-A
Zuber, Conrad	2	1805-1826	E	57

Copied by:

/s/ Mrs. John D. Rogers

INDEX TO

PICKENS COUNTY WILLS

VOLUME NO. 1
1828-1862

This index is compiled from W.P.A. copies of
wills filed in the COUNTY PROBATE COURTS.
The volumes indexed are a part of the
South Carolina Collection of the
University of South Carolina
Library.

Columbia, S.C.
1939

Name	Vol.	Date	Section	Page
Abbett, John	1	182801862	1	256
Ables, John M.	1	1828-1862	1	250
Ables, John W., see - - - - - - - - - - - - -			Ables, John M.	
Addis, Samuel	1	1828-1862	1	305
Alexander, Daniel	1	1828-1862	1	214
Alexander, Elisha	1	1828-1862	1	23
Alexander, Thomas	1	1828-1862	1	243
Alexander, William	1	1828-1862	1	139
Allgood, Barnett	1	1828-1862	2	335
Anderson, John	1	1828-1862	1	230
Anderson, Susan	1	1828-1862	1	71
Armstrong, Benjamin	1	1828-1862	1	29
Arnold, William (Sr.)	1	1828-1862	1	221
Baker, Lemuel M.	1	1828-1862	2	378
Baker, Richard	1	1828-1862	2	352
Ballenger, John L.	1	1828-1862	1	187
Barker, James (Sr.)	1	1828-1862	1	44
Barnett, Elijah	1	1828-1862	1	113
Barrett, William	1	1828-1862	1	286
Barton, Caleb	1	1828-1862	1	54
Barton, David	1	1828-1862	1	105
Boatwright, William	1	1828-1862	1	185
Boggs, G. W. B.	1	1828-1862	2	348
Bowen, John	1	1828-1862	1	27
Bowen, William	1	1828-1862	1	269
Brewer, James	1	1828-1862	1	280
Brown, Lewis	1	1828-1862	1	155
Burdine, Davis Talley	1	1828-1862	1	179
Cane, William	1	1828-1862	2	344
Capehart, Leonard	1	1828-1862	2	325
Carne, Thomas William	1	1828-1862	1	79
Cassell, John	1	1828-1862	2	331
Clayton, John	1	1828-1862	1	162
Cleveland, Benjamin	1	1828-1862	1	16
Cleveland, Eli	1	1828-1862	1	192
Cobb, John	1	1828-1862	1	98
Cobb, Robert	1	1828-1862	1	177
Cooper, Sion	1	1828-1862	1	19
Craig, John	1	1828-1862	1	102
Davis, Eli	1	1828-1862	1	25
Davis, Joseph	1	1828-1862	1	267
Davis, Sarah L.	1	1828-1862	1	66
Day, William	1	1828-1862	1	94
Dendy, James	1	1828-1862	1	151
Dickson, William	1	1828-1862	1	6
Dodd, William (Sr.)	1	1828-1862	1	170
Drummonds, James	1	1828-1862	1	162
Drummons, James, see - - - - - - - - - - - - -			Drummonds, James	

Duff, Mary	1	1828-1862	1	99
Durham, Charles	1	1828-1862	1	34
Earle, Samuel	1	1828-1862	1	38
Ellis, Gideon (Sr.)	1	1828-1862	1	296
Evatt, Hundley	1	1828-1862	1	203
Ferguson, Andrew	1	1828-1862	1	127
Ferguson, Elisha A.	1	1828-1862	2	333
Ferguson, Nancy	1	1828-1862	1	180
Field, John (Sr.)	1	1828-1862	1	111
Fitzgerald, Ambrose	1	1828-1862	1	48
Fleming, John L.	1	1828-1862	2	347
Foster, Robert S. C.	1	1828-1862	1	261
Freeman, Benton	1	1828-1862	1	208
Freeman, David	1	1828-1862	2	383
Gaines, Henry	1	1828-1862	1	14
Gaines, James	1	1828-1862	1	96
Gaines, Richard G.	1	1828-1862	1	20
Garner, Nancy	1	1828-1862	1	185-b
Gassaway, Thomas	1	1828-1862	1	205
Gibson, Zachariah W.	1	1828-1862	2	350
Gilliland, John	1	1828-1862	2	368
Gordon, Nathaniel	1	1828-1862	1	134
Grant, James	1	1828-1862	1	200
Grant, William	1	1828-1862	1	303
Grisham, Elizabeth	1	1828-1862	1	138
Grisham, John (Sr.)	1	1828-1862	1	59
Guyton, Jacob	1	1828-1862	1	167
Hall, Hugh	1	1828-1862	1	307
Hall, Jesse (Planter)	1	1828-1862	1	52
Hallum, Richard	1	1828-1862	1	174
Hallum, Thomas, see - - - - - - - - - - - - - - -			Hallums, Thomas	
Hallums, Thomas	1	1828-1862	1	300
Hamilton, Davis (Sr.)	1	1828-1862	1	72
Hamilton, Jane	1	1828-1862	1	114
Hanes, John	1	1828-1862	1	76
Harbin, Thomas William	1	1828-1862	1	212
Hardin, Richard Carol	1	1828-1862	1	266
Hayes, Solomon (Sr.)	1	1828-1862	1	232
Hembree, Edward	1	1828-1862	1	274
Hendricks, Larkin (Sr.)	1	1828-1862	2	359
Hendricks, Moses	1	1828-1862	1	164
Hester, Alfred	1	1828-1862	1	275
Hill, George	1	1828-1862	1	77
Holland, D. T.	1	1828-1862	1	265
Hughes, Henry R.	1	1828-1862	2	351
Humphres, Catherine, see - - - - - - - - - - - -			Humphreys, Catherine	
Humphreys, Catherine	1	1828-1862	1	36
Humphreys, David (Sr.)	1	1828-1862	1	82
Hunt, H. C.	1	1828-1862	2	337

Isbell, Pendleton	1	1828-1862	1	158
Isbell, Sydney S.	1	1828-1862	2	258
Ivester, Hugh	1	1828-1862	1	238
Jenkins, Andrew	1	1828-1862	2	363
Jolly, William (Sr.)	1	1828-1862	1	17
Jones, Garland F.	1	1828-1862	2	375
Jones, Jabez	1	1828-1862	1	294
Keith, John	1	1828-1862	1	202
Keith, Warren Davis	1	1828-1862	1	283
Keith, William L.	1	1828-1862	1	239
Kilpatrick, John C. (Jr.)	1	1828-1862	1	90
Kilpatrick, John C. (Sr.)	1	1828-1862	1	129
Kirksey, Silas	1	1828-1862	1	210
Lamar, Bird - - - - - - - - - - - - - - - - - -			Listed in Index but not found in Will Book	
Land, Isaac	1	1828-1862	1	118
Lanier, Bird	1	1828-1862	1	245
Lawrence, Joseph N.	1	1828-1862	2	381
Lawrence, Rachel	1	1828-1862	1	168
Lay, Charles	1	1828-1862	1	8
Lay, James	1	1828-1862	1	308
Lay, John	1	1828-1862	1	288
Lewis, Davis - - - - - - - - - - - - - - - - - -			Listed in Index but not found in Will Book	
Lewis, Jacob	1	1828-1862	1	271
Lewis, Jesse P.	1	1828-1862	1	143
Lewis, Lindamina	1	1828-1862	1	68
Lidai, John	1	1828-1862	1	108
Liddell, George Washington	1	1828-1862	2	327
Lively, Thomas (Sr.)	1	1828-1862	1	85
Lodon, Jesse P.	1	1828-1862	1	282
Looper, Jeremiah (Sr.)	1	1828-1862	2	322
McAdams, Joseph (Planter)	1	1828-1862	2	376
McDonald, Henry	1	1828-1862	1	172
McWhorter, Jeremiah	1	1828-1862	1	133
McWhorter, John (Planter)	1	1828-1862	1	81
Mansell, Joshua	1	1828-1862	1	223
Maret, John	1	1828-1862	2	343
Maret, Stephen	1	1828-1862	1	198
Mauldin, Jane	1	1828-1862	1	130
Maxwell, Richard D.	1	1838-1862	1	291
Mayfield, Tempy	1	1828-1862	1	285
Melear, Richard H.	1	1828-1862	1	237
Messer, Samuel	1	1828-1862	1	152
Miller, Elisha	1	1828-1862	1	87
Miller, Isaac	1	1828-1862	1	137
Miller, John C.	1	1828-1862	2	365
Miller, Richard L.	1	1828-1862	2	313

Moody, Daniel	1	1828-1862	1	226
Moody, Martin	1	1828-1862	1	273
Moore, Burt	1	1828-1862	1	64
Morgan, Morgan	1	1828-1862	1	61
Moss, Frederick	1	1828-1862	1	194
Mullinix, William G.	1	1828-1862	2	320
Mullinnex, William G.	1	1828-1862, see Mullinix, William G.		
Murphree, Levi	1	1828-1862	1	69
Murphree, Moses	1	1828-1862	1	147
Neal, John, see - - - - - - - - - - - - - - - - -			Neel, John	
Neel, John	1	1828-1862	1	62
Neel, John (Jr.)	1	1828-1862	1	233
Neville, Jesse	1	1828-1862	1	110
Nicholson, Hannah	1	1828-1862	1	117
Niebuhr, John P.	1	1828-1862	1	228
Niebuhr, Rebeccah	1	1828-1862	2	362
Norris, Robert	1	1828-1862	1	259
Norton, Jepthah	1	1828-1862	2	340
Ostendorff, John O.	1	1828-1862	1	277
Parsons, James	1	1828-1862	2	354
Pentte, Burrell	1	1828-1862	1	281
Perritt, Burrell, see - - - - - - - - - - - - - - - -			Pentte, Burrell	
Perry, Benjamin	1	1828-1862	1	119
Perry, E. M.	1	1828-1862	2	380
Petty, Ambrose	1	1828-1862	1	46
Phillips, Levi	1	1828-1862	1	160
Pickens, Eliza	1	1828-1862	1	298
Poe, Richard	1	1828-1862	1	146
Porter, Mary	1	1828-1862	1	186
Pugh, David	1	1828-1862	1	122
Reeder, A. P.	1	1828-1862	1	251
Reeder, Elizabeth	1	1828-1862	1	190
Reeder, Thomas Milton	1	1828-1862	1	89
Reid, Joseph	1	1828-1862	1	1
Rice, Isaac	1	1828-1862	1	254
Richardson, Noah T.	1	1828-1862	2	371
Roberson, Jeremiah, see - - - - - - - - - - - - -			Robinson, Jeremiah	
Robinson, Allen	1	1828-1862	1	219
Robinson, James	1	1828-1862	2	373
Robinson, Samuel	1	1828-1862	1	216
Robinson, William (Farmer)	1	1828-1862	1	278
Rogers, Felix	1	1828-1862	2	370
Rogers, James (Major)	1	1828-1862	1	166
Roper, Gideon	1	1828-1862	2	339
Roper, Joshua	1	1828-1862	1	235
Russell, David	1	1828-1862	2	315
Russell, Edy	1	1828-1862	1	248

Sanders, James	1	1828-1862	1	312
Sanders, William	1	1828-1862	2	310
Sandford, William - - - - - - - - - - - - - -		Listed in Index but		
		not found in Will Book		
Shell, Henry	1	1828-1862	1	11
Simpson, William	1	1828-1862	1	135
Smith, Benjamin	1	1828-1862	1	50
Smith, Job	1	1828-1862	1	74
Southerland, James, see - - - - - - - - - - -		Sutherland, James		
Steele, Esther	1	1828-1862	1	183
Stephens, Daniel	1	1828-1862	1	32
Stribling, Jesse	1	1828-1862	1	101
Sugg, Jesse (Sr.)	1	1828-1862	1	125
Sutherland, James	1	1828-1862	1	140
Swofford, John	1	1828-1862	2	384
Terrell, Aaron	1	1828-1862	2	317
Thomas, Bryant	1	1828-1862	1	181
Trammel, Thomas	1	1828-1862	1	289
Trotter, Henry	1	1828-1862	2	364
Trotter, James	1	1828-1862	1	196
Verner, John	1	1828-1862	1	218
Visage, Thomas	1	1828-1862	1	189
White, Alexander	1	1828-1862	1	202-b
Whitmire, Henry (Sr.)	1	1828-1862	1	263
Williams, Joseph	1	1828-1862	1	92-b
Williams, William (Planter)	1	1828-1862	2	356
Winchester, Willoughby	1	1828-1862	1	126
Wood, Joseph	1	1828-1862	1	4
Young, Stephen	1	1828-1862	1	10
Yow, Demcy	1	1828-1862	2	346

Copied by:

/s/ Mrs. John D. Rogers

INDEX

TO

RICHLAND COUNTY WILLS.

Volume No. 1
1787-1853

Volume No. 2
1787-1853

Volume No. 3
1787-1853

Volume No. 4
1854-1864

This index is compiled from W.P.A. copies of
wills filed in the COUNTY PROBATE COURTS.
The volumes indexed are a part of the
South Carolina Collection of the
University of South Carolina
Library.

Columbia, S.C.
1939

Name	Vol.	Date	Section	Page
Abbott, John	2	1787-1853	H	31
Adams, Ann	3	1787-1853	L	345
Adams, Harry W.	1	1787-1853	E	149
Adams, Harry N.	2	1787-1853	K	165
Adams, James	3	1787-1853	L	18
Adams, James H.	4	1854-1864	L	248
Adams, Joel (Sr.)	2	1787-1853	H	114
Adams, Joel	4	1854-1864	L	182
Adams, Joel Belton	3	1787-1853	L	303
Adams, Joel R. (Planter)	4	1854-1864	L	210
Adams, Margaret	2	1787-1853	K	114
Adams, Richard	1	1787-1853	B	9
Adams, Richard	1	1787-1853	E	14
Adams, Robert (Planter)	3	1787-1853	L	204
Adams, Robert J.	3	1787-1853	L	152
Adams, Sarah	3	1787-1853	L	291
Adams, Sarah H.	3	1787-1853	L	158
Adger, Susan	4	1854-1864	L	285
Alison, Andrew (Planter)	1	1787-1853	B	11
Anderson, James S.	4	1854-1864	L	30
Arthur, Rebecca L.	3	1787-1853	L	28
Aumann, Sophia	4	1854-1864	L	345
Bailey, Samuel P.	3	1787-1853	L	347
Baker, Jesse	2	1787-1853	G	84
Barnwell, Richard W. (Jr.)	4	1854-1864	L	358
Barnwell, William Hazzard N.	4	1854-1864	L	366
Barrilon, Christopher	2	1787-1853	H	83
Beard, Ulrick (Planter)	1	1787-1853	D	21
Beard, William	3	1787-1853	L	258
Bell, Benjamin F.	2	1787-1853	A	27
Bell, Elizabeth	4	1854-1864	L	334
Belton, John (Sr.)	1	1787-1853	B	31
Black, Joseph A.	4	1854-1864	L	92
Black, Margaret	3	1787-1853	L	182
Blain, Joseph	2	1787-1853	G	67
Blake, Eliza H.	2	1787-1853	K	69
Blanchard, Benjamin	1	1787-1853	B	15
Blanchard, Wm. (Planter)	1	1787-1853	E	5
Blanding, Shubel	4	1854-1864	L	176
Boatwright, James	4	1854-1864	L	99
Boatwright, James S.	4	1854-1864	L	88
Boile, Mary, see - - - - - - - - - - - - - - - Jones, Mary				
Bolton, Robert	2	1787-1853	H	21
Bookter, C.	4	1854-1864	L	123
Bookter, E. F.	4	1854-1864	L	438
Bookter, Jacob (Planter)	1	1787-1853	D	40
Bookter, Nathan	4	1854-1864	L	417
Bougle, Sarah	3	1787-1853	L	292
Bowers, Charlotte	3	1787-1853	L	7
Boyle, Cunningham	2	1787-1853	K	129
Boyle, Louisa C.	4	1854-1864	L	146
Braswell, Hannah	1	1787-1853	C	36

Bremar, Peter	1	1787-1853	E	104
Brennan, Luke C.	4	1854-1864	L	19
Brevard, Alexander	2	1787-1853	H	134
Brisbane, Adam F.	1	1787-1853	C	52
Brizna, Elizabeth	2	1787-1853	K	6
Brizna, Francis	4	1854-1864	L	32
Brodie, Alexander	4	1854-1864	L	97
Bronson, Hiram C.	4	1854-1864	L	329
Brown, Elizabeth	1	1787-1853	E	110
Brown, Elizabeth D.	4	1854-1864	L	38
Brown, John B.	2	1787-1853	H	124
Brown, John D.	2	1787-1853	H	157
Brown, John Richard	4	1854-1864	L	217
Brown, Mary	2	1787-1853	G	100
Brown, Sarah	4	1854-1864	L	244
Brown, William	2	1787-1853	H	129
Bruns, Henry	4	1854-1864	L	416
Bryan, Sarah (Widow)	4	1854-1864	L	435
Bryce, John	3	1787-1853	L	336
Bryce, Peter	3	1787-1853	L	196
Bull, Henry D.	4	1854-1864	L	36
Busby, Jesse (Planter)	1	1787-1853	E	69
Busbe, Winney	1	1787-1853	E	9
Bynum, Drury	2	1787-1853	K	86
Bynum, William	3	1787-1853	L	176
Caldwell, Davis	3	1787-1853	L	298
Calwell, Howard H.	4	1854-1864	L	219
Calvert, John	1	1787-1853	D	22
Carew, John	1	1767-1853	E	90
Carrell, Jacob (Sr.)(Planter)	1	1787-1853	E	133
Carroll, William	2	1787-1853	K	31
Carter, Cracy	2	1787-1853	H	23
Cary, Ann	2	1787-1853	G	110
Cary, Lemuel	2	1787-1853	H	150
Chandler, Jesse (Sr.)	2	1787-1853	G	106
Chapman, Gersham	2	1787-1853	K	9
Chapman, John William	2	1787-1853	L	244
Chappell, Hicks Major	2	1787-1853	K	59
Chappell, Robert	1	1787-1853	C	55
Cheves, Langdon	4	1854-1864	L	109
Church, Richard	1	1787-1853	E	92
Clark, John (Shoemaker)	1	1787-1853	E	20
Clarke, Richard	1	1787-1853	E	51
Clarke, Sterling	1	1787-1853	E	34
Clarkson, Aaron L.	1	1787-1853	D	24
Clarkson, William	4	1854-1864	L	160
Clifton, Charles	1	1787-1853	E	43
Clifton, Claiborne	2	1787-1653	H	64
Clifton, Mary	2	1787-1853	K	154
Olive, Henry	2	1787-1853	K	138
Cohen, Bella (Spinster)	4	1854-1864	L	327
Coogler, Jacob	2	1787-1853	K	107
Coon, Adam	1	1787-1853	E	127
Coon, Casper	1	1787-1853	B	49
Cooper, Jesse	4	1854-1864	L	105

Cooper, Thomas (Dr.)	2	1787-1853	K	162
Coosmouls, Henry	1	1787-1853	B	43
Cosby, James	4	1854-1864	L	413
Coulter, David	2	1787-1853	H	37
Cross, William T.	4	1854-1864	L	44
Croswell, John (Planter)	1	1787-1853	E	151
Curry, Jane	1	1787-1853	C	9
Daniel, Richard	1	1787-1853	B	45
Davis, David	4	1854-1864	L	174
Davis, David T.	4	1854-1864	L	246
Davis, James (Dr.)	2	1787-1853	L	132
Davis, James	3	1787-1853	L	155
Davis, Mary Ann	2	1787-1853	G	64
Davis, Mary T.	3	1787-1853	L	276
DeBruhl, Jesse	4	1854-1864	L	222
Delahunt, Robert	2	1787-1853	G	40
DeLeon, Jacob	2	1787-1853	H	97
De Lozear, Hannah	4	1854-1864	L	56
Delozeair, Asa	2	1787-1853	G	117
Denley, William (Jr.)	1	1787-1853	D	16
Denley, Wright (Planter)	4	1854-1864	L	264
Dial, James	3	1787-1853	L	40
Diseker, Jacob (Planter)	2	1787-1853	H	193
Dobbins, Joseph L.	1	1787-1853	D	26
Dodd, John	1	1787-1853	B	38
Donlevy, Frances W.	2	1787-1853	G	119
Dority, Henry	4	1854-1864	L	34
DuBard, Catherine E.	3	1787-1853	L	164
Dubard, William	2	1787-1853	K	160
Duggins, William	2	1787-1853	K	52
Duncan, Matthew	1	1787-1853	B	3
Dunlap, David Ellison	1	1787-1853	D	30
Edgar, Adam	3	1787-1853	L	270
Edgar, Francis	4	1854-1864	L	275
Edmunds, Thomas	2	1787-1853	H	142
Edwards, Jane	4	1854-1864	L	178
Egan, Thomas H.	2	1787-1853	G	60
Ellis, William (Boatbuilder)	2	1787-1853	G	16
Ellison, Joseph (Merchant)	3	1787-1853	L	87
Ellison, Margaret	3	1787-1853	L	317
Entzminger, Christian	4	1854-1864	L	24
Entzminger, John	4	1854-1864	L	48
Entzminger, Peter	3	1787-1853	L	335
Evans, John	4	1854-1864	L	134
Evans, Ludwell (Planter)	1	1787-1853	E	1
Evans, Richard	1	1787-1853	E	116
Everett, Benjamin, see				Everit, Benjamin
Everit, Benjamin	1	1787-1853	B	44
Falls, Alexander	4	1854-1864	L	268
Fannin, Elizabeth	2	1787-1853	H	178
Farrow, Daniel	2	1787-1853	K	4
Faust, Burrell	1	1787-1853	E	138
Faust, Daniel	2	1787-1853	K	56

Faust, Jacob (Planter)	1	1787-1853	C	6
Faust, Jane A.	2	1787-1853	K	2
Faust, Jasper	3	1787-1853	L	172
Faust, John Henry	1	1787-1853	B	5
Faust, Mary	1	1787-1853	D	4
Faust, Parthenia	4	1854-1864	L	195
Faust, Peter	2	1787-1853	H	15
Faust, William	1	1787-1853	C	51
Fetner, Archibald	4	1854-1864	L	238
Fisher, Edward	2	1787-1855	K	54
Fitch, Augustus	4	1854-1864	L	116
Fitzpatrick (Wm.) (Planter)	1	1787-1853	E	55
Fitzpatrick, William	2	1787-1853	G	20
Fitzsimons, Mrs. Catherine	3	1787-1853	L	32
Fleming, Mrs. Mary (Widow)	2	1787-1853	K	61
Flinn, Robert	4	1854-1864	L	356
Ford, Daniel	1	1787-1853	D	9
Forshaw, William M.	3	1787-1853	L	191
Fox, William (Planter)	2	1787-1855	G	6
Freeman, Benjamin	2	1787-1853	H	7
Friday, Samuel D.	4	1854-1864	L	428
Friedberg, Joseph	4	1854-1864	L	299
Frost, Kiziah	2	1787-1853	G	47
Gaffney, Peter	4	1854-1864	L	12
Gandy, Uriah	2	1787-1853	H	52
Garner, Sarah	3	1787-1853	L	11
Gary, Robert	3	1787-1853	L	166
Geiger, Dorthy	4	1854-1864	L	127
Gibson, Sarah	3	1787-1853	L	78
Gill, Agnes (Widow)	2	1787-1853	G	39
Gill, John	1	1787-1853	B	19
Gill, Lucy	4	1854-1864	L	420
Giradin, Margaret, see - - - - - - - - - - - - - -			Girardin, Margaret	
Girardin, Margaret	3	1787-1853	L	99
Goodwyn, Elizabeth	2	1787-1853	G	122
Goodwyn, John (Planter)	1	1787-1853	E	73
Goodwyn, John T	4	1854-1864	L	27
Goodwyn, Robert	1	1787-1853	E	47
Goodwyn, Robert H.	4	1854-1864	L	236
Goodwyn, Sarah	2	1787-1853	G	86
Goudy, Andrew	2	1787-1853	H	177
Gracy, Emma Winn	4	1854-1864	L	295
Gracy, John J.	4	1854-1864	L	228
Graddick, John	3	1787-1853	L	130
Green, Elizabeth W.	4	1854-1864	L	197
Green, Henry C.	3	1787-1853	L	399
Green, Robert L.	2	1787-1853	H	41
Green, Sarah	2	1787-1853	K	102
Green, Selina	3	1787-1853	L	52
Green, Thomas	1	1787-1853	C	64
Gregg, Cornelia M.	4	1854-1864	L	291
Gregg, Maxcy	4	1854-1864	L	320
Grey, David	1	1787-1853	E	122
Griffin, Charlotte	4	1854-1864	L	187
Griffin, William B.	4	1854-1864	L	262
Guignard, Elizabeth	1	1787-1853	E	113

Guignard, James Sanders	4	1854-1864	L	69
Guignard, John G.	2	1787-1853	G	103
Gunter, Brian (Planter)	4	1854-1864	L	165
Haig, John James (Planter)	1	1787-1853	E	9
Hall, Ainsley	2	1787-1853	H	1
Hall, James	2	1787-1853	H	25
Hamilton, John	1	1787-1853	E	55
Hamiter, Adam F.	2	1787-1853	G	127
Hampton, Gale	1	1787-1853	E	96
Hampton, Mary (Widow)	4	1854-1864	L	540
Harris, Barton	2	1787-1853	G	158
Harris, Elizabeth	2	1787-1853	H	62
Harris, Margaret	4	1854-1864	L	433
Harrison, Benjamin	2	1787-1853	K	108
Hart, Benjamin	3	1787-1853	L	296
Hart, Margaret E.	4	1854-1864	L	107
Haswell, Robert	1	1787-1853	B	59
Hay, William	1	1787-1853	C	8
Hayes, Lavinia	3	1787-1853	L	47
Hays, Charles	1	1787-1853	E	16
Heath, Ethel (Planter)	1	1787-1853	C	37
Heath, Harris	1	1787-1853	E	35
Heath, John (Planter)	1	1787-1853	C	56
Heath, Mary	1	1787-1853	E	29
Heath, Thomas (Jr.)	2	1787-1853	H	99
Heath, Thomas	3	1787-1853	L	324
Hendrick, Robert (Dr.)	1	1787-1853	D	47
Henry, Frances	4	1854-1864	L	213
Henry, James (Planter)	3	1787-1853	L	105
Herbemont, Alexander	4	1854-1864	L	370
Herbemont, Caroline (Mrs.)	2	1787-1853	K	64
Herbemont, Nickolas	2	1787-1853	K	118
Herron, Samuel	2	1787-1853	G	76
Hicks, Robert	1	1787-1853	C	58
Hicks, William B.	4	1854-1864	L	391
Higgins, Benjamin (Planter)	2	1787-1853	H	17
Higgins, Elizabeth R.	4	1854-1864	L	325
Higgins, William	3	1787-1853	L	351
Hill, Robert	1	1787-1853	C	28
Hillegas, Mary (Widow)	4	1854-1864	L	204
Hinsdale, Martin	4	1854-1864	L	233
Hinson, William	1	1787-1853	C	12
Hinton, Micajah	2	1787-1853	H	70
Hodge, Nancy	3	1787-1853	L	103
Hogan, Rosannah	3	1787-1853	L	217
Holliday, Mary	2	1787-1853	K	143
Hollis, Edward	1	1787-1853	C	19
Hollis, John H.	2	1787-1853	K	50
Hood, Frederick	3	1787-1853	L	135
Hooker, John	1	1787-1853	E	141
Hopkins, Amy	3	1787-1853	L	48
Hopkins, David T.	2	1787-1853	K	78
Hopkins, Francis M.	4	1854-1864	L	378
Hopkins, James	3	1787-1853	L	83
Hopkins, John (Planter)	2	1787-1853	H	169
Hopkins, Sarah T.	3	1787-1853	L	42
Hopkins, Williams	4	1854-1864	L	368

Hornsby, Christina	4	1854-1864	L	192
Horry, Peter (Planter)	1	1787-1853	E	124
House, Thomas	1	1787-1853	C	52
Howell, Arthur	1	1787-1853	B	51
Howell, Grace	2	1787-1853	K	48
Howell, Grace	4	1854-1864	L	350
Howell, Harriet	3	1787-1853	L	199
Howell, Jesse M.	4	1854-1864	L	114
Howell, Jessie Malachi	2	1787-1853	K	11
Howell, Lucy	2	1787-1853	G	95
Howell, Malachi	2	1787-1853	G	92
Howell, Margaret	1	1787-1853	E	153
Howell, Martha (Mrs.)	3	1787-1853	L	238
Howell, Mary	2	1787-1853	H	45
Howell, Mathew R.	3	1787-1853	L	309
Howell, Robert	1	1787-1853	D	28
Howell, Thomas	1	1787-1853	B	21
Howell, William	4	1854-1864	L	441
Hoxie, Norton A.	4	1854-1864	L	121
Hoyt, Smith	4	1854-1864	L	90
Hugg, Stephens	2	1787-1853	K	76
Huggins, Samuel	2	1787-1853	H	196
Huggins, William (Planter)	1	1787-1853	B	50
Hughes, John (Surgeon)	2	1787-1853	K	97
Hunt, James Green	1	1787-1853	C	17
Hutchinson, Thomas	2	1787-1853	G	30
Jackson, Samuel	1	1787-1853	B	47
Jameson, David	2	1787-1853	H	173
Johnston, Robert C.	4	1854-1864	L	215
Johnstone, Andrew	4	1854-1864	L	426
Jones, Mary	4	1854-1864	L	143
Jones, Mathew	3	1787-1853	L	349
Jones, Matthew	2	1787-1853	H	28
Jones, William Hl.	4	1854-1864	L	430
Jumper, Martha J.	4	1854-1864	L	360
Keenan, Alexander	4	1854-1864	L	172
Kelley, Benjamin	4	1854-1864	L	58
Kelley, H.H.	4	1854-1864	L	136
Kelly, Alexander (Planter)	1	1787-1853	E	3
Kelly, Jane (Spinster)	1	1787-1853	E	27
Kennedy, John A.	3	1787-1853	L	37
Kensler, Daniel	1	1787-1853	C	5
Killingsworth, Francis R.	4	1854-1864	L	180
Killingsworth, Jesse	2	1787-1853	G	24
Killingsworth, Jessie	4	1854-1864	L	60
Kinman, James D.	4	1854-1864	L	273
Kinster, Christine	1	1787-1853	B	27
Kinsler, Elizabeth (Widow)	2	1787-1853	G	58
Kinsler, Herman	2	1787-1853	H	100
Kinsler, John J.	4	1854-1864	L	119
Kirk, Susannah	3	1787-1853	K	89
Latta, Robert	3	1787-1853	L	283
Law, William	3	1787-1853	L	248
Leadingham, William	2	1787-1853	H	49

Learmont, Thomas	4	1854-1864	L	260
Legran, Elizabeth	2	1787-1853	H	55
Legran, Oliver	2	1787-1853	G	28
Levy, Samuel M.	2	1787-1853	K	157
Libecap, Mathias (Planter)	1	1787-1853	B	36
Lieber, Oscar M.	4	1854-1864	L	288
Lightner, George (Planter)	1	1787-1853	E	106
Lightner, George (Sr.)	2	1787-1853	H	153
Lightner, Jacob	3	1787-1853	L	92
Lipman, Mary	3	1787-1853	L	26
Livingston, William	2	1787-1853	G	133
Longbothern, Bulckley Thos.	1	1787-1853	E	130
Loomis, Cyrenius	4	1854-1864	L	396
Lott, John S.	3	1787-1853	L	1
Lowe, Pleasant	3	1787-1853	L	209
Lucious, John	2	1787-1853	G	54
Lykes, Frederick (Sr.)(Planter)	3	1787-1853	L	150
Lyon, Isaac	3	1787-1853	L	59
Lyons, Henry	4	1854-1864	L	162
McCawley, James	2	1787-1853	G	46
Mack, Conral	1	1787-1853	C	43
McClellan, James	2	1787-1853	G	15
McCord, D.J.	4	1854-1864	L	40
McCord, David	1	1787-1853	D	3
McCormick, Samuel	3	1787-1853	L	278
McCormick, William	3	1787-1853	L	113
McDonald, Alexander	2	1787-1853	G	8
McDonald, William	3	1787-1853	L	9
McDowell, Alexander	2	1787-1853	H	146
McDowell, Alexander	2	1787-1853	K	44
McGuire, Michael	1	1787-1853	C	47
McGuire, Peter	2	1787-1853	K	136
McIlwain, John	2	1787-1853	G	23
McKinna, Charles	4	1854-1864	L	424
McKinstrey, John	1	1787-1853	C	30
McLaughlin, Benjamin L.	3	1787-1853	L	267
McLaughlin, John	2	1787-1853	H	132
McLaughlin, Mary	4	1854-1864	L	51
McLemore, Joel	1	1787-1853	C	21
McLemore, John	2	1787-1853	K	90
McMillan, William (Planter)	2	1787-1853	K	116
McQueen, William C.	4	1854-1864	L	407
Malone, John	1	1787-1853	D	18
Malone, Mary	3	1787-1853	L	65
Marks, Frances	3	1787-1853	L	185
Marshall, C.G.	4	1854-1864	L	22
Marshall, John	3	1787-1853	L	306
Marshall, John	1	1787-1853	D	12
Marshall, John Francis	4	1787-1853	L	112
Marshall, Martin (Planter)	2	1787-1853	K	41
Marshall, Sarah	3	1787-1853	L	132
Martin, Frances	2	1787-1853	H	54

Martin, Joseph	1	1787-1853	E	100
Martin, Joseph (Sr.)	2	1787-1853	H	179
Martin, Joseph (Sr.)	1	1787-1853	D	56
Martin, Mary Wright	3	1787-1853	L	85
Martin, William	2	1787-1853	H	106
Maxwell, Janet	3	1787-1853	L	64
May, James	1	1787-1853	E	41
Medlin, Colvin	4	1854-1864	L	382
Medlin, Joel (Jr.)	3	1787-1853	L	156
Medlin, Robert	3	1787-1853	L	294
Miers, John (Planter)	1	1787-1853	C	40
Milling, Jane	1	1787-1853	E	7
Montague, Susan Ann Eliz.	4	1854-1864	L	270
Monteith, Galloway	4	1854-1864	L	158
Monteith, William	2	1787-1853	G	72
Moody, Joseph	2	1787-1853	H	19
Moore, Henry	1	1787-1853	D	49
Moore, John A.	4	1854-1864	L	66
Moore, William	4	1854-1864	L	149
Mordecai, Isaac D.	4	1854-1864	L	375
Morris, Mary	3	1787-1853	L	3
Morris, Mary	1	1787-1853	E	166
Morrison, Mary	3	1787-1853	L	80
Mulder, Abel	2	1787-1853	G	124
Munds, James Theus	4	1854-1864	L	332
Munson, Harriet Maria	2	1787-1853	K	110
Munson, Robert	3	1787-1853	L	34
Myer, William	2	1787-1853	G	130
Myers, David (Planter)	2	1787-1853	K	25
Myers, Phalby	4	1854-1864	L	7
Myers, William (Planter)	2	1787-1853	K	73
Mylling, Jane, see - - - - - - - - - - - - - - - - - - - Milling, Jane				
Nagel, Albert H.	4	1854-1864	L	64
Neal, Benjamin	2	1787-1853	H	47
Neal, Lewis	1	1787-1853	E	58
Nelson, Joseph H.	3	1787-1853	L	138
Nertz, Milley (Widow)	3	1787-1853	L	162
Neuffer, Harmon F	4	1854-1864	L	256
Neville, C.B.	3	1787-1853	L	216
Newsom, Benjamin	4	1854-1864	L	158
Nipper, Temperance	3	1787-1853	L	234
Nixon, Stephen (Sr.)	2	1787-1853	G	1
Norton, Catherine	4	1854-1864	L	97
Nutting, Mary	2	1787-1853	H	126
O'Conner, Eliza Harriet	1	1787-1853	E	88
Odom, J.J.	4	1854-1864	L	447
O'Hanlon, James (Planter)	4	1854-1864	L	443
O'Hanlon, John C.	3	1787-1853	L	304
Oliver, Mary Ann	2	1787-1853	H	175
O'Neal, Charles	4	1854-1864	L	352
Parker, Gabriel	1	1787-1853	E	75
Parker, Lucy	2	1787-1853	G	44

Parr, John	2	1787-1853	K	55
Parr, Mary (Widow)	3	1787-1853	L	140
Partridge, John	2	1787-1853	H	59
Partridge, Phillip	1	1787-1853	C	53
Partridge, William	1	1787-1853	B	13
Patterson, Andrew	1	1787-1853	D	1
Patterson, James	3	1787-1853	L	159
Patterson, Samuel	2	1787-1853	K	57
Pearse, John	2	1787-1853	H	89
Peirce, William	1	1787-1853	D	58
Pemberton, A.H.	3	1787-1853	L	125
Pemberton, John	1	1787-1853	C	42
Phelps, Mary	2	1787-1853	G	4
Pierce, John	1	1787-1853	E	108
Player, Susan Jane	3	1787-1853	L	213
Pollock, David	2	1787-1853	H	59
Poole, George	1	1787-1853	E	102
Porcher, Augustus H.	3	1787-1853	L	256
Powers, Paul (Planter)	1	1787-1853	D	15
Prescott, Aaron (Planter)	1	1787-1853	E	145
Prescott, Jesse (Planter)	3	1787-1853	L	43
Preston, William C.	4	1854-1864	L	221
Price, John	1	1787-1853	E	95
Pullig, Anthony	2	1787-1853	H	92
Purvis, Mary	3	1787-1853	L	313
Purvis, William	2	1787-1853	H	66
Quilter, Timothy F.	3	1787-1853	L	5
Raiford, Isaac	1	1787-1853	E	143
Randall, Joseph	4	1854-1864	L	293
Raoul, Carolina	2	1787-1853	K	146
Raoul, J.L.	2	1787-1853	H	68
Rawlinson, Benj. (Blacksmith)	1	1787-1853	E	77
Raynal, Mary Martha	2	1787-1853	H	130
Reapsamen, John (Planter)	1	1787-1853	C	44
Reddock, C.D.	4	1854-1864	L	206
Reese, Jesse	2	1787-1853	G	90
Reese, John Al.	3	1787-1853	L	75
Reese, Joseph (Minister)	1	1787-1853	C	23
Reese, Mary Howell	4	1854-1864	L	140
Reese, Sarah	3	1787-1853	L	95
Reese, Timothy	2	1787-1853	K	112
Reilly, Bernard	4	1854-1864	K	384
Reynolds, George N.	4	1854-1864	L	404
Richter, Christian F.	4	1854-1864	L	283
Rivers, William	2	1787-1853	G	54
Rives, Herbert	1	1787-1853	C	16
Rives, Precilla	1	1787-1853	D	5
Rives, Robert	1	1787-1853	C	1
Rives, Timothy	2	1787-1853	G	79
Roach, Simeon	1	1787-1853	E	59
Roberson, John W. (M.D.)	1	1787-1853	D	43
Roberts, Phillips	3	1787-1853	L	274
Robertson, Robert	1	1787-1853	E	49
Robinson, John	1	1787-1853	D	45
Rodgers, Ol. B. (Soldier)	3	1787-1853	L	136
Romanstine, George	2	1787-1853	G	52
Romanstine, John	3	1787-1853	L	97

Rosborough, Alexander	4	1854-1864	L	208
Rose, Martin D.	4	1854-1864	L	554
Ross, James	1	1787-1855	B	40
Rowan, James	5	1787-1855	L	71
Rowan, Robert	5	1787-1855	L	123
Rowan, Samuel (Planter)	1	1787-1855	B	41
Russell, Robert E.	4	1854-1864	L	1
Salisbury, Pettigrew	1	1787-1855	C	10
Scott, Benjamin	1	1787-1855	E	119
Scott, James S.	4	1854-1864	L	155
Scott, Samuel	2	1787-1855	H	76
Scott, William	2	1787-1855	G	155
Scott, William (Sr.)	1	1787-1855	E	71
Seay, John	2	1787-1855	H	91
Seubt, Annie	4	1854-1864	L	17
Sharp, John C.	5	1787-1855	L	245
Shaver, Margaret (Widow)	1	1787-1855	E	52
Sheppard, John E.	1	1787-1855	E	45
Shirling, James	1	1787-1855	B	17
Simmons, Claude	1	1787-1855	E	57
Singelton, M.R.	5	1787-1855	L	322
Sistrunk, Jasper	2	1787-1855	H	53
Slappy, Christina	1	1787-1855	E	25
Sledd, Seten	1	1787-1855	B	54
Smiley, Dorthy	5	1787-1855	L	315
Smiley, William	5	1787-1855	L	21
Smith, Edward D.	2	1787-1855	G	49
Smith, George	4	1854-1864	L	151
Smith, George (Sr.)	2	1787-1855	G	12
Smith, Peter	1	1787-1855	C	49
Smith, Richard	2	1787-1855	G	42
Smith, William (Barber)	1	1787-1855	E	80
Smyth, Robert·	1	1787-1855	C	61
Snowden, Gilbert T.	5	1787-1855	L	299
Soloman, Phineas	5	1787-1855	L	194
Sondlay, Richard	4	1854-1864	L	159
Sowden, Joshua	4	1854-1864	L	46
Sowter, George	2	1787-1855	G	70
Spelling, William	2	1787-1855	H	152
Spigner, Frederick (Plant.)	2	1787-1855	G	62
Stack, Elizabeth (Widow)	5	1787-1855	L	108
Stack, William	5	1787-1855	L	56
Stanley, Samuel	2	1787-1855	G	26
Stanton, Joseph	5	1787-1855	L	256
Stark, Mrs. Grace	5	1787-1855	L	23
Stark, Robert	2	1787-1855	H	121
Stevens, James	5	1787-1855	L	232
Stowe, Susan	4	1854-1864	L	226
Strange, Henry	1	1787-1855	C	14
Stubbs, John	4	1854-1864	L	347
Sturgun, Martha M.	4	1854-1864	L	364
Sturgeon, William (Sr.)	2	1787-1855	H	145
Suling, John	5	1787-1855	L	75
Surginer, Wm.	2	1787-1855	G	88
Taylor, Ann Timothy (Widow)	4	1854-1864	L	393
Taylor, Benjamin E.	5	1787-1855	L	251

Taylor, John (Blacksmith)	1	1787-1853	E	155
Taylor, Margaret	3	1787-1853	L	174
Taylor, Mary	1	1787-1853	B	29
Taylor, Mary (Widow)	3	1787-1853	L	110
Taylor, Sarah (Mrs.)	3	1787-1853	L	220
Taylor, Teresa	4	1854-1864	L	26
Taylor, Thomas (Sr.)(Col.)	2	1787-1853	H	181
Taylor, William	2	1787-1853	H	43
Thayer, Harriet G.	4	1854-1864	L	410
Thompson, Gouvenuer M.	4	1854-1864	L	189
Thompson, Grace G.	2	1787-1853	K	151
Thompson, Mary	2	1787-1853	G	56
Thompson, Sarah C.	3	1787-1853	L	91
Trapp, John T.	3	1787-1853	L	116
Threewits, Joel	2	1787-1853	K	100
Tidwell, Gnumon	2	1787-1853	H	80
Tomlinson, William (Sr.)	1	1787-1853	E	159
Trice, William	1	1787-1853	E	12
Tucker, Isaac	1	1787-1853	E	85
Tucker, Joel A.	2	1787-1853	H	148
Tucker, Sarah W.	3	1787-1853	L	118
Tucker, Wood	2	1787-1853	G	18
Turnipseed, George (Plant.)	2	1787-1853	K	167
Turnipseed, Harriet E.	4	1854-1864	L	86
Turnipseed, Herman (Plant.)	1	1787-1853	E	18
Turnipseed, John B. (Planter)	2	1787-1853	H	167
Turnipseed, Mary Sybil	4	1854-1864	L	267
Turnipseed, Nancy	3	1787-1853	L	14
Turquand, Catherine	2	1787-1853	G	75
Tyler, Mary (Widow)	3	1787-1853	L	192
Tyson, Mason B.	2	1787-1853	H	109
Vinson, Andrew W.	3	1787-1853	L	279
Waddell, John	4	1854-1864	L	15
Wade, George	2	1787-1853	H	10
Wages, Dawson	3	1787-1853	L	242
Wages, Rebecca	3	1787-1853	L	240
Wages, William	3	1787-1853	L	201
Waggoner, Martin	1	1787-1853	C	18
Walker, Joseph	1	1787-1853	E	98
Wallace, Andrew	4	1854-1864	L	301
Walsh, Thomas	2	1787-1853	K	47
Walshe, John (Dr.)	2	1787-1853	G	140
Walter, Sarah T. (Widow)	4	1854-1864	L	242
Ward, Henry D.	2	1787-1853	G	10
Ward, Henry Dana A.	2	1787-1853	H	73
Watkins, Samuel (Sr.)	2	1787-1853	H	57
Watson, Effa	2	1787-1853	G	108
Watson, Jonh	1	1787-1853	E	21
Watts, Thomas	2	1787-1853	G	65
Wayre, Richard (Merchant)	1	1787-1853	E	60
Weir, Samuel	3	1787-1853	L	120
Wescott, David	1	1787-1853	B	7
Wescott, Ebenezer	1	1787-1853	C	34
Wessinger, Penelope	3	1787-1853	L	101
Weston, Christian G.	4	1854-1864	L	3
Weston, Francis H.	4	1854-1864	L	362

Weston, Robert (Sr.)	2	1787-1853	H	188
Whitaker, William (Jr.)	1	1787-1853	B	1
Whitaker, William (Sr.)	1	1787-1853	B	23
White, Ann	4	1854-1864	L	372
White, James	1	1787-1853	E	82
White, Mary S. (Spinster)	2	1787-1853	G	56
Whitecotton, Axton	2	1787-1853	H	165
Williams, Eli	2	1787-1853	H	111
Williams, William	1	1787-1853	D	34
Williamson, Chestian E.	2	1787-1853	H	8
Williamson, James	1	1787-1853	D	7
Williamson, Richard	1	1787-1853	D	23
Wilson, John Du Bose (Clerk)	3	1787-1853	L	62
Wilson, Olivia	3	1787-1853	L	16
Wimberly, Mary	1	1787-1853	B	25
Wood, James R.	4	1854-1864	L	93
Wood, Sampson S.	2	1787-1853	G	74
Woodward, Isom	3	1787-1853	L	128
Woodward, Lieuellan	4	1854-1864	L	297
Woodward, Mary	2	1787-1853	H	78
Wootan, Mark	2	1787-1853	H	155
Yates, Robert	2	1787-1853	K	54
Young, James	2	1787-1853	K	1
Young, Mary (Widow)	3	1787-1853	L	332
Young, Napolean B.	4	1854-1864	L	258
Zanony, John	2	1787-1853	K	141

Copied by:

/s/   Mrs. John D. Rogers

INDEX

TO

SPARTANBURG COUNTY WILLS.

Volume No. 1
1787-1820

Volume No. 2
1830-1835

Volume No. 3
1840-1858

This index is compiled from W.P.A. copies
of wills filed in the COUNTY PROBATE
COURTS. The volumes indexed are a
part of the South Carolina collection
of the University of South Carolina
Library.

Columbia, S. C.
1939

SPARTANBURG COUNTY

WILLS

Name	Vol.	Date	Section	Page
Abbott, Solomon	3	1840-1858	D	451
Alexander, Robert	3	1840-1858	D	416
Allen, Caleb	3	1840-1858	D	244
Allen, James	1	1821-1829	B	66
Allen, John	1	1821-1829	B	26
Allen, Willis	3	1840-1858	D	131
Anderson, David	1	1821-1829	B	99
Anderson, Denny. (Sr.)	2	1830-1835	C	40
Anderson, Rebeccah	2	1830-1835	C	16
Anderson, Samuel	2	1830-1835	C	8
Arndell, Reddick	2	1830-1835	C	43
Arnold, John	1	1787-1820	A	35
Austell, Joseph	1	1821-1829	B	33
Bagwell, Sarah	1	1840-1858	D	248
Ballenger, Edward	1	1821-1829	B	30
Ballenger, James (Sr.)	1	1787-1820	A	31
Barnett, Agnes	3	1840-1858	D	284
Barnett, Edward	1	1787-1820	A	130
Barnett, Micajah (Planter)	2	1830-1835	C	87
Barry, Andrew	1	1787-1820	A	16
Barry, Margaret	1	1821-1829	B	44
Barry, Richard	1	1787-1820	A	82
Bates, Anthony	3	1840-1858	D	37
Bates, George	2	1830-1835	C	77
Bearden, Isaac	2	1830-1835	C	45
Bearden, John	3	1840-1858	D	127
Bennett, James (Sr.)	1	1821-1829	B	62
Bennett, William	2	1830-1835	C	89
Benson, Robert	1	1787-1820	A	33
Bishop, Eli	3	1840-1858	D	484
Bishop, Isaac	1	1821-1829	B	13
Bishop, William	2	1830-1835	C	71
Blackstock, William	3	1840-1858	D	8
Bobo, Absalom	3	1840-1858	D	143
Bobo, Burrell	2	1830-1835	C	19
Bobo, Salley	1	1787-1820	A	69
Bobo, Spencer	1	1787-1820	A	77
Bomar, Edward	3	1840-1858	D	358
Bonner, Anny	3	1840-1858	D	220
Bonner, Benjamin (Plant.)	1	1787-1820	A	48
Brewton, George	1	1787-1820	A	60
Brewton, John	3	1840-1858	D	282
Brewton, Jonas (Sr.)	3	1840-1858	D	454
Brewton, see also — — — — — — — — — — — — — — — — Bruton				
Brice, Samuel	3	1840-1858	D	200
Brockman, James	3	1840-1858	D	476
Brown, James	3	1840-1858	D	64
Brown, Jesse	3	1840-1858	D	190
Brown, John (Farmer)	3	1840-1858	D	424
Brown, Wylie S.	1	1821-1829	B	108
Bruton, David (Sr.)	1	1787-1820	A	71
Bruton, Susannah	2	1820-1835	C	114
Bruton, see also — — — — — — — — — — — — — — — — — Brewton				
Buise, Jonathan	3	1840-1858	D	111

Buise, David (Sr.)	3	1840-1858	D	340
Bullington, Mary	3	1840-1858	D	304
Bullington, Robert	3	1840-1858	D	278
Burnett, Mathias	2	1840-1858	D	9
Burnett, Sarah	3	1840-1858	D	246
Burns, James	3	1840-1858	D	439
Burton, Thomas	2	1830-1835	C	46
Byers, Joseph	3	1840-1858	D	301
Caldwell, Andrew (Farmer)	3	1840-1858	D	329
Caldwell, James	3	1840-1858	D	411
Caldwell, William	3	1840-1858	D	2
Callicot, Asa (Sr.)	1	1787-1820	A	139
Camp, Adam S.	3	1840-1858	A	175
Camp, James	1	1737-1820	D	94
Camp, Joseph	2	1830-1835	C	117
Cannon, Jesse	3	1840-1858	D	225
Cannon, John	3	1840-1858	D	216
Cannon, William	3	1840-1858	D	128
Cantrell, James	2	1830-1835	C	113
Casey, Casandra	3	1840-1858	D	138
Casey, John	1	1737-1820	A	81
Casey, Mary	3	1840-1858	D	162
Casey, Moses (Sr.)	2	1830-1835	C	9
Casey, Sarah	1	1821-1829	B	113
Cathcart, Samuel (Mason)	1	1787-1820	A	142
Chambers, Edmond	1	1821-1829	B	8
Chamblin, James	3	1840-1858	D	318
Chapman, Elizabeth	3	1840-1858	D	402
Chapman, John (Sr.)	3	1840-1858	D	387
Chapman, William	3	1840-1858	D	350
Chesney, Hester	2	1820-1829	C	136
Chesney, Richard	1	1737-1820	A	87
Chesney, Thomas	3	1840-1858	D	370
Clark, John	3	1840-1858	D	86
Clark, William G.	3	1840-1858	D	342
Clayton, Mary	3	1840-1858	D	68
Clement, Edward	3	1840-1858	D	119
Coan, Andrew	2	1830-1835	C	64
Coan, James	3	1840-1858	D	79
Cole, Thomas	1	1787-1820	A	74
Collins, John	3	1840-1858	D	12
Compton, Thomas	1	1737-1820	A	109
Cooper, Adam	3	1840-1858	D	10
Cooper, Mathew	3	1840-1858	D	400
Cooper, William	1	1787-1820	A	13
Copeland, Alexander	2	1830-1835	C	74
Cothren, Gabriel	3	1840-1858	D	254
Couch, Benjamin	1	1787-1820	A	91
Couch, Mathew	1	1821-1829	B	11
Cox, Paul	3	1840-1858	D	82
Crocker, Anthony	3	1840-1858	D	152
Crocker, Dorcus	2	1830-1835	C	141
Crook, Jesse	3	1840-1858	D	89
Crow, Isaac	1	1787-1820	A	100
Crow, Jonathan	3	1840-1858	D	125
Cudd, John	3	1840-1858	D	421
Daniel, Elizabeth	2	1830-1835	C	28
Daniel, Frances	3	1840-1858	D	112

Daniel, Reuben	1	1828-1829	B	92
Daniel, Robert M.	2	1830-1835	C	140
Dantzler, David	3	1840-1858	D	149
Darby, Thomas	2	1830-1835	C	83
Davidson, Alexander	2	1830-1835	C	1
Davis, Jesse	1	1787-1820	A	20
Davis, Joseph	3	1840-1858	D	192
Davis, Thompson	3	1840-1858	D	228
Dean, H. J. (Lawyer)	3	1840-1858	D	364
Dean, John	3	1840-1858	D	257
Demsey, Lucretia	1	1821-1829	B	81
Devine, George	1	1821-1829	B	53
Dickson, Robert	3	1840-1858	D	322
Dickson, William	3	1840-1858	D	316
Divine, George, see - - - - - - - - - - - - - - - - Devine, George				
Dobbins, Ezekial	3	1840-1858	D	451
Drummond, Ephraim	3	1840-1858	D	24
Drummond, Harrison	3	1840-1858	D	383
Drummond, Samuel W.	3	1840-1858	D	405
Dunaway, Samuel (Planter)	1	1787-1820	A	99
Durham, John	2	1830-1835	C	92
Earl, Theron	3	1840-1858	D	25
Eison, John	1	1821-1829	B	68
Ellis, Samuel	3	1840-1858	D	409
Farmer, William	2	1830-1835	C	108
Farrow, Samuel	1	1821-1829	B	57
Farrow, Thomas	3	1840-1858	D	70
Farrow, Waters	3	1840-1858	D	118
Finch, James A.	3	1840-1858	D	482
Fleming, Alexander	3	1840-1858	D	135
Fleming, James	2	1830-1835	C	12
Ford, Dolly	3	1840-1858	D	309
Foster, Anthony	1	1787-1820	A	153
Foster, Anthony	3	1840-1858	D	453
Foster, Henry (Planter)	1	1821-1829	B	3
Foster, Isham (Planter)	1	1787-1820	A	112
Foster, J ohn (Planter)	1	1787-1820	A	107
Foster, John (Planter)	2	1830-1835	C	95
Foster, Moses (Planter)	1	1787-1820	A	39
Foster, Sarah	3	1840-1858	D	324
Foster, Simpson	1	1821-1829	B	39
Foster, William (Planter)	1	1787-1820	A	118
Foster, William	2	1830-1835	C	134
Fowler, Dempsey	2	1830-1835	C	129
Fowler, John	3	1840-1858	D	58
Friar, Jonathan, see - - - - - - - - - - - - - - Fryer, Jonathan				
Frie, Peter	1	1787-1820	A	28
Fryer, Jonathan	3	1840-1858	D	315
Fryer, Richard	1	1821-1829	B	1
Gaffney, M ichael	3	1840-1858	D	332
Gaston, Joseph	3	1840-1858	D	148
Gaston, Robert	3	1840-1858	D	168
Gaston, Samuel	3	1840-1858	D	459
Gennings, William	3	1840-1858	D	208
Gentry, Nathaniel	3	1840-1858	D	267
Gilbert, Baldam	3	1840-1858	D	252

Gillespie, Edward F.	3	1840-1858	D	349
Golightly, Amy	1	1787-1820	A	50
Golightly, Christopher	3	1840-1858	D	206
Golightly, David	3	1840-1858	D	53
Goodlett, Ann	1	1787-1820	A	127
Goodlett, Robert	1	1821-1329	B	35
Gorden, Isaac	2	1830-1835	C	125
Gosnell, John	3	1840-1858	D	442
Gosnett, Gabriel	2	1820-1835	C	62
Gowen, John	1	1787-1820	A	2
Grant, Daniel (Sr.)	1	1821-1829	B	95
Greer, Isabel	3	1840-1858	D	480
Griffin, Bowen	3	1840-1858	D	337
Griffin, Jesse	3	1840-1858	D	250
Grist, John	1	1787-1820	A	79-A
Grist, John	1	1787-1820	A	79-B
Guinn, John, see - - - - - - - - - - - - - - - - - -			Gwinn, John	
Guttery, Absalom	2	1830-1835	C	76
Gwinn, John (Farmer)	3	1840-1858	D	265
Hall, David	3	1840-1858	D	390
Ham, James	1	1787-1820	A	135
Hannah, Thomas	2	1830-1835	C	104
Harmon, Samuel, see - - - - - - - - - - - - - - - -			Hermon, Samuel	
Harris, Balus	3	1840-1858	D	14
Harris, Sylvira	3	1840-1858	D	441
Harrison, Thomas	1	1787-1820	A	132
Hatchett, Josiah	1	1828-1829	B	45
Henry, Ann Eliza	3	1840-1858	D	352
Henry, James E. (Attorney)	3	1840-1858	D	211
Hering, Edward, see - - - - - - - - - - - - - - - -			Herring, Edward	
Hermon, John	2	1830-1835	C	11
Hermon, Samuel	3	1840-1858	D	166
Herring, Edward	1	1787-1820	A	27
Hester, Charles (Farmer)	2	1830-1835	C	49
Hewatt, John	1	1787-1820	A	21
High, Benjamin	1	1787-1820	A	92
Hill, Leonard (Sr.)	3	1840-1858	D	5
Hindman, John	1	1787-1820	A	146
Hindman, William	3	1840-1858	D	292
Hines, Whitney	3	1840-1858	D	15
Hobby, John (Farmer)	1	1821-1829	B	96
Hobby, Zachariah	2	1820-1835	C	109
House, Thomas (Planter)	1	1787-1820	A	15
Howard, Benjamin	1	1787-1820	A	126
Hughs, Ann	2	1830-1835	C	37
Humphries, Jesse	3	1840-1858	D	151
Jackson, Thomas	1	1821-1829	B	74
Jamerson, Rosey	3	1840-1858	D	126
Jamerson, Samuel	3	1840-1858	D	195
Jamerson, Sarah	3	1840-1858	D	281
James, Charles	1	1821-1829	B	15
James, John	1	1821-1829	B	28
Jamison, Henry	3	1840-1858	D	348
Jamison, Samuel, see - - - - - - - - - - - - - - - -			Jamerson, Samuel	
Jamison, Sarah, see - - - - - - - - - - - - - - -			Jamerson, Sarah	
Johnson, Christopher	1	1787-1820	A	4
Johnson, David	3	1840-1858	D	344
Johnson, John	3	1840-1858	D	461

Johnson, Rowland	3	1840–1858	D	113
Jones, Benjamin	2	1830–1835	C	111
Jones, John	1	1787–1820	A	116
Jordan, Margaret	1	1821–1829	B	64
Kelly, Thomas	3	1840–1858	D	147
Kelly, Williamson	3	1840–1858	D	466
Kennedy, Lionel H. (Atty.)	3	1840–1858	D	141
Kestler, Henry	3	1840–1858	D	209
King, John, Jr.	3	1840–1858	D	44
King, John	3	1840–1858	D	303
Kirby, Lovicy	3	1840–1858	D	156
Kirby, Oliver	3	1840–1858	D	261
Lamaster, Richard	1	1821–1829	B	54
Lamb, Jesse	2	1830–1835	C	122
Lambright, Benjamin F.	3	1840–1858	D	462
Lancaster, Absolom	1	1787–1820	A	67
Lancaster, Samuel	1	1787–1820	A	5
Lancaster, William	1	1821–1820	B	40
Langston, Nathan	2	1830–1835	C	47
Law, John (Sr.)	1	1821–1829	B	78
Layton, James	3	1840–1858	D	291
Layton, James	3	1840–1858	D	339
Leatherwood, John	1	1787–1820	A	140
Leatherwood, Zachariah	1	1787–1820	A	45
Lee, Levi	1	1821–1820	B	25
Lee, Selah	2	1830–1835	C	106
Leonard, Thomas	3	1840–1858	D	202
Leonard, William	3	1840–1858	D	367
Lewess, George	1	1787–1820	A	125
Lewis, Joel (Planter)	1	1787–1820	A	56
Lewis, John	1	1787–1820	A	43
Linder, John	2	1830–1835	C	56
Linder, Lee (Planter)	3	1840–1858	D	46
Lipscomb, David (Farmer)	1	1787–1820	A	85
Lipscomb, Elizabeth	3	1840–1858	D	66
Lipscomb, John (Sr.)	1	1821–1829	B	101
Lipscomb, Smith (Sr.)	3	1840–1858	D	239
Lipscomb, William	1	1787–1820	A	10
Littlejohn, Elizabeth	3	1840–1858	D	305
Littlejohn, Henry L.	3	1840–1858	D	286
Lively, Joseph	1	1821–1829	B	84
Loftis, John	3	1840–1858	D	169
McArthur, Abram (Planter)	3	1840–1858	D	31
McBee, Matthew	1	1787–1820	A	105
McCarter, George (Planter)	1	1787–1820	A	65
McClain, Charles	1	1821–1829	B	14
McClintock, Elizabeth F.	3	1840–1858	D	262
McClure, John	3	1840–1858	D	17
McElrath, John	1	1821–1829	B	47
McElrath, Robert T.	3	1840–1858	D	478
McKie, Alexander	2	1830–1835	C	30
McWilliams, Wm. (Planter)	1	1821–1829	B	37
Martin, Barrett, L.	3	1840–1858	D	4
Mason, Francis	1	1821–1829	B	63
Mason, Posey	3	1840–1858	D	260
Mason, Ransom	3	1840–1858	D	198

Mathis, Mathew	3	1840-1858	D	438
Mayer, Thomas	1	1787-1820	A	151
Mayes, Thomas G.	3	1840-1858	D	62
Meaders, George	3	1840-1858	D	444
Meaders, William	1	1821-1829	B	18
Meadows, Thomas (Planter)	1	1787-1820	A	70
Miles, Mary	3	1840-1858	D	396
Miller, James A.	3	1840-1858	D	327
Miller, Michael	1	1787-1820	A	54
Miller, Samuel	3	1840-1858	D	287
Montgomery, John	3	1840-1858	D	154
Moore, Andrew Barry	3	1840-1858	D	158
Moore, Elsworth	3	1840-1858	D	430
Moore, Michael (Merchant)	1	1821-1829	B	72
Moore, Thomas (Gen.)	1	1821-1829	B	21
Moore, Wesley	3	1840-1858	D	325
Morris, John	2	1830-1835	C	53
Morrow, Samual (Sr.)	1	1787-1820	A	150
Morrow, Samual (Farmer)	3	1840-1858	D	42
Mullinax, John	2	1830-1835	C	80
Murph, John	3	1840-1858	D	81
Murray, John N.	3	1840-1858	D	255
Nesbitt, James (Sr.)	2	1830-1835	C	130
Nesbitt, Jonathan	2	1830-1835	C	56
Nesbitt, Samuel	1	1787-1820	A	96
Nesbitt, Samuel	3	1840-1858	D	106
Newman, Davis	3	1840-1858	D	307
Newman, Reuben	3	1840-1858	D	196
Nicholls, Benjamin	2	1830-1835	C	17
Nicholls, Catherine	3	1840-1858	D	335
Nicholls, George	3	1840-1858	D	194
Oaland, Peter C.	3	1840-1858	D	210
O'Neill, Henry (Planter)	1	1787-1820	A	51
Otts, Samuel	1	1787-1820	A	73
Owen, William	1	1787-1820	A	114
Owens, John	1	1821-1829	B	16
Paden, Thomas	1	1821-1829	B	50
Page, Christian	3	1840-1858	D	372
Page, James	3	1840-1858	D	413
Page, Robert (Sr.)	1	1821-1829	B	90
Palmer, John D.	1	1787-1820	A	134
Parham, Drury	3	1840-1858	D	49
Patterson, Adonijah	3	1840-1858	D	22
Payterson, David	3	1840-1858	D	272
Patterson, Edward	3	1840-1858	D	56
Pearson, Robert N.	2	1830-1835	C	137
Pearson, Robert N.	3	1840-1858	D	1
Peden, Eleanor	2	1830-1835	C	54
Peden, Elizabeth	2	1830-1835	C	26
Penny, Sarah	1	1787-1820	A	72-a
Penny, Thomas	1	1787-1820	A	72-b
Peterson, Peter	2	1830-1835	C	35
Pettit, Joshua	1	1821-1829	B	104
Petty, Charles	3	1840-1858	D	76
Pickenpack, John	3	1840-1858	D	312
Pickenpack, Mary Dorothy	3	1840-1858	D	404
Pollard, William	2	1830-1835	C	110

Poole, John	3	1840–1858	D	182
Poole, Thomas	2	1830–1835	C	123
Pope, Thomas	1	1821–1829	B	43
Posey, Thomas	3	1840–1858	D	164
Prewitt, Rosannah	3	1840–1858	D	245
Prewitt, Peter (Planter)	1	1787–1829	B	32
Price, Joseph	2	1830–1835	C	57
Price, Thomas	1	1787–1820	A	158
Prince, Richard	1	1787–1820	A	19
Pruitt, Rosannah, see – – – – – – – – – – – – – – – – – – Prewitt, Rosannah				
Raines, Caty	2	1830–1835	C	2
Rakestraw, Jesse	2	1830–1835	C	72
Rakestraw, Rufus	3	1840–1858	D	85
Red, John	1	1821–1829	B	48
Reid, William	3	1840–1858	D	356
Reynolds, James	1	1821–1829	B	87
Rhodes, Christopher	1	1787–1820	A	24
Rhodes, Christopher	2	1830–1835	C	127
Rhodes, William	3	1840–1858	D	446
Richards, James	3	1840–1858	D	204
Richardson, James T	3	1840–1858	D	33
Richardson, Moses	3	1840–1858	D	229
Richeson, Moses, see – – – – – – – – – – – – – – – – – –Richardson, Moses				
Robuck, George	3	1840–1858	D	176
Rogers, John	3	1840–1858	D	256
Rogers, Robert (Sr.)	2	1830–1835	C	4
Rogers, William (Planter)	2	1830–1835	C	14
Ross, Samuel	2	1830–1835	C	51
Rowland, George	1	1787–1820	A	128
Rutland, Reddick	1	1821–1829	B	85
Sarratt, John	3	1840–1858	D	320
Sarratt, Thomas	1	1787–1820	A	115
Scruggs, Richard	3	1840–1858	D	362
Seay, Reuben	2	1830–1835	C	51
Sexton, Morgan	3	1840–1858	D	422
Shippey, Elijah	3	1840–1858	D	449
Shippey, Samuel	2	1830–1835	C	84
Simmons, Joseph	1	1821–1829	B	111
Smith, Charles (Farmer)	1	1821–1829	B	55
Smith, Charles (Planter)	3	1840–1858	D	40
Smith, Eber (Physician)	2	1830–1835	C	138
Smith, Edward (Planter)	1	1787–1820	A	58
Smith, Edward	3	1840–1858	D	483
Smith, Holeman	3	1840–1858	D	360
Smith, Isaac	3	1840–1858	D	448
Smith, Jane	3	1840–1858	D	170
Smith, John	1	1787–1820	A	76-a
Smith, John	1	1787–1820	A	76-b
Smith, John	3	1840–1858	D	407
Smith, Perry	3	1840–1858	D	479
Smith, William	2	1830–1835	C	98
Smith, William	3	1840–1858	D	455
Snoddy, Elizabeth	3	1840–1858	D	399
Snoddy, Isaac (Jr.)	2	1830–1835	C	78
Snoddy, Isaac	3	1840–1858	D	33
Snoddy, John (Jr.)	3	1840–1858	D	186
Snoddy, Samuel	1	1787–1820	A	98
Stacey, Robert	3	1840–1858	D	184

Stewart, Samuel	1	1787–1820	A	120
Stone, Lewis	2	1830–1835	C	23
Stone, Moses	3	1840–1858	D	92
Stone, Samuel	1	1821–1829	B	89
Stone, William	1	1787–1820	A	47
Story, George	3	1840–1858	D	428
Takewell, John	3	1840–1858	D	108
Thomason, Elizabeth	3	1840–1858	D	376
Thompson, Alex. (Planter)	3	1840–1858	D	19
Thompson, Frances	3	1840–1858	D	109
Thompson, James	1	1787–1820	A	135
Thompson, James (Planter)	2	1830–1835	C	5
Thompson, Richard	3	1840–1858	D	95
Thomson, Henry H.	3	1840–1858	D	467
Thomson, Jane	1	1787–1820	A	133
Timmons, Hannah	1	1787–1820	A	103
Tolleson, John	1	1821–1829	B	6
Tracy, William	3	1840–1858	D	55
Trail, David (Planter)	2	1830–1835	C	24
Traylor, Joel (Planter)	1	1787–1820	A	1
Tucker, Ann	3	1840–1858	D	389
Turner, Darby	2	1830–1835	C	94
Turner, Henry (Sr.)	3	1840–1858	D	27
Turner, James	3	1840–1858	D	486
Turner, John	1	1787–1820	A	125
Turner, Mathais	1	1787–1820	A	122
Turner, William	3	1840–1858	D	380
Turner, William B.	3	1840–1858	D	374
Underwood, William	1	1787–1820	A	22
Vandiver, James	2	1830–1835	C	135
Vernon, Margaret	3	1840–1858	D	139
Vise, Reuben	3	1840–1858	D	295
Vionset, John	1	1787–1820	A	144
Wakefield, Jesse	3	1840–1858	D	433
Walden, Asa	1	1821–1829	B	107
Walding, Henry (Sr.)	1	1821–1829	B	79
Waldrop, William	3	1840–1858	D	247
Waldrupe, William, see - - - - - - - - - - - - - - - - - - -Waldrop, William				
Walker, Absalom	3	1840–1858	D	556
Walker, Charles S. (Rev.)	3	1840–1858	D	419
Walker, John	1	1787–1820	A	41
Walker, John	2	1830–1835	C	59
Walker, William	3	1840–1858	D	464
Wall, Robert I.	3	1840–1858	D	223
Wall, Zachariah	3	1840–1858	D	381
Walling, Daniel	1	1787–1820	A	23
Waters, Jane	3	1840–1858	D	293
Watkins, Jonas	3	1840–1858	D	88
Weaver, Thomas J.	1	1787–1820	A	58
Wells, John	3	1840–1858	D	115
Weson, Amos	2	1820–1835	C	67
West, James	3	1840–1858	D	117
West, Asborn (Farmer)	1	1787–1820	A	44
West, Thomas	3	1840–1858	D	593
Whetstone, David	3	1840–1858	D	299
White, Daniel	3	1840–1858	D	180

White, John	1	1828-1823	B	19
White, John	2	1830-1835	C	55
White, William	3	1840-1858	D	373
Wilbanks, Phebe	1	1821-1829	B	71
Wilbanks, William	1	1787-1820	A	89
Wilkins, Moses	3	1840-1858	D	121
Wilkins, Robert	3	1840-1858	D	171
Wilkins, William	1	1787-1820	A	155
Wilkins, William	3	1840-1858	D	385
Williams, Edward	3	1840-1858	D	145
Williams, Isaac	2	1830-1835	C	86
Williams, John	3	1840-1858	D	269
Williams, Richard	3	1840-1858	D	163
Williamson, Henry	1	1787-1820	A	151
Williamson, Thomas	1	1787-1820	A	25
Williamson, Thomas	3	1840-1858	D	52
Wilson, Alexander	2	1830-1835	C	7
Wingo, Abner	1	1787-1820	A	49
Wingo, John	3	1840-1858	D	297
Wingo, Obediah	1	1821-1829	B	115
Wingo, Ranson	2	1830-1835	C	135
Wofford, Benjamin (Rev.)	3	1840-1858	D	230
Wofford, Catherine	1	1821-1829	B	70
Wofford, Comfort	3	1840-1858	D	410
Wofford, Isaac (Sr.)	3	1840-1858	D	178
Wofford, James	1	1787-1820	A	63
Wofford, Jesse	2	1830-1835	C	63
Wofford, John (Sr.)	1	1787-1820	A	57
Wofford, Joseph	1	1821-1829	B	109
Wofford, Joseph	3	1840-1858	D	378
Wolf, John	3	1840-1858	D	173
Wolf, Sarah	3	1840-1858	D	395
Wood, Benjamin P.	2	1830-1835	C	58
Wood, Henry (Sr.)	3	1840-1858	D	60
Wood, John (Carpenter)	1	1787-1820	A	156
Wood, Maiden	3	1840-1858	D	29
Wood, Nancy	3	1840-1858	D	156
Wood, Pennuel	1	1787-1820	A	8
Wood, William	1	1787-1820	A	149-a
Wood, William	1	1787-1820	B	149-b
Wood, William	2	1830-1835	C	120
Wood, William	3	1840-1858	D	129
Woodruff, H.P.	3	1840-1858	D	93
Woodruff, Joseph	1	1787-1820	A	110
Woodruff, Samuel (Sr.)	2	1830-1835	C	68
Wright, John	1	1787-1820	A	59
Wright, Joseph	1	1821-1829	B	97
Wyatt, Vincent	2	1830-1835	C	115
Young, Richard	2	1830-1835	C	112
Young, William	3	1840-1858	D	310
Younger, James	1	1821-1829	B	98

Copied by:

/s/ Mrs. John D. Rogers

INDEX

TO

SUMTER COUNTY WILLS.

Volume No. 1
1774-1849

Volume No. 2
1823-1853

This index is compiled from W.P.A. copies of
wills filed in the COUNTY PROBATE COURTS.
The volumes indexed are a part of the
South Carolina Collection of the
University of South Carolina
Library.

Columbia, S. C.
1939

Name	Vol.	Date	Section	Page
Adams, Elizabeth	2	1823-1853	D-1	50
Ammonett, Charles	1	1774-1849	A	53
Anderson, David (Planter)	1	1774-1849	Wills not recorded	11
Anderson, Frances	2	1823-1853	D-2	291
Anderson, John	1	1774-1849	A	103
Anderson, John (Sr.)(Plant.)	1	1774-1849	AA	190
Anderson, Joseph	2	1823-1853	D-1	29
Anderson, Joseph W.	2	1823-1853	D-2	152
• Anderson, Mary	1	1774-1849	M	22
Andrews, Harriet Ann	2	1823-1853	D-2	114
Armstrong, James	1	1774-1849	A	120
Atkinson, James (Planter)	1	1775-1849	Wills not recorded	1
Atkinson, Mary	2	1823-1853	D-2	80
Baggs, Thomas	1	1774-1849	A	157
Bagnal, Isaac	1	1774-1849	AA	104
Baker, Rachel	2	1823-1853	D-2	202
Baker, Thomas (Planter)	2	1823-1853	D-2	50
Ballard, Elizabeth	2	1823-1853	D-1	247
Barber, Agnes	1	1774-1849	A	8
Barfield, Willis	2	1823-1853	D-2	42
Barnes, James (Planter)	2	1823-1853	D-1	39
Barret, I. D.	2	1823-1853	D-2	48
Beard, William (Sr.)	2	1823-1853	D-2	132
Bell, Archy	1	1774-1849	M	47
Bell, Jonathan	1	1774-1849	AA	60
Bell, Samuel	2	1823-1853	D-2	53
Bell, William Rafor (Plant.)	1	1774-1849	A	147
Belser, Jacob (Planter)	2	1823-1853	D-1	158
Belvin, Wilie	2	1823-1853	D-1	177
Benbow, Evan (Planter)	2	1823-1853	D-1	234
Benbow, Gershon	2	1823-1853	D-2	147
Benbow, Martha	2	1823-1853	D-2	129
Benbow, Richard (Planter)	1	1774-1849	A	6
Bennet, Esther	1	1774-1849	A	145
Birch, Michael	1	1774-1849	A	26
Bishop, Penlope	2	1823-1853	D-2	131
Blackwell, Michael (Plant.)	2	1823-1853	D-1	139
Blither, William	2	1823-1853	D-1	24
Bosher, Thomas	1	1774-1849	AA	203
Bostwick, J.F.	2	1823-1853	D-2	21
Bowman, John	2	1823-1853	D-1	12
Boykin, Drury (Sr.)	1	1774-1849	M	12
Boyd, John	2	1823-1853	D-2	241
Boykin, Jonathan	1	1774-1849	M	43
Bracey, Charlotte	2	1823-1853	D-1	162
Bracey, Sackfield	1	1774-1849	A	222
Bracey, Theodosia	1	1774-1849	AA	165
Bracey, Thomas	2	1823-1853	D-2	247
Bradford, John	2	1823-1853	D-1	168
Bradford, Matthew (Planter)	2	1823-1853	D-2	178
Bradford, Nathaniel	1	1774-1849	A	260
Bradford, Richard (Planter)	2	1823-1853	D-1	78
Bradford, Robert	2	1823-1853	D-2	253
Bradham, Henry	2	1823-1853	D-2	245
*Anderson, Thomas	2	1823-1853	D-1	185

Bradley, Eliza	2	1825-1853	D-2	172
Bradley, Elisabeth	1	1774-1849	A	98
Bradley, James (Planter)	1	1774-1849	AA	188
Bradley, John	1	1825-1853	D-2	265
Bradley, Marth M.	1	1774-1849	M	33
Bradley, Roger	1	1774-1849	A	129
Bradley, Samuel	1	1774-1849	AAA	24
Bradley, Samuel	1	1774-1849	Wills not recorded	28
Bradley, Theodocia, see - - - - - - - - - - - - - - - - - Bracey, Theodosia				
Brewer, Royal	2	1825-1853	D-2	207
Britton, Henry	2	1825-1853	D-2	82
Britton, Thomas	1	1774-1849	A	125
Broadway, Elizabeth	1	1774-1849	AA	173
Brock, Charles	2	1825-1853	D-1	225
Brock, Patrick	1	1774-1849	A	27
Broughton, Edward	2	1825-1853	D-2	316
Brown, Elizabeth	2	1825-1853	D-2	112
Brown, Jacob	2	1825-1853	D-2	29
Brown, James	2	1825-1853	D-2	128
Brownfield, Sussannah	2	1825-1853	D-2	75
Brumby, Thomas (Planter)	1	1774-1849	A	183
Brunson, James	2	1825-1853	D-2	36
Brunson, Mary	1	1774-1849	M	24
Bryson, Ann	1	1774-1849	AA	20
Burgess, Andrew	2	1825-1853	D-2	282
Burket, James	1	1774-1849	A	33
Byrd, Henry	2	1825-1853	D-2	107
Byrd, Rhodecy	1	1774-1849	M	16
Cain, Mary	2	1825-1853	D-2	278
Cain, William (Farmer)	2	1825-1853	D-2	15
Cameron, John	2	1825-1853	D-1	71
Campbell, Alexander(Plant.)	1	1774-1849	Wills not recorded	3
Cannon, John	1	1774-1849	A	154
Cantey, Charles	1	1774-1849	A	150
Cantey, Mary	2	1825-1853	D-1	35
Cantey, Rebekah	2	1825-1853	D-1	51
Carter, Margaret	1	1774-1849	A	237
Carter, William	2	1825-1853	D-1	20
Cater, George (Sr.)	1	1774-1849	AA	163
Chandler, Samuel	1	1774-1849	AA	45
Chandler, Thomas	1	1774-1849	AA	78
Chewning, Ann (Widow)	2	1825-1853	D-1	176
Chewning, Richard W.(Plant.)	1	1774-1849	AA	166
Chisholm, John (Merchant)	1	1774-1849	A	76
Christmas, John	1	1774-1849	A	172
Christmas, Lidia	1	1774-1849	M	44
Christmas, Moses	1	1774-1849	AA	91
Clark, Ann	1	1774-1849	A	189
Coker, Joshua (Sr.)	1	1774-1849	A	255
Coker, Robertson	2	1825-1853	D-2	149
Coker, Wiley	1	1774-1849	A	139
Colclough, Alexander	1	1774-1849	AA	32
Colliette, Thomas	1	1774-1849	AA	67
Commander, Joseph (Sr.)	2	1825-1853	D-1	118

Commander, R. L.	2	1825-1855	D-2	71
Commander, Samuel (Sr.)(Planter)	1	1774-1849	Wills not recorded	4
Connell, Thomas (Planter)	2	1825-1855	D-1	14
Conners, Charles (Planter)	2	1825-1855	D-2	84
Conyers, James (Jr.)	1	1774-1849	Wills not recorded	6
Conyers, James	1	1775-1849	Wills not recorded	167
Conyers, John	1	1774-1849	AA	14
Conyers, Margaret Reily	1	1774-1849	AA	7
Conyers, Stranghan	2	1825-1855	D-1	188
Cook, Jos. B. (Rev.)(Plant.)	2	1825-1855	D-1	220
Cooper, George	2	1825-1855	D-1	124
Copeland, Ripley (Sr.)	2	1825-1855	D-2	154
Copplay, Elizabeth, see - - - - - - - - - - - - - - - - - - Coppy, Elizabeth				
Coppy, Elizabeth	1	1774-1849	Wills not recorded	8
Corbett, James (Planter)	2	1825-1855	D-1	98
Corbett,James(Sr.)(Plant.)	2	1825-1855	D-2	173
Corbett, Susannah	2	1825-1855	D-1	214
Coskray, John E. (Planter)	2	1825-1855	D-2	205
Coulliette, Thomas, see - - - - - - - - - - - - - - - - - -Colliette, Thomas				
Cousar, John (Minister)	1	1774-1849	M	19
Cox, John	2	1825-1855	D-L	97
Cox, Joseph D.	1	1774-1849	AA	202
Cubbage, Philemon	2	1825-1855	D-1	4
Cubbage, Thomas	2	1825-1855	D-1	66
Daniel, Edward	2	1825-1849	D-1	145
Daniel, Tabitha	1	1774-1849	AA	44
Daniel, William	1	1774-1849	Wills not recorded	151
Daniels, Elizabeth	1	1774-1849	Wills not recorded	115
Dargan, John M. (Planter)	2	1825-1855	D-2	192
Davies, Amos (Planter)	2	1825-1855	D-2	220
Davis, Benjamin (Planter)	1	1774-1849	Wills not recorded	50
Davis, Elizabeth	1	1774-1849	AA	76
Davis, James	1	1774-1849	AA	51
Davis, John G. (Planter)	2	1825-1855	D-1	15
Davis, Martha H.G.	2	1825-1855	D-2	169
Davis, Nabar Burrows	1	1774-1849	Wills not recorded	204
Davis, Thomas	2	1825-1855	D-2	44
Dearington, Thomas	1	1774-1849	Wills not recorded	19
Dearington, Thomas	1	1774-1849	Wills not recorded	252
Deas, Simon	1	1774-1849	AA	102
Dennis, Littleton	2	1825-1855	D-2	18
Denson, James	1	1774-1849	AA	80
Denson, Simon	1	1774-1849	AA	80
DesChamps, Francis(Plant.)	1	1774-1849	AA	160
Diggs, Judith	2	1825-1855	D-2	105
Dingle, Robert	1	1774-1849	AA	123
Doney, Charles	2	1825-1855	D-2	171
Dow, John	1	1774-1849	M	1
Dow, Robert (Planter)	1	1774-1849	AA	27
DuBose, Peter	2	1825-1855	D-2	195
Dukes, James	2	1825-1855	D-2	98
Dunn, Burrel	2	1825-1855	D-2	346
Dunn, Janet	1	1774-1849	Wills not recorded	144
Dunn, Sylvester (Sr.)	1	1774-1849	Wills not recorded	30
Durant, Henry	1	1774-1849	Wills not recorded	102
Dwyer, Samuel	1	1774-1849	AA	200

Name		Date	Type	Page
Edward, William	1	1774-1849	Wills not recorded	10
Edwards, Elizabeth	1	1774-1849	Wills not recorded	218
English, Robert (Planter)	2	1823-1853	D-1	225
Evans, Frederick	2	1823-1853	D-1	171
Faris, John W.	1	1774-1849	Wills not recorded	192
Felder, James	2	1823-1853	D-1	86
Fitzpatrick, Micagah	1	1774-1849	Wills not recorded	42
Fitzpatrick, Peter (Plant.)		1774-1849	Wills not recorded	44
Flemming, Elizabeth	2	1823-1853	D-1	134
Fley, Samuel	1	1774-1849	Wills not recorded	134
Ford, Mary	1	1774-1849	Wills not recorded	253
Fort, Burrell	2	1823-1853	D-1	172
Foxworth, Zackariah (Plant.)	1	1774-1849	Wills not recorded	206
Francisco, John	1	1774-1849	Wills not recorded	124
Franklin, Lawrence	2	1823-1853	D-1	2
Fraser, John Baxter (Plant.)	1	1774-1849	AA	106
Freeman, Harriet	2	1823-1853	D-2	310
Freeman, Jose	1	1774-1849	M	42
Frierson, Aaron	1	1774-1849	AA	132
Frierson, John (Sr.)	2	1823-1853	D-2	1
Frierson, John I. (Plant.)	1	1774-1849	M	39
Fullwood, James C. (Plant.)	2	1823-1853	D-2	54
Fulwood, Sarah	1	1774-1849	AA	19
Fulwood, Wm. I. (Planter)	2	1823-1853	D-1	160
Furman, Wood	1	1774-1849	Wills not recorded	23
Gamble, Catherine	1	1774-1849	AA	194
Gamble, Robert	1	1774-1849	M	45
Gardner, Alister	2	1823-1853	D-2	116
Gardner, Nathan	1	1774-1849	AA	129
Garlington, Christopher	1	1774-1849	Wills not recorded	127
Gayle, Josiah	1	1774-1849	AA	168
Gerald, Alice M.	2	1823-1853	D-2	63
Gibbons, Jesse (Planter)	2	1823-1853	D-2	150
Gibson, Phineas	1	1774-1849	Wills not recorded	239
Gidians, Abram	2	1823-1853	D-2	141
Gilley, Susanna	2	1823-1853	D-1	128
Graham, William	1	1774-1849	AA	162
Grant, William	1	1774-1849	Wills not recorded	197
Graves, Massey (Widow)	2	1823-1853	D-2	222
Green, Joel L.	2	1823-1853	D-2	289
Green, Lewis	2	1823-1853	D-1	130
Green, William	2	1823-1853	D-2	219
Greening, John (Planter)	1	1774-1849	AA	40
Groomes, Isaac	1	1774-1849	AA	75
Guerry, Legrand (Planter)	1	1774-1849	Wills not recorded	170
Haley, Peter (Planter)	1	1774-1849	Wills not recorded	214
Hamilton, Henry K.	2	1823-1853	D-2	61
Hampton, Amy	2	1823-1853	D-2	120
Hampton, Naomi	1	1774-1849	AA	87
Hampton, Richard	1	1774-1849	Wills not recorded	58
Harvin, James E.	1	1774-1849	AA	174
Harvin, Richard (Planter)	1	1774-1849	Wills not recorded	107
Harvin, Richard (Sr.)	2	1823-1853	D-1	107
Haynsworth, Henry	2	1823-1853	D-1	25
Haynsworth, Josiah	2	1823-1853	D-2	154

Name		Dates	Type	Page
nsworth, Sarah	2	1823-1853	D-1	149
lton, James	1	1774-1849	Wills not recorded	71
nderson, Susannah	1	1774-1849	AA	49
Heriot, John Ouldfield(Plant.)	2	1823-1853	D-1	164
Hiatt, Charles	2	1823-1853	D-1	140
High, Joseph	1	1774-1849	Wills not recorded	259
Hilton, John J.	2	1823-1853	D-2	277
Hilton, William	2	1823-1853	D-2	78
Hodge, Benjamin (Planter)	1	1774-1849	Wills not recorded	224
Hodge, Benjamin Dupre	2	1823-1853	D-2	313
Hodge, Martha	2	1823-1853	D-2	39
Holladay, John, see - - - - - - - - - - - - - - - - - - --- Holliday, John				
Holladay, Susannah, see - - - - - - - - - - - - - - - - - - Holliday, Susann				
Holland, Sylvia	2	1823-1853	D-1	233
Holliday, John	1	1774-1849	AA	36
Holliday, Susannah	1	1774-1849	AA	93
Holloway, James	2	1823-1853	D-1	132
Horan, John	1	1774-1849	AA	96
Howard, James (Dr.)	1	1774-1849	AA	69
Howard, Joseph (Dr.)	1	1774-1849	Wills not recorded	16
Hudnall, Willis	1	1774-1849	AA	34
Hudson, Janet	2	1823-1853	D-2	181
Humphrey, Thomas.(Rev.)(Plant.)	1	1774-1849	AA	119
Humphrey, William	1	1774-1849	Wills not recorded	92
Humphrey, William	2	1823-1853	D-2	245
Hurst, Henry	2	1823-1853	D-2	165
Hutcherson, John	2	1823-1853	D-2	127
Ivar, Elizabeth	1	1774-1849	Wills not recorded	227
Ivar, George (Planter)	1	1774-1849	Wills not recorded	158
Jackson, Mary	2	1823-1853	D-2	7
Jackson, Thomas	1	1774-1849	Wills not recorded	29
James, George Ford	2	1823-1853	D-1	224
James, John (Planter)	1	1774-1849	Wills not recorded	9
James, John (Planter)	1	1774-1849	AA	54
James, Mathias	1	1774-1849	AA	117
James, Robert	2	1823-1853	D-2	33
James,Shearwood (Planter)	1	1774-1849	Wills not recorded	1
James, Walter (Planter)	1	1774-1849	AA	139
James, Walter Dobein	2	1823-1853	D-1	121
Jennings, James	2	1823-1853	D-1	211
Johnson, Elijah (Sr.)	1	1774-1849	M	11
Johnson, Mary	1	1774-1849	AA	47
Johnson, Thomas N.	1	1774-1849	Wills not recorded	66
Johnston, James	2	1823-1853	D-1	155
Jones, John H.	2	1823-1853	D-1	72
Jordan, Jacob	2	1823-1853	D-2	162
Jordan, Joseph T.	2	1823-1853	D-2	175
Kelly, Daniel	2	1823-1853	D-2	40
Kelly, Simon	2	1823-1853	D-2	307
Kennedy, Cherry	2	1823-1853	D-2	161
Kersey, Janet	1	1774-1849	AA	4
King, Robert	1	1774-1849	Wills not recorded	208
King, William	2	1823-1853	D-2	59
Kingswood,Jacob (Planter)	1	1774-1849	AA	57

Name		Dates	Type	Page
Kingswood, Margaret	1	1774-1849	AA	98
Kinlock, Cleveland	2	1823-1853	D-1	7
Kolb, Thomas	2	1823-1853	D-2	311
LaCoste, Stephen	2	1823-1853	D-2	321
Langstaff, John Matthew	1	1774-1849	Wills not recorded	90
Law, Jared	2	1823-1853	D-2	342
Laws, George (Planter)	2	1823-1853	D-1	105
Lee, Anthony	1	1774-1849	Wills not recorded	94
Lenoir, Isaac	1	1774-1849	Wills not recorded	140
Lenoir, John (Sr.)	1	1774-1849	AA	25
Lenoir, Thomas J.	1	1774-1849	AA	26
Lenud, Henry (Planter)	1	1774-1849	Wills not recorded	56
Lenud, Henry	1	1774-1849	Wills not recorded	165
Lesesne, William	2	1823-1853	D-1	212
Lisk, Mary	2	1823-1853	D-1	204
Long, Reuben	1	1774-1849	M	37
Lowery, James (Merchant)	1	1774-1849	Wills not recorded	16
Lowry, James, see - Lowery, James				
Lowry, Samuel (Planter)	2	1823-1853	D-1	63
Lynam ,Cassanda	2	1823-1853	D-2	100
McBride, Samuel	2	1823-1853	D-2	269
McCallum, Kenneth (Plant.)	1	1774-1849	Wills not recorded	54
McCants, James	1	1774-1849	AA	187
McCants, Samuel	1	1774-1849	AA	79
McCaskell, Daniel	2	1823-1853	D-1	61
McClendon, Lewis	1	1774-1849	AA	3"
McCollough, Mary	1	1774-1849	Wills not recorded	186
McCoy, James	1	1774-1849	M	30
McCoy, John (Sr.)	1	1774-1849	AA	53
McCoy, John (Planter)	2	1823-1853	D-1	153
McCoy, Reddin	2	1823-1853	D-2	69
McDonald,Archibald Contur	2	1823-1853	D-2	136
McDonald, Daniel	1	1774-1849	AA	122
McDonald, Hugh	2	1823-1853	D-2	43
McDonald, John	2	1823-1853	D-2	73
McDonald, John	2	1823-1853	D-2	257
McDonald, William	2	1823-1853	D-1	37
McDonnell,John(Surveyor)	2	1823-1853	D-1	33
McEachern, James	1	1774-1849	AA	1
McElveen, John (Sr.)	1	1774-1849	AA	2
McFadden, Eli (Planter)	1	1774-1849	AA	11
McFaddin, John (Sr.)	2	1823-1853	D-1	55
McFaddin, John (Planter)	2	1823-1853	D-1	111
McFaddin, R.S.	2	1823-1853	D-2	361
McFaddin, Sarah I.	2	1823-1853	D-2	318
McFaddin, Theodore	2	1823-1853	D-1	231
McFaddin, Thomas	2	1823-1853	D-1	21
McFaddin, William	2	1823-1853	D-2	13
McGirth, Mary	1	1774-1849	Wills not recorded	13
McIntosh, Joshua	1	1774-1849	M	7
McIntosh, Peter (Planter)	2	1823-1853	D-1	87
McIntosh, William	2	1823-1853	D-2	91
McIntosh, William D.	2	1823-1853	D-2	137
McKay, John	2	1823-1853	D-2	101
McKenzie, William (Farmer)	2	1823-1853	D-2	365
McKinnery, Eli	1	1774-1849	AA	118

McKinney, Sarah	2	1823-1853	D-1	159
McKnight, Esther	2	1823-1853	D-2	233
McKnight, John (Planter)	1	1774-1849	M	17
McKnight, Robert	1	1774-1849	AA	182
McLendon, Jacob	2	1823-1853	D-2	295
McLeod, Alexander	2	1823-1853	D-1	244
McLeod, Catherine	2	1823-1853	D-2	372
McLeod, Margaret	2	1823-1853	D-1	115
McLeod, Thomas	2	1823-1853	D-2	203
McMahan, Benjamin	1	1774-1849	AA	133
Manning, Elizabeth	1	1774-1849	Wills not recorded	250
Manning, Moses	1	1774-1849	Wills not recorded	171
Manning, Richard I.	2	1823-1853	D-2	185
Maples, Elizabeth	2	1823-1853	D-1	44
Maples, Mary	2	1823-1853	D-2	123
Maples, Richard	1	1774-1849	Wills not recorded	111
Maples, Rosanna	1	1774-1849	Wills not recorded	238
Marsden, Elizabeth	1	1774-1849	Wills not recorded	236
Mathis, William	2	1823-1853	D-2	314
Matthews, Isaac	1	1774-1849	Wills not recorded	86
Mayrant, Charles	2	1823-1853	D-1	203
Mayrant, William	2	1823-1853	D-2	5
Mayrant, William (Sr.)	2	1823-1853	D-1	183
Mellett, Peter(Plant.)	1	1774-1849	Wills not recorded	19
Micheau, Noah	1	1774-1849	M	27
Miller, Charles	1	1774-1849	AA	130
Miller, Jesse	2	1823-1853	D-2	60
Miller, John Blout(Plant.)	2	1823-1853	D-2	335
Mills, William	2	1823-1853	D-1	75
Mitchel, Stephen	1	1774-1849	AA	115
• Montgomery, Jas.H.(Plant.)	1	1774-1849	Wills not recorded	216
Montgomery, William	1	1774-1849	Wills not recorded	64
Moody, Charles	2	1823-1853	D-2	287
Moody, Solomon (Sr.)	2	1823-1853	D-1	205
Moody, William	1	1774-1849	Wills not recorded	164
Moore, Isham	1	1774-1849	Wills not recorded	73
Moore, John Isham	2	1823-1853	D-2	347
Moore, Mary	2	1823-1853	D-2	215
Moore, Matthew L.	2	1823-1853	D-1	69
Muldrow, Mary	2	1823-1853	D-2	363
Muldrow, Robert	2	1823-1853	D-2	356
Muliedy, Thomas	2	1823-1853	D-1	68
Mullin, Edward	1	1774-1849	Wills not recorded	114
Mullin, John	1	1774-1849	Wills not recorded	194
Mullin, Wm. L. (Planter)	1	1774-1849	AA	16
Murphy, Malachi (Sr.)	1	1744-1849	AA	195
Murphy, Malachi (Planter)	2	1823-1853	D-1	82
Murray, John	1	1774-1849	AA	21
Murrell, William	2	1823-1853	D-1	116
Neilson, Samuel	1	1774-1849	Wills not recorded	22
Nelson, James (Planter)	2	1823-1853	D-1	208
Nelson, Mary	1	1774-1849	AA	83
Nelson, Samuel E.	2	1823-1853	D-2	327
Nelson, Samuel James	2	1823-1853	D-1	135
Nesbitt, Elizabeth	2	1823-1853	D-2	164
* Montgomery, Samuel (Plant.)	1	1774-1849	AA	100

Nettles, Jesse (Planter)	1	1774-1849	M	26
Nettles, Jesse	2	1823-1853	D-1	59
Newman, Elizabeth	1	1744-1849	AA	23
Newman, Ethelial	2	1823-1853	D-1	32
Newman, Thomas	1	1774-1849	Wills not recorded	122
Newman,William(Sr.)(Plant.)	1	1774-1849	Wills not recorded	211
Nichols, Bershaba	1	1774-1849	Wills not recorded	241
Norton, Daniel	2	1823-1853	D-2	96
Norton, Temperance	2	1823-1853	D-2	244
Orr, Thomas (Dr.)	2	1823-1853	D-1	101
Osteen, Jacob	2	1823-1853	D-2	189
Pack, Joseph (Planter)	2	1823-1853	D-1	92
Pearson, William (Planter)	1	1774-1849	Wills not recorded	4
Peebles, Jesse	2	1823-1853	D-1	249
Peeples, William	2	1823-1853	D-2	117
Perdrian,Samuel (Planter)	2	1823-1853	D-2	103
Perry, John (Sr.)	1	1774-1849	Wills not recorded	59
Perry, John	1	1744-1849	AA	189
Perry, Philip	1	1774-1849	Wills not recorded	249
Pettypool, John	1	1774-1849	Wills not recorded	210
Pitts, Joseph M.	1	1774-1849	M	3
Player, Thomas (Jr.)	1	1774-1849	AA	10
Plowden, Edward	1	1774-1849	A	89
Polk, Tabitha	1	1774-1849	AA	158
Pollard, John (Planter)	1	1774-1849	Wills not recorded	63
Potts, Wm. (Sr.)(Planter)	2	1823-1853	D-1	241
Pringle, John	2	1823-1853	D-2	250
Pritchard, Stephen	2	1823-1853	D-2	231
Pyland, George	1	1774-1849	Wills not recorded	247
Rafield, John	1	1774-1849	Wills not recorded	41
Ragan, Charles C.	2	1823-1853	D-2	232
Ragan, John	1	1774-1849	Wills not recorded	61
Ragan, Richard	2	1823-1853	D-2	352
Ragan, William	1	1774-1849	Wills not recorded	14
Ramsey, James	1	1774-1849	Wills not recorded	205
Ramsey, John	2	1823-1853	D-2	113
Rawlins, Richard	2	1823-1853	D-2	12
Rees, Huberd	1	1774-1849	Wills not recorded	77
Rees, Isham	1	1774-1849	Wills not recorded	47
Rees, Mary	1	1774-1849	M	35
Rees, Mary	1	1774-1849	Wills not recorded	213
Rees, Nancy, (Widow)	2	1823-1853	D-2	158
Rees, William	1	1774-1849	Wills not recorded	173
Rees, William J.	2	1823-1853	D-2	259
Rees, William J.(Planter)	2	1823-1853	D-2	344
Rembert, Abigah	1	1774-1849	Wills not recorded	96
Rembert, Edward (Dr.)	1	1774-1849	AA	85
Rembert, Hubert	1	1774-1849	Wills not recorded	169
Rembert, James (Planter)	1	1774-1849	Wills not recorded	201
Rembert, Thomas (Planter)	1	1774-1849	AA	127
Reynolds, John (Planter)	2	1823-1853	D-2	211
Rhame, Bradley (Planter)	2	1823-1853	D-1	181
Rhame, Jeremiah (Planter)	1	1774-1849	AA	185
Rhame, Obadiah	2	1823-1853	D-1	218
Rhame, Thomas D.	2	1823-1853	D-2	326

Rhodus, John	2	1823-1853	D-2	177
Richardson, Ann Cantey	2	1823-1853	D-2	238
Richardson, Dorcas	2	1823-1853	D-1	199
Richardson, James Burchill	2	1823-1853	D-1	251
Richardson, John P.	1	1774-1849	Wills not recorded	179
Richardson, John S.(Judge)	2	1823-1853	D-2	262
Richardson, Richard (Sr.)	1	1774-1849	AA	5
Richardson, William	1	1774-1849	Wills not recorded	12
Richardson, William D.	2	1823-1853	D-2	303
Richbourgh,Claudius(Plant.)	1	1774-1849	AA	94
Richburg, James (Sr.)	1	1774-1849	Wills not recorded	80
Ridgeway, James	2	1823-1853	D-2	198
Ridgeway, James F.	2	1823-1853	D-2	297
Ridgeway, William (Jr.)	1	1774-1849	AA	13
Ridgill, Richard	1	1774-1849	Wills not recorded	199
Ridgill, Robert	2	1823-1853	D-2	199
Ridgill, William	1	1774-1849	AA	31
Ridgway, William, see - - - - - - - - - - - - - - - - - - - Ridgeway, William
Roach, Ann E.	2	1823-1853	D-2	240
Roberson, Willis	2	1823-1853	D-1	77
Robinson, Alexander	1	1774-1849	Wills not recorded	17
Robinson, William	1	1774-1849	Wills not recorded	34
Rose, Daniel (Merchant)	2	1823-1853	AA	73
Rose, Thomas (Sr.)	2	1823-1853	D-2	167
Rutledge, Ann	2	1823-1853	D-2	94
Rutledge, John H.	2	1823-1853	D-2	302
Rutledge, Mary Golightly	2	1823-1853	D-1	226
Sabb, E.W.	2	1823-1853	D-2	304
Sabb, Morgan (Planter)	1	1774-1849	Wills not recorded	178
Sabb, Thomas (Jr.)	2	1823-1853	D-2	168
Sanders, Sarah	2	1823-1853	D-1	42
Sanders, William (Planter)	1	1774-1849	AA	63
Savage, William	1	1774-1849	Wills not recorded	136
Scarborough, Martha	2	1823-1853	D-2	234
Scurry, Jesse (Planter)	2	1823-1853	D-1	57
Severance, Margaret	2	1823-1853	D-2	280
Shaw, James (Planter)	2	1823-1853	D-1	147
Shaw, Lillis	2	1823-1853	D-2	374
Sherriff, James W.	2	1823-1853	D-2	49
Silliman, Alexander	1	1774-1849	AA	183
Simonton, Robert	2	1823-1853	D-1	88
Simpson, John	1	1774-1849	Wills not recorded	161
Simms, William	1	1774-1849	AA	9
Sims, Margaret	2	1823-1853	D-1	151
Singletary, Hannah	1	1774-1849	Wills not recorded	69
Singletary, Mary	2	1823-1853	D-2	4
Singleton, Elizabeth	1	1774-1849	AA	179
Singleton, H. Blanchard	2	1823-1853	D-2	187
Singleton, James Sherwood	2	1823-1853	D-1	161
Singleton, John (Sr.)(Plant)	2	1823-1853	D-1	52
Singleton, John	1	1774-1849	AA	143
Singleton, Joseph	1	1774-1849	Wills not recorded	244
Singleton, Louisa (Widow)	2	1823-1853	D-2	109
Singleton, Rebecca	2	1823-1853	D-1	232
Singleton, Richard	2	1823-1853	D-2	379
Singleton, Robert	1	1774-1849	Wills not recorded	22

Skinner, Charles	2	1823-1853	D-1	17
Skinner, Harvey	2	1823-1853	D-2	344
Smart, Alexander	1	1774-1849	Wills not recorded	209
Smith, Arthur	2	1823-1853	D-2	65
Smith, Henry I.(Planter)	2	1823-1853	D-2	275
Smith, Jannet (Widow)	2	1823-1853	D-1	216
Smith, Jesse	2	1823-1853	D-2	350
Smith,John (Sr.)(Planter)	2	1823-1853	D-1	18
Smith, William	2	1823-1853	D-1	137
Solomons, Esdaile	2	1823-1853	D-2	6
Solomons, Mark	1	1774-1849	M	10
Spann, Anna	1	1774-1849	M	28
Spann, Charles	2	1823-1853	D-2	143
Spann, Elizabeth	2	1823-1853	D-2	26
Spann, James	2	1823-1853	D-1	117
Spann, James (Sr.)	2	1823-1853	D-1	196
Spann, John N.	2	1823-1853	D-2	9
Spann, Richard	2	1823-1853	D-2	57
Sparrow, Eli	1	1774-1849	M	32
Spears, Mason (Planter)	1	1744-1849	Wills not recorded	257
Spears, Obidiah	2	1823-1853	D-2	10
Sprey, Henry	1	1774-1849	Wills not recorded	88
Sprott, Joseph	2	1823-1853	D-2	182
Stafford, Charity	2	1823-1853	D-2	27
Stafford, Joshua	1	1774-1849	AA	43
Stafford, L.C.	2	1823-1853	D-2	46
Stamper, Robert	1	1774-1849	Wills not recorded	149
Stevenson, Samuel	2	1823-1853	D-2	294
Stokes, Vine (Planter)	1	1774-1849	M	48
Stucky, Edmund	2	1823-1853	D-1	143
Sumter, Natalie D.	2	1823-1853	D-2	30
Sumter, Thomas	2	1823-1853	D-2	20
Sylvester, Asberry(Planter)	1	1774-1849	Wills not recorded	151
Sylvester, Joseph	1	1774-1849	Wills not recorded	251
Taylor, John	1	1774-1849	AA	192
Taylor, William	1	1774-1849	AA	141
Terry, Alice	1	1774-1849	AA	198
Terry, William	1	1774-1849	Wills not recorded	24
Thames, John (Jr.)	1	1774-1849	AA	61
Thompson, William	1	1774-1849	AA	38
Tisdale, Francis(Planter)	2	1823-1853	D-1	28
Tisdale, John	1	1774-1849	AA	28
Tisdale, John	1	1774-1849	AA	42
Tobias, Mary	2	1823-1853	D-1	46
Tock, Mary	1	1774-1849	AA	71
Tomlin, Hiram	1	1774-1849	AA	157
Tomlinson, Richard	1	1774-1849	Wills not recorded	132
Truluck, George	1	1774-1849	M	21
Vasser, Daniel H.	1	1774-1849	M	9
Vaughan, Hannah	2	1823-1853	D-2	299
Vaughan, Noel (Planter)	2	1823-1853	D-2	200
Vaughn, Mary	1	1774-1849	Wills not recorded	162
Vaughn, Henry (Jr.)	1	1774-1849	Wills not recorded	242

Vaughn, John (Sr.)	1	1774-1849	Wills not recorded	25
Vaughn, Noel (Sr.)(Planter)	2	1823-1853	D-1	131
Walter, John C.	1	1774-1849	Wills not recorded	233
Walter, Richard Charles	1	1774-1849	Wills not recorded	36
Walter, William D.(Plant.)	1	1774-1849	Wills not recorded	230
Ward, Benjamin	2	1823-1853	D-1	49
Waties, John	2	1823-1853	D-1	9
Waties, Thomas	2	1823-1853	D-1	103
Watson, John	2	1823-1853	D-2	186
Watson, Sarah	2	1823-1853	D-1	163
Watson, William (Planter)	1	1774-1849	AA	17
Watts, Julius (Planter)	2	1823-1853	D-2	331
Weeks, Chosel	2	1823-1853	D-2	338
Wells, Edward (Planter)	2	1823-1853	D-2	51
Wells, Margaret	2	1823-1853	D-2	37
Wells, Mary	2	1823-1853	D-2	209
Wells, Thomas	2	1823-1853	D-1	221
West, Joseph	2	1823-1853	D-2	208
Wheeler, Keziah	2	1823-1853	D-1	1
Wheeler, Sarah	1	1774-1849	Wills not recorded	52
Wheeler, William	2	1823-1853	D-2	293
Whilden, William	2	1823-1853	D-1	190
White, Ellen	1	1774-1849	Wills not recorded	155
White, Hannah	2	1823-1853	D-1	229
White, Henry	1	1774-1849	Wills not recorded	112
White, Jared	1	1774-1849	Wills not recorded	220
White, John	1	1774-1849	Wills not recorded	212
White, Joseph B.	2	1823-1853	D-2	333
Whitworth, Isaac	1	1774-1849	AA	172
Wilder, Jesse	1	1774-1849	Wills not recorded	40
Wilder, Jonathan(Planter)	2	1823-1853	D-2	218
Wilder, Josiah	2	1823-1853	D-2	95
Wilder, Spencer(Planter)	1	1774-1849	AA	125
Wilder, Wm. S. (Planter)	2	1823-1853	D-1	3
Williams, John (Planter)	2	1823-1853	D-2	312
Williams, Mary	1	1774-1849	AA	30
Williams, Peter	1	1774-1849	Wills not recorded	38
Williams, Roland John	1	1774-1849	AA	170
Willis, Wills	1	1774-1849	AA	66
Wilson, David	2	1823-1853	D-2	138
Wilson, David E.	2	1823-1853	D-2	236
Wilson, Elizabeth	2	1823-1853	D-1	214
Wilson, James H.	1	1774-1849	M	5
Wilson, Richard (Planter)	1	1774-1849	AA	50
Wilson, Robert	2	1823-1853	D-1	193
Wilson, Roger	2	1823-1853	D-1	47
Wilson, William	2	1823-1853	D-2	285
Windham, Solomon (Planter)	1	1774-1849	Wills not recorded	138
Windom, Benjemin	2	1823-1853	D-1	6
Windom, Solomon, see - Windham, Solomon				
Witherspoon, John	2	1823-1853	D-1	10
Witherspoon,John(Planter)	1	1774-1849	Wills not recorded	105

Copied by:

/s/ Mrs. John D. Rogers

INDEX

TO

UNION COUNTY WILLS.

Volume No. 1
1777-1814

Volume No. 2
1815-1849

This index is compiled from W.P.A. copies of
wills filed in the COUNTY PROBATE COURTS.
The volumes indexed are a part of the
South Carolina Collection of the
University of South Carolina
Library.

Columbia, S.C.
1939

WILLS

Name	Vol.	Date	Section	Page
Adams, Charmer	2	1815-1849	B	279
Adams, Margaret	1	1777-1814	A	220
Addington, James	1	1777-1814	A	120
Alexander, Randolph	1	1777-1814	A	119
Anderson, Elijah	2	1815-1849	B	142
Armstrong, Thomas H.	2	1815-1849	B	385
Ashford, Moses	2	1815-1849	B	84
Askew, Lemuel (Dr.)	2	1815-1849	B	561
Bailey, Harrison	2	1815-1849	C	51
Bailey, John	1	1777-1814	A	156
Bailey, Susannah	1	1777-1814	A	63
Baker, Leonard	2	1815-1849	B	462
Ballard, John	2	1815-1849	B	328
Bankhead, James	1	1777-1814	A	94
Bankhead, James	1	1777-1814	A	208
Barnett, Marion	2	1815-1849	C	47
Beard, Eleanor	2	1815-1849	B	122
Beaty, Robert	1	1777-1814	A	151
Bell, Thomas	1	1777-1814	A	215
Belue, Renny (Sr.)	1	1777-1814	A	78
Belue, Renny (Jr.) (Plant.)	1	1777-1814	A	98
Belue, Reuben (Saddler)	1	1777-1814	A	216
Benson, James	1	1777-1814	A	151
Berry, Richard	2	1815-1849	B	59
Beuford, James	1	1777-1849	A	70
Beuford, Joshua	1	1777-1849	A	106
Bevis, Zacharia	1	1777-1849	A	284
Birdsong, Patte	1	1777-1814	A	296
Birdsong, John	1	1777-1849	A	326
Black, Robert	2	1815-1849	C	106
Blackstock, William	1	1777-1814	A	92
Blasingame, John	1	1777-1814	A	248
Blasingame, Thomas	2	1815-1849	B	1
Boatman, Waterman	1	1777-1814	A	518
Bobo, Barrum	2	1815-1849	B	210
Bobo, Lewis	1	1777-1814	A	239
Bobo, Mary	2	1815-1849	C	110
Bobo, Tillman	2	1815-1849	B	415
Bogan, Isaac	1	1777-1814	A	198
Bogan, John (Farmer)	1	1777-1814	A	182
Booker, Bird	2	1815-1849	B	74
Bowles, John	2	1815-1849	B	298
Boyce, Alexander	2	1815-1849	B	154
Boyd, John	2	1815-1849	B	12
Brandon, Christopher	2	1815-1849	B	459
Brandon, George	2	1815-1849	B	165
Brandon, Thomas (Gen.)	1	1777-1814	A	156
Brandon, William	1	1777-1814	A	130
Brock, George	2	1815-1849	B	218
Brock, Joseph	2	1815-1849	B	94
Brock, William O.	2	1815-1849	B	19
Brock, William O.	2	1815-1849	B	67
Brooks, Thomas	1	1777-1814	A	166
Brown, Richard	2	1815-1849	C	86

Browning, Robert	2	1815-1849	B	275
Browning, Thomas	2	1815-1849	B	141
Bull, William A.	2	1815-1849	B	570
Cain, Alexander	1	1777-1814	A	204
Caldwell, James	2	1815-1849	B	29
Carothers, John	2	1815-1849	C	100
Chislom, David	1	1777-1814	A	5
Clanton, Charles	1	1777-1814	A	22
Clark, Henry	1	1777-1814	A	65
Clark, Henry	1	1777-1814	A	68
Clark, Jesse (Jr.)	2	1815-1849	A	543
Clark, Jesse (Jr.)	2	1815-1849	B	411
Clark, John	1	1777-1814	A	58
Clowney, Samuel	2	1815-1849	B	145
Clowney, William K.	2	1815-1849	C	22
Cobb, Nathaniel	1	1777-1814	A	304
Cole, John (Planter)	1	1777-1814	A	104
Cole, Richard	1	1777-1814	A	229
Coleman, Joseph	1	1777-1814	A	522
Coleman, Reuben	2	1815-1849	C	105
Coleman, Robert	2	1815-1849	B	117
Comer, Daniel	1	1777-1814	A	9
Comer, Daniel	2	1815-1849	B	155
Comer, James	2	1815-1849	B	46
Comer, John	2	1815-1849	B	167
Cook, Robert	1	1777-1814	A	214
Cooper, Elizabeth	1	1777-1814	A	46
Cooper, Elijah	1	1777-1814	A	65
Cooper, Jerimah	1	1777-1814	A	56
Cooper, Samuel	1	1777-1814	A	28
Cooper, Stacy	2	1815-1849	B	100
Corry, Ann, see - Currey, Anne				
Corry, Nicholas	2	1815-1849	B	409
Corry, Robert	2	1815-1849	B	273
Cotter, Willia (Planter)	1	1777-1814	A	207
Cotter, William (Planter)	2	1815-1849	B	26
Crenshaw, Robert (Sr.)	1	1777-1814	A	268
Crenshaw, Robert	2	1815-1849	B	56
Crossley, George	1	1777-1814	A	16
Cunningham, Arthur	2	1815-1849	B	157
Cunningham, Henry	1	1777-1814	A	168
Curry, Ann	2	1815-1849	B	404
Curtis, Nancy	2	1815-1849	C	48
Dadds, Nathaniel (Plant.)	1	1777-1814	A	114
Darby, Benjamin	1	1777-1814	A	179
Darby, Josiah (Planter)	2	1815-1849	B	96
Davidson, Samuel	2	1815-1849	C	92
Davis, Amos	2	1815-1849	B	148
Davis, James	2	1815-1849	B	213
Davis, John M.	2	1815-1849	B	244
Davis, John M	2	1815-1849	B	458
Davis, Nathaniel	1	1777-1814	A	66
Dawkins, B.F.	2	1815-1849	B	475
Dawkins, Nancy (Mrs.)	2	1815-1849	C	115
Develin, Michael	2	1815-1849	B	166
Donaldson, Hugh	1	1777-1814	A	290
Drake, Francis	1	1777-1814	A	25
Drake, Joyce	1	1777-1814	A	189

Drake, Richard	1	1777–1814	A	309
Draper, Thomas	1	1777–1814	A	277
Duncan, Robert	2	1815–1849	B	159
Duncan, Susannah	2	1815–1849	B	220
Easter, Robert	2	1815–1849	B	454
Edwards, Edward	2	1815–1849	B	102
Eison, Fredrick	1	1777–1814	A	160
Ellis, Edmon	1	1777–1814	A	157
Evans, John	2	1815–1849	B	454
Ezell, William	2	1815–1849	B	254
Fairbarn, Christian	1	1777–1814	A	174
Fant, William	2	1815–1849	C	84
Faris, Dorcas	2	1815–1849	B	21
Farr, James	2	1815–1849	B	130
Farr, Jas.	2	1815–1849	C	46
Farr, Richard	1	1777–1814	A	252
Farr, William	1	1777–1814	A	20
Farr, William B.	2	1815–1849	B	444
Farr, William B.R.	2	1815–1849	B	457
Farrow, Elisabeth	2	1815–1849	B	270
Faucett, Nancy	2	1815–1849	C	17
Fincher, Aaron	1	1777–1814	A	40
Fincher, Aaron	1	1777–1814	A	170
Fincher, Hannah	1	1777–1814	A	255
Fincher, Jesse	2	1815–1849	B	269
Fincher, John	2	1815–1849	B	287
Fitch, Daniel (Planter)	2	1815–1849	B	518
Floyd, Enoch	1	1777–1814	A	150
Foster, John	2	1815–1849	B	158
Foster, John	2	1815–1849	B	285
Foster, William	2	1815–1849	B	250
Fowler, Ellis (Sr.)	1	1777–1814	A	257
Fowler, Ephriam	2	1815–1849	B	104
Fowler, John (Sr.)	2	1815–1849	B	58
Fowler, John	2	1815–1849	B	267
Fowler, William	1	1777–1814	A	279
Fowler, Wymac	2	1815–1849	C	3
Frost, Mary	1	1777–1814	A	56
Gage, John (Jr.)	2	1815–1849	B	449
Garner, Lewis	1	1777–1814	A	250
Gault, Robert	2	1815–1849	A	356
Gibbs, James	1	1777–1814	A	54
Gibbs, James (Farmer)	2	1815–1849	B	35
Gibson, Joseph	1	1777–1814	A	188
Giles, John	2	1815–1849	C	21
Giles, William	2	1815–1849	C	53
Gilky, Samuel	2	1815–1849	B	56
Gist, Francis (Col.)	2	1815–1849	B	494
Gist, William F.	2	1815–1849	B	179
Glass, Mary	2	1815–1849	B	207
Glenn, William C.	2	1815–1849	B	174
Good, Robert	1	1777–1814	A	90
Good, Sarah	2	1815–1849	B	161
Goodwin, John	2	1815–1849	B	134
Goodwin, Sampson	1	1777–1814	A	196
Gore, Joshua (Sr.)	2	1815–1849	B	432

Gossett, Fielder	2	1815-1849	C	16
Goudelock, Adam (Planter)	1	1777-1814	A	48
Gray, Daniel (Rev.)	2	1815-1849	B	38
Greer, Thomas (Sr.)	1	1777-1814	A	261
Greer, Thomas	2	1815-1849	C	62
Greer, William	1	1777-1814	A	249
Gregory, Benjamin Tl.	2	1815-1849	C	55
Gregory, Gerald	1	1777-1814	A	185
Gregory, Isaac	1	1777-1814	A	61
Gregory, Isaac	2	1815-1849	B	139
Gregory, John	2	1815-1849	B	68
Gregory, John	2	1815-1849	B	408
Gregory, John	2	1815-1849	C	54
Gregory, Robert	1	1777-1814	A	299
Guyton, Abraham	2	1815-1849	B	25
Guyton, Hannah	2	1815-1849	B	41
Guyton, Isaac (Planter)	2	1815-1849	B	405
Guyton, Joseph	2	1815-1849	B	65
Guyton, Martha E.	2	1815-1849	B	516
Guyton, Nathaniel	1	1777-1849	A	255
Haile, John (Carpenter)	2	1815-1849	B	54
Haile, John	2	1815-1849	B	164
Hall, William	2	1815-1849	B	4
Hames, Charles (Sr.)(Farm.)	1	1777-1814	A	224
Hames, Charles	1	1777-1814	A	329
Hames, Charles	2	1815-1849	B	429
Hames, Edmund	2	1815-1849	B	366
Hames, Faithy (Widow)	1	1777-1814	A	154
Hames, Thomas (Farmer)	2	1815-1849	B	30
Hames, William	2	1815-1849	B	125
Hamilton, Jermiah	1	1777-1814	A	305
Haney, Hannah	2	1815-1849	B	116
Haney, Hiram	1	1777-1849	A	246
Harlan, George	1	1777-1814	A	324
Harlan, Samuel	1	1777-1814	B	246
Harland, George	1	1777-1814	A	88
Harland, George	1	1777-1814	A	301
Harrington, John	1	1777-1814	A	15
Harris, James	2	1815-1849	B	73
Harris, Mark	1	1777-1814	A	146
Harris, Moses	1	1777-1814	A	510
Harris, Robert	1	1777-1814	A	242
Harris, Salley	1	1777-1814	A	254
Harris, Thomas	1	1777-1814	A	50
Haselwood, Thomas	1	1777-1814	A	100
Hawkins, James	1	1777-1814	A	10
Hawkins, William	1	1777-1814	A	218
Haward, Thomas, see - - - - - - - - - - - - - - - - - - - Howard, Thomas				
Hedgepath, Peter	1	1777-1814	A	292
Henderson, John	2	1815-1849	B	135
Henderson, Thomas	1	1777-1814	A	51
Hendley, John	1	1777-1814	A	222
Hendley, William	1	1777-1814	A	18
Hendley, Edward T.	2	1815-1849	B	250
Heyward, Thomas, see - - - - - - - - - - - - - - - - - Howard, Thomas				
Hobson, William	2	1815-1849	B	339
Hodge, Samuel	2	1815-1849	C	90

Holcomb, Benjamin	1	1777-1814	A	44
Holcombe, Neville	2	1815-1849	B	260
Holcombe, Phillip	2	1815-1849	B	82
Holder, Daniel	2	1815-1849	B	400
Hollingsworth, Benjamin	2	1815-1849	B	23
Hollingsworth, Enoch	1	1777-1814	A	515
Hollingsworth, Isaac	1	1777-1814	A	287
Hollingsworth, Jacob	2	1815-1849	B	28
Hollingsworth, Posey	2	1815-1849	C	42
Hope, James	2	1815-1849	B	51
Hopkins, John	1	1777-1814	A	202
Howard, Clemmons	2	1815-1849	B	327
Howard, Mary	2	1815-1849	B	329
Howard, Thomas	2	1815-1849	A	547
Howard, Thomas	2	1815-1849	C	20
Howell, David	1	1777-1814	A	72
Huey, John	1	1777-1814	A	24
Hughes, Joseph	1	1777-1814	A	101
Humphries, Charlie (Sr.)	2	1815-1849	B	513
Humphries, Elisabeth	2	1815-1849	B	489
Hunt, Thomas B.	1	1777-1814	A	64
Hunt, Thomas B.	1	1777-1814	A	263
Hunter, James	2	1815-1849	B	446
Hyatt, Thomas	2	1815-1849	B	395
Ivey, Lucy	2	1815-1849	B	487
Jackson, Frederick	2	1815-1849	B	295
Jackson, Ralph	2	1815-1849	B	47
Jasper, John	1	1777-1814	A	107
Jasper, John	1	1777-1814	A	266
Jasper, Susannah	2	1815-1849	B	194
Jefferies, Francis	2	1815-1849	B	389
Jeffries, John	2	1815-1849	C	18
Jenkins, Charles G. (Jr.)	2	1815-1849	B	511
Jenkins, Jesse	2	1815-1849	B	17
Jenkins, Randolph	2	1815-1849	B	157
Jennings, Jno.	2	1815-1849	C	80
Jeter, Argulanus V.	2	1815-1849	C	8
Jeter, David S.	2	1815-1849	C	116
Jeter, James	2	1815-1849	B	554
Jeter, James B.	2	1815-1849	C	124
Johns, Isaiah	2	1815-1849	B	98
Johnson, Benjamin	1	1777-1814	A	80
Johnson, Hannah, see - - - - - - - - - - - - - - - - - - - Haney, Hannah				
Johnson, James	2	1815-1849	B	178
Johnson, James	2	1815-1849	B	251
Johnson, Zachariah	2	1815-1849	B	114
Johnston, David	1	1777-1814	A	175
Jones, John	2	1815-1849	B	42
Jones, John (Sr.)	2	1815-1849	B	393
Jones, John	2	1815-1849	B	396
Jones, Joseph	1	1777-1814	A	273
Jones, William	2	1815-1849	B	493
Kennedy, Abraham	2	1815-1849	B	334
Kennedy, Archelaus	2	1815-1849	B	331
Kennedy, Benjamin (Plant.)	2	1815-1849	B	95

Kennedy, James	2	1815-1849	B	307
Kennedy, William	2	1815-1849	B	76
Killian, Geo. B.	2	1815-1849	C	40
Kingsborough, William	2	1815-1849	B	63
Kirby, John	1	1777-1814	A	236
Lamb, Robert	2	1815-1849	C	112
Lamb, Thomas	1	1777-1814	A	158
Lancaster, Larkin	2	1815-1849	C	65
Lancaster, Lemuel	2	1815-1849	B	558
Langston, Caleb	1	1777-1814	A	127
Lawrence, James	2	1815-1849	B	227
Lawrence, William	1	1777-1814	A	286
Lawson, Sion	2	1815-1849	B	394
Lawson, William	2	1815-1849	B	185
Layton, Susannah	2	1815-1849	B	445
Layton, Thomas	1	1777-1814	A	43
Ledbetter, Lewis	1	1777-1814	A	164
Lee, Amos	2	1815-1849	B	407
Lee, Drusilla (Widow)	1	1777-1814	A	514
Lee, John	2	1815-1849	B	127
Lee, Joseph	1	1777-1814	A	281
Lee, Michael	1	1777-1814	A	235
Lee, William	1	1777-1814	A	54
Lee, William	2	1815-1849	B	326
Linam, Charles	1	1777-1814	A	297
Linam, George	2	1815-1849	B	5
Lindsey, Jane	1	1777-1814	A	306
Lipham, Daniel	2	1815-1849	B	197
Lipsey, Rickston	2	1815-1849	C	98
Little, Jonas	2	1815-1849	B	92
Littlefield, Lucy	2	1815-1849	B	206
Littlejohn, Samuel	1	1777-1814	A	293
Lockhart, James (Sr.)	1	1777-1814	A	185
Long, Elizabeth	2	1815-1849	B	341
Long, William	2	1815-1849	B	16
Lovell, Daniel	1	1777-1814	A	298
Lyles, Susannah	2	1815-1849	B	52
Lynum, Charles, see - Linam, Charles				
McBeth, Alexander (Sr.)	2	1815-1849	B	71
McBeth, John	2	1815-1849	B	402
McBride, Daniel	1	1777-1814	A	116
McBride, Isaac	2	1815-1849	B	91
McBride, William	2	1815-1849	B	286
McClure, John	2	1815-1849	C	66
McCool, Adam (Yeoman)	1	1777-1814	A	128
McCraw, Edward	2	1815-1849	B	456
McCrlight, Wm. (Sr.)(Plant.)	2	1815-1849	B	77
McCollock, Martha	2	1815-1849	B	416
McCullough, Elizabeth	2	1815-1849	C	122
McDonald, Thomas	1	1777-1814	A	117
McElwain, James (Planter)	1	1777-1814	A	271
McFetrick, Johnn	2	1815-1849	B	576
McGarity, Clemmons	2	1815-1849	B	108
McJunkin, Mary	2	1815-1849	B	79
McJunkin, William	1	1777-1814	A	97
McKissick, Isaac	2	1815-1849	B	277
McKissick, Joseph	2	1815-1849	B	245

McMahan, Daniel M.	2	1815-1849	B	467
McPherson, Stephen (Plant.)	2	1815-1849	B	240
McWhirter, James (Sr.)	2	1815-1849	B	597
Malone, Jones	2	1815-1849	B	152
Mardis, Moses	2	1815-1849	C	115
Mayes, Edward	2	1815-1849	B	324
Mayes, Thomas	1	1777-1814	A	155
Mayhew, James C.	2	1815-1849	B	192
Means, Hugh (Gen.)	2	1815-1849	B	180
Means, James	2	1815-1849	B	474
Means, James	2	1815-1849	B	476
Means, Joseph	2	1815-1849	B	8
Miller, Elisabeth	1	1777-1814	A	57
Miller, Jerome	2	1815-1849	B	350
Miller, Rebecca	2	1815-1849	B	196
Minton, Thomas	1	1777-1814	A	155
Mitchell, Mary	2	1815-1849	B	479
Mitchell, William	2	1815-1849	B	172
Mitchell, William	2	1815-1849	B	436
Mobley, Mary	2	1815-1849	C	53
Moore, John	2	1815-1849	B	385
Moseley, Baxter	2	1815-1849	B	86
Moseley, James	2	1815-1849	B	549
Morgan, Spencer	1	1777-1814	A	44
Morgan, Spencer	1	1777-1814	A	244
Murphy, Bird	2	1815-1849	C	57
Murphy, Mark	2	1815-1849	B	216
Murphy, Susanna	2	1815-1849	C	25
Murrell, David	2	1815-1849	B	106
Murrell, Drurry	1	1777-1814	A	122
Musgrove, Sarah	2	1815-1849	B	372
Nance, Thomas	2	1815-1849	B	575
Nance, Zachariah	2	1815-1849	B	189
Narvell, Jane	2	1815-1849	B	283
Nedarman, John	1	1777-1814	B	181
Nelson, Hugh	1	1777-1814	A	172
Nelson, John (Jr.)	1	1777-1814	A	176
Nelson, Susannah	2	1815-1849	B	160
Nix, Benjamin	2	1815-1849	B	305
Nix, Moses	2	1815-1849	B	358
Noger, Daniel (Shoemaker)	1	1777-1814	A	102
Norman, Dicey	2	1815-1849	B	296
Norman, George	1	1777-1814	A	51
Norman, John (Sr.)	2	1815-1849	B	561
Norman, Jusith	2	1815-1849	C	78
Norman, Thomas	2	1815-1849	C	28
Nott, Abram	2	1815-1849	B	224
Nuckols, W.T.	2	1815-1849	C	102
O'Neal, John	1	1777-1814	A	148
O'Neille, John, see - - - - - - - - - - - - - - - - - - -				O'Neal, John
Orio, James (Sr.)	2	1815-1849	B	140
Page, Richard	2	1815-1849	B	53
Pair, Allen	2	1815-1849	B	484
Pair, Claybourn	2	1815-1849	B	229
Palmer, Daniel	2	1815-1849	C	12

Palmer, James	2	1815-1849	B	451
Palmer, Jefferies	2	1815-1849	B	591
Palmer, John	2	1815-1849	B	180
Palmer, Joshua (Sr.)(Farmer)	2	1815-1849	B	290
Palmer, Rhoda	2	1815-1849	B	574
Plmer, T.R.H.	2	1815-1849	C	51
Palmer, Thomas	1	1777-1814	A	159
Parham, Francis	2	1815-1849	B	263
Parham, John	2	1815-1849	B	170
Park, George	1	1777-1814	A	201
Park, James (Farmer)	2	1815-1849	B	208
Parnell, James	1	1777-1814	A	74
Parr, Darky	2	1815-1849	C	5
Patrick, Charles	2	1815-1849	B	231
Patrick, Gabriel	1	1777-1814	A	275
Patrick, John	2	1815-1849	B	320
Patton, Samuel	1	1777-1814	A	194
Paulk, Phebe	2	1815-1849	C	82
Pearson, Isaac	2	1815-1849	B	252
Pearson, Tabitha	1	1777-1814	A	83
Peek, Jonthan	1	1777-1814	A	156
Peterson, Peter	2	1815-1849	B	272
Peterson, Sarah	1	1777-1814	A	305
Petty, Absolem (Farmer)	1	1777-1814	A	165
Petty, Jesse	1	1777-1814	A	47
Petty, James	1	1777-1814	A	252
Petty, Joshua	2	1815-1849	B	20
Pickens, Martha	2	1815-1849	B	451
Plaxico, Henry (Farmer)	2	1815-1849	B	288
Plummer, William	1	1777-1849	A	5
Porter, Edward Sanders	1	1777-1814	A	8
Porter, Hancock	2	1815-1849	C	45
Porter, Jedethan	1	1777-1814	A	191
Porter, Lucy	2	1815-1849	C	6
Porter, William (Sr.)	2	1815-1849	B	61
Posey, Farr	2	1815-1849	B	24
Potter, Adam	1	1777-1814	A	145
Potts, George	1	1777-1814	A	161
Powell, Richard	1	1777-1814	A	145
Prewitt, David	2	1815-1849	B	151
Prewitt, Mary	2	1815-1849	B	177
Prince, Daniel (Planter)	1	1777-1814	A	13
Prince, David	1	1777-1814	A	230
Pruitt, John	2	1815-1849	C	96
Pruitt, Mary, see - Prewitt, Mary				
Puckett, Ephram	1	1777-1814	A	112
Putman, James	1	1777-1814	A	316
Putman, John	2	1815-1849	B	88
Quay, Catherine	2	1815-1849	C	27
Ray, William	2	1815-1849	B	427
Reid, J.L., see - Reed, Jethro L.				
Reid, Judith	1	1775-1814	A	240
Reid, Jethro L.	2	1815-1849	B	182
Rhodes, Mary	2	1815-1849	B	14
Rice, Hezekiah (Planter)	2	1815-1849	B	305
Rice, Mary	2	1815-1849	B	259
Rice, Sarah p. (Widow)	2	1815-1849	C	23

Rice, William	2	1815-1849	B	577
Rochester, Ann	2	1815-1849	B	584
Rochester, Nicholas	2	1815-1849	B	245
Rogers, James	2	1815-1849	B	500
Rogers, John	2	1815-1849	B	321
Rogers, John	2	1815-1849	B	464
Rogers, William	2	1815-1849	B	111
Roundtree, James	2	1815-1849	B	483
Roundtree, Turner	1	1777-1814	A	76
Sandage, Nathan	2	1815-1849	B	70
Sanders, Reuben S.	1	1777-1814	A	512
Sartor, William (Planter)	2	1815-1849	B	200
Savage, James	1	1777-1814	A	180
Savage, James	2	1815-1849	B	242
Savage, John (Captain)	1	1777-1814	A	282
Savage, Sarah	2	1815-1849	B	325
Savage, William S.	2	1815-1849	C	75
Scott, Thomas	2	1815-1849	B	419
Selby, Samuel	2	1815-1849	B	256
Sharp, William	2	1815-1849	B	185
Simmons, Carpenter	2	1815-1849	B	590
Simmonson, Magnus	1	1777-1814	A	45
Simpson, Edmond	2	1815-1849	B	501
Sims, Elizabeth	2	1815-1849	B	80
Sims, James	1	1777-1814	A	58
Sims, Nathan	2	1815-1849	B	442
Sinclair, John	2	1815-1849	B	428
Sinclair, Rob (Tailor)	1	1777-1814	A	251
Smith, Abraham	1	1777-1814	A	210
Smith, David	1	1777-1814	A	205
Smith, David	1	1777-1814	A	209
Smith, David	1	1777-1814	A	274
Smith, Fleet	2	1815-1849	B	252
Smith, George	2	1815-1849	B	459
Smith, George L.	2	1815-1849	B	441
Smith, Henry	2	1815-1849	C	64
Smith, James	2	1815-1849	B	552
Smith, Martha	2	1815-1849	B	556
Smith, Sarah, see - - - - - - - - - - - - - - - - - - -			Smith, Samuel	
Smith, Samuel	2	1815-1849	B	509
Souter, Margaret	2	1815-1849	C	1
Sparks, Josiah	2	1815-1849	C	50
Sparks, Mitchell	2	1815-1849	B	295
Spears, William	2	1815-1849	B	257
Spivey, Charles	1	1777-1814	A	289
Steen, Gideon	2	1815-1849	C	94
Steen, John	2	1815-1849	B	481
Steen, William	1	1777-1814	A	125
Stevens, Edward	2	1815-1849	B	256
Stevens, Henry	1	1777-1814	A	256
Stockton, David	1	1777-1814	A	4
Stokos, John	2	1815-1849	B	222
Stribling, Clayton	2	1815-1849	B	258
Summer, Mill	2	1815-1849	B	265
Swink, Catherine	2	1815-1849	C	45
Tate, James	2	1815-1849	B	575
Tate, James	2	1815-1849	B	587
Taylor, John	1	1777-1814	A	55

Taylor, Langhorn	2	1815-1849	B	115
Taylor, Thomas C.	2	1815-1849	B	261
Thomas, James	1	1777-1814	A	42
Thompson, Charles	1	1777-1814	A	113
Thomson, Sarah	2	1815-1849	B	281
Tindall, Robert	1	1777-1814	A	226
Torbert, Samuel	1	1777-1814	A	82
Tosh, James (Farmer)	1	1777-1814	A	212
Townsend, James	1	1777-1814	A	87
Townsend, Tabitha	1	1777-1814	A	258
Trainum, Obediah, see				Tranum, Obediah
Tranum, Obediah	2	1815-1849	B	153
Travilla, Henry	1	1777-1814	A	247
Tucker, George Beauford	1	1777-1814	A	187
Tucker, Joseph	2	1815-1849	B	168
Tucker, Lucy	2	1815-1849	B	89
Tucker, Mary	2	1815-1849	B	54
Van Lew, John V.	2	1815-1849	B	342
Vaughan, Cynthia	2	1815-1849	B	452
Vaughan, Randolph	2	1815-1849	B	215
Walker, J.F.	2	1815-1849	C	108
Walker, Janett	2	1815-1849	B	152
Wallace, Robert	1	1777-1814	A	109
Wallace, William	2	1815-1849	B	186
Waters, Francis	2	1815-1849	B	44
Watkins, Thomas	2	1815-1849	B	50
Weldon, Moses	1	1777-1814	A	84
West, Benjamin	2	1815-1849	C	2
West, Rachel	2	1815-1849	C	26
White, Isaac (Sr.)	1	1777-1814	A	141
White, Isaac	2	1815-1849	B	163
White, John	1	1777-1814	A	200
White, Nancy	2	1815-1849	B	87
White, Richard (Sr.)	2	1815-1849	B	485
White, Stephen	1	1777-1849	A	177
Whitlock, Mary	1	1777-1849	A	295
Whitlock, Robert	1	1777-1849	A	190
Whitlock, William	1	1777-1814	A	193
Whitson, Solmon (Shoemaker)	1	1777-1814	A	85
Wilkins, Aaron	2	1815-1849	B	360
Williams, John (Sr.)	2	1815-1849	B	120
Williams, John Wyatt	2	1815-1849	B	519
Wilson, John	1	1777-1814	A	29
Woodson, Benjamin	1	1777-1814	A	108
Woodson, James	1	1777-1814	A	96
Wright, Roderick	1	1777-1814	A	192
Wright, Thomas	1	1777-1814	A	33
Young, Catherine (Widow)	1	1777-1814	A	320

Copied by:

/s/   Mrs. John D. Rogers

INDEX TO

WILLIAMSBURG COUNTY WILLS.

VOLUME NO. I

1802-1853

This index is compiled from W.P.A. copies of
wills filed in the COUNTY PROBATE COURTS.
The volumes indexed are a part of the
South Carolina Collection of the
University of South Carolina
Library.

Columbia, S.C.
1939

Name	Vol.	Date	Section	Page
Barate, Agnes	1	1802-1853	B	217
Barr, George A.	1	1802-1853	B	273
Barr, James (Sr.)	1	1802-1853	A	77
Barr, Jane	1	1802-1853	B	210
Barr, Jannet	1	1802-1853	D	375
Barrett, Agnes, see - - - - - - - - - - - - - - - - - - - Barate, Agnes				
Barrineau, Isaac (Sr.)	1	1802-1853	A	4
Barrineau, Margaret	1	1802-1853	D	310
Bellin, John B.	1	1802-1853	C	318
Bennett, Henry (Planter)	1	1802-1853	B	306
Bennett, Robert S.	1	1802-1853	B	258
Bennett, Samuel	1	1802-1853	D	389
Benton, Moses	1	1802-1853	A	100
Benton, Richard	1	1802-1853	A	116
Bird, Joel	1	1802-1853	B	314
Blake, James (Farmer)	1	1802-1853	C	366
Bostwick, Jonathan (Planter)	1	1802-1853	A	69
Bradley, James	1	1802-1853	A	85
Bradley, Mary	1	1802-1853	A	143
Bradshaw, Samuel (Farmer)	1	1802-1853	A	141
Braveboy, Morris (Planter)	1	1802-1853	D	394
Britton, Benjamin (Planter)	1	1802-1853	B	296
Britton, Thomas G. (Planter)	1	1802-1853	B	249
Brockington, Martha	1	1802-1853	C	326
Brockington, W.S. (Planter)	1	1802-1853	B	239
Brockington, John (Planter)	1	1802-1853	D	475
Brown, Abner (Planter)	1	1802-1853	D	384
Brown, Mary	1	1802-1853	B	188
Brown, William	1	1802-1853	D	444
Brown, William (Sr.)	1	1802-1853	D	453
Buford, William	1	1802-1853	A	48
Buford, Wm. (Planter)	1	1802-1853	A	50
Buford, William I. (Planter)	1	1802-1853	D	402
Burdick, Eliphatel H.	1	1802-1853	A	32
Burgess, James	1	1802-1853	A	90
Burgess, John D. (Planter)	1	1802-1853	A	9
Burrows, George (Planter)	1	1802-1853	A	8
Cade, Richard	1	1802-1853	B	203
Calhoun, James G.	1	1802-1853	A	29
Campbell, Archable	1	1802-1853	D	407
Campbell, James	1	1802-1853	C	357
Campbell, Rebecca	1	1802-1853	A	94
Campbell, William	1	1802-1853	A	99
Cantey, Joseph	1	1802-1853	B	247
Carter, William H.	1	1802-1853	D	438
Chandler, Hannah	1	1802-1853	D	373
Clark, Alexander	1	1802-1853	A	31
Coachman, Joseph	1	1802-1853	A	68
Cockfield, Joseph (Planter)	1	1802-1853	B	171
Cockfield, Josiah	1	1802-1853	B	279
Cockfield, W.W.	1	1802-1853	D	467
Coleman, Jacob	1	1802-1853	A	75
Connell, R.E.	1	1802-1853	D	474

Connor, John McNicholl	1	1802-1853	A	65
Cooper, William James	1	1802-1853	A	24
Cormick, Patrick	1	1802-1853	A	36
Daniel, James	1	1802-1853	B	212
Dickey, Catherine	1	1802-1853	B	181
Dickey, Catherine	1	1802-1853	A	121
Douglass, Elizabeth	1	1802-1853	D	411
Durnot, Benjamin	1	1802-1853	A	39
Eaddy, Edward D.	1	1802-1853	D	433
Eaddy, James	1	1802-1853	A	142
Eddy, Samuel	1	1802-1853	C	368
Ellis, Mary	1	1802-1853	D	451
Epps, Daniel (Planter)	1	1802-1853	B	189
Epps, Martha	1	1802-1853	D	482
Ervin, J.	1	1802-1853	A	110
Ervin, Joseph	1	1802-1853	A	107
Feagin, Richardson	1	1802-1853	D	377
Ferdon, Joanna	1	1802-1853	C	362
Ferndon, Wm. (Planter)	1	1802-1853	D	465
Fleming, John	1	1802-1853	A	88
Folly, James	1	1802-1853	B	223
Frierson, Richard (Sr.)	1	1802-1853	B	185
Frierson, William (Sr.)	1	1802-1853	B	233
Fulmore, John C.	1	1802-1853	B	309
Gamble, James (Sr.)	1	1802-1853	B	264
Gamble, James (Planter)	1	1802-1853	D	477
Gamble, Richard	1	1802-1853	A	35
Gamble, William H.	1	1802-1853	D	424
Gibson, Ebenzer (Sr.)	1	1802-1853	A	14
Gibson, George (Planter)	1	1802-1853	D	416
Gibson, James	1	1802-1853	C	352
Gibson, John	1	1802-1853	A	22
Glass, Alexander (Planter)	1	1802-1853	A	108
Gordon, Benjamin E.	1	1802-1853	B	260
Gotea, John (Sr.)	1	1802-1853	A	18
Gowdy, James	1	1802-1853	A	12
Graham, Charles N.	1	1802-1853	B	311
Graham, Elizabeth	1	1802-1853	B	194
Graham, Hugh	1	1802-1853	A	37
Graham, James (Planter)	1	1802-1853	D	447
Graham, John (Dr.)	1	1802-1853	A	64
Graham, John	1	1802-1853	B	266
Graham, Sarah	1	1802-1853	B	237
Graham, Susannah	1	1802-1853	D	422
Graham, William (Planter)	1	1802-1853	C	328
Green, George (Planter)	1	1802-1853	D	392
Hambleton, Margaret	1	1802-1853	A	103
Hanna, Hugh (Planter)	1	1802-1853	D	382

Hannah, William	1	1802-1853	D	419
Hawthorn, George	1	1802-1853	A	157
Haselden, Samuel	1	1802-1853	A	166
Hedleston, William	1	1802-1853	B	220
Hewit, Eliphalet H.	1	1802-1853	A	83
Hicks, Jesse	1	1802-1853	D	437
Hickson, John	1	1802-1853	A	76
Howard, Edward	1	1802-1853	A	1
James, Edward	1	1802-1853	C	361
James, Gavin	1	1802-1853	A	159
James, Gavin	1	1802-1853	C	369
James, Jane	1	1802-1853	A	54
James, John (Planter)	1	1802-1853	C	339
Jaudon, Paul (Planter)	1	1802-1853	A	73
Johnson, Jacob	1	1802-1853	B	275
Johnson, William (Sr.)	1	1802-1853	C	354
Jolly, Susannah	1	1802-1853	D	397
Jones, Samuel	1	1802-1853	A	156
Keels, George W. (Planter)	1	1802-1853	B	243
Keels, Isaac	1	1802-1853	B	196
Keels, John (Planter)	1	1802-1853	A	33
Kelty, John	1	1802-1853	A	138
Knox, Samuel (Planter)	1	1802-1853	B	252
Leger, John	1	1802-1853	A	114
Lesesne, Charles	1	1802-1853	B	283
Lesesne, Francis J.	1	1802-1853	D	471
Lifrage, William (Sr.)	1	1802-1853	B	255
Lister, Richard	1	1802-1853	B	262
Lowry, John	1	1802-1853	A	168
Lowry, Richard (Planter)	1	1802-1853	B	205
Lowry, Sarah M.	1	1802-1853	D	396
McAllister, John	1	1802-1853	D	479
McBride, James	1	1802-1853	A	95
McCants, Ann	1	1802-1853	B	201
McClam, Solomon (Sr.)	1	1802-1853	A	145
McClary, David (Planter)	1	1802-1853	B	169
McClary, John	1	1802-1853	B	224
McCollister, John	1	1802-1853	A	26
McConnell, George	1	1802-1853	A	105
McConnell, George	1	1802-1853	B	236
McConnell, James	1	1802-1853	A	92
McConnell, James	1	1802-1853	C	320
McConnell, Rachel	1	1802-1853	C	336
McConnell, Thomas (Planter)	1	1802-1853	B	286
McConnell, William	1	1802-1853	B	213
McCottry, Mary	1	1802-1853	B	192
McCrea, Esther	1	1802-1853	D	480
McCrea, Thomas	1	1802-1853	B	218
McCrea, Thomas (Jr.)	1	1802-1853	A	97
McCutchen, George (Sr.)	1	1802-1853	C	359
McCutchen, Hugh	1	1802-1853	D	428
McCutchen, Mary Baxter	1	1802-1853	D	459

McCutchen, Thomas	1	1802-1853	B	183
McDaniel, James (Planter)	1	1802-1853	C	333
McDonald, William (Planter)	1	1802-1853	A	135
McElroy, William	1	1802-1853	A	20
McElveen, Joseph P.	1	1802-1853	D	468
McFadden, James (Planter)	1	1802-1853	D	484
McGill, Elizabeth	1	1802-1853	B	231
McGill, Mary Ann	1	1802-1853	D	449
McGill, Mary Ann	1	1802-1853	D	455
McGill, Mary M.	1	1802-1853	D	457
McIlveen, William (Sr.)	1	1802-1853	A	16
McKee, Elizabeth	1	1802-1853	A	46
McKee, Joseph	1	1802-1853	A	42
McKinzie, Daniel	1	1802-1853	B	230
McLam, Bryant	1	1802-1853	D	435
McMurray, John	1	1802-1853	A	67
Matthews, Isaac	1	1802-1853	A	60
Matthews, John M.	1	1802-1853	D	371
Micheau, Paul (Sr.)	1	1802-1853	A	58
Montgomery, James (Planter)	1	1802-1853	D	486
Montgomery, John	1	1802-1853	B	199
Montgomery, John	1	1802-1853	C	331
Montgomery, Samuel Srpy	1	1802-1853	D	426
Moore, William (Planter)	1	1802-1853	A	112
Morris, Richard (Planter)	1	1802-1853	D	431
Morris, Richard W.	1	1802-1853	D	405
Mouzon, Samuel R.	1	1802-1853	D	378
Mouzon, Susannah	1	1802-1853	A	118
Mouzon, Susanna D.	1	1802-1853	A	3
Murphy, Archibald (Planter)	1	1802-1853	B	173
Murphy, Jane	1	1802-1853	B	235
Nesmith, Lemuel	1	1802-1853	C	358
Nesmith, Richard (Planter)	1	1802-1853	B	271
Nesmith, Samuel (Sr.)	1	1802-1853	A	133
Oliver, Peter M. (Planter)	1	1802-1853	D	398
Owens, Lucy	1	1802-1853	A	63
Owens, Sealy	1	1802-1853	B	282
Owens, Stephen	1	1802-1853	A	28
Paisley, Hannah	1	1802-1853	A	79
Paisley, Hugh (Farmer)	1	1802-1853	B	187
Paisley, Jannet	1	1802-1853	D	464
Parsons, Mary	1	1802-1853	C	364
Patterson, Jannet	1	1802-1853	A	164
Pendergrass, Sarah A.	1	1802-1853	D	415
Perdrian, Ann	1	1802-1853	D	462
Perdrian, John (Planter)	1	1802-1853	D	381
Perritt, Ann	1	18021853	C	355
Pressley, James F.	1	18021853	B	254
Pressley, John	1	1802-1853	A	161
Pressley, Mary B.	1	1802-1853	D	441
Pressley, William J.	1	1802-1853	B	232
Price, Henry	1	1802-1853	A	44

Rhodus, Solomon	1	1802-1853	A	6
Rogers, John	1	1802-1853	D	408
Rogers, Thomas (Merchant)	1	1802-1853	A	52
Salters, Sarah	1	1802-1853	D	488
Scott, Jennet	1	1802-1853	A	81
Scott, John (Sr.)	1	1802-1853	A	148
Singletary, Jacob	1	1802-1853	A	119
Singletary, John	1	1802-1853	B	179
Singletary, Samuel (Planter)	1	1802-1853	D	386
Singletary, Sarah	1	1802-1853	B	176
Singletary, Thomas D.	1	1802-1853	B	244
Smith, Abner	1	1802-1853	A	101
Snowden, Abner	1	1802-1853	A	152
Speights, E.M. (Planter)	1	1802-1853	B	312
Spring, Ann	1	1802-1853	A	19
Spring, Richard	1	1802-1853	C	322
Staggers, Martin	1	1802-1853	C	324
Steele, Thomas (Planter)	1	1802-1853	B	302
Steele, Thomas M.	1	1802-1853	B	299
Stone, Leonard	1	1802-1853	D	469
Stretch, Mary	1	1802-1853	A	111
Strong, Ann	1	1802-1853	B	215
Strong, Robert (Planter)	1	1802-1853	D	400
Strong, Samuel (Planter)	1	1802-1853	A	147
Sutton, Richard (Planter)	1	1802-1853	C	349
Turner, Benjamin	1	1802-1853	A	155
Walsh, Francis	1	1802-1853	A	163
Ward, James	1	1802-1853	B	177
Watson, Andrew	1	1802-1853	A	129
Watson, John (Planter)	1	1802-1853	C	316
Watson, Sarah	1	1802-1853	A	131
Wilson, David I.	1	1802-1853	D	376
Wilson, Elizabeth	1	1802-1853	C	337
Wilson, Elizabeth M.	1	1802-1853	B	301
Wilson, Jane	1	1802-1853	B	229
Wilson, Mary P.	1	1802-1853	B	307
Wilson, Samuel	1	1802-1853	A	123
Witherspoon, Elizabeth	1	1802-1853	A	150
Witherspoon, Gavin	1	1802-1853	A	127
Witherspoon, Robert L.	1	1802-1853	A	71
Woody, John	1	1802-1853	B	269
Young, Martha	1	1802-1853	D	413
Zuill, James	1	1802-1853	A	40

Copied by:

/s/   Mrs. John D. Rogers

INDEX TO

YORK COUNTY WILLS.

Volume No. 1
1770-1815

Volume No. 2
1816-1859

Volume No. 3
1840-1853

This index is compiled from W.P.A. copies of
wills filed in the COUNTY PROBATE COURTS.
The volumes indexed are a part of the
South Carolina Collection of the
University of South Carolina
Library.

Columbia, S.C.
1959

WILLS

Note: York County Wills not divided into books.

Name	Vol.	Date	Page
Adams, Brixene	3	1840-1855	113
Adams, Francis	2	1816-1859	170
Adams, James S.	3	1840-1855	21
Adams, Margaret	2	1816-1859	57
Adams, Robert	1	1770-1815	154
Adams, Robert	1	1770-1815	243
Adams, William	1	1770-1815	220
Adkins, Samuel (Planter)	1	1770-1815	263
Akin, William	1	1770-1815	551
Albright, John	3	1840-1855	212
Alexander, Catherine I.	3	1840-1855	115
Alexander, Herman	2	1816-1859	252
Alexander, Hester	2	1816-1859	154
Alexander, Joseph (Minister)	1	1770-1815	444
Allen, Andrew (Planter)	1	1770-1815	475
Allison, Albert	2	1816-1859	93
Allison, Alexander	1	1770-1815	535
Allison, Hugh	1	1770-1815	222
Allison, John	1	1770-1815	538
Allison, Robert	2	1816-1859	276
Amberson, William	3	1840-1855	246
Anderson, Ann	3	1840-1855	177
Anderson, Eliza Ann	2	1816-1859	206
Anderson, John	3	1840-1855	143
Anderson, John, (Sr.)	1	1770-1815	506
Anderson, William Henry	3	1840-1855	23
Andrey, William	2	1816-1859	519
Armstrong, Arthur	2	1816-1859	292
Armstrong, James	2	1816-1859	1-b
Armstrong, Mary	2	1816-1859	555
Armstrong, Robert L.	2	1816-1859	155
Armstrong, Sarah	3	1840-1855	1
Arnold, Josephus	1	1770-1815	289
Ash, John	1	1770-1815	16
Ash, William	2	1816-1859	131
Ashmore, Walter	1	1770-1815	87
Bailey, Elijah (Sr.)	1	1770-1815	426
Barnes, John	2	1816-1859	517
Barnet, Alexander	3	1840-1855	277
Barnet, Thomas	1	1770-1815	509
Barnett, John (Sr.)	1	1770-1815	598
Barnett, Rachel	3	1840-1855	571
Barnett, Thomas	2	1816-1859	171
Barnett, Thomas	2	1816-1859	295
Barnette, Richard	2	1816-1859	448
Barnhill, Isabella	1	1770-1815	572
Barnhill, John	2	1816-1859	487
Barnwell, Cynthia E.	3	1840-1855	179
Barnwell, Mary C.	3	1840-1855	160
Barron, John (Sr.)	2	1816-1859	552
Barron, Thomas	2	1816-1859	133

Barron, William	3	1840-1853	25
Bartlett, Daniel	2	1816-1839	135
Barry, Jane	2	1816-1839	488
Barry, John (Sr.)	2	1816-1839	297
Barry, John H.	3	1840-1853	79
Barry, Roger	2	1816-1839	207
Barry, Samuel	2	1816-1839	209
Barry, William	1	1770-1815	295
Barry, William A.	3	1840-1853	2
Bates, Elizabeth	3	1840-1853	247
Bates, John (Sr.)	2	1816-1839	418
Bates, Robert	2	1816-1839	107
Baxter, Andrew	1	1770-1815	209
Baxter, Margaret	1	1770-1815	210
Baxter, Mary	2	1816-1839	464
Baxter, William (Planter)	2	1816-1839	108
Beaird, David	1	1770-1815	291
Beamgarde, Godfrey	2	1816-1839	554
Beard, James	1	1770-1815	61
Beard, Jane	2	1816-1839	173
Beatty, Jesse	1	1770-1815	342
Beatty, Jonathan	1	1770-1815	554
Beatty, William	1	1770-1815	224
Bell, Robert	1	1770-1815	294
Bennett, John	3	1840-1853	181
Benoist, James	1	1770-1815	265
Benson, Jacob	2	1816-1839	335
Berry, Catherine	1	1770-1815	24
Bigger, Esther	3	1840-1853	351
Bigger, James	1	1770-1815	244
Bigger, James	3	1840-1853	299
Bigger, Joseph	1	1770-1815	44
Bigger, Mathew	1	1770-1815	63
Bigger, Moses	2	1816-1839	450
Bigger, William M.	2	1816-1839	556
Birk, Francis	1	1770-1815	158
Black, Alexander	1	1770-1815	125
Black, Alexander	1	1770-1815	492
Black, Jacob (Farmer)	3	1840-1853	3
Black, John	2	1816-1839	558
Black, Joseph	3	1840-1853	352
Black, Merriba	3	1840-1853	44
Black, Robert(Sr.)(Yeoman)	1	1770-1815	10
Black, Robert	1	1770-1815	400
Black, Thomas	1	1770-1815	475
Blair, John	3	1840-1853	182
Blair, Samuel	2	1816-1839	420
Blake, John	3	1840-1853	248
Bland, Edward (Farmer)	1	1770-1815	196
Blaylock, Jeremiah	2	1816-1839	321
Boggs, Aaron	2	1816-1839	490
Boggs, Joseph	1	1770-1815	156
Boleyn, Britton	3	1840-1853	373
Boyd, Jane	3	1840-1853	214
Boyd, John	2	1816-1839	210
Boyd, John	3	1840-1853	117
Boyd, Joseph	2	1816-1839	134
Boyd, Thomas	2	1816-1839	452

Boyls, Mary	1	1770–1815	109
Bogwell, Robert	2	1816–1839	94
Bradley, Ellfyday	2	1816–1839	301
Bradley, Samuel	2	1816–1839	560
Bradshaw, Thomas	3	1840–1853	145
Brandon, John (Sr.)	1	1770–1815	225
Bratton, Martha	2	1816–1839	279
Bratton, Robert (Sr.)	1	1770–1815	535
Bratton, William	1	1770–1815	511
Brian, Mary	3	1840–1853	45
Bridges, Thomas	2	1816–1839	363
Bridges, William	3	1840–1853	301
Brown, John	3	1840–1853	82
Brown, John	3	1840–1853	250
Brown, Joseph	2	1816–1839	254
Brown, Robert	2	1816–1839	466
Brown, William	1	1770–1815	127
Brown, William (Sr.)	3	1840–1853	146
Brumfield, Charles	1	1770–1815	573
Brumfield, Elizabeth	2	1816–1839	336
Bryan, James (Sr.)	2	1816–1839	558
Buchanan, Samuel (Sr.)	2	1816–1839	105
Burns, Elizabeth	3	1840–1853	279
Burns, Laughlin	1	1770–1815	344
Burris, Elizabeth	3	1840–1853	118
Burris, Robert	3	1840–1853	574
Burris, William (Sr.)	1	1770–1815	477
Byers, David	1	1770–1815	128
Byers, David	3	1840–1853	303
Byers, Sarah	3	1840–1853	388
Cairnes, Elisabeth	3	1840–1853	27
Cally, William	1	1770–1815	198
Campbell, Elisabeth (Widow)	2	1816–1839	110
Campbell, James	1	1770–1815	362
Campbell, James	1	1770–1815	459
Campbell, James	3	1840–1853	26
Carnahan, John	1	1770–1815	89
Carothers, James	3	1840–1853	378
Carothers, William	3	1840–1853	84
Carrall, Joseph	1	1770–1815	517
Carrel, Joseph	1	1770–1815	20
Carrel, Joseph (Planter)	1	1770–1815	51
Carrell, Jeanett	1	1770–1815	183
Carroll, Elijah	3	1840–1853	306
Carroll, Henry	3	1840–1853	376
Carroll, John	2	1816–1839	521
Carroll, Joseph	2	1816–1839	519
Carroll, Thomas	2	1816–1839	175
Carroll, Thomas	2	1816–1839	365
Carruth, John	2	1816–1839	157
Carson, William (Farmer)	1	1770–1815	428
Chambers, Elizabeth (Sr.)	2	1816–1839	213
Chambers, James	1	1770–1815	519
Chambers, John (Farmer)	2	1816–1839	178
Chambers, John	3	1840–1853	324
Chambers, Samuel	2	1816–1839	523

Chambers, William	2	1816–1839	62
Chambers, William	2	1816–1839	525
Champion, Richard	1	1770–1815	185
Champion, William	2	1816–1839	2
Cherry, Peter	2	1816–1839	537
Chesney, Nancey	1	1770–1815	478
Childers, Jacob (Planter)	3	1840–1853	47
Choat, William	2	1816–1839	340
Clark, Eli	3	1840–1853	86
Clark, John	2	1816–1839	508
Clark, John	3	1840–1853	120
Clark, Joseph	1	1770–1815	461
Clarke, Ann	1	1770–1815	576
Clendinen, Thomas	2	1816–1839	38
Conley, Patrick	1	1770–1815	514
Cooper, Isles	1	1770–1815	515
Cooper, John	1	1770–1815	495
Cooper, Margaret	2	1816–1839	180
Cooper, Robert	3	1840–1853	48
Coulter, Jedidiah	3	1840–1853	327
Craig, Henry	1	1770–1815	363
Craig, James	1	1770–1815	8
Craig, Mary (Widow)	2	1816–1839	64
Craig, William	1	1770–1815	266
Crawford, Agness	2	1816–1839	456
Crawford, Alexander	3	1840–1853	329
Crawford, Ann	3	1840–1853	121
Crawford, James	2	1816–1839	66
Crawford, James (Sr.)	2	1816–1839	581
Crawford, Jane	3	1840–1853	50
Crawford, Walter	1	1770–1815	389
Crawford, William	1	1770–1815	516
Crow, James	1	1770–1815	246
Currence, Hugh	3	1840–1853	331
Currence, Rebecka	2	1816–1839	468
Currence, William	3	1840–1853	201
Curry, Charles	2	1816–1839	4
Cushman, Xerxes H.	2	1816–1839	280
Dale, Ann (Widow)	1	1770–1815	537
Dale, William	1	1770–1815	211
Daniel, Holway W.	3	1840–1853	333
Darby, Zadock	2	1816–1839	182
Darval, James	2	1816–1839	367
Darwin, John	2	1816–1839	492
Darwin, John B.	3	1840–1853	354
Davidson, Elizabeth	3	1840–1853	87
Davidson, John (Sr.)	1	1770–1815	518
Davidson, Margaret	2	1816–1839	421
Davis, Thomas	2	1816–1839	112
Davis, Vincent	3	1840–1853	358
Davis, William (Sr.)	2	1816–1839	95
Dennis, John	3	1840–1853	89
Denton, Samuel	1	1700–1815	46
Dickson, William	2	1816–1839	342
Dicky, John	1	1770–1815	26
Dicky, John	1	1770–1815	268
Donahy, Eleanor	1	1770–1815	111

Donaldson, Tabitha	3	1840–1853	251
Donnally, James	2	1816–1839	69
Donnally, Martha	2	1816–1839	369
Donnom, Isaac	2	1816–1839	590
Dowdlw, Allen	1	1770–1815	579
Drennan, Thomas	1	1770–1815	402
Drennan, Mary	1	1770–1815	447
Duglass, George (Planter)	1	1770–1815	578
Dulin, James	3	1840–1853	90
Dun, James	1	1770–1815	462
Duncan, Thomas (Sr.)	1	1770–1815	430
Dunkin, Mary	1	1770–1815	479
Dunlap, Benjamin	3	1840–1853	308
Dunlap, Susanna	2	1816–1839	561
Dunlap, William	2	1816–1839	184
Dunwoody, John	2	1816–1839	215
Durham, John	2	1816–1839	322
Dyson, Maddox	1	1770–1815	539
Eakin, Alexander	1	1770–1815	365
Eakin, Alexander (Jr.)	1	1770–1815	345
Ekin, William	1	1770–1815	531
Ellis, Benjamin (Planter)	1	1770–1815	404
Ellis, John (Planter)	2	1816–1839	370
Ellis, Robert	1	1770–1815	540
Ellis, Sarah Sumner	2	1816–1839	136
Elwell, Hannah	3	1840–1853	382
Enloe, Isaac	2	1816–1839	59
Enlow, Mary	1	1770–1815	3
Erwin, William (Sr.)	1	1770–1815	543
Erwin, William R.	3	1840–1853	215
Evans, Rebecca	3	1840–1853	51
Falls, John	2	1816–1839	509
Faries, James	1	1770–1815	297
Faries, James	3	1840–1853	123
Faries, William	1	1770–1815	367
Faris, Jean	1	1770–1815	406
Farres, Alexander	2	1816–1839	186
Farries, Robert	1	1770–1815	320
Farris, Samuel	3	1840–1853	125
Farris, William	3	1840–1853	53
Farris, William	1	1770–1815	367
Feemster, James	2	1816–1839	457
Feemster, John	2	1816–1839	6
Feemster, John	2	1816–1839	42
Feemster, Joseph	1	1770–1815	347
Ferguson, James	1	1770–1815	112
Ferris, Alexander, see – – – – – – – – –		Farres, Alexander	
Fewell, John (Planter)	3	1840–1853	127
Floyd, Andrew	2	1816–1839	527
Floyd, James	3	1840–1853	252
Forbes, John (Sr.)	2	1816–1839	302
Foreman, James	1	1770–1815	448
Foreman, Samuel (Farmer)	1	1770–1815	391
Fowler, James	1	1770–1815	270
Fulton, A.S.	3	1840–1853	334
Fulton, Daniel	3	1840–1853	93

Gabbie, Joseph	2	1816-1859	216
Gabby, John	2	1816-1859	8
Gallagher, Jane	2	1816-1859	592
Gallimore, Edward	1	1770-1815	271
Galloway, Alexander	2	1816-1859	188
Galloway, Alexander (Sr.)	2	1816-1859	589
Galloway, William (Planter)	2	1816-1859	255
Garvin, John	1	1770-1815	228
Gault, Elizabeth	2	1816-1859	159
Gay, Samuel	1	1770-1815	230
Gazaway, William (Sr.)	2	1816-1859	394
Gibson, James	1	1770-1815	522
Gibson, Matthew	1	1770-1815	570
Gill, Mary (Widow)	2	1816-1859	218
Gillam, Ezekiel	3	1840-1853	217
Gillespie, James R.	3	1840-1853	254
Gillespie, Margaret (Widow)	2	1816-1859	78
Gillham, Charles	1	1770-1815	272
Gillham, Charles	1	1770-1815	248
Gilmore, Frances (Sr.)	1	1770-1815	480
Given, Mary	3	1840-1853	359
Given, William	3	1840-1853	129
Givens, Daniel (Sr.)	1	1770-1815	450
Glenn, James	3	1840-1853	94
Glover, James (Farmer)	1	1770-1815	200
Good, Ann	2	1816-1859	395
Good, James B.	3	1840-1853	510
Good, John (Sr.)	1	1770-1815	572
Gordan, John	1	1770-1815	101
Gordan, John	1	1770-1815	299
Gordan, Mansfield	3	1840-1853	383
Gordan, Nanny	1	1770-1815	99
Graham, James	3	1840-1853	259
Graham, Jean	1	1770-1815	91
Green, Abraham	2	1816-1859	70
Greer, Agnes	2	1816-1859	469
Greer, Henry M.	3	1840-1853	280
Greer, Mary	3	1840-1853	55
Greer, Susanna	2	1816-1859	529
Grier, Robert	2	1816-1859	220
Grier, Thomas	2	1816-1859	223
Guinn, Thomas	2	1816-1859	563
Gunning, Edward H.	3	1840-1853	361
Gwin, Richard	2	1816-1859	583
Gwin, Samuel	3	1840-1853	256
Gwin, Thomas, see - - - - - - - - - - - - - - - - - - -			Guinn, Thomas
Gwinn, Elizabeth	3	1840-1853	54
Hacket, William	3	1840-1853	219
Hagan, William	2	1816-1859	402
Haggens, Mary	1	1770-1815	407
Hall, John	1	1770-1815	188
Hall, John	1	1770-1815	451
Hall, William	2	1816-1859	258
Hambright, Frederick (Sr.)	2	1816-1859	44
Hambright, Frederick	3	1840-1853	130
Hambright, Jefferson	3	1840-1853	262
Hambright, Josiah	2	1816-1859	259
Hamilton, David	1	1770-1815	202

Hamilton, Jean	1	1770–1815	409
Hamilton, Patrick	2	1816–1839	72
Hamilton, William	2	1816–1839	565
Hammel, Archibald	3	1840–1853	132
Hanna, Archibald C.	2	1816–1839	459
Hanna, James	1	1770–1815	204
Hanna, Sarah (Widow)	2	1816–1839	191
Hannah, Rosanah	2	1816–1839	138
Harbison, John	1	1770–1815	393
Harp, Thomas	1	1770–1815	349
Harper, Alexander	3	1840–1853	95
Harper, Matthew (Sr.)	2	1816–1839	304
Harris, Henry G. (Planter)	3	1840–1853	335
Harris, James	2	1816–1839	396
Harris, Mary	2	1816–1839	231
Harris, Nathaniel	2	1816–1839	10
Harris, Prudence	2	1816–1839	470
Harris, Robert (Jr.)	2	1816–1839	161
Harrison, Henry	2	1816–1839	372
Harshaw, Daniel	1	1770–1815	497
Hart, John	1	1770–1815	213
Hart, John	2	1816–1839	162
Hart, Priscilla	2	1816–1839	195
Hart, William	1	1770–1815	581
Hart, William T.	3	1840–1853	338
Hartness, Robert	1	1770–1815	233
Hawser, Christina	3	1840–1853	385
Hays, Jesse	3	1840–1853	57
Hays, Robert	3	1840–1853	58
Hemingway, William	2	1816–1839	193
Hemphill, Alexander	1	1770–1815	65
Hemphill, John	3	1840–1853	6
Hemphill, Margaret	3	1840–1853	339
Hemphill, Mary	2	1816–1839	424
Hemphill, Samuel (Sr.)	2	1816–1839	96
Henderson, Esther	1	1770–1815	73
Henderson, James (Planter)	3	1840–1853	148
Henderson, John	2	1816–1839	400
Henderson, Nathaniel (Sr.)	1	1770–1815	130
Henderson, Nathaniel	2	1816–1839	399
Henry, Alexander	2	1816–1839	326
Henry, James	1	1770–1815	482
Henry, William	2	1816–1839	12
Hetherington, William	3	1840–1853	134
Hill, Soloman	2	1816–1839	229
Hill, William	1	1770–1815	235
Hill, William	1	1770–1815	545
Hoff, Powell	2	1816–1839	15
Hogg, James	2	1816–1839	373
Hogg, Thomas	2	1816–1839	97
Hoggs, John	2	1816–1839	495
Holt, Akillas	2	1816–1839	530
Hood, George	2	1816–1839	17
Hood, John	1	1770–1815	553
Horsby, Susannah	3	1840–1853	312
Houser, Henry	2	1816–1839	140

Houser, Henry	2	1816–1859	140
Houser, John	2	1816–1859	404
Howe, Joseph	1	1770–1815	258
Howie, Robert	2	1816–1859	18
Hutchinson, David	5	1840–1855	151
Hutchinson, Samuel	2	1816–1859	471
Irwin, Nathaniel	1	1770–1815	114
Jackson, David (Sr.)	2	1816–1859	74
Jackson, Elizabeth	5	1840–1855	96
Jackson, John	2	1816–1859	426
Jackson, John	5	1840–1855	224
Jackson, Joseph (Farmer)	2	1816–1859	255
Jackson, Margaret	5	1840–1855	226
Jackson, Will	1	1770–1815	484
Jackson, William B.	5	1840–1855	540
James, John	5	1840–1855	228
Jamieson, Joseph	5	1840–1855	60
Jenkens, Benjamin	2	1816–1859	80
Johnston, David	1	1770–1815	155
Johnston, David	2	1816–1859	197
Johnston, David	5	1840–1855	62
Johnston, John	2	1816–1859	429
Johnston, Margaret	5	1840–1855	64
Johnston, Sarah	2	1816–1859	506
Jordan, John	1	1770–1815	101
Julian, Jacob	1	1770–1815	240
Kenmure, James	1	1770–1815	324
Kendrick, William	2	1816–1859	198
Kenedy, William	1	1770–1815	190
Kerr, Jane	1	1770–1815	465
Kerr, William	1	1770–1815	374
Kimbral, Nancy	2	1816–1859	567
King, George (Planter)	1	1770–1815	107
King, John	2	1816–1859	374
Kingy, Barbra	1	1770–1815	585
Knox, Samuel	1	1770–1815	155
Kolb, James	1	1770–1815	500
Kuykendal, Samuel	1	1770–1815	465
Kuykendal, Sarah	1	1770–1815	594
Kuykendall, Jonathan	2	1816–1859	260
Lambeth, Margaret	2	1816–1859	164
Laney, Joseph	1	1770–1815	67
Latham, James	2	1816–1859	20
Lattimore, Robert (Farmer)	1	1770–1815	29
Laurance, Joseph	2	1816–1859	199
Leathem, Andrew	1	1770–1815	95
Leathem, Marey	2	1816–1859	142
Leathem, Richard (Planter)	1	1770–1815	68
Leech, James	1	1770–1815	560
Leech, William	1	1770–1815	105
Leeper, Robert	1	1770–1815	162
Lesley, Samuel	1	1770–1815	575
Lindsay, John M.	5	1840–1855	250
Lindsey, John	2	1816–1859	46
Lipscomb, Wyatt (Planter)	2	1816–1859	545

Litle, William	2	1816–1859	165
Love, Alexander	1	1770–1815	12
Love, Andrew	1	1770–1815	326
Love, Robert	1	1770–1815	192
Love, Robert	2	1816–1859	281
Love, Robert	2	1816–1859	576
Love, William	2	1816–1859	262
Lowry, Samuel	2	1816–1859	349
Lusk, Elizabeth (Widow)	1	1770–1815	1
Lusk, Jane (Widow)	2	1816–1859	98
McAdorry, Thomas	1	1770–1815	74
McAfee, Abner	3	1840–1855	198
McCall, Gussell	2	1816–1859	569
McCants, John	1	1770–1815	452
McCarter, Christopher	2	1816–1859	113
McCarter, James A.	2	1816–1859	474
McCarter, Sarah (Sr.)	3	1840–1855	29
McCarter, Sarah	2	1816–1859	498
McCarter, Walter	2	1816–1859	353
McCaw, John (Sr.)	2	1816–1859	115
McCaw, John	2	1816–1859	473
McCaw, Nancy	3	1840–1855	156
McCleland, Hugh	1	1770–1814	164
McCleland, William	1	1770–1815	467
McCleland, Robert	3	1840–1855	98
McClelland, Robert	1	1770–1815	274
McClenahan, Finney	2	1816–1859	76
McClenahan, Jane	3	1840–1855	282
McClure, John	3	1840–1855	284
McConnel, John	2	1816–1859	284
McCord, James	1	1770–1815	116
McCorkle, Joseph W.	3	1840–1855	10
McCreight, Robert	2	1816–1859	307
McCully, James	3	1840–1855	362
McCully, Samuel	3	1840–1855	364
McCurday, Robert	1	1770–1815	329
McDaniel, Thomas	2	1816–1859	258
McElmoyle, John (Sr.)	1	1770–1815	486
McElwain, John	2	1816–1859	116
McElwee, J.R.	3	1840–1855	255
McElwee, John (Sr.)	3	1840–1855	100
McElwee, William	3	1840–1853	387
McFadden, Isaac	3	1840–1855	391
McFadden, Patrick	1	1770–1815	167
McFarline, John	2	1816–1859	236
McGarity, Michal	1	1770–1815	52
McGuown, William	2	1816–1859	48
McKee, James	3	1840–1855	344
McKee, Samuel	1	1770–1815	576
McKenzie, Joseph (Sr.)	2	1816–1859	117
McKinney, Neal	1	1770–1815	277
McKnight, John	1	1770–1815	59
McKoy, John	3	1840–1855	341
McLean, William	2	1816–1859	267
McLenahan, John S.	3	1840–1855	50
McMackin, Thomas	2	1816–1859	511
McMeans, James	2	1816–1859	355

McMurray, Nancy	1	1770–1815	499
McNeel, John	3	1840–1853	235
McNeel, Mary	2	1816–1839	328
McNeely, Robert	3	1840–1853	65
McPhilimey, James	1	1770–1815	350
McSwain, George	2	1816–1839	460
McSwain, John	1	1770–1815	410
McWhorter, Hugh	1	1770–1815	169
Manion, Thomas	1	1770–1815	304
Manning, Thomas (Sr.)	3	1840–1853	9
Mannon, Massy	2	1816–1839	407
Marley, Jameison	2	1816–1839	432
Martin, Michal	2	1816–1839	357
Martin, Thomas	3	1840–1853	204
Mason, James	2	1816–1839	144
Meacham, Bartlett	2	1816–1839	512
Meed, Adam	1	1770–1815	411
Meek, Jane	1	1770–1815	140
Meek, Moses	1	1770–1815	587
Mellon, George	1	1770–1815	242
Millen, John	1	1770–1815	278
Miller, Abraham	2	1816–1839	264
Miller, David	1	1770–1815	561
Miller, Elvy	2	1816–1839	431
Miller, Francis	3	1840–1853	31
Miller, Hugh	2	1816–1839	202
Miller, John	1	1770–1815	38
Miller, John	1	1770–1815	306
Miller, John	3	1840–1853	11
Miller, Joseph (Sr.)	2	1816–1839	119
Miller, Joseph	2	1816–183?	433
Miller, Robert	1	1770–1815	252
Miller, Robert	3	1840–1853	392
Miller, Samuel	2	1816–1839	497
Miller, Stephen	1	1770–1815	76
Miller, William	1	1770–1815	500
Milom, John	1	1770–1815	80
Minter, John	2	1816–1839	571
Minter, William	1	1770–1815	413
MisCelly, Frances	1	1770–1815	50
Miskelly, James	1	1770–1815	35
Miskelly, Jean (Widow)	1	1700–1815	307
Mitchal, James	1	1770–1815	563
Mitchel, Robert R.	3	1840–1853	285
Mollenax, William	1	1770–1815	309
Montgomery, Rebecca	1	1770–1815	468
Moar, Elener (Widow)	1	1770–1815	522
Moare, Alexander	1	1770–1815	520
Moare, Elizabeth	3	1840–1853	287
Moare, Gordan	2	1816–1839	573
Moare, James	3	1840–1853	160
Moare, James	3	1840–1853	289
Moare, Jean	1	1770–1853	104
Moare, John	3	1840–1853	33
Moare, John (Sr.)	2	1816–1839	123
Moare, John	2	1816–1839	378
Moare, Nathan	2	1816–1839	329

Moare, Hugh	2	1816–1839	580
Moare, Samuel	2	1816–1839	100
Moare, William (Sr.)	2	1816–1839	584
Morgan, Peter	3	1840–1853	292
Morris, John	1	1700–1815	415
Moss, Gilly	3	1840–1853	35
Muldoon, David (Planter)	1	1700–1815	279
Muldoon, John	2	1816–1839	235
Mullin, Mary Unity	2	1816–1839	587
Murphy, James	1	1700–1815	54
Nance, William	3	1840–1853	36
Nash, Lucy	1	1700–1815	453
Neely, David	2	1816–1839	21
Neely, Elizabeth	2	1816–1839	380
Neely, Elizabeth	3	1840–1853	39
Neely, Jackson (Sr.)	1	1770–1815	41
Neely, Jean	2	1816–1839	82
Neely, John	3	1840–1853	161
Neely, Jonathan	2	1816–1839	125
Neely, Martha (Widow)	1	1770–1815	564
Neely, William	2	1816–1839	535
Neely, William	3	1840–1853	41
Nelly, Samuel	2	1816–1839	532
Nelson, William (Farmer)	1	1770–1815	378
Nesbitt, Francis	2	1816–1839	309
Nichels, James	1	1770–1815	170
Niven, John (Sr.)(Planter)	3	1840–1853	313
Oldrage, Hannah	2	1816–1839	275
Orr, John H.	2	1816–1839	408
Packard, Zedoc	2	1816–1839	381
Pair, Miel	2	1816–1839	104
Parker, Thomas	1	1770–1815	380
Parks, William	3	1840–1853	345
Patterson, Andrew	2	1816–1839	23
Patterson, Benjamin	3	1840–1853	197
Patterson, Elizabeth	3	1840–1853	393
Patterson, John	1	1770–1815	523
Patterson, Mary	2	1816–1839	311
Patterson, Robert (Farmer)	1	1770–1815	6
Patteson, John	1	1770–1815	171
Patton, David S.	3	1840–1853	395
Patton, Joseph	1	1770–1815	503
Patton, Robert	1	1770–1815	417
Patton, William (Blacksmith)	1	1770–1815	173
Patrick, Elias	3	1840–1853	42
Patrick, Elizabeth	3	1840–1853	163
Patrick, Mary	3	1840–1853	294
Patrick, Robert (Blacksmith)	1	1770–1815	501
Patrick, Robert	2	1816–1839	382
Patrick, William	2	1816–1839	168
Patrick, William H.	3	1840–1853	264
Peters, James	2	1816–1839	382
Peters, John (Sr.)	2	1816–1839	102
Peters, John	3	1840–1853	102
Peters, Martha (Jr.)	2	1816–1839	384

Pettus, George	2	1816-1839	25
Pettus, George	3	1840-1853	135
Pettus, John D.	2	1816-1839	86
Pettus, William (Farmer)	2	1816-1839	49
Plaxeco, John T.	3	1840-1853	397
Plaxico, James	3	1840-1853	265
Polk, Eleanor	1	1770-1815	331
Polk, John	1	1770-1815	310
Polk, William	2	1816-1839	204
Porter, David (Sr.)	1	1770-1815	281
Porter, Samuel	1	1770-1815	4
Powell, James	1	1770-1815	253
Powell, James	1	1770-1815	332
Pursley, James (Planter)	1	1770-1815	70
Pursley, James	2	1816-1839	84
Pursley, Robert	2	1816-1839	476
Quinn, James	3	1840-1853	15
Rainey, William	2	1816-1839	312
Ramsey, Jane	1	1770-1815	454
Ramsey, John	2	1816-1839	147
Ramsey, Martha	3	1840-1853	17
Ramsey, Martha	3	1840-1853	267
Randall, Jacob	1	1770-1815	381
Ratchford, George	3	1840-1853	317
Ratchford, John	3	1840-1853	400
Ratchford, Mary	1	1770-1815	565
Ratchford, William (Sr.)	1	1770-1815	284
Ray, Henery (Sr.)	1	1770-1815	81
Rea, Frances	1	1770-1815	351
Rea, Henry	3	1840-1853	66
Rea, Mary	3	1840-1853	165
Rea, Sarah (Widow)	2	1816-1839	28
Reeves, Cynthia	2	1816-1839	538
Reynicks, Mary (Widow)	1	1770-1815	256
Richardson, James	1	1770-1815	193
Riddle, George	2	1816-1839	53
Roberts, Andrew	2	1816-1839	438
Roberts, James	2	1816-1839	51
Roberts, Jasse	2	1816-1839	315
Roberts, John	2	1816-1839	478
Robertson, John	2	1816-1839	480
Robertson, Rebecca	3	1840-1853	346
Robertson, Thomas	3	1840-1853	236
Robeson, James	1	1770-1815	144
Robinson, Mary	2	1816-1839	87
Robinson, Patrick	1	1770-1815	117
Robinson, William (Sr.)	2	1816-1839	127
Robison, William	2	1816-1839	539
Rogers, Isaac	2	1816-1839	30
Rogers, Michael	1	1770-1815	286
Ross, George	3	1840-1853	541
Ross, James (Sr.)	2	1816-1839	240
Ross, Rachel	1	1770-1815	94
Rowell, William F.	2	1816-1839	440
Sadler, Elizabeth	2	1816-1839	513
Sadler, Jane	2	1816-1839	1-a

Sadler, Jane (Widow)	2	1816–1859	101
Sadler, Mary R. (Widow)	3	1840–1855	67
Sadler, Richard	2	1816–1859	442
Sadler, Joseph	1	1770–1815	504
Sadler, Richard (Sr.)(Plant.)	1	1770–1815	354
Sadler, Richard	1	1770–1815	590
Sandefur, Phillip	2	1816–1859	55
Sandifer, Elizabeth	2	1816–1859	410
Sandlin, Randal (Sr.)	1	1770–1815	356
Scott, Alexander	2	1816–1859	504
Scott, David	1	1770–1815	258
Scott, Mary	1	1770–1815	567
Shane, John	1	1770–1815	525
Shearer, Hugh	1	1770–1815	85
Sherer, Thomas	2	1816–1859	578
Shurley, Elizabeth	3	1840–1855	43
Simeral, Jean	1	1770–1815	419
Simerill, James B. W.	2	1816–1859	500
Simril, James	3	1840–1855	519
Simmons, Daniel	2	1816–1859	545
Sinclair, Duncan	1	1770–1815	383
Sitgraves, John	1	1770–1815	177
Smith, Edward	3	1840–1855	269
Smith, George	3	1840–1855	206
Smith, Henry	1	1770–1815	96
Smith, James (Planter)	2	1816–1859	128
Smith, Henry	2	1816–1859	358
Smith, James	1	1770–1815	146
Smith, John (Planter)	1	1770–1815	148
Smith, John	1	1770–1815	420
Smith, John	1	1770–1815	527
Smith, John	2	1816–1859	36
Smith, John	2	1816–1859	385
Smith, Josiah	1	1770–1815	591
Smith, Lillis (Widow)	2	1816–1859	360
Smith, Nicholas (Planter)	1	1770–1815	568
Smith, Rhoda	3	1840–1855	273
Smith, Robert	3	1840–1853	401
Smith, Samuel D.	3	1840–1855	166
Smith, Sarah E.	3	1840–1855	405
Smith, William	1	1770–1815	505
Smith, William	3	1840–1855	347
Smith, William H.	2	1816–1859	588
Smith, William M.	3	1840–1853	157
Smith, Winefred	2	1816–1859	291
Smith, Winefred	3	1840–1855	258
Spence, John	1	1770–1815	287
Spratt, Andrew	1	1770–1815	353
Spratt, James	3	1840–1855	104
Spratt, Thomas	1	1770–1815	423
Springs, John	3	1840–1855	406
Springs, Richard	2	1816–1859	443
Stanton, Eleanor	3	1840–1855	68
Stanton, William A.	2	1816–1859	482
Starnes, Jacob	3	1840–1855	413
Starr, Arthur	1	1770–1815	208
Starr, John	3	1840–1853	106
Steedman, Michael	2	1816–1859	485

Steel, Archibald	1	1770-1815	194
Steel, Joseph	1	1770-1815	179
Steel, William	2	1816-1839	331
Steele, Mary	2	1816-1839	485
Stephenson, Darcus M.	3	1840-1853	296
Stephenson, James M. (Farmer)	3	1840-1853	69
Stephenson, William (Sr.)	2	1816-1839	57
Steward, Margaret	1	1770-1815	97
Stewart, Michael	1	1770-1815	434
Stary, Benjamin	3	1840-1853	138
Stuart, Alexander	1	1770-1815	260
Stuart, Archibald	2	1816-1839	317
Sturges, Daniel	1	1770-1815	56
Sturgis, Jane	1	1770-1815	215
Sturgis, Laban	1	1770-1815	119
Suggs, Laban	2	1816-1839	501
Summerford, William	3	1840-1853	139
Surley, Elizabeth, see - - - - - - - - - - Shurley, Elizabeth			
Sutton, Mary	3	1840-1853	297
Swann, Ann	2	1816-1839	548
Swann, John	2	1816-1839	32
Swann, Mary H.	2	1816-1839	546
Talbert, Regin	3	1840-1853	108
Tate, James	2	1816-1839	285
Thomasson, James (Sr.)	3	1840-1853	239
Thomasson, Nathaniel	2	1816-1839	549
Thompson, Alexander	2	1816-1839	287
Thompson, Ann	1	1770-1815	570
Thompson, James	1	1770-1815	436
Thompson, John	2	1816-1839	416
Thompson, Samuel	1	1770-1815	488
Thompson, Thomas	1	1770-1815	121
Thompson, William	2	1816-1839	149
Thompson, William	1	1770-1815	217
Tharne, Hezekiah	3	1840-1853	168
Thrift, Abraham	1	1770-1815	397
Ticer, Clark	1	1770-1815	335
Ticer, Hugh	1	1770-1815	385
Tilghman, Joshua	2	1816-1839	412
Tipping, Henry	3	1840-1853	70
Tipping, James	1	1770-1815	18
Turner, Robert	2	1816-1839	130
Turner, Thomas	2	1816-1839	77
Turner, Thomas	2	1816-1839	169
Venable, John (Jr.)	1	1770-1815	261
Venables, John (Sr.)	1	1770-1815	438
Venables, Richard	1	1770-1815	489
Vennable, Jane	2	1816-1839	205
Vennable, William	2	1816-1839	589
Vickers, Ralph	1	1770-1815	469
Waddel, David	2	1816-1839	89
Waddell, Joseph	1	1770-1815	59
Wagner, George	1	1770-1815	490

Walker, Elizabeth (Widow)	1	1770–1815	387
Walker, Hugh	2	1816–1839	551
Walker, Thomas	1	1770–1815	181
Walker, Thompson	3	1840–1853	72
Wallace, McCastland	3	1840–1853	243
Wallace, Oliver (Jr.)	1	1770–1815	85
Wallis, Martha	2	1816–1839	91
Wallis, Mary	3	1840–1853	73
Watson, David	2	1816–1839	387
Watson, Deborah	3	1840–1853	207
Watson, George	1	1770–1815	440
Watson, James	1	1770–1815	311
Watson, James Franklin	3	1840–1853	170
Watson, Samuel	1	1770–1815	455
Watson, Violet	1	1770–1815	594
Watson, William (Sr.)	1	1770–1815	218
Watson, William	1	1770–1815	458
Watson, William	3	1840–1853	366
Weathers, Edmund	3	1840–1853	171
Weathers, Isaac	1	1770–1815	357
Webb, Eleanor	2	1816–1839	486
Webb, James	1	1770–1815	336
Wells, Hugh	2	1816–1839	243
Wherry, Darcas	1	1770–1815	470
Wherry, William	3	1840–1853	323
Whisonant, Michael	3	1840–1853	414
White, Hugh	2	1816–1839	244
White, Jessie	3	1840–1853	18
White, Joseph	1	1770–1815	359
White, Margaret	2	1816–1839	361
White, Sarah	2	1816–1839	447
Whitesides, Hugh	2	1816–1839	247
Whitley, Jonathan	1	1770–1815	122
Wilkins, Smith	2	1816–1839	506
Williams, Charles	2	1816–1839	249
Willkie, William	1	1770–1815	313
Willson, Richard	1	1770–1815	151
Willson, William	1	1770–1815	262
Wilson, Hugh (Planter)	1	1770–1815	315
Wilson, John (Yeoman)	1	1770–1815	105
Wilson, John	3	1840–1853	244
Wilson, Robert	3	1840–1853	275
Wilson, Thomas	2	1816–1839	515
Withers, Randolph (Planter)	3	1840–1853	74
Withers, Sarah M.	3	1840–1853	208
Witherspoon, Isaac D. (Atty.)	3	1840–1853	416
Wood, Aaron	2	1816–1839	461
Wood, Dorothy	3	1840–1853	78
Wood, Foster H.	3	1840–1853	211
Wood, James	3	1840–1853	368
Workman, John (Sr.)	1	1770–1815	442
Workman, John	2	1816–1839	34
Workman, John	3	1840–1853	349
Workman, Robert	3	1840–1853	110
Wright, Wm. (Sr.)(Planter)	1	1770–1815	471
Wright, William	1	1770–1815	529

Wright, William	3	1840-1853	419
Wylie, Joseph	3	1840-1853	112
Wylie, Nancy	2	1816-1839	446
Wylie, William	1	1770-1815	153
Wylie, William (Planter)	3	1840-1853	173
Yarborough, Ann	3	1840-1853	298
Young, James	1	1770-1815	124
Young, James	1	1770-1815	596

Copied by:

-s- Mrs. John D. Rogers